Data-Driven Design and Construction

Data-Driven Design and Construction

25 STRATEGIES FOR CAPTURING, ANALYZING, AND APPLYING BUILDING DATA

Randy Deutsch, AIA, LEED AP

WILEY

Published by John Wiley & Sons, Inc., Hoboken, New Jersey

Published simultaneously in Canada

Cover image: Copyright © NBBJ
Cover design: Wiley

Library of Congress Cataloging-in-Publication Data:

Deutsch, Randy.
   Data-driven design and construction : 25 strategies for capturing, analyzing and applying building data / Randy Deutsch.
       pages cm
   Includes index.
   ISBN 978-1-118-89870-3 (hardback); ISBN 978-1-118-89921-2 (ebk.); ISBN 978-1-118-89926-7 (ebk.)
   1. Building—Data processing.   I. Title.
   TH437.D48 2015
   720.285—dc23
                                                                        2015021964
Printed in the United States of America

10 9 8 7 6 5 4 3 2 1

To my son, Simeon,
who taught me to seek out primary sources
in writing and in life.

If we have data, let's look at data. If all we have are
opinions, let's go with mine.

—Jim Barksdale

CONTENTS

Foreword xiii
James Timberlake, FAIA, Partner, KieranTimberlake

Preface xv

Acknowledgments xxiii

Introduction: Measuring the Immeasurable, Validating the Ineffable 1
Not One More Thing 1
Strategies for Practice 2
Benefits of Gathering, Analyzing, and Applying Building Data 4
Challenges of Gathering, Analyzing, and Applying Building Data 13
Strategy No. 1: Hone in on Key Information 17
Strategy No. 2: Demonstrating Works, Explaining Doesn't 20

PART I

Why Data, Why Now? ———————————————— **27**

Chapter 1

THE DATA TURN 29
Five Factors Leading to the Leveraging of Data and Industry Change 29
Strategy No. 3: Look Outside the Industry 32
Case Study Interview with Robert Yori 37
Strategy No. 4: Not Big Data, Smart Data 54
Case Study Interview with Sean D. Burke 55
Data versus Documents 61
Case Study Interview with Jonatan Schumacher 63

Chapter 2

A DATA-DRIVEN DESIGN APPROACH FOR BUILDINGS 71
    Five Trends Leading to the Rise of Data in the AECO Industry   71
    Strategy No. 5: Eight Questions to Ask for Data Preparedness   73
    Case Study Interview with Zigmund Rubel 75
    Data-Centric Approaches   84
    Case Study Interview with Andrew Heumann   86
    Strategy No. 6: Four Steps toward Making the Change to Be More
        Data-Centric   87
    Strategy No. 7: Ask Good Questions   88
    Case Study Interview with Jonathon Broughton   96

Chapter 3

LEARNING FROM DATA   107
    Five Factors Ensuring Data Preparedness   107
    Training, Learning, and Working with Data   110
    Case Study Interview with Brian Ringley   113
    Strategy No. 8: Play with Data   123
    Case Study Interview with Toru Hasegawa   126
    Case Study Interview with Aimee Buccellato   134

PART II

Capturing, Analyzing, and Applying Building Data ——————— 141

Chapter 4

CAPTURING AND MINING PROJECT DATA   143
    Public Sources of Data   143
    Case Study Interview with Ryan Mullenix   145
    Private Data Sources   153
    Case Study Interview with Sam Miller   157
    Having a Data Collection Strategy   169

Strategy No. 9: Create a Data Collection Strategy   169
Case Study Interview with Gregory Janks   170
Strategy No. 10: First Steps to Becoming Data-Centric   174

Chapter 5

ANALYZING DATA   179
Analysis versus Analytics   179
Strategy No. 11: First Steps in Applying Data Analysis   180
Predictive Analytics   180
Case Study Interview with Mads Jensen   182
Strategy No. 12: Two Ways to Think about Energy Analysis   191
Strategy No. 13: Analysis for Sustainable Design   192
Case Study Interview with Chris Pyke, PhD   198
Strategy No. 14: How Analysis Informs Decision Making   201
Strategy No. 15: Start Simple, Technology Optional   202
Strategy No. 16: Leverage Data as Means to an End   203
Case Study Interview with Brendon Levitt   203
Dhour Case Study   209

Chapter 6

APPLYING DATA   213
First Steps   213
Strategy No. 17: First Steps Before Applying Data   214
Strategy No. 18: Plan for the Data   215
Case Study Interview with Billie Faircloth   216
Data-Enabled Project Teams   222
Strategy No. 19: Should the Data Team Be Integrated or
   Stationed in the Corner?   225
Case Study Interview with Andrew Witt   226
Data-Intensive Roles   230
Strategy No. 20: Computer Scientist vs. Emerging Professional   231
Case Study Interview with Greig Paterson   235
Leadership in Data   238

PART III

What Data Means for You, Your Firm, Profession, and Industry —————— 241

Chapter 7

DATA IN CONSTRUCTION AND OPERATIONS 243
  Data in Construction 244
  Strategy No. 21: Construction-Related Data
    Questions 245
  Case Study Interview with Tyler Goss 246
  Responding to Change 250
  Case Study Interview with Mani Golparvar-Fard, PhD 250
  Linking Design, Construction, and Operations 259
  Strategy No. 22: Extract and Transfer What Matters 261
  Case Study Interview with Bill East, PhD 262
  Standards and Interoperability 266
  Case Study Interview with Greg Schleusner 267

Chapter 8

DATA FOR BUILDING OWNERS AND END USERS 273
  Benefits to the Owner 273
  Case Study Interview with Sukanya Paciorek 274
  Direction to Work with Data 277
  Case Study Interview with Peter Pellerzi 279
  Strategy No. 23: with Data, the Heart of the Issue Is
    Culture 280
  AECO Firms as Data Intermediaries 281
  Case Study Interview with Brian Skripac 282
  Data Visualization Helps Owners Make
    Decisions 285
  Case Study: Data Viz Using Revit 286
  Case Study Interview with Evelyn Lee 293
  Data-Driven Design Driven by Owners 296

Chapter 9

BUILDING A CASE FOR LEVERAGING DATA   297
   Business Intelligence (BI) and Current-State Assessment   297
   Fee and Profitability Data Case Study   298
   Case Study Interview with David Fano and Dr. Daniel Davis   300
   Strategy No. 24: Big Data in Practice   301
   Security and Privacy   310
   Case Study Interview with Mark Frisch, FAIA, LEED AP BD+C   312
   Sharing Data   324
   Case Study Interview with David Sawdey   325
   Strategy No. 25: Use Data to Provide Better Service   326

Epilogue

THE FUTURE OF DATA IN AEC   331
   Our Data-Driven Future   331
   The Future Is Already Here   333

Appendix   337

   Experts, Innovators, and Thought Leaders Interviewed   337
   Organizations and Universities Represented   338
   The 25 Data-Driven Strategies   339
   Software Mentioned   339
   Recommended Reading   341

Index   343

FOREWORD

In this comprehensive book, Professor Randy Deutsch has unlocked and laid bare the twenty-first-century *codice nascosto* of architecture. It is *data*. Big data. Data as driver. The word alone sends shivers down most architects' spines. It is seen as cold, analytic, devoid of art—a word that suggests formlessness. For some in the design industry, especially those trained before the turn of the millennium, it portends the death of architecture as they were taught it and have come to know it. But data, a building block of information, is an essential strand of architecture's DNA in the twenty-first century.

Like many who became interested in architecture at a very young age and then were educated and trained in the 1970s using T-squares, triangles, and slide rules, I have seen momentous changes in the profession over the past 40-plus years. There has likely been more transformation (much of it revolutionary) in that time, in terms of how design has been affected, production changed, and outcomes altered, than in the previous five centuries. My generation had to learn architecture, and the making of it, all over again. No longer are we reliant on pens, pencils, and mechanical hardware informed by intuition and limited analysis. Instead, we can rely upon real analysis, real research, real information, broken down and shared into zeros and ones, data bits, and software that alters our understanding exponentially, turning analysis into fact-based performative form.

Zeroes and ones break down words, numbers, and images into a commonly shared language that in turn takes on many forms. The zeroes and ones code data. They are analytic and virtual, replacing the intuitive and virtuous nature of architecture and design that we were taught was timeless. Le Corbusier's Modulor, his riff on the Golden Section and measurement, can be interpreted as an early zeroes-and-ones analogue, even though most architects choose to see it as solely a yardstick or a cubic and volumetric definer of space and form. This was simple data in the form of a rule-set, or principles, which helped to engender form.

Information is a word that for most architects has real and true meaning—particularly if it ensures for them an exchange of facts and ideas that could potentially lead to realizing design intentions. Information-based design seems harmless enough, but for many architects it has a multiplicity of meanings. Information in the twenty-first century is data-driven and data-based. At its root, *in-form-ation* is a word that as a basic building block of architecture crosses generation, meaning, and outcome.

Form is a word that most architects embrace. At its root, it means the most to design-oriented architects. Pre-form, per-form, form-ulate—all actively modify the root into more meaning and depth, through prefix or suffix modifications. In this new architecture, zeroes and ones, and therefore data, give form meaning, extend form, and make form performative. Twenty-first-century form, especially as imagined by architects, can only be produced through data, modified by data, realized with data, and measured by data.

Professor Deutsch takes data, information, and form, and explains not only how they are used, but also how they are useful. More important, he discusses the benefits and positive outcomes of employing big data. Those zeroes and ones become architecture, through data, making up information and helping to form performative form. How novel an idea that is: that architecture can become informed, smart, offer feedback, continuously adjust, and continue to improve—not just because we, as architects, say it can, but because the data either tells us it is working or helps us to adjust and accommodate for that which is not working. Our architecture can be responsive to our environment, and to us, and in turn, it can continuously inform the architecture that follows it.

But here we are, 15 years into the new millennium, and still many architects and constructors do not see it that way. In spite of this, architecture can, and will, be made better through information, realized by gathering, analyzing, and maneuvering data. It will be improved by more of it, in real time, during predesign, design development, and documentation phases, enhancing designs performatively and measurably rather than intuitively. Lastly, data doesn't stop with conception and design. As stated in this tome, it is important not only throughout the design industry among suppliers and constructors alike, but also well beyond the time when clients occupy the buildings they have commissioned. The influence of data is a full cycle, continuously informing and reforming architecture.

This book offers us the chance to become informed and knowledgeable pursuers of data and the opportunities it offers for making architecture a wonderful, useful, and smart art form. Architecture as we were taught, but now architecture that can both fulfill a dream and tell a greater truth.

James Timberlake, FAIA
Partner, KieranTimberlake

PREFACE

Sherlock Holmes was highly intuitive, but only after he had collected sufficient data to eliminate the false positives.

—Jonathon Broughton, Data Wrangler

The impetus for this book goes back to my time as a university student. Upon graduation from architecture graduate school, as a graduation gift, my mentor—a professor—gave me a draft outline of a book he never got around to writing. "Here, you write this," he said, as though he was giving me a book to read. The book—had it been written—was on the topic of architectural justification, a subject that had at the time and long since interested me. I found the opportunity for design professionals to provide ultimate justifications for their architectural acts compelling. While that book so far has not been written (and this is not that book), a focus on process, decision making, and professional judgment prevail in my thinking, in my public speaking, and—informing my research on data in the AECO industry—in the pages that follow.

More recently, I served as the lead design architect on a team of talented designers and researchers on a prototype apartment building. Only this wasn't your typical housing project: This building would inconspicuously tap residents for their data. Data, in other words, would be extracted from the building's inhabitants in exchange for subsidizing their rent. My task, as the sole architect on the team, was partly to design attractive, functioning, buildable housing; but, as I soon discovered (and more importantly to the team in the success of the outcome), the charge was to assure that the 24/7 collecting of valuable data from the residents didn't feel like eavesdrop-

ping, wiretapping, or the intervention of Big Brother. In other words, the data gathering had to feel seamless and invisible. Most importantly, it couldn't feel *creepy*. It wasn't the first time an architect has been called upon to design something that needed to disappear, but it proved to be the most important. And the client's fascination with data goes a long way toward explaining why, as an architect, I am drawn to the topic of data-driven design. For the first time in my career, design and data met head to head. It wouldn't be the last.

The real revelation for me as a licensed architect, building designer, and professor was that the housing project—the building—was treated by all on the team as something almost incidental. Sure, it needed to be there: The residents needed to live *somewhere*. *Something* needed to keep rain and snow out of their bedrooms. But, to be sure, the focus of every meeting was on the data: how it would be gathered in such a way that people didn't feel like someone was watching their every move, however private. No one in the building, for example, could be aware of conspicuous data-gathering devices. How one went about tapping the building inhabitants for their data was the real design assignment. The goal was to make the data capturing innocuous, undetectable, and appear to be *humane*.

In my career as a building designer, I am continuously challenged by the need to persuade clients to go with—or as often dissuade them from going in—a particular design direction. There is only so much arm-waving an architect can do to recommend a preferred design direction. Early on, I realized that this process was a whole lot more successful—

faster and less painful—when the decisions (our so-called *preferences*) were backed with reliable data.

To take one example, when approached by a client to expand their headquarters due to projected growth, there was some guesswork as to whether the completed project would accommodate the owner's needs at time of move-in and beyond. I watched as the addition, nearing completion, accommodated the company's anticipated expansion needs, but *not* their severely underestimated future needs. Data, and data analytics' ability to predict outcomes—as several individuals and cases in this book attest—would have prevented these stressful and unhappy outcomes.

In my parallel career as a university professor—whether teaching a comprehensive- or integrated-design studio, sequence of building construction courses, professional practice or mixed-reality construction management (virtual and real)—I have come to realize that the subject of data permeates the heart of the curriculum. Yet, just try getting a course approved on the topic of "buildings as data" over the long-used standbys: buildings as buildings, or buildings as documents. It is disheartening to recognize that what students need to know in order to thrive in the new work environment isn't always, if ever, taught. Something needs to change.

While writing my last book, *BIM and Integrated Design: Strategies for Architectural Practice* (John Wiley & Sons, 2011), I started paying more and more attention to the often cited "I" in BIM, which stands for "information." I noticed that, for most users, the BIM model was treated as a receptacle or place for safekeeping. People would say the model "holds" objects, the building code, specifications, and other types of information the way a shelf holds books. As analogies go, this wasn't a very sophisticated one.

While recognizing the value of BIM, most individuals and firms use BIM today as a document creation tool,

when instead design and construction professionals need to recognize BIM's real value as a database, and start treating it like one. Additionally, it has become increasingly clear—through the ongoing research of Paul Teicholz and others at CIFE—that BIM alone won't improve labor productivity in the AEC industry, which, after more than 50 years of tracking, still lags other nonfarm industries. To improve productivity we will need something more. In *BIM and Integrated Design*, I suggested that we needed to collaborate and integrate while using BIM to see steeper and swifter gains. As of the writing of this book, those gains have yet to be realized.[1] Something else—in combination with working on integrated teams—will need to do the heavy lifting if we are to see progress in our lifetimes. (See Figure 1.1)

Here, in this book, I am proposing that leveraging, capturing, analyzing, and applying of building data is the answer to our industry's collective productivity woes.

Asking the Right Questions

Starting with data, without first doing a lot of thinking, without having any structure, is a short road to simple questions and unsurprising results. Picking the right techniques has to be secondary to asking the right questions.

—Max Shron[2]

As conferences are where the questions of what matter most to a field are asked, as a member of Notre Dame University's Sustainable Data Community, I spoke recently at their Forum where I posed the following 12 questions:

- The AEC industry is the last to use data—why?
- What's driving data use in other industries?

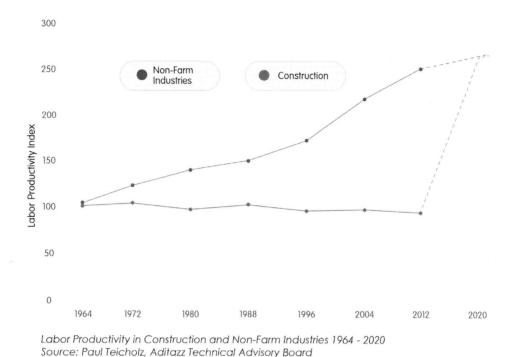

Labor Productivity in Construction and Non-Farm Industries 1964 - 2020
Source: Paul Teicholz, Aditazz Technical Advisory Board

Figure P1: BIM alone won't improve labor productivity in the AEC industry, which, after 50-plus years of tracking, still lags other nonfarm industries. © *Aditazz*

- Why is this happening now?

- What forces are conspiring to come together to make the time ripe to leverage data in our practices and organizations, in our businesses, jobsites, habitations, and offices?

- What's the business case for incorporating data into our industry?

- How exactly will design professionals have a competitive advantage when working with data?

- Will architects have to adapt to working with quants? How will they do so?

- Will we need to modify the architectural curriculum to incorporate learning of the gathering, analysis, and use of data in design projects?

- Can data be crunched into a form that can be analyzed and communicated by nonexperts?

- Where do knowledge and judgment come in? And how, using data, does one arrive at insights?

- How can we ensure that our data is of high quality?

- Can we legally allow others to rely on the data in our models? Can we guarantee that data? Who is liable?

After conducting 40 in-depth interviews with design, construction, and operations professionals and educators around the globe for this book, I feel that all of these questions—except one—remain warranted. That would be the first: *The AEC industry is the last to use data—why?* It turns out that design professionals, at firms large and small, using sophisticated digital tools and hand tools, intelligence and intuition, have been using data to great effect and equally impressive results in their work. It is just that we, as a profession and industry, have not given voice to it—until now. In this book, I have sought to respond to each and every one of these questions, and many more.

The other week I found myself on a long road trip with a university facilities and operations director. The conversation got around to the topic of my research. I mentioned my book—the one that you are now holding, *Data-Driven Design and Construction*. He looked at me as though to ask, *How will that help me?* This book shows him—and now you—how. Using practice-based research and in-depth interviews with industry and academic leaders, this book seeks to answer these and other urgent questions and propose actionable strategies that design and construction professionals can begin to put to use to help convince clients concerning design direction, move projects forward, grow their organizations, remain competitive, and innovate.

Depending on what are you trying to accomplish, data plays a role now in every facet of practice. Data of course can be used in design and planning to generate form and create interesting geometry. But that's only the beginning of what data can do:

- Data can ensure that your designs remain innovative and relevant.

- Data helps increase building performance and improve productivity, as well as enhance human and operational performance, as it predicts a facility's future performance.

- Data helps teams, firms, and owners achieve business results, by winning projects or by convincing a client that a particular design option is superior, and can be used to reduce risk for the owner, contractor, and architect.

- Data helps eliminate emotion from the decision-making process and allows teams to make decisions with more confidence by proving that their initial concepts were right. It helps designers to get answers out of the information they are already dealing with that will ultimately validate their outcomes.

- Data provides objective evaluations of all aspects of our built environment and helps us to justify design decisions and anticipate consequences for proposed courses of action.

Additional benefits and challenges of working with data in design and construction—for architects, engineers, building owners, and facility managers—can be found in the Introduction, and for owners in Chapter 8. This book introduces professionals and their organizations that are enabled, informed, or driven by data, and shares their recommendations, insights, and strategies for doing so. It also seeks to address and rectify a gap in our learning, by explaining to architects, engineers, contractors, and owners—and students of these fields—how to acquire and use data to make more informed decisions. Further, it raises—and attempts to answer—important questions that design and construction professionals, owners, and their teams need to clarify in order to grow their practices and proceed with their design agendas.

This book isn't about yet another new movement or trend in architecture. In fact, there is nothing *new* about data use in architecture (the use of data in architecture goes back at least to the Renaissance, if not earlier). "Data," according to one practitioner, "is something that has been shaping architecture, planning, and design for generations knowingly or not. It is being collected in so many ways it's scary to fathom."

What *is* the start of a trend in architecture that is just beginning to gain notice (one that hasn't been formally documented until now) is how data-driven design is the new frontier of the convergence between BIM and architectural computational analyses and its associated tools. We are seeing computational design tools develop in parallel with BIM as a game-changer for winning projects and changing owners' perspectives on the value of model-based studies. A small number of current practitioners are utilizing it today, so the value of making the ROI and methodology available to students to train for as they enter the profession will enable practice to prosper as they enter the workforce.

The current professional discourse has been focused more on BIM than on the equally game-changing computational analytics. Aimed at all members of the project team, this book seeks to rectify this situation by reaching across the boundaries of design, construction, ownership, and operations of buildings. It's unique in its approach to looking at BIM as the source of data in *data-driven design* (D³). Having a book that brings attention to the topic will, I hope, incentivize schools and universities to begin to tackle the subject of data-driven design in their curricula, which does not happen often enough today. Students are surprisingly unaware of this issue within architecture and construction management schools. It is time for that to change.

Because data-driven design affects so many facets of the building lifecycle, this book attempts to be as inclusive as possible. The title is *Data-Driven Design and Construction*, but would include planning, educators, owners, operators, facility managers, energy consultants, strategy, R&D, *and* real estate if there were available *real estate* on the book's front cover. For my research I rely on many sources, including my own experience, among more traditional sources, but especially on first-hand interviews with thought leaders in the AECO industry who work day-to-day with data.

Innovators and Thought Leaders Leveraging Data throughout the Building Lifecycle

The material in this book grew from the author's recent conversations with firm leaders and other industry executives at companies ranging in size from sole proprietorships to large multinational organizations. The interviewees' responses were recorded, transcribed by the author, and condensed for publication. Their job titles reflect their status at the time they were interviewed. The conversations occurred between February and July of 2014. Those interviewed for the book (40 of them) include people who are driving this transformation of the industry. In many cases, the interviewees used the occasion of the interview to clarify their own thinking about data in their work and practices. Together, these views and my attendant commentary paint a cohesive (if not entirely comprehensive) picture of where things in the AECO industry are headed.

The practitioners and academics who appear in the book represent a cross-section of the profession and industry; they are predisposed to think in terms of data: architects, engineers, contractors, building owner/operators, energy consultants, predictive analytic and digital consultants. Some are in management and leadership positions. Some have a design role, whereas others work in construction or operations. Some work on the front lines and some in trenches, from firms both large and small. Some hail from academia, some from marketing and strategy. Some are immersed in software, consulting on digital technology or climate engineering, with some inventing tools as the need arises. Some will be familiar names, some will be new to you—but in a short time all will become familiar presences in your work, career, and thinking.

What the practitioners and academics you'll meet in this book all have in common is that they each have a strong interest and opinions on the topic of data; they all have a proven track record for utilizing data in their work to achieve outstanding results; and, together, they represent how data is currently leveraged in the AECO induslry. Practitioners in architecture, engineering, computer science, informatics, and those affiliated with this research are currently studying methods to create new ways for gathering and broadly disseminating data—including sustainability data—to help improve our habitable built environment. This book identifies individuals and firms who are using the software effectively, creatively, and for higher purposes and uses; taps into their knowledge base and shares their latest findings, best practices, and insights; and presents factual information on how data is being used by those who are leading the way. It presents people with interesting applications of data in the AECO industry, and for the first time, looks inside practices to take a closer look at how those in the AECO are working with data and what lessons they've learned.

Throughout the first half of 2014, I spoke with people around the globe who are working with data in design and construction, in planning and research, in fabrication and strategy, in real estate and academia, and have collected their experiences, words of advice, hard-earned insights, and strategies, and made them available to you in this book. So many books show you how the 1 percent does it. Then when it comes time for you to try to do it at home or the office, you are unable to repeat the results. So I also sought out people who are struggling to

include data in their design and construction process and practices.

The research for this book has been based on today's technology and practices. Since leveraging data in architectural practice, construction, and operations is at a point of inception and rapid evolution, updates will be posted to the author's blog (http://datadrivendesignblog.com) as well as the publisher's book page as they occur. Book writing itself could be thought of as an exercise in data mining, where the first-hand expert testimony is the raw data leveraged—through queries and data dives—to test working hypotheses and evidence to support the author's claims. In the writing of this book I often found myself data mining for insights from the interview database. The book you hold in your hands is the result.

What This Book Will Do for You

Data-Driven Design and Construction: 25 Strategies for Capturing, Applying, and Analyzing Building Data addresses how innovative individuals and firms are using data to remain competitive while advancing their practices, and how firms can benefit from creating a data plan and putting data to use in their projects. There's a need for a book that shows not only why design, construction, and operations professionals need to understand where data and analysis fit into their work and practices, but also how they can go about using data and analysis to meet and exceed expectations.

This book will help you recognize the data you already have: data that you are sitting on, data that is available to you today in abundance, data that you may not have realized was there. It will prepare you—*ready* you—for the necessity of making the capture, analysis, and application of data a central part of your practice, culture, and—importantly—

mindset. This book will help you to see data as central to your firm's arsenal of tools and resources; and help you understand data's impact on learning, recruitment and training, human resources, finance and accounting, branding, strategy, design, innovation, project management, and leadership.

This book explores the most commonly encountered obstacles to a firm's successful application of data on projects and teams, as well as the challenges the data creates for individuals as they strive to establish a data strategy for their organization. These challenges include interoperability, workflow, impacts on firm culture, training, technological challenges, data's influence on who works on teams, communication, cost, data sharing, and privacy and security. Design decisions, when challenged, have to be justified, and there is no better way to defend these courses of action than to provide data to back up these decisions.

Show Me the Data

The secret to success in business—and no less in design and construction—is to speak your client's language, and more and more of that language is spoken in terms of data. Owners no longer accept designers' and contractors' reasons at face value. They ask for evidence, and data, to back up those claims and reasons, and then base their decisions to move forward with their projects on that data. If you want to see your preferred design scheme selected, and buildings built, and want others to continue to come to you for the services you provide, you will need to add new tools to your toolkit. This book will help you identify and use them effectively, and introduce you to people who can help you along the way.

This book won't quote trends and statistics. *Ninety percent of the world's data has been produced in the last two years.*[3] How does knowing that help *you*?

You won't find many factoids like that in this book. As interesting as they are in and of themselves, you don't want factoids. What you want is *information* that enables you to do your job better. All this data-related trivia tells you is that *there's a lot of data*. We get that. What these statistics don't do is help you do your job better. And *that* is the purpose of this book.

There are two types of people who will react differently to the title of this book: those who count themselves amongst the analog (some might call themselves Luddites or *close to retirement* and thus immune to change), and those who want to prepare for the future, because they recognize that the future is already here. To this second group, using data is common sense. They don't need convincing: they just want to be shown the way. That is what this book is for and sets out to accomplish.

This book is about saving the architecture profession from extinction and construction from languishing in 100-year-old habits. This book is about making the AEC industry more productive, about helping firms become more competitive and giving architects a purpose again. This book is about rebuilding credibility in the eyes of building owners, and adding substance to spurious arguments about beauty and design. This book is about creating better buildings with better information, and it is about all of the things that can't be captured in a book title (Data-Driven *Everything*?) This book is about building a bridge between design intent and the outside world; it's about the "I" in BIM, and it's about how big data can be leveraged in our industry, long after we stop calling it *big data*. This book is about making firms perform more efficiently and effectively; about optimizing energy use in buildings; and about making smarter decisions. This book is about the future, and it's about what is happening right now. I hope you enjoy reading it as much as I enjoyed writing it.

Please go to www.wiley.com/go/datadrivendesign for instructor materials.

Notes

Unless otherwise indicated, quoted text throughout the book is from interviews with the author that took place between February and July of 2014.

1. "Data-driven planning & design: How data is driving architecture, planning, and design," January 15, 2012; www.hugewindow.com/alpha/data-driven/.

See also Paul Tiecholz, "Labor-productivity declines in the construction industry: Causes and remedies (Another look)." *AECBytes*, March 14, 2013; www.aecbytes.com/viewpoint/2013/issue_67.html.

2. Max Shron, *Thinking with Data: How to Turn Information into Insights* (Kindle Locations 112–113). O'Reilly Media, 2014.

3. SINTEF, May 22, 2013; www.sciencedaily.com/releases/2013/05/130522085217.htm.

ACKNOWLEDGMENTS

Thank you to John Wiley & Sons' Amanda Miller, VP and publisher; Helen Castle, executive commissioning editor for the Global Architecture program, for sharing her guidance and expert insights; assistant editor Calver Lezama, from whom I benefited greatly; and to Kathryn Malm Bourgoine, who recognized the promise in my book proposal.

A big thank you to James Timberlake for his daily inspiration and generosity in writing the foreword, and to Carin Whitney of KieranTimberlake for her assistance and perseverance. To all of the industry innovators and thought leaders for sharing their insights, time, and experience. A shoutout to architect-in-the-making Joseph Palmer for his excellent illustrations.

At the University of Illinois Urbana-Champaign School of Architecture, I would like to thank director Peter Mortensen, and especially professors Jeff Poss, Bill Worn, and David Chasco for their ongoing support and encouragement.

To Sharon, Simeon, and Michol for standing by me throughout the writing of this book.

INTRODUCTION: MEASURING THE IMMEASURABLE, VALIDATING THE INEFFABLE

Buildings are decisions.

—Markku Allison

Being a design and construction professional today is a balancing act. Many are overwhelmed: at capacity in terms of time, resources, and mind-space; struggling to keep up with the latest technologies and work processes, let alone considering getting ahead. Meanwhile, they know—despite dwindling margins—that they need to remain competitive in order to compete for work, move projects forward, and get work done in an efficient manner.

You might think that design and construction professionals have already dealt with successive disruptive technologies—CAD, BIM, digital-, parametric-, and computational-design tools, to name a few—and aren't sure if they're ready for *another*. Aren't architecture, engineering, and construction already complex and complicated enough?

Not One More Thing

Some will balk: *We're not ready—we're unprepared—* to deal with data on top of everything else we have going on. Or, *we're just trying to make ends meet—* trying to compete for projects on threadbare budgets and miserly fees. *Do we really need another thing on top of everything else we have to contend with?* These are all ways of saying the same thing: that data is *one more thing*.

But capturing, engaging with, analyzing, and applying data is *not* one more thing. As this book will try to make clear, data is not something *added on* to all you are currently doing. It is integral to what you do and have been doing for some time. All activities that we undertake today can be transformed into data. Data always informs our designs. The data is already there; you just need to know where to look to find it. It already exists—in abundance—and represents an opportunity too big to pass up. You cannot afford to ignore it. This book will help you to see the data you have available to you more clearly and readily.

Something Old, Something New

Architects, engineers, and even contractors have been working with data for ages. What *is* new are the myriad ways we have to capture, analyze, and apply the data that is available to us. Likewise, many data sources are new, and many industry players—and their titles and backgrounds—may be unfamiliar, even to those in the industry.

Data is recognized by many in the architecture, engineering, construction, and operations (AECO) industry as the elephant in the room. Data and especially the catchall term *big data* is an important topic and, specific labels aside, is poised to remain so. To their credit, many design and AECO industry professionals already realize that data is the answer to their most perplexing professional and business problems—but they are unfamiliar with the steps necessary to acquire and use the data that will enable them to do their jobs better, remain competitive, and achieve a higher return on their technology and training investment. Even more than the acquisition of new skill sets and technological capabilities, to reclaim their roles as leaders, architects in particular need to simultaneously account for data and information derived from their digital models, and also be able to gather, navigate, and communicate this information while working collaboratively throughout the complete design and construction cycle.

Strategies for Practice

In this book you will find step-by-step instructions for working with data, but, because no two firms are alike, only a scant few one-size-fits-all solutions. That's because this is a book of adaptable strategies you and your organization can apply today to make the most of the data you have at your fingertips—much of which you may not be aware of. This book also reflects the trend toward a real-time convergence of technologies and processes that aren't reflected in linear first-this-now-this checklists. This book looks inside practices to observe how people in the AECO industry are leveraging data in their day-to-day work—*today*.

We need to get better at leveraging data to remain competitive, to satisfy our clients' need for evidence, and to help make our claims credible. We need to learn how to work with data to verify our intuition and instinctive hunches, to bridge the gut/data divide, and to remain relevant in a business-oriented, STEM-centric world. (See Figure I.1.)

Why Start Now?

You've gone this long without consciously using data, so why start now? In fact, you have been using—gathering, analyzing, and applying—building data all along and likely didn't realize it. This book shows you how to do so more intentionally, purposefully, and effectively, and helps you see the opportunity that has been there all along.

Data is changing the way we work in the AECO industry. Design and construction professionals need to increase productivity. Building owners have charged us with the task of verifiably increasing value while simultaneously decreasing waste, realizing the promise of our digital tools, integrated processes, and workflows. This book covers the role that data plays in our profession's and industry's continued relevance, improved prospects, and brighter future—because an industry is a terrible thing to waste.

Learning to work more effectively with data will require the acquisition of some new skills. But even more important, especially at the beginning, is the development of effective mindsets. BIM (building information modeling) is a case in point. While recognizing the value of BIM, most still use BIM tools today for document creation, at a time when design and construction professionals need to recognize BIM's real value—as a database—and start treating it like one. How we use and interact with the data generated in BIM-enabled projects is the next step in BIM adoption. Learning to capture, analyze, and apply data is how many of us will take BIM beyond visualization, clash detection, and coordination to

Figure I.1: A spectrum of decision-making criteria: Data increases credibility. © R Deutsch

the next level. In fact, *Data-Driven Design and Construction: 25 Strategies for Capturing, Applying, and Analyzing Building Data* was written, in part, to help design practitioners and their project teams to make better use of BIM. Many firms are already doing this—you will meet them in the chapters that follow—but up until now, there has been little to guide those who would like to explore a similar path.

Data's PR Problem

Data admittedly has a public relations problem. Why focus on something so seemingly small when there are many large and complex problems demanding our attention? Most people are indifferent when it comes to data. Data is not as interesting or sexy as design. Some are hesitant to talk about data because they see it as a commodity. Some, especially academics, are threatened by data, the study of which culturally and institutionally originates outside of design and architecture proper. Some see it as one more thing threatening to minimize the architect's strength and core competency—*design*—or don't see how these things relate to or support one another. Some fear that data is the antithesis of craft: why crunch numbers when you can use your hands to create something beautiful and of everlasting value? All of this combines to ask: *Do we really need one more intervention, trend, or movement to move architects away from their art, and contractors from their craft?* There's an attitude that data should be something left to the "quants." The basic question is: *Why should design professionals and contractors concern themselves with data?*

You work with data not because you like to work with numbers, but so you can design with more confidence. As you'll learn in the chapters that follow, data isn't the antithesis of design and craft; rather, data enhances craft and, importantly, ensures that what is designed and crafted gets built. Working with data doesn't preclude you from using your

imagination or from designing innovative buildings. In fact, data makes each more likely to happen. Because it leads to quicker, more assured decisions, working with data frees you up to spend more time in design.

Is data a *nice-to-have*, but not yet a *must-have*, for design and construction firms? The point isn't for you to become an expert at working with data for its own sake, but to learn how to leverage the data you already have available to you to increase the chances that your design will get approved and built, so you, your clients, and the building users benefit from your built work. By this definition, data is indeed a *must-have*.

There are just too many ways that data can be gathered and utilized for you and your organization to ignore it. As we move forward, *not* recognizing this could be a mortal blow to the sustenance of untold firms. No matter where you find yourself in the building lifecycle, data can help you achieve your goals. This book will explain in clear terms what you need to have in place to make data part of your practice, and will help you determine how prepared you are to use data. You wouldn't go hiking or camping without the right supplies and tools. This book will let you know what you need to have in place to make this journey.

We need to start thinking of buildings, and our work as building professionals, in terms of data, to tell better data stories to our clients and stakeholders. We need educators who recognize the value of data and share this knowledge with their students, who are the future of the profession and industry. We need to continue to identify problems that can be addressed with data, and a way of thinking about those problems to render them amenable to computational analysis. This book will help you ask questions that others don't ask—or don't know to ask—that will lead to more assured decisions and insights. (See Figure I.2.)

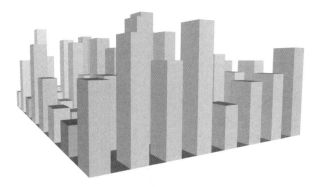

Figure I.2: Bar-chart city: The importance of starting to see the urban environment in terms, and comprised, of data. © R Deutsch

Benefits of Gathering, Analyzing, and Applying Building Data

The benefits of using data on building projects are many, and some may surprise you. These and other benefits—and challenges involved in working with data—are covered in greater detail in the chapters that follow.

Globally Shared Benefits

In addition to benefits specific to the owner, architect, and contractor, there are several benefits that are equally shared by all involved parties. Global benefits of data include the elimination of emotion from the decision-making process and fostering of behavioral changes, as well as a reduction in risk, management of complexity, and an improved project definition.

Data Brings an Analytical Approach to the Building Process

Many AECO professionals use data to help eliminate emotion from the decision-making process. As Evelyn Lee, strategist at MKThink, noted, "It helps our clients find thought processes that are objective when it comes to the ultimate solutions we help

them to create using data that supports how we move forward in the project."

Data Leads to Behavior Change

Behavior change is one of the more startling results of leveraging data in building projects, especially on the user end. Daniel Davis of CASE lived in an apartment where tenants had to prepay for their power. "Right beside the door was a meter displaying how much credit you had left—how much power was remaining," explains Davis. "You could turn on the oven and see the remaining power quickly diminish. I became acutely aware of how much power I was using in that apartment." No longer was a unit's power usage an abstract number sent as part of a bill every month, says Davis, "it was something I constantly saw, every day. Through this constant exposure I came to better understand my power usage and how to better control it. This was just a single metric, a single data point, and it had a noticeable effect on my behavior. Using data in this way has great potential."

Data Reduces Risk

Owners are convinced by data. Evelyn Lee points out that data's ability to convince has the added benefit of reducing an owner's sense of risk. "The fact that

An Incomplete List of Things That Can Be Made Better with Data

- Answering a factual question
- Telling a story
- Exploring a relationship
- Discovering a pattern
- Making a case for a decision
- Automating a process
- Judging an experiment[1]

we can turn what is seen as subjective solutions into objective ones supported by data is very meaningful to them. Ultimately, they feel that they are reducing their risk associated with any future architectural project because we've done the research and the data has challenged them."

Data Manages Complexity

Today's building projects are enormously complex undertakings, ones that no individual person can manage by himself or herself. Data—more specifically, the leveraging of data—helps building teams manage this complexity. (See Figure I.3).

Data Helps Define the Project

"Data helped us understand what the client needed," explains Tom Mulhern, formerly with Gensler. "Not just I need this project on time and on budget. That's what it often devolves to, unfortunately. But more of a vivid understanding of the social or cultural objective of the client." As a building owner, Sukanya Paciorek, Vice President of Corporate Sustainability at Vornado Realty Trust, understands that the data they collect can be valuable to whoever chooses to use it, perhaps best stating the case that data provides globally shared benefits. "The reason we set up a system where the interface is intended for multiple users is that we feel the end-use can be widespread," explains Paciorek.

As a landlord, we benefit from it in that our operators and building engineers have people like me and my team to look at it to enhance our operations and improve what it is that we do every day. Our tenants are enabled to look at that same data through their own lens and figure out how to make their operations better—to lower their expenses and their needs for electricity. In general, the more meaningful data you collect, the more people for which it is actionable. As our buildings become more efficient, the grid and the community-at-large receive the benefit of that, as we are not calling upon as many resources from the broader society in which we live. Overall, the benefit is pretty widespread.

Benefits to the Architect

Data provides several benefits specific to the architect. Among the most familiar, having data to back-up one's decisions creates confidence, serves as a learning tool, and improves intuition, all leading to better, more assured, decisions and insights. Some of data's less familiar benefits to the architect are nonetheless impactful.

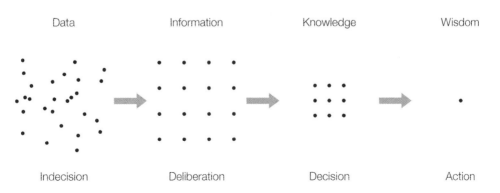

Figure I.3: DIKW progression: Leveraging data to manage complexity. © R Deutsch

Data Provides More Certainty and Confidence

The opposite of leveraging data isn't using one's intuition; it's *gambling*. The most important thing Aditazz knows about data is that it will provide them with more confidence in predicting outcomes, explains Zigmund Rubel. "If we have all of these analyses showing us why a certain outcome will be provided, we'll have more confidence that a particular outcome will be achieved. If we just hope that it will work, then we are gambling, and unfortunately that's what many design practices do in their work product." (See Figure I.4.)

Data Helps Team Members to Learn Quickly

Sam Miller, partner at LMN Architects, describes a benefit from using data on an acoustic reflector project: real-time learning on the job. "The outcome was a shape and a geometry that was unexpected. There were surprises as we were defining the geometry. The acoustical consultant really learned something. And even though he is a seasoned veteran, and was doing this for many years, he's never analyzed the geometry and had the ability to manipulate geometry to the level he had. In that process, he learned quite a bit about what is going to be effective."

Data Leads to Better Design Decisions and Insights

Leveraging data leads not only to more assured business decisions, but to better design performance decisions as well. "We did some work on a school where the architects and engineers had anticipated that the classrooms would need a substantial HVAC system to handle overheating," says Brendon Levitt, LOISOS + UBBELOHDE. "Using a detailed thermal model, we assumed that the building would have no heating or cooling systems and we simulated the resultant indoor temperatures over the course of a year. We found that by increasing natural ventilation, installing ceiling fans, and shading the windows, indoor temperatures stayed in a comfortable range. This not only saved money for the school district, but it improved comfort conditions for the students." See Figure I.5.

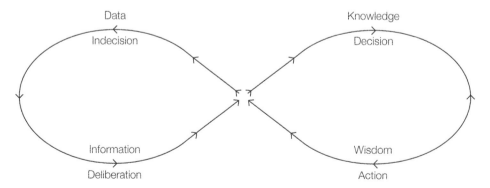

Figure I.4:   Typically illustrated as a pyramid or continuum, DIKW can be thought of as a continuous loop toward increasing certainty. © *R Deutsch*

ZERO NET ENERGY DESIGN DASHBOARD

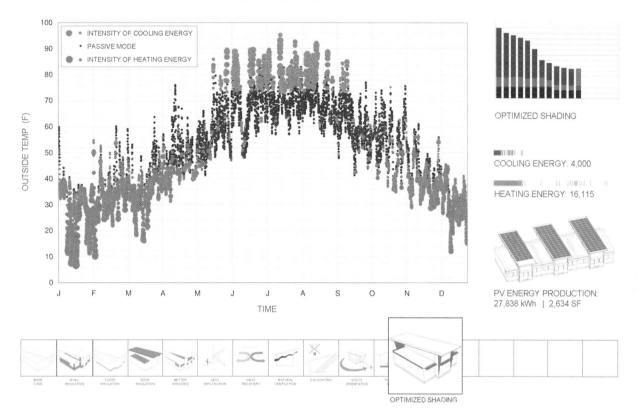

Figure I.5:   Visualization enables clients to walk through iterations of the building as indicated by icons along the bottom of the image: the base case; adding wall insulation; better windows. The less "orange," the less "blue," the more white, the better. The bigger the dot, the more energy used. © *LOISOS + UBBELOHDE*

Data Enables Teams to See the Impacts of Multiple Factors Simultaneously

Today's computational tools enable near real-time analysis in the cloud. "It's 30X faster than traditional energy modeling because you're actually using your design model to generate the energy model tool," explains Sean D. Burke, LEED AP, Digital Practice Leader at NBBJ, Seattle. "Then it's processed online, off of your computer, so you can continue working."

Data Helps the Architect Make Better Business Decisions

Working with data helps architects make better business decisions—not only for themselves, but for all involved. "The architect, the owner, needs to say the implications of space could result in these business outcomes," says David Fano. "What do we need to do then? I doubt many architects ask their clients for their sales records. There needs to be a transformation of the architect to business consultant. Data

VIEWS
Overall View Analysis Diagram

Scheme B

Scheme B	% OF OVERALL AREA					
VIEW	Plot 1	Plot2	Plot3	Plot4	TOTAL VIEW AVERAGE %	Summary
Guggenheim, Sheikh Zayed Museum and Full Sea View	1%	4%	7%	0	7%	
Guggenheim and Full Sea View	17%	16%	18%	25%	19%	50%
Full Sea View	26%	24%	25%	19%	23%	
Sheikh Zayed Museum and Full Sea View	4%	24%	11%	4%	11%	
Sheikh Zayed Museum and Partial Sea View	16%	2%	17%	18%	13%	39%
Sheikh Zayed Museum View	17%	14%	13%	17%	15%	
Partial Sea View and Partial Sheikh Zayed Museum View	0%	7%	5%	0%	3%	
Partial Sea View	17%	4%	0%	0%	5%	11%
Base	2%	5%	4%	0%	3%	
	100%	100%	100%	100%	100%	

Figure I.6:   Overall View Analysis Diagram. © *RTKL*

is going to help make a lot of those decisions." (See Figures I.6 and I.7.)

Data Convinces

Data speaks the language that clients/owners speak, in terms they understand and can appreciate. It speaks the language that those owners rely on to make the hard decisions—the financial team, reps, actuaries, and accountants. Communication is improved not by explaining the project in strictly architectural terms, but by doing so in a language clients understand: by describing the client's

projects in the client's terms, not those of designers. See Figure I.8.

Data Allows You to Use Your Experience—and Past Projects—as a Searchable Database

Using BIM as a database yields an almost infinite number of benefits. Data is already present within the model; through analysis and visualization, this data becomes the information and knowledge needed to support design decisions. (See Figure I.9.)

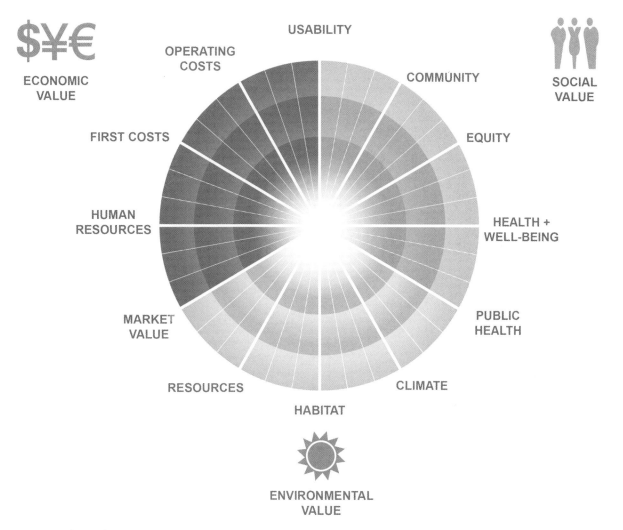

Figure I.7: The performance wheel is RTKL's version of the triple bottom line—economic, environmental, and social—that lays out the firm's design values. © RTKL

Data Supports, Backs Up, and Improves One's Intuitions

"[A]lgorithmic design, data analysis, is a means to an end. To make our lives better. To empower the architect to make his or her intuitions."

—Jonathon Broughton, Data Wrangler, Allies and Morrison

Architects act—and make professional judgments—from a combination of experience, knowledge, and intuition. "What better way to reinforce intuition if you can prove it right?" asks Jonathon Broughton. "And when it is wrong, we can demonstrate that it is wrong." Leveraging data helps architects design better buildings by using the data that is available

Figure I.8:   An early version of the CASE Building Analytics dashboard. The dashboard helps architects and building owners see trends in their projects' geographic locations, sizes, and program types. © *CASE Inc.*

Figure I.9: Beyond BIM, the Dashboard provides a concise interface to compare metrics of a number of SOM projects. The color-coding indicates percentile ranking relative to all SOM buildings of that same type. Metrics include: Net and Gross areas, Building Efficiency, MEP Systems, Glass Types, Lease Span, Elevatoring, and sustainability metrics. © *Skidmore, Owings and Merrill LLP*

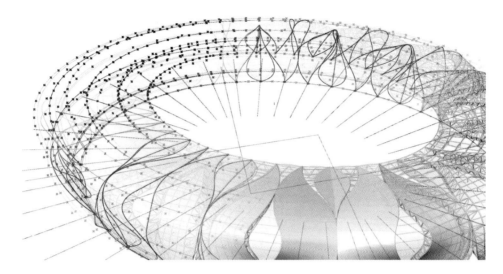

Figure I.10:   Hangzhou Stadium. External "Petal" structure: Parametric components of stadium design. © *NBBJ*

to them to inform their designs. There's a place for hunches and intuition, but better buildings are backed up by ample data.

Data Eliminates False Positives

What, exactly, is it that data does for architects and their building projects that standard knowledge, experience, or intuition can't? It eliminates paths that don't lead anywhere: hunches and assumptions that were enabled by preconceived notions that turn out to be incorrect. The beauty of gathering and leveraging data in building projects is that it enables designers to save time and valuable resources by eliminating false positives.

Data Moves the Design Along

Data is not an end in itself. Rather, it is a means to help firms sell their ideas more effectively. So, is the benefit in the tool or in the data? The two are interrelated. Data, in conjunction with analytic tools, speeds up the process of early analysis, which allows teams to move on to the design phase more quickly and assuredly. (See Figure I.10.)

Benefits to the Contractor

Benefits to the contractor include competitive advantage and enhanced information management—and data makes it more likely that buildings will get built. Contractors collect data concerning the procurement and cost of materials, when possible in real time, as well as on the quality of workmanship. These kinds of data allow contractors to make more confident decisions concerning cost and quality, which, along with time, are of primary concern to any successful construction undertaking. Because contractors are notoriously slow to try novel processes and take on unproven risks, construction industry-related benefits remain a work in progress.

Think to the Third Sweater

Jill Bergman, Healthcare Principal and Vice President at HDR, shares a story that argues for leveraging data and demonstrates the value of querying data in building projects. In its telling, it also provides a basis for how we may derive wisdom from data. "My favorite story to share on benefits and outcomes of investing in data and databases has nothing to do with computers," explains Bergman.

> It goes back to when I gave my mother a gift certificate for sweater knitting classes for her birthday. I thought I was so brilliant to give a gift and get a sweater back. My older, and some-times wiser, brother asked for the third sweater. And in that split moment, I knew he was right. The first sweater was going to be a mess; it was the learning sweater. It was not made for com-fort, nor beauty, nor longevity, but for learning. The second sweater is striving, applying, reus-ing knowledge, and following previous paths. But the third sweater is applying knowledge, a commitment to creating, and an understand-ing of the whole sweater, not just the data—knitting. Databases and working with data is lo think to the third sweater. When we start over on a new project every time, it is like going back to the first sweater every time.

Challenges of Gathering, Analyzing, and Applying Building Data

Data can be a powerful resource for design and construction professionals, owners, and end users of buildings. Nevertheless, working with data on building projects in the AECO industry is not without its challenges.

Globally Shared Challenges

Just as there are obstacles specific to the owner, architect, and contractor, there are several chal-lenges that are shared by all involved parties. Global challenges of data include technical chal-lenges, risk aversion, firms size, and the granularity and quality of the data being captured, analyzed, applied, and leveraged throughout the building lifecycle.

Easy Data

Numbers convince—but achieving those numbers can be fraught with obstacles and hardships. "Data is convincing because it's numeric and tangible. It's easy data, you can't really argue it," argues Brian Skripac, Director of Digital Practice at Astorino. "You're trying to validate a design strategy one way or another. In the end, you have to have numbers to do it."

As with benefits, there are challenges that affect stakeholders, including the owner, the public, and the specific end users. The construction industry is complex, fragmented, and rife with problems such as delays, rework, standing time, material waste, poor communication, conflict, and being over budget, compounded by the global slow-down and the need to address sustainability issues.[2] AECO professionals are challenged on two fronts: in terms of adapting new technolo-gies and in terms of implementing new work pro-cesses. These two types of challenges have been identified as technical and adaptive (or behavioral) challenges brought about by change. *Technical challenges* are those that can be solved by the knowledge of experts and, however complex or difficult, can be solved using well-honed skills applied to well-defined problems. In contrast, *adaptive challenges* are tangled, poorly defined, open-ended, call for a host of different skills and approaches that are rarely transparent, and require new learning.[3] Working with and leverag-ing data in organizations in the building industry involves both types of challenges, and they are addressed differently.

Risk Aversion

When it comes to working with new technologies and work processes, whether it involves working in the cloud or working with data, it does not bode well that the construction industry takes a wait-and-see approach. "There is always a part of the market that likes to try things early, and others that prefer to wait and see," says Mads Jensen, CEO of Sefaira. See Figure I.11.

To realize many of the benefits listed earlier, changes in attitudes and mindsets must first take

place within the AECO industry. "The AECO industry has fundamental challenges to full participation in big data," says Chris Pyke of USGBC, "including but not limited to market fragmentation, professional specialization, risk aversion, and low (relative) rates of R&D investment." Pyke suggests a cure:

Most professional publications in the AECO industry place a strong emphasis on celebrating success. For example, *ASHRAE Journal* provides monthly features on exceptionally high-performing buildings. Yet, these publications provide

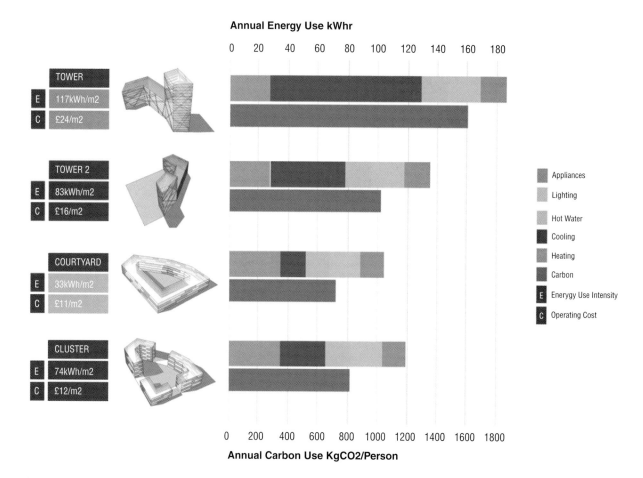

Figure I.11:   Sefaira allows architects to compare design options and measure their performance using chosen parameters. © *Sefaira*

relatively little coverage of failures and under-performance. Contrast this emphasis with journals for professional pilots, these publications focus overwhelming[ly] on failures. "Plane lands safely" is not a story. "Building performs as designed" shouldn't be a story. We should want to talk about underperformance and failure. We need to find ways to talk about these issues in ways that address the real, practical circumstances in the AECO industry (e.g., our litigious culture). Clearly, if the aviation industry can find a way, so we can we."

> *"Plane lands safely ..." is not a story. "Building performs as designed" shouldn't be a story.*
> —Chris Pyke, USGBC

Firm Size

Does the size of one's firm pose a challenge when attempting to work with data? What about small firms? Is data meant only for large practices? (See Figure I.12.)

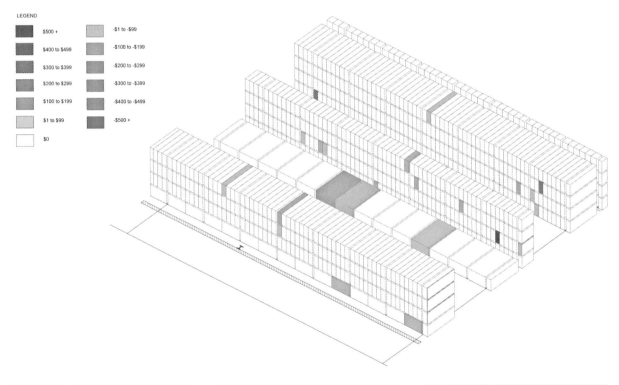

LEGEND

Color	Range		Color	Range
	$500 +			-$1 to -$99
	$400 to $499			-$100 to -$199
	$300 to $399			-$200 to -$299
	$200 to $299			-$300 to -$399
	$100 to $199			-$400 to -$499
	$1 to $99			-$500 +
	$0			

			CATEGORY	TOTAL
95	05	37	CANDY-COUNT GOODS	13.20
95	05	42	GRANOLA BARS-GROCERY	-24.96
95	05	46	CANDY BARS	23.28
95	05	84	CHEWING GUM	-6.84
95	05	95	DIET AIDS-NUTRITIONAL FOOD/BEVERAGE-HBC	-14.40
95	06	14	BAKEWARE/GLASSWARE-GM	122.40
95	07	73	CANDY-MISC.	-158.40
95	08	02	SEASONAL GENERAL MERCHANDISE-GM	-199.00
95	09	30	CHEWING GUM-COUNT GOODS	-6.25

			CATEGORY	TOTAL
95	09	85	CANDY BARS	15.52
96	25	77	SEASONING	9.84
96	26	65	HERB & SPICES	138.60
96	26	71	EXTRACTS	-43.08
96	26	72	PET SUPPLIES-GM	-27.28
96	26	12	MCK SPECIALTY ITEMS	8.10
96	26	20	SEASONING	3.78
96	26	22	SEASONING	59.04
96	26	27	SEASONING	19.68

			CATEGORY	TOTAL
96	26	37	SPICES	-9.27
96	27	62	HERB & SPICES	-8.52
96	28	16	HERB & SPICES	101.52
96	28	25	GARLIC & ONIONS	-8.64
96	29	42	CANDY-COUNT GOODS	15.12
96	29	44	MISCELLANEOUS HBC-HBC	35.70
96	30	15	SEASONING	-10.32
96	30	26	EYE CARE	-1118.40
				-1069.58

Figure I.12:   Building information modeling (BIM) is a tool to document and manage the construction process. But can it be used as a data visualization tool? © *Space Command*

"It's a potential problem for the profession in that there is a kind of the haves and have-nots situation developing," says Sam Miller. "There are resources required to take this on. Some of the smaller firms are going to struggle."

Garbage In, Garbage Out

Like all things, if used poorly, it will result in poor outcomes.

—David Fano, CASE

One challenge for anyone who works with data is ensuring the quality and reliability of the data one uses, as well as its source.

Work Needs to Happen Up Front

As with the early contributions of the integrated project delivery method—namely, team knowledge and expertise—gathering, analyzing, and using data

on a project will have the greatest impact, at the least expense, early in the process. But this work needs to be planned for, with a corresponding outlay of resources. See Figure I.13.

Need to Separate the Signal from the Noise

It is not just the amount of data, but the contextualizing of the data, that makes it more valuable, and this carries its own set of challenges. "One of the hardest things in our business is that everyone knows there's a lot of data. The hardest thing is to show you the right amount of data—and the right kind—in a way that makes sense to you. Enough information for you to make a decision off of," says Jennifer Johnson, Senior Director of Product Development at Reed Construction Data. "It's really easy to paralyze people with data. The hardest thing is to really boil it down to the 3-5 factors that are really going to make a difference in your business."

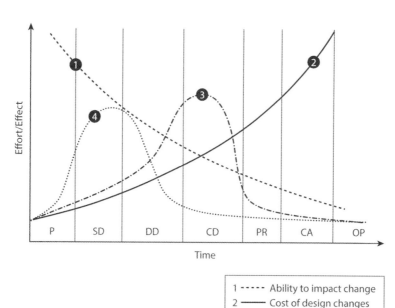

1 ----- Ability to impact change
2 ——— Cost of design changes
3 ·—·—· Traditional design process
4 ········· Preferred design process

Figure I.13: MacLeamy Graph. Patrick MacLeamy advocates for shifting the bulk of design effort earlier in the project to reduce the impact of design changes. © *HOK*

Strategy No. 1: Hone in on Key Information

The quantity of data matters but the context also matters, and to discern the data's context you have to ask a lot of questions. Jennifer Johnson recommends:

> You need to know what the construction activity is. What the forecast is. What are the handful of things you need to know? How do I expose that view so the trends become very clear? Once those trends are clear, go and dive deep into the data and do any kind of analysis that you need to. Let's not miss the forest for the trees. You need to hone in on just a few key pieces of information that are exposed to you that are most relevant to your business.

Each person and project team needs to ask and determine how much data is the right amount for what they are trying to accomplish. "What we're looking at now, and what the industry will have to deal with moving forward, now that the data store is open, there's a real issue of what is signal and what is noise," says Sukanya Paciorek, Vice President of Corporate Sustainability at Vornado Realty Trust. "Being able to figure out which is which requires a very practical orientation. What is the goal? What is the direction we are trying to take? Because more data is not better data. More data just gets in the way."

More data is not better data. More data just gets in the way.
—Sukanya Paciorek, Vornado

Vast Amounts of Data Can Challenge Computer Hardware

Up until recently, we have had to rely on internally managed computer hardware to collect and store the data that we use in our projects. Will cloud-based data-driven design bring a whole new level of analysis to the industry? If so, how?

Interoperability and Cross-Referencing of Datasets

While an abundance of data is available to those in the AECO industry, we can seek to benefit only if the various platforms and technologies speak to and "play well with" each other.

Seeing the Impacts of Multiple Factors Simultaneously

Because data is not rule-based, it enables teams to see the impacts of multiple factors simultaneously, which can be seen as a benefit. But doing so also has its challenges, such as those that occur when one wants to cross-check multiple datasets. (See Figure I.14.)

Working with Unstructured Data

Although other markets and sectors have purported to find some success at doing so, the AECO industry is not ready to work with unstructured data of massive size.

Overcoming the Fear That Computers Will Be Making Decisions

This fear is actually a misperception: that jobs will become automated and data-driven computers and algorithms will be put in charge. No matter how much data we have, or how sophisticated the algorithms, no matter how automated our processes are, or how learned our machines become, humans will still be making the decisions. There are places in the planning process where the computer can give us great gains, but some important parts of the process will always remain in the human domain. There are people

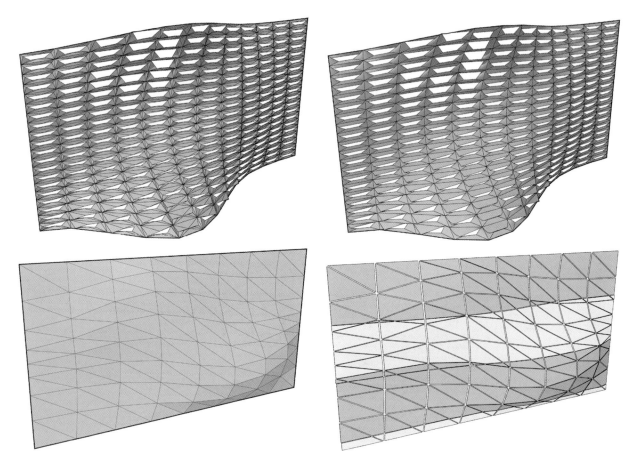

Figure I.14:   Using proxy models to satisfy a variety of deliverables with a single data set. Parametric platforms allow users to create multiple versions of a model based upon a shared data set. In doing so, different deliverable requirements are satisfied without the need to manually remodel.© *Brian Ringley*

who believe that architecture and construction will become a computer/robotic culture in the end and that there won't be a place for them. To this, Zigmund Rubel, AIA, co-founder of Aditazz Inc., says, "In all fairness, to some degree they're right." (See Figure I.15.)

The fear is that people think computers are going to make the decision. I don't see that happening any time soon.

—Zigmund Rubel, Aditazz

Data Sharing and Transparency

Privacy and security are big concerns of AECO organizations, and they have good reason to be concerned. First and foremost, AECO practices and organizations need to become aware and informed of the benefits that can be received by the transparent sharing of data, the means by which the data can be best shared, and the software interoperability challenges that create potential obstacles to the open sharing of data. As the technology and data-related issues work themselves out, those in the

Figure I.15: The Aditazz Realization Platform wheel integrates design, construction, and building of products. © *Aditazz*

design professions and construction industry need to commit to the transparent sharing of data for the full benefits to be realized.

Challenges to the Architect

There are several challenges that are particular to the architect. Key among them is the fact that data is seen as too abstract to be incorporated into the design process. While architects recognize that architecture is both an art and a science, data is perceived by some architects as being foreign to the art and craft of designing buildings. Or worse, data

is seen as a commodity. Coupled with these challenges is the fear that data will require the architect to validate their choices, something that some architects would prefer to leave to the engineers or consultants.

Data Is Too Abstract for Architects

Architects trust what they can see and touch. There's a basic distrust of something as abstract as data, especially among nontechnical architects, architects with design leanings, and architects who see themselves first and foremost as artists.

Data isn't seen as sexy as design…. [Most people] see it as almost clerical.

– Andy Hamer, CEO CodeBook[4]

In the face of increasing amounts of data, and the need to leverage data in one's work, one might ask: *Hasn't architecture already become abstract enough?*

Strategy No. 2: Demonstrating Works, Explaining Doesn't

Some who work with data find themselves having to explain what they do and the value they provide in a document-centric process or organization. I asked Jonathon Broughton, Data Wrangler at Allies and Morrison, if he finds that others, even within his organization, understand what he does. "No," he admitted.

> I try my hardest not to explain myself because if I try to explain what it is I do, it is so far from what people understand that it is counterproductive. Because they're thinking, he's occupying a desk, I'm occupying a desk; I'm working all hours getting these drawings out, he's just having fun in the corner. It's much better for me to ask: Do you have something that's causing you a particular problem? Is there something in the way that you are working right now that—even if you don't know why or how—could probably be better? Then it's a much easier conversation to describe what I would do if I were in your position. If they have time to try it, they realize it is saving them X hours/week. That may be the thing that makes him go home and see his kids on a Friday night. That's when they suddenly understand what it is that I do. Demonstrating works. Explaining doesn't.

Past Experience

When working with data, your past experience can actually work against you. This happens because you are up against the tried and true. Risk-averse contractors and facilities personnel don't trust the data. They prefer to move forward based on past experience. This attitude shows up throughout the building lifecycle.

The Need to Validate

Along with risk aversion comes a fear of having to validate a decision, whether one's own or a decision by another party. "We're scared to validate," says David Fano of CASE. "All of the energy calculations on the building model said it is going to be this. Then they go back and measure it and it is not anywhere near that. We can't be scared of that. We have to embrace those failures, learn from them."

Firm Culture, Demographics, and Generations

Firm culture, along with the demographics and generations that makes up the workforce, makes working with data challenging. "Data is different—it's new and it's scary," says Evelyn Lee, Strategist at MKThink, concluding that the challenges surrounding data begin in school. "With the current architecture curriculums, I don't think any of the students graduating right now have an issue with working with data. A lot of these programs have a cross-over with GIS and energy modeling, which requires data. If you asked any of these graduates, they would tell you they would love to find a firm where I could put all of this into action." (See Figure I.16.)

It is as if once the data is there, common sense just falls to the wayside. That is a huge danger of data … there is trust in data that removes our critical thinking.

—Brian Ringley

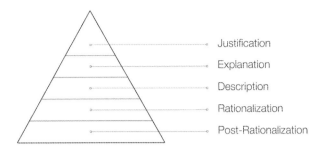

Figure I.16: Data as the ultimate justification for a course of architectural action. © *R Deutsch*

Data Can Be Too Specific and Restrictive

Does data help to create projects that are more flexible and adaptable? Or is working with data too specific and restrictive? "One of the biggest hurdles for using data in our industry is going to be embracing certainty," says David Fano. "Being able to say, yes, I *know* it's that. Most people want to be able to say, it could be this. It could be that."

Good News for the Owner Can Be Bad News for the Architect

In the pages that follow, a number of design professionals describe situations where running the numbers resulted in good news for the owner, but what could be interpreted as bad news for the design team. For example: "Despite our RFP, the data doesn't support the need for an anticipated addition for three years."

Working with Data Requires Additional Time and Effort

Similar to working in BIM, working with data requires some work up front. Doing so requires additional effort and manpower beyond what is typi-

cally involved in the predesign phase of projects. We cannot be assured that we will gain materially from such efforts, or if—like BIM—it will come to be expected, as opposed to being regarded as an additional design service. As with BIM, we might soon be asking, "Who will pay for the additional efforts that working with data requires?" (See Figure I.17.)

Challenges to the Contractor

Challenges to the contractor are unique in that some can be thought of as self-created or self-inflicted: for example, an aversion to taking on what is perceived to be additional risks, instead of looking at the addition of data into the construction process as potentially reducing, or managing, risks. Because budget, schedule, and safety are primary concerns of the contractor, there is sometimes an unwillingness to try a new technology or process if they will require resources, time, or training, or if unproven.

Introducing Technology Requires Training, Resources, and Time

Contractors are especially sensitive to the additional time and effort required when working with data on building projects, in part because their work is judged in terms of time (meeting a schedule) and cost (meeting a budget). So much so, that researchers who innovate in the construction space know that they want their efforts to be implemented into practice, they need to build on top of existing technologies and processes, over and above attempting to introduce new tools and workflows that require time for training and use of tightly allocated resources. Simply gathering data can be more time-consuming than one might anticipate. The time factor has to be considered when incorporating data in decisions, from structural systems to interior finishes.

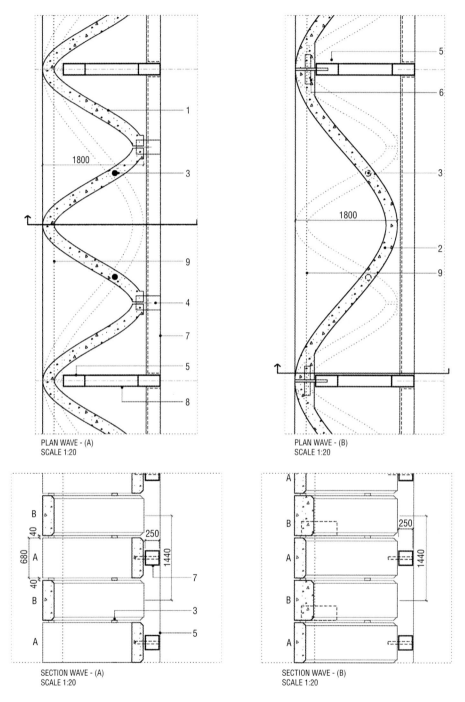

Figure I.17: Cooling tower (Doha, Qatar): Over-clad façade to cooling infrastructure in an urban context. Design data work is extended into construction to automate the manufacture of the formwork shuttering. © *Allies and Morrison*

Risk of Unproven or Untried Processes

How receptive is the risk-averse construction industry to change, and the introduction of new apps, gadgets, and processes? Mani Golparvar-Fard builds data-enabled technologies on top of existing processes rather than inventing new tools, partly to save contractors' time and cost, but also—primarily—because no one has time to learn a new technology or resources to pay for a new tool. (See Figure I.18.)

In proposing platforms, what I ran up against cultur-ally was: show me the 150 projects where this has been deployed successfully.

—Tyler Goss, CASE

To summarize, there are many benefits, but also considerable challenges, facing any design or construction professional, owner, or facility manager who is looking to incorporate data in the decision-making

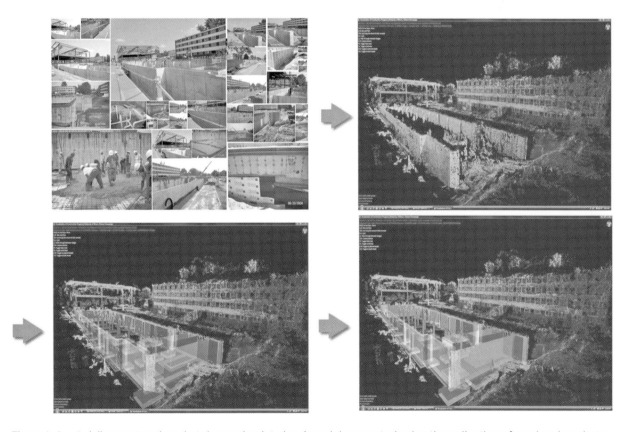

Figure I.18:   A daily construction photolog and point cloud model generated using the collection of overlapping photos. The elements detected as behind-schedule are color-coded in "red," and the elements on schedule are color-coded in "green." © *Mani Golparvar-Fard, PhD.*

process. Benefits and challenges to the owner are covered in Chapter 8. How does the AECO industry, as a discipline, capitalize on data to drive innovation in architecture, as other disciplines and industries have, despite the considerable challenges? This question is addressed and answered in the chapters that follow.

How the Book Is Organized

The book is divided into three parts, successively emphasizing justifications for, explanations for, and descriptions of data use, and asking (in this order) *why*, *how*, and *what*. Each part is more granular in terms of information than what preceded it. (See Figure I.19.)

In Part I, Chapters 1 through 3 look at justifications for using data in the AECO industry. Chapter 1 defines what we mean by data, examines how data differs from information and knowledge, and explores data's relationship with BIM. The benefits and challenges of different types of data are explored, as is a big question: *Who really needs to hear the message of data-driven design?*

Chapter 2 asks where we are today, as an industry, on the data front. This chapter looks at what it

means to be a data-driven, in contrast to a data-enabled or data-informed, practice. The chapter concludes with a look at the human side of data: our need while working with data to leverage intuition—the so-called human override of data—in the face of increased automation, resulting in man-machine collaboration. Chapter 3 focuses on ways to teach and work with data in school, opportunities for effective training in practice, and the role of unlearning past habits that may stand in the way of moving forward with a data initiative.

Part II looks at explanations for how data is used in the AECO industry. Chapter 4 is an exploration of how firms mine project data; where data is found and the ways it can be collected, including sensors, laser scanning/point cloud, and card swipes; and the types of data that can be captured, from monitoring air quality to acoustics.

Chapter 5 is concerned with the analysis of data, and the various tools used in the analysis and analytics of data, including parametric tools and processes such as BIM as well as computational design tools and algorithms. Building performance—including energy, sustainability, commissioning, lifecycle, human performance, operational performance, and business performance—is discussed, as are the metrics used in measuring and benchmarking results. The chapter concludes with a discussion of predictive analytics through building simulation, and the importance of visualizing and communicating data. Chapter 6 looks at the application of project data, and the new and existing roles of those who work with data in the AECO industry. Talent acquisition and leadership opportunities are explored.

Part III describes applications for data use throughout the project lifecycle, focusing on the role of data in construction, facilities, and operations. Chapter 7 focuses on how data is currently used in construction, and the impact of construction culture on data-driven efforts. Standards and interoperability

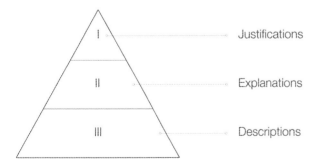

Figure I.19: Organized into three parts, this book provides—in this order—justifications for, explanations for, and descriptions of data use in the AECO industry. © R Deutsch

are discussed, as are linked data, open source and open data, open BIM, and buildingSMART initiatives. Chapter 8 continues the discussion beyond construction, looking at how data can be leveraged by building owners, operators, and end users; the impact of data on various building types, including data centers and technology projects; and what role, if any, data plays in the planning, design, construction, and operation of these building types.

Chapter 9 looks at ways to manage risk while using data. How much are security and privacy issues when collecting data? What are the potential barriers to sharing data in organizations? The book concludes with what's in store in the years ahead and where opportunities exist for data use in the AECO industry. There is a brief discussion of the future of BIM for architecture, construction, and facilities management; the so-called Internet of things, including the Internet of buildings; and what role data will play in all things "smart": smart buildings, objects, devices, manufacturer's products, infrastructure, landscapes, and cities.

1. Max Shron, *Thinking with data: How to turn information into insights* (Kindle Locations 33-34). O'Reilly Media, 2014.
2. Andera Al Saudi, "Empowering the world's BIM community," *The BIM Hub*, July 23, 2014; http://www.adjacentgovernment.co.uk/pbc-edition-004/bim-community/
3. "Perspectives on change: Ronald A. Heifetz," Change Theorists Wiki; http://changetheorists.pbworks.com/w/page/15475032/FrontPage?ie=UTF8&refRID=1Q32H7MCBH2HX1B8VBSR
4. Andy Hamer, CEO CodeBook Solutions, in email to author dated June 19, 2014.

We are in a race now to produce better and better information, instead of better and better buildings.

—Paul Fletcher

Data-Informed Decision-Making

Design and construction professionals often find themselves in situations where they are asked to defend their decisions—their choices, preferences, designs, or actions. The way professionals go about justifying their decisions is central to the shaping of their work and determining what gets built.

Throughout history, it has been the architect's role to make the arbitrary believable and rational. How do architects currently go about justifying their actions? What results are they finding? How successful are their efforts? It's not that there is more arbitrariness in architecture today, but that design professionals are having a harder time convincing others of their authority and the soundness of their selections. In school, design-professionals-in-the-making are trained to justify not their choices, but rather themselves.

What design and construction professionals really mean when they use the words *justify* or *justification* is often other terms and concepts used in handling the defense of design decisions: rationalization, self-justification, explanation, description, and excuse-making. These all add up to after-the-fact rationalization of design decisions.

There is a need for design and construction professionals, starting in school, to abandon self-justifying behavior. What we want to do is back our decisions up with data. *Get the data on it.* For some, data is something that is addressed after the fact: a rationalization of or support for actions already taken. These post-facto rationalizations are detected by everyone, seen as such, and therefore less effective in justifying and more importantly, convincing.

Owners are looking for reasons, not rationalizations. Can convincing grounds for decisions be found? Have design professionals been looking in the wrong places to ground their decisions? Is there an a priori ranking of the types of justifications that can take precedence? In other words, are there ultimate justifications, or only those that are most effective in a given situation?

1 The Data Turn

Model quality is certainly improving, but we are still not seeing enough valuable embedded data.

—David W. Light

Until recently, the discussion of data wasn't a daily occurrence in most architecture, engineering, and construction companies. Why then is there a need today for an understanding of how data is being leveraged in architecture, engineering, and construction, and by owners and operators? In other words: specifically for the AECO industry, why is this happening now?

Five Factors Leading to the Leveraging of Data and Industry Change

What forces and technologies have come together in the second decade of the twenty-first century that make the gathering and use of data possible for industry practitioners in firms small, medium, and large?

Technology

Technology has played a large part in the rise of data availability and use, including increased computer power, enabling the ability to crunch large quantities of data and provide higher-resolution communications, access to the cloud, and less expensive storage options. Software has a role in all of this as well. We have started to ask how building information can be better leveraged using data mining, and have started to investigate new directions for accelerating the flow of building information throughout a facility's life cycle. In turn, we have started to see where BIM data is being used in decision making in design, construction, and building operations. (See Figures 1.1 and 1.2.)

Many design and construction professionals—and also their clients—are justifiably frustrated that promised results from BIM tools are not being more readily achieved. The reason for this delay is that so-called higher uses of BIM—analyses, including scheduling, cost estimating, energy, sustainability, facilities management, and facility operations—require not only collaboration on integrated teams, but also the collection and strategic application of building data. Another factor is higher-resolution communications. Soon people will be able to share vastly more information than they are currently. I asked Andrew Witt, Director of Research at Gehry Technologies, if this can be attributed to an increase in the need to share or something else. "It's the opportunistic availability of both data and the means to share

Figure 1.1: BIM Benchmark measures real-world performance of computer hardware. Users are presented with a series of statistics concerning how quickly their computer executed a series of tasks in a BIM model, allowing them to make more informed hardware-purchasing decisions. © *CASE*

Figure 1.2: A version of the BIM Benchmark tool prototyped at CASE. © *CASE*

it," says Witt. "It's not necessarily based on some new requirement to share. There's a greater and greater expectation of higher and higher fidelity communication. People will have the means to execute high-resolution communication. People won't necessarily be communicating more frequently. But the resolution of that communication will be much higher."

The higher resolution will enable more data and information—and more exact data and information—to be shared more quickly and more reliably. Part of this is being brought about by cloud computing. Mads Jensen, CEO of Sefaira, admits that he wouldn't have a product if not for the cloud: "With cloud computing, we can now analyze everything in far greater detail, thereby using the analysis of our design data to actually shape the next design decision." (See Figures 1.3 and 1.4.)

Strategy No. 3: Look Outside the Industry

The architecture profession and construction industry have always trailed mainstream technology. CASE's David Fano suggests one way to keep up or even stay ahead: "If you want to see what's coming up for the AEC industry, just look at articles in *TechCrunch*[1] from five years ago. You can see where the world is going. If anything, we're behind."

Fano takes a contrarian view, holding everything that appears new today has actually been with us for some time: "How long has business intelligence been around? It's old news. For the AEC industry, it's a new, innovative, groundbreaking thing—it's really not. That's what I tell people—others have figured this out for us already. The technology's figured out. The software's figured out. Processes are mostly figured out. We just have to readapt them to our industry."[2]

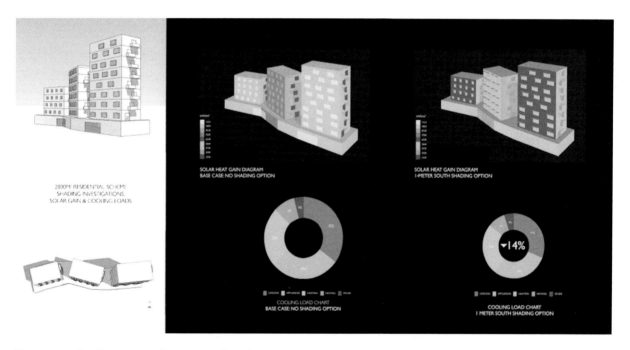

Figure 1.3:   Shading tests and corresponding changes to cooling loads. © *Sefaira*

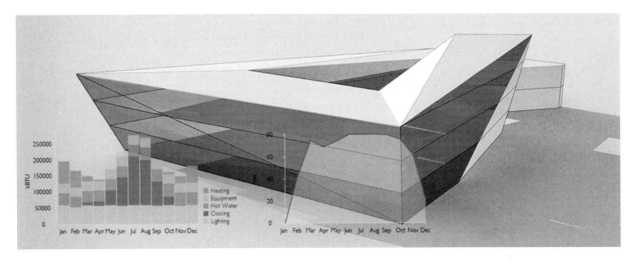

Figure 1.4:   Sefaira's outputs include clear informative graphs that can exported and edited to fit the designer's brand. © *Sefaira*

"To us, the cloud is simply a server. There is nothing particularly new about this technology. Architecture firms in the 1970s were using servers for the same reason we use the cloud today: servers can store and process orders of magnitude more data than can be done on a local machine," adds Fano. "Rather than throwing data away, we can keep it in the cloud. We can create massive databases of every model a firm has produced. Not just the final model; we can save every version of the model's development."[3]

"The short answer is that we are really just standing on the shoulders of the phenomenal advances we've seen in computer science in the last three decades," concludes Mads Jensen, CEO of Sefaira. "We live in an incredible age."[4]

Technology is not limited to solutions available to us within our organizations. As Jensen points out, "In many ways, computer games have pioneered models for data-driven decision making. Games like Sim City were way ahead of business software in terms of giving users a data-rich and immersive environment in which to make decisions, and a continuous

feedback loop enabling more iterations and ultimately better decisions." (See Figures 1.5 and 1.6.)

People

It's not only about the technology and tools: people make a difference. People are an important force that helps make the gathering, analysis, and application of data a reality today. But not just any people: the *right* people—people with a certain inclination—are helping to make the leveraging of data in AECO industry possible. What these inclinations are vary from person to person, but some patterns can be discerned. The ability to identify and recognize these qualities in others can have implications for human resources, as well as for attracting and retaining talent.

Firm cultures that encourage, or at the very least accept, that working with data is now a significant part of the project team effort can make a difference. In particular, we will need cultures that encourage and uphold the attitudes and mindsets necessary to work with people who are as comfortable working with data and analytics as they are

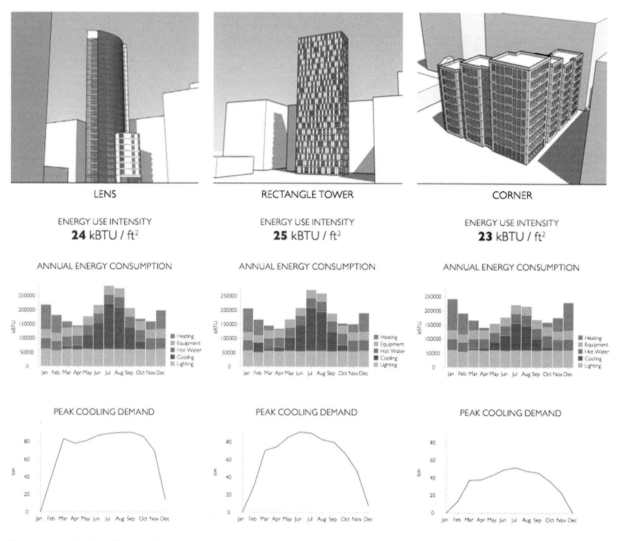

Figure 1.5: Sefaira allows architects to compare design options and measure their performance using chosen parameters. (EUI/ Annual Energy Consumption/ Peak Cooling Demand) © *Sefaira*

putting buildings together. Sean D. Burke, LEED AP, Digital Practice Leader at NBBJ, Seattle, discussed the convergence of parametric and computational tools in terms of people: "From a tools perspective—and tools aren't the only thing causing this convergence—it's the maturity of the design community, everyone being able to take advantage of both ways of working; and a generational thing as well." Due to access to information, ubiquitous training, and the sharing of information, today people are perceived as being more capable of developing the processes and technology necessary to manage data.

Figure 1.6: Users make comparisons to set the project on the right track early, refine the design as it progresses, and test the effects of design changes (including value engineering). © Sefaira

Performance

We're already starting to see a change in the focus of the current generation of architects, from form to performance, away from the media attention of the so-called *starchitect* and creation of monumental, iconic buildings to more site-specific, earth-friendly building interventions. Erik Olsen, PE, Managing Partner, and CEO at Transsolar Climate Engineering, has witnessed the fascination with form taking on a change. "In the younger generation of architects, the fascination with form is not what it was for the older generation of architects practicing today. It's already changing." The move away from an exclusive focus on form has provided an opening for the discovery of data.

Access

There is a lot of data available today, in many formats, and all of it is easier to access today than at any previous time. Although interoperability remains a recurring concern, this is as much due to improved interoperability of software tools as it is to the collaborative, open sharing of information among various parties.

Awareness

Whether through education, enlightenment, or awareness through experience, we are finally coming to accept the nature of the construction industry as being fragmented. In other words, it's an industry built on one-of-a-kind, one-off designs, with geographically dispersed production sites and project stakeholders. Teams come together for a brief time to construct the project, then disperse; notably, these team efforts are marked by a lack of single entities doing it all. The industry is moving from construction being historically risk-averse to assessing and managing risk on a project-by-project basis. Mark Frisch, FAIA, Managing Principal at Solomon Cordwell Buenz, notes that today, "There is a generally greater appreciation of how data can positively inform a variety of processes in our profession." All of these have a role to play in making this time ripe for a data turn. (See Figure 1.7.)

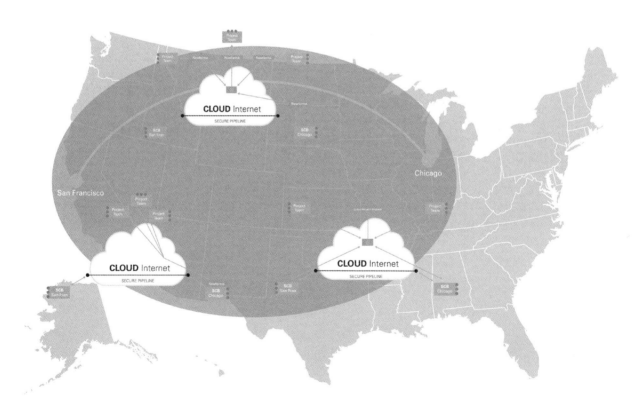

Figure 1.7:   Horizon Cloud. Cloud technology enables a secure pipeline for sharing data across offices and project teams.
© Solomon Cordwell Buenz

Case Study Interview with Robert Yori

Robert Yori is a senior digital design manager at the New York office of Skidmore, Owings and Merrill (SOM), where he co-manages the office's Digital Design efforts and co-leads SOM's firmwide BIM/Digital Design initiatives. He develops BIM curricula for, and teaches at, New York University and elsewhere, and you can often see him presenting at industry conferences, including Autodesk University, ACADIA, and RTC.

Is data something that you just work with and take for granted? Are we potentially fetishizing it by even talking about it?

Robert Yori (RY): *Data* itself is such a broad term. Something that was produced with ink is also data. It's really a question about how it's absorbed, shared, and processed. In the broad sense, dealing with massive amounts of data is something architects have always done, although much of it hasn't historically been computational. The core question is this: How can we utilize the myriad types of data in a way to better our projects? Utilizing computers to do that is also a long and storied history. So the granularity and explicit nature of that data, that's the relatively new part of the challenge. Plus, everyone adopts things at a different pace.

Talk a little about the database work SOM has been doing with CASE Inc.

RY: Some of our recent work echoes an effort we've undertaken in analog form in years past. We've collectivized our knowledge and our expertise about different building types in certain markets. Towers, for example, are a staple of our business. We have a really good sense of the particulars about tower metrics through all of the projects that the firm has completed, through a combination of anecdotal knowledge and rigorous analysis, and we're pretty good about documenting and sharing that. We thought it would be useful to take that to the next level—by moving it out of the analog realm and translating it into the digital realm—for a couple of reasons. One, it allows us some flexibility. It frees the information from the paper documentation that we produce. In paper form, for example, we might decide we're going to publish data internally on eight buildings. If we want to add a ninth, there's a fair amount of effort required to revise the publication, reprint, redistribute, and so on. If the information is part of a database, we're able to flexibly add and remove buildings, markets, and other unforeseen information. More importantly, it enables us to selectively filter in ways that we might not have thought of when we were initially publishing the paper documents. We've been digging deep into analyzing our best projects and putting the results into a database, which becomes a powerful resource for precedent research. [See Figures 1.8 through 1.11.]

> *We could ask the database: "How many buildings have we done in New York with this particular type of glass?" When a client comes to us and says, "I really love that project you did in midtown Manhattan. Can you do something similar for our site in China?" we can begin to analyze our building's key design metrics almost instantaneously, to understand how they may translate to another building in another region. To see whether the glass type is appropriate in terms of solar gain, daylight, or transparency, or R value. To evaluate the cooling and ventilation strategies and determine if they would be applicable in China. It gives us thorough, quick access to a body of knowledge that has historically been difficult to gather at this level of comprehensiveness.*
>
> —Robert Yori, SOM

(Continued)

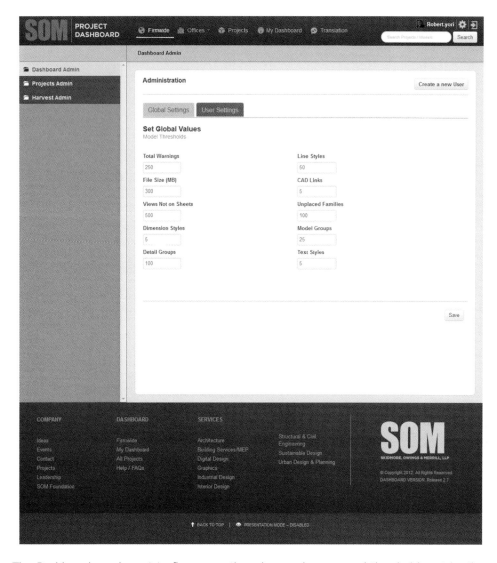

Figure 1.8: The Dashboard can be set to flag properties whose values exceed thresholds set by the user. As the Dashboard grows in functionality, roles can be added or modified. © *Skidmore Owings and Merrill LLP*

How important is it that others in the firm understand that—in addition to their work on buildings and urban spaces—they're also working on databases?

RY: Project leaders and senior architects are juggling vast amounts of data in their heads, and the teams are making it explicit through drawings, specifications, project briefs, and renderings. Over the last decade, as teams have started utilizing Revit, it's been an easier conversation to have. After teams begin to get familiar and comfortable with the tool, I

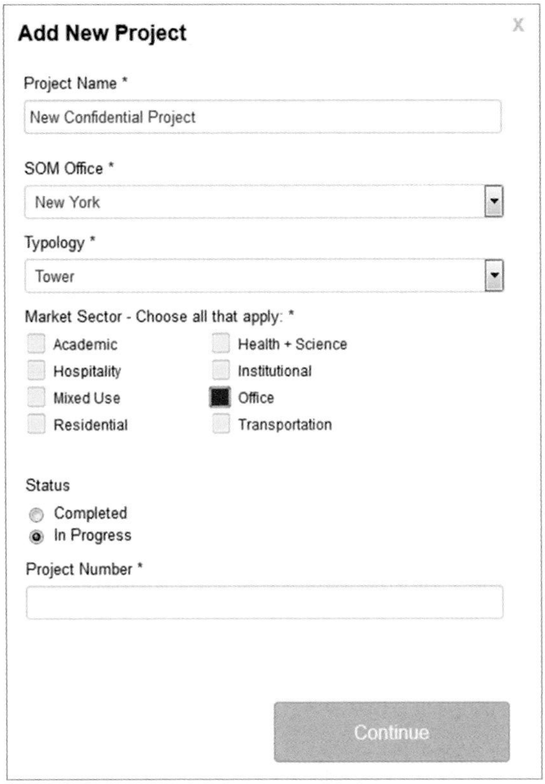

Figure 1.9: Adding a new project involves inputting a number of fields, including market sector, building typology, and status, which can be sourced from an existing database to minimize redundancy and promote data validity. © Skidmore Owings and Merrill LLP

say, "You know that's a database you're working in, right?" And many of them respond, "Yeah, I know." It's really a graphic introduction into what a database is and what it might be useful for. Similar potentials existed with CAD, because CAD was a database—if it was used that way.

There are different approaches and varying degrees of understanding and facility with the notion of "drawings as database," just like when computers were first introduced into architecture. As a profession we struggled with the idea of tangibles versus intangibles, what's more difficult to embody digitally, and what can and should be embodied. Overall, we're all having to deal with increasing amounts of data. Those that are computationally inclined naturally would look to some sort of database solution. But I don't necessarily like to call it that from the start—it can scare people off. [See Figures 1.12 through 1.14.]

In the best of all possible worlds, would everyone see buildings in terms of data?

RY: A knee-jerk response would be, "Sure, I wish everybody could do that." I wouldn't be anywhere wise enough to be able to say what the prescription is for the industry. Architecture is manifold. Everybody comes to it with their own

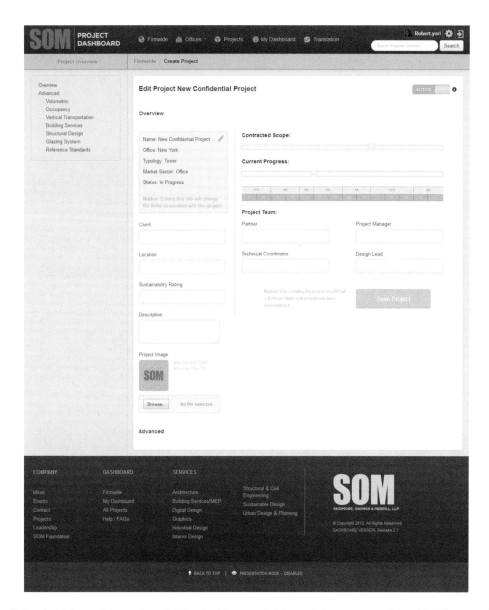

Figure 1.10:   Extended information, such as Contracted Scope and Current Progress, can be added for querying projects at a particular phase. © *Skidmore Owings and Merrill LLP*

interests and their own personalities. That's one of the things that make it so fascinating—that it's not simply one set of ideas. As much as I love data, and working informationally, sometimes I'm just drawn to things that are incredibly simple and crafted entirely by hand. It's like the classical music enthusiasts who can't get enough of the three-chord rock-and-roll song. It takes all kinds. So, sure, in some ways it would make our lives easier if everyone would see buildings in terms of data. But I'd be afraid we'd all be missing out if everyone approached it only one way.

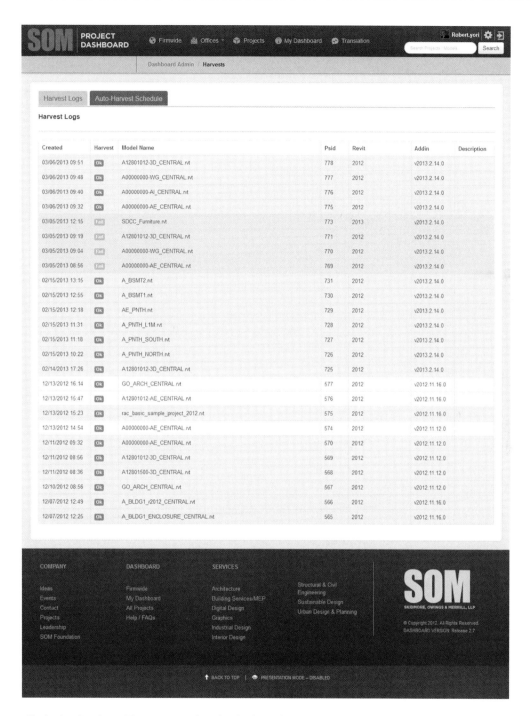

Figure 1.11:   Project uploads, or Harvests, can be checked, tracked, and verified. © *Skidmore Owings and Merrill LLP*

(Continued)

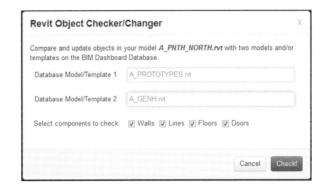

Figure 1.12   A Comparison Engine enables a user to check one or more Family Types against Types in another file, such as a Standards file. Results display discrepancies in Families' Parameter values. © Skidmore Owings and Merrill LLP

300LOD 22D CMU 150 2 - Side GYP 1HR	Values Mismatch	⟳	Matches
300LOD 22E CMU 150 2 - Side GYP 2HR	Values Mismatch	⟳	Matches
300LOD 22F CMU 150 2 - Side GYP + 1 - Side CB 1HR	Values Mismatch	⟳	Matches

Parameter	Value	Parameter	Value	Parameter	Value
Spacing		Spacing		Spacing	
Adjust for Mullion Size		Adjust for Mullion Size		Adjust for Mullion Size	
Join Condition		Join Condition		Join Condition	
Manufacturer		Manufacturer		Manufacturer	
Assembly Code		Assembly Code		Assembly Code	
Layout		Layout		Layout	
Border 1 Type		Border 1 Type		Border 1 Type	
Model		Model		Model	
Border 2 Type		Border 2 Type		Border 2 Type	
Keynote		Keynote		Keynote	
Type Comments		Type Comments		Type Comments	
Interior Type		Interior Type		Interior Type	
Type Mark		Type Mark		Type Mark	
URL		URL		URL	
Curtain Panel		Curtain Panel		Curtain Panel	
Cost	0.00	Cost	0.00	Cost	0.00
Fire Rating		Fire Rating		Fire Rating	
Function		Function	1	Function	
Automatically Embed		Automatically Embed		Automatically Embed	
Assembly Description		Assembly Description		Assembly Description	
Description		Description		Description	
Workset	14	Workset	14	Workset	14
Width	245	Width		Width	245
Coarse Scale Fill Pattern		Coarse Scale Fill Pattern		Coarse Scale Fill Pattern	
Wrapping at Inserts		Wrapping at Inserts		Wrapping at Inserts	
Coarse Scale Fill Color		Coarse Scale Fill Color		Coarse Scale Fill Color	
Wrapping at Ends		Wrapping at Ends		Wrapping at Ends	
Edited by		Edited by		Edited by	
Span At 16" On Center		Span At 16" On Center		Span At 16" On Center	
Stud Size		Stud Size		Stud Size	
Unbraced Length L/240		Unbraced Length L/240		Unbraced Length L/240	

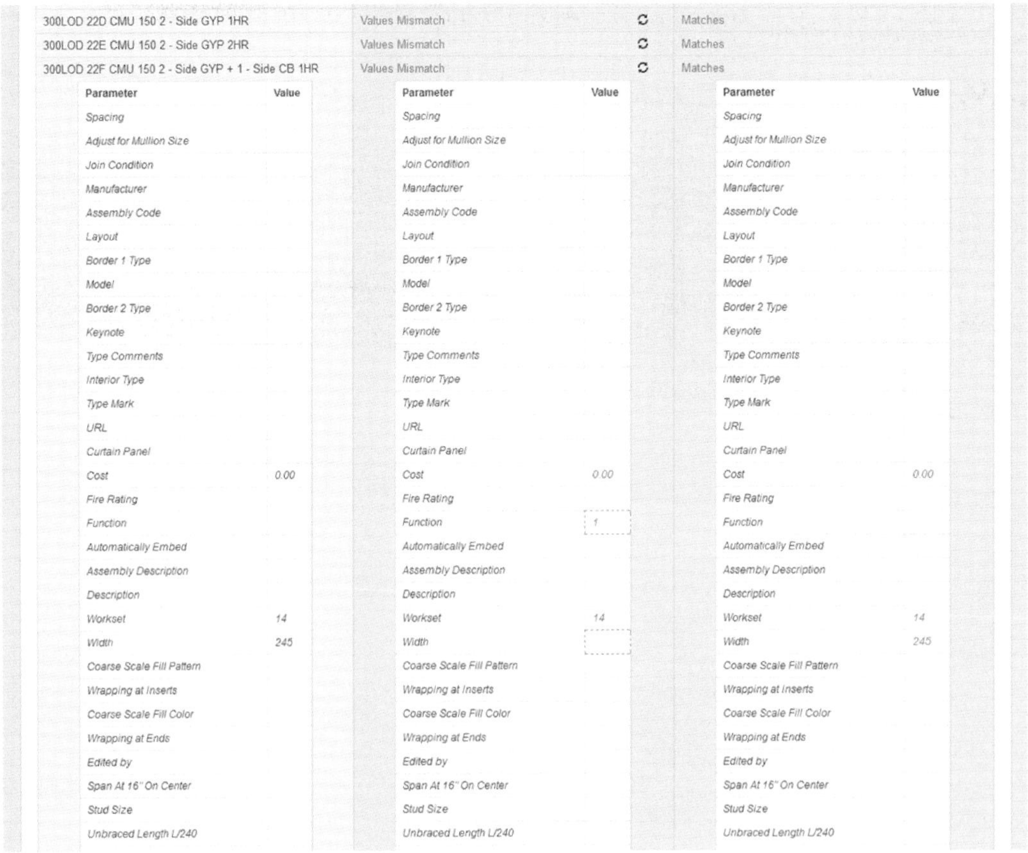

Figure 1.13:   Results display discrepancies in Families' Parameter values for easy management of multi-model projects. © Skidmore Owings and Merrill LLP

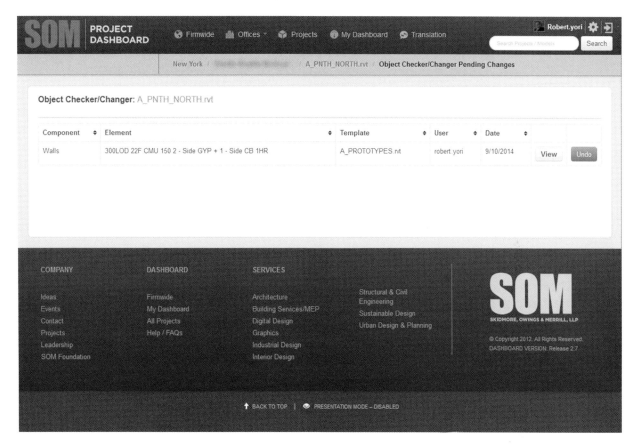

Figure 1.14:   Corrections can be made from the Dashboard console and propagated back to their respective models.
© *Skidmore Owings and Merrill LLP*

Are there particular technologies that are better at handling project data? Is this ever a factor in your considering working with these tools?

RY: One that is fairly ubiquitous and a great entry point is Excel. How many people create lists in Microsoft Excel? Nearly everybody works in it, many without even realizing that it can be the basis for a database. I've seen that happen a lot—not just here at SOM but all over. I've seen it in my own use. I write down a number of things, then think, well, if I put it in Excel I can do a number of calculations. After a while I say "wouldn't it be great if I could take that and extend it out, and include 'x,' 'y,' and 'z,' and do some calculations, and validate my ideas…" and then the spreadsheet becomes a tremendously useful, ad hoc database. The lowest-threshold, lowest-cost, lowest-hanging fruit that you can do to begin to understand how to utilize what you have is in Excel. Revit is good for this, too, because it provides a database with a graphic front end. For hardcore data gathering, it's a gateway drug of sorts. You see the value of good data, and the possibilities, and begin to look elsewhere for more capable and more sophisticated tools. Oftentimes that requires a more sophisticated or deeper level of knowledge such as SQL databases or more sophisticated modeling programs. But Excel is ubiquitous for so many people that it's a great place to start.

(Continued)

Revit is good for this, too, because it provides a database with a graphic front end. For hardcore data gathering, it's a gateway drug of sorts.

—Robert Yori, SOM

Back to CAD for a moment, it has a tremendous capacity to be informational, but, as I mentioned, only if it's used that way. Through my early career I've seen many people not understand the data value of putting things on the proper layer. Or naming blocks properly so they can be counted. One of the complications of any of the computational tools is that their perceived validity can be an all-or-nothing prospect. It has to be perfect. Once someone begins to cast doubt on the legitimacy of the information that's driving it, it can cast doubt on the legitimacy of the entire procedure.

For many design professionals, the subject of data isn't nearly as compelling as the generation of interesting form. Do you see this as an impediment to data use in the AEC industry?

RY: Data is a means to an end. So much of what we do can be classified that way, too. Understanding the motivations behind the data wrangling, and finding value in those motivations, is a conversation that should be had. Putting out data for its own sake might be interesting as part of the process, but it is very much part of the process and not an end goal or solution. People don't generally get into architecture to data wrangle. People get into architecture to solve particular problems or pursue particular interests that they want to pursue. Sure, some are interested in minute problems of great detail—which is great because not everybody is. Understanding data and computational process as a means to an end is really, really important. Because as adults learn, we need a motivation to understand why we should do things differently than we're comfortable with. If we can't find a personally compelling and beneficial reason to change, we won't.

In the near future, what do you see as an ideal firm approach: to strive to be a data-enabled, data-informed, or data-driven practice? What is your firm's approach? Why?

RY: Like any good academic, we should define what each of these three terms means. "Data-enabled" may be being aware of the data but not leveraging it. "Data-informed" might be using data as a factor in the decision-making process. "Data-driven" could imply—I don't know if it's a good thing—that it is your primary priority. I can't characterize the whole firm one way, but certainly aspects of what we do at SOM are data-driven. And some are data-informed. There is some information that is better suited to being data-driven and some that is less so. So holistically, when we are approaching design, I would have to go with data-informed. Because there are some things that we do that are incredibly data-intensive. Some things that we do aren't so much.

I see the ideal approach for the industry as being data-informed, although it is hard to generalize at that level. There are certain types of practice that are more data-driven. For example, my good friend has recently gone to work for a firm that focuses on healthcare. There are lots of fantastic, incredibly fascinating conversations about evidence-based design. A firm doing that kind of intensive work may be closer to data-driven. If you as a client want to go to a more sculptural architect, because you may be looking for something maybe a little less programmatically defined or rigorous, and want something that's more emblematic, perhaps you're closer to data-enabled. Being aware of data and understanding the role it can and should play in one's practice is very, very important. Having an awareness of it. In school, our professors often told us that architecture is about the problems you choose to solve—I would extend that and say "and how we choose to solve them." As long as you are aware of the "data factor," and you're understanding when

When I hear the term "data-inspired," it sounds as if there's an attempt to make it appear as though data was used in an integral way but really wasn't. Is "data-washing" a term yet?

—Robert Yori, SOM

it might make sense to use it in your practice, and to what degree, that's key.

How much of leveraging data is technology and how much is mindset?

RY: You've got to have the mindset first. If you're not motivated to do it you're not going to do it.

What mindsets would you recommend others in our organizations, profession, and industry develop in order to work with data?

RY: If the goal is to get that motivation, I would look to work that is data-driven or data-informed. Dig in and find out how data-driven or data-informed work is improving the quality of the projects and process. And it's got to be fun. You've got to have fun while you're doing it. That's the greatest motivator for anybody.

Can you describe a project where use of data led to an improved decision, insight, or outcome?

RY: We could cite any number of our performance-oriented buildings. So much of that design is data-driven. It has to be. A recent tower project in Guangzhou, China, made significant use of simulation and data-driven analysis in shaping the building to channel high-velocity wind through energy-generating turbines. We're using a similar strategy on a tower in Indonesia that also employs geothermal strategies. We're doing a net-zero energy school in Staten Island, New York, and using data-driven strategies to exceed our goals for solar panel surface area requirements.

Another good example, although not a building, is our Revit and BIM standards initiative. A number of years ago I gave a lecture at Autodesk University on the crossing over from pioneering use to mainstream platform use of BIM, including Revit. I referenced Geoffrey A. Moore's *Crossing the Chasm* very heavily. A lot of that transition involved creating standards for everyone—guidelines, best practices, and so forth. We knew that we had amassed a number of successful projects in Revit done by our pioneers and their teams. And we wanted to figure out how we could triangulate those successes into a body of documentation to be a guide on

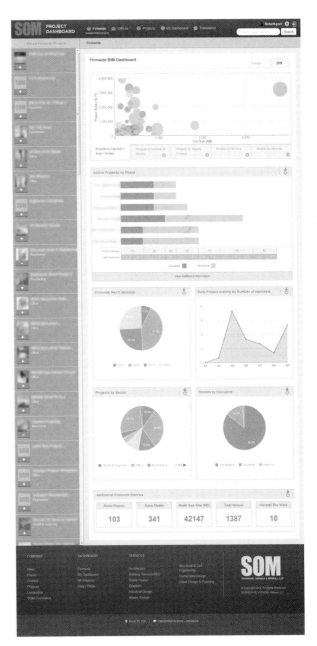

Figure 1.15: The BIM Dashboard's front page gives the user an at-a-glance, high-level understanding of norms for file size, project versions, models by discipline, status of most recent and active projects, and more. © *Skidmore Owings and Merrill LLP*

(Continued)

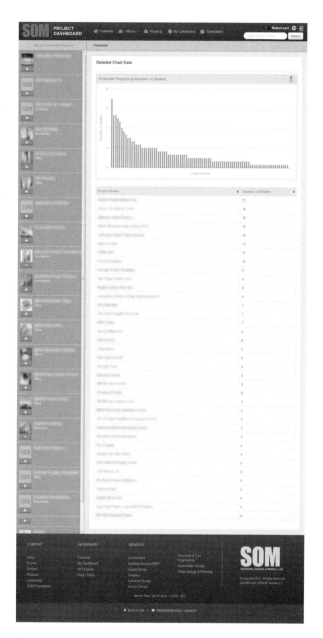

Figure 1.16: Users can drill down and visualize specific anomalies. The graph indicates that the largest project has a third more models than the next largest one, and that the majority of projects have one to six models. © *Skidmore Owings and Merrill LLP*

Figure 1.17: The Project page shows information about all of the models that constitute the Federated Model. The file size and aggregate number of warnings for the overall project remain constant—a sign that the project is very well managed. © *Skidmore Owings and Merrill LLP*

Figure 1.18: The Project Model Page gives an immediate status of the health of a project based on a number of commonly agreed-upon metrics. The Model's history is also included, providing additional insight as to future performance. © *Skidmore Owings and Merrill LLP*

(Continued)

future projects—in essence, a standards effort. [See Figure 1.15 through 1.18.]

We were faced with two options: Option one, to do what everybody does when it comes to standards. Sit around the table and verbally duke it out over which process is better, what we think this parameter should be named, why we should put it here or there, and so on. Option two was an entirely different approach—to find a way to transform the data, information, and knowledge embodied and embedded in the projects that we had already completed successfully. We chose option two, and began our engagement with data and CASE. We talked to CASE and it seemed like a much better idea to build a tool to query and extract the information out of those models and analyze it.

For example, we looked at our walls. A typical question was how to indicate fire ratings. Should they be described as "1 hr.," or "1," or "60," for minutes? We selected 10 projects that we had all agreed were the most successful ones, harvested the data from them all, and analyzed that data to see how it had been done. It helped us determine a trajectory for moving forward. We weren't blindly guessing. In the Option 1 scenario, the people sitting around that table verbally duking it out, they had that data, but it was only in their heads. It wasn't made explicit and analyzable to the degree that it was in Option 2, when we all analyzed it together. Out of that process we were able to understand amazing things from our projects. Different modeling and logical approaches, naming techniques—everything from the mundane to the sublime. It informed us tremendously in what we should do moving forward.

We got very little resistance because we, as a firm, knew the projects had already worked. This was an evolution of what we had already done and was an attempt to broaden that usage out. This is how we had done it at SOM successfully so far, and used that knowledge to move forward. [See Figures 1.19 thru 1.21.]

Figure 1.19: The Warnings functionality logs each warning from a model and remembers elements associated with that warning, allowing the user to track unique warning instances. © *Skidmore Owings and Merrill LLP*

Figure 1.20: A text box provides easy copy/paste access to Warning Element IDs so they can quickly be selected in Revit. © *Skidmore Owings and Merrill LLP*

Figure 1.21: Any of the Warnings can be expanded, revealing Element IDs that are indicated below. Each grouping indicates a unique Warning Instance. © *Skidmore Owings and Merrill LLP*

Data Defined

For a book dedicated to the subject of data, when starting out it is important to define our terms. What exactly do we mean when we say *data*? Is it a raw resource? How is it distinguished from information? Is the term so inclusive that it cannot be defined? To define data, we need to look at the various types and quantities of data.

Types of Data

Brian Ringley, Fuse Lab Technology Coordinator at City University of New York and on the Global Design Technology Team at Woods Bagot, clarifies how he approaches and defines data in his work with AEC technology and AEC education. "In my mind, there are three primary categories of data that AEC technologists and professionals deal with, and I define them relative to their relationship to an element of geometry:

Inherent geometrical data, or the data that's intrinsic to the generation of an element of geometry. For example, the inherent data of a nurbs [non-uniform rational basis spline] surface would include data items such as parameter space, boundary edges, and vertices; a guid [globally unique identifier]; control point and degree counts; and analysis data such as measurements of curvature and draft angle, to name a few.

External generative data, or data that is externally sourced from the generation of a piece of geometry for the purpose of affecting said geometry or iteratively generating new geometry. An example of this is the data used to measure insolation of the surface of a building. The actual data items that can be used to measure insolation are things like a Radiance sky model, Radiance material files, an EPW weather file, and definitions of time

durations and intervals for measurement. These data items must interact with inherent geometrical data such as surface normal direction and basic object occlusion to compute insolation values, which can then be used to modify existing geometry or generate new geometry. (This is the bulk of what is considered big data.)

Supplemental BIM data, or data for the purposes of building construction and building operation/life cycle that supplement geometrical data, generally produced within spreadsheets or BIM software. IFC data is an excellent example of this, but even simple data items such as the indication of whether or not a wall is structural within the Revit interface would be an example of this. [See Figure 1.22.]

What makes data valuable rather than serving solely as a commodity? The answer may be in the outcomes we seek and how the data is ultimately put to use. Ryan Mullenix, Design Partner at NBBJ, sees the value not in the data itself but in how the data is used. "One of the most intriguing comments I've heard recently, from a San Francisco futurist,[5] is that data is just data. Data doesn't answer a question. Data is just information. Its importance is in how you take that data and use it to address the problem you are trying to solve. That's been a big focus of ours."

DIKW

Is data the same thing as information? How, beyond granularity, can data be distinguished from information? The "I" in BIM, for example, stands for information. How are data and information different? Is it just semantics? Are the two terms interchangeable? "I use data interchangeably with information," admits David Fano of CASE. "It's such a nuanced distinction. When I talk about them, I tend to use them interchangeably." But are the terms truly interchangeable?

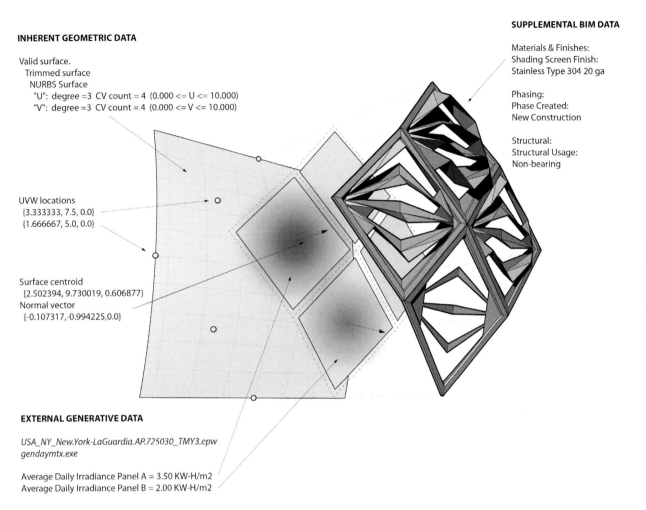

INHERENT GEOMETRIC DATA

Valid surface.
  Trimmed surface
    NURBS Surface
    "U": degree =3 CV count = 4 (0.000 <= U <= 10.000)
    "V": degree =3 CV count = 4 (0.000 <= V <= 10.000)

UVW locations
{3.333333, 7.5, 0.0}
{1.666667, 5.0, 0.0}

Surface centroid
{2.502394, 9.730019, 0.606877}
Normal vector
{-0.107317,-0.994225,0.0}

SUPPLEMENTAL BIM DATA

Materials & Finishes:
Shading Screen Finish:
Stainless Type 304 20 ga

Phasing:
Phase Created:
New Construction

Structural:
Structural Usage:
Non-bearing

EXTERNAL GENERATIVE DATA

USA_NY_New.York-LaGuardia.AP.725030_TMY3.epw
gendaymtx.exe

Average Daily Irradiance Panel A = 3.50 KW-H/m2
Average Daily Irradiance Panel B = 2.00 KW-H/m2

Figure 1.22: Three basic data types in AEC parametric modeling: inherent geometric data, external generative data, and supplemental BIM data. © *Brian Ringley*

We can define data in terms of a continuum, sometimes referred to as the DIKW spectrum or pyramid, where DIKW stands for data, information, knowledge, and wisdom. With the application of data on building projects, "insight" might be substituted for wisdom as a more beneficial goal for leveraging data: data, information, knowledge, and *insight*. Daniel Davis of CASE notes that "most of our industry is based on knowledge and information where

we derive insights—whether insights from data or computational tools." See Figure 1.23.

"Conceptually, I believe in the data, information, knowledge, wisdom (DIKW) progression," says Fano. He continues,

What the industry needs to realize is this is what they've been doing. Part of the reason

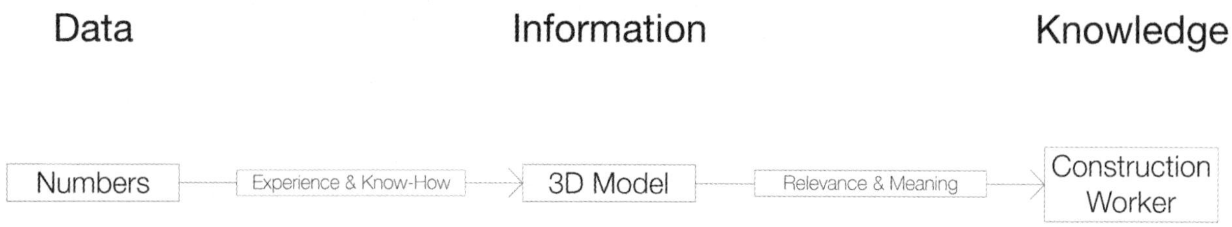

Data	Information	Knowledge

| Numbers | → Experience & Know-How → | 3D Model | → Relevance & Meaning → | Construction Worker |

Figure 1.23: DIKW Progression. To arrive at relevant and meaningful decisions, data must first pass through the BIM model. © R Deutsch

architects are so valuable and come into trouble later in their career is because they have accumulated a lot of wisdom. I don't think that can be trivialized. What I think is happening is—if we can capture this stuff which is really only in passive knowledge— now we have all of this more retrievable stuff we can expose the wisdom to a different demographic and one that thinks about things in a different way. I do see this as a watershed moment for the AEC industry. When we could end some of these long-lasting traditions—modes of working—as people begin to leverage information.

Fano describes the DIKW progression in terms of increasing structure to the data: "In its simplest terms, it's using past insight to make future decisions. When it's raw, it's data. When it's a little more structured, it's information. It's about decision making and equipping ourselves with the right things to make better decisions." With the DIKW continuum, it is clear that without data there would be no upstream information, knowledge, or wisdom. Data, in other words, can be thought of as a lower-order or more granular form of information.

One further distinction between data and information can be made. We keep hearing about the "I" in BIM. How is data related to the "I" in BIM? The "I" in

BIM is often described as a bookshelf or file cabinet in which manufacturer's manuals and product cut sheets are kept. The BIM is said to *hold* the specifications, the project manual—for safekeeping—so one knows where to find it. In contrast to information, data is at once less specific and more fluid and applicable. With data, the model becomes something more than a receptacle or container where information is stored, more than a retrieval system or long-term storage container. Data in BIM is different in that the data in BIM is fluid and can be queried.

Massive Quantities of Data Defined

As discussed, use of data in the AECO industry is not new. The built environment has long been an abundant source of data. What is new is the amount of data that is available to us; our capacity to measure and ability to capture, process, and act on that data; and, frankly, our industry's urgent need to do so.[6] The use of large quantities of data in decision making in design and construction involves securing a commitment within teams and the organization, reinventing internal and external processes, and modifying organizational behavior.[7] How we refer to massive amounts of data in our industry is still being debated. (See Figure 1.24.)

It is a contention of this book that use of the term *big data*, still popular at the time of publication,

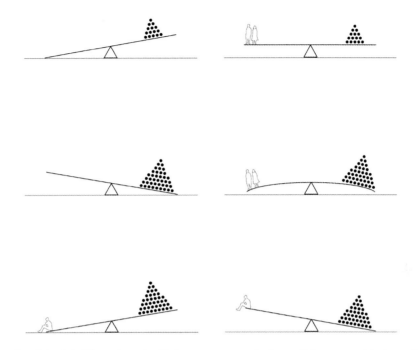

Figure 1.24: Leveraging "big data." Experiment with how your organization will leverage data to make better decisions, bring about better insights, and make better buildings. © *R Deutsch*

will rapidly diminish, and that massive amounts of data will just be referred to as *data*. "Technology is evolving rapidly," acknowledges Mads Jensen, CEO of Sefaira, "and so is the language we use to talk about it. Because of the rapid evolution, we don't always manage to get full consensus on what terms actually mean, before they are either replaced or their meaning morphs again." Jensen took a stab at defining big data: "Big data: Often used as a term for what we can do with statistics once we have lots of data available. We may not understand or be able to model everything that is going on, but there are enough potential relationships that you can start to infer causation and try to draw some conclusions about how things relate."

David Fano finds trying to define big data for the AECO industry as a futile exercise. "If you look at big data, it's just like BIM," says Fano.

That term came from a marketing depart-ment. That term didn't come from anyone actually doing the work. It doesn't matter if it goes away any time soon—it isn't worth wast-ing energy on. We should embrace it for what it is. It's a mindset. There are definitely ide-ologies around it that I agree with. So I'll just cherry-pick the ones that work for me to talk about it the way I want to talk about it. To waste any time trying to come to a singular defini-tion I don't see as valuable. When I talk about it, I define it in my terms. I'm going to tell you how I define this term when I talk about it. You can still use your definition. We're all using the same language here. [See Figure 1.25.]

Chris Pyke of USGBC believes that we are getting a little ahead of ourselves with the use of the term *big data*, finding value in the traditional big data

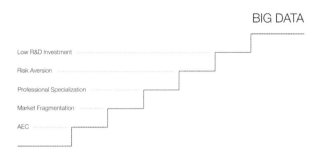

BIG DATA

Low R&D Investment
Risk Aversion
Professional Specialization
Market Fragmentation
AEC

Figure 1.25: AECO industry's considerable challenges to fully participating in big data. © *R Deutsch*

concepts of volume, velocity, variety, and verac-ity. "Today, our data volumes are relatively mod-est, velocities relatively low, variety is growing, and veracity is widely (wildly) variable. So, we have some of the elements, but we are hardly approaching big data as it is understood in e-commerce or finance." Pyke continues:

> Big data will come to our industry when we begin to collect and integrate spatially and temporally specific information from mil-lions of buildings associated with billions of occupants using energy and creating social, economic, and environmental impacts on a second-by-second basis. We are creating the foundation for this future, but it remains over the horizon.

Andrew Heumann, leader of NBBJ's Design Computation team, defines massive amounts of data as datasets large enough to require specialized computational infrastructure—such as cloud com-puting, or farms of machines like supercomputers—in order to process it, and says "under that definition I wouldn't say we're using big data." Heumann goes on to say:

> However, with a slightly more liberal definition, a server with hundreds of BIM models on it is big data—and in that case we use it every day,

not just as individuals accessing specific proj-ects, but with our tools that analyze and moni-tor the performance of all the projects in the firm, taking a look at all the models at once.

Clayton Starr of RTKL defines big data more tradi-tionally, as information gathered to inform the gath-erer of trends and to predict future outcomes. "This can be a passive harvest such as my local grocery store loyalty program or a weather station collecting bits of data daily to actively tracking the movement of people and equipment. The biggest surprise is always what you perceive the outcome will be to what it actually is. It can be startling to see how much waste we have in our daily routine, misuse of resources, or how much Kraft Mac and Cheese you actually buy." There are unquestionably fewer spe-cific applications for big data when defined this way.

Strategy No. 4: Not Big Data, Smart Data

Each organization has to define big data in terms that are meaningful for the specific situation and way they intend for its use. For example, Evelyn Lee, a strategist at MKThink, doesn't think about massive amounts of data points solely in terms of size, but rather in terms of what it can do for the client, and says that it's about finding the right balance in everything. Her approach? "We try to pull the smart data from big data." Lee continues,

> Whenever development people say if you want to have the most sustainable building on the block, never turn the lights on. Never run any of the mechani-cal systems. At the same time, we're trying to produce a productive workplace for your employees. What is the right amount of everything that will get you the highest level of productivity? We do use "big data," and we have a system that can mine it really quickly, but it's really about being smart about the data you're collecting. So we talk about it as smart data.

"Big data companies typically harvest data that is constantly being generated in real time," adds Andrew Witt. "That's never happening on a building project. There may be some collateral information on building projects, but I don't think it can really qualify as big data." Witt doesn't classify his work in terms of working with big data. "When I think of big data, I think of billions of data points. On the projects that we have worked with at GT, they have been more in the hundreds of thousands of data points or maybe millions of data points. In terms of building information, it is really hard to get to that big data threshold with a single project." Witt continues,

> Big data presumes that that sort of data is structurally homogenous and that there's a comparability across all the separate data points. One of the difficulties of talking about big data in the context of BIM is that, taken as a whole, there's a lot of heterogeneous information in the model. All of that information is structurally distinct and it isn't really comparable. You aren't going to compare the meta-

data of a window with the metadata from a building's concrete slab. They're two different animals. That's one of the challenges when you talk about big data in a context like that. Individual comparable datasets are actually relatively small.

Others contend that big data allows for the comparison of seemingly incompatible datasets. "Look at site selection decisions," suggests Tom Mulhern SVP, Chief Innovation Officer at Dātu Health:

> The real estate data is their data. They're looking at market analyses. They're looking at branch data. At resale value. Their business is built around the mastery of that data. Their ability to process that data on behalf of their client. One of the things that's definitional about big data is overlapping datasets that typically haven't been overlapped. Uniting data about one thing with data about another. Data about the economics of a building overlapped with data about the design of the building.

Case Study Interview with Sean D. Burke

Sean D. Burke, LEED AP, is a senior associate at NBBJ in Seattle, Washington. As the Digital Practice Leader for BIM, Sean is responsible for developing best practices, conducting research and development on new processes and tools, and working closely with the Design Computation group to identify areas where technology can help evolve the practice. Sean has presented at Autodesk University and at conferences around the world.

What implications do some of the new tools have for the sharing of data and even big data?

Sean D. Burke (SB): They're still immature right now. It's hard to say where they're going to go. They're solving an initial niche of peer-to-peer collaboration, in lieu of big, more heavy-handed administration sites that require a lot of IT involvement. I think that's a good thing because it democratizes the idea of project teams. It makes it a lot more agile and reduces the barrier to entry. You can poke into the tool and invite your coworkers and collaborators from other design firms in an ad hoc manner rather than having it be so formalized, where you have to set up an account, give everybody access. It's entirely left up to the individual, which is a good thing. It has disadvantages as well: it's harder to control the flow of information if you have projects that have some sensitivity to the information. The majority of projects, though, don't fall under that category.

(Continued)

As for implications for big data, when it comes down to aggregating things across multiple projects or teams, the cloud becomes a pretty rich information source if it can be mined properly, and if access to that data is available in an open way. Currently, the providers of these cloud services, such as Autodesk, are mining that data and creating big data. They might be anonymizing that data and using it for their own internal sales and marketing needs. It's happening already, whether we are benefiting directly or not.

Talk about how big data fits into the BIM workflow. What are some of the ways NBBJ is harnessing big data?

SB: There are a couple different ways. One, we're starting to experiment with ways of getting data out of Revit, and managing it in more of a computer database platform. There are commercial tools out there like dRofus, CodeBook, Trelligence Affinity that are really good on the front end. When you're meeting with a client on a large project like a hospital, and you have to suck in all this data that you have been getting from them, and have to put it somewhere before you've drawn a single line or modeled a single wall. And you want that data to be validated against the model later on once you've built it. Those tools are great for that. We're trying to figure out if there's more opportunity there than those planning tools currently have. We're trying to think about the next step in that area.

On the other hand, we're keeping a real close eye on CASE's Project Dashboard. [See Figures 1.26 and 1.27.] The idea of aggregating data across multiple projects, then putting it in a dashboard-type interface so you can learn several different things, both at the project team level and the business intelligence (BI) level for the firm, is quite interesting.

On the subject of geometry versus data, you've written that[8]"Moving geometry between tools is trivial. Moving data between tools is key." Can you explain how these are different and why the ability to move data is key?

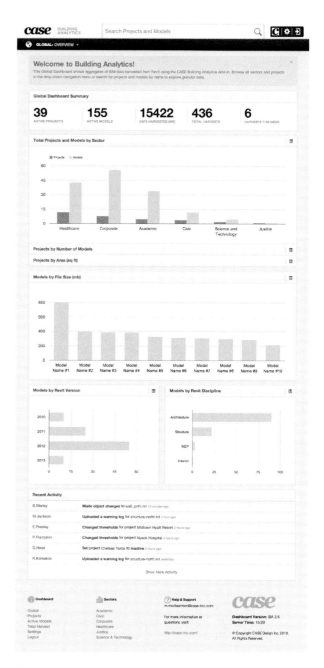

Figure 1.26: The global overview gives a quick snapshot of key statistics that are monitored daily; here the number of active projects and the activity in the BIM models are displayed. © *CASE*

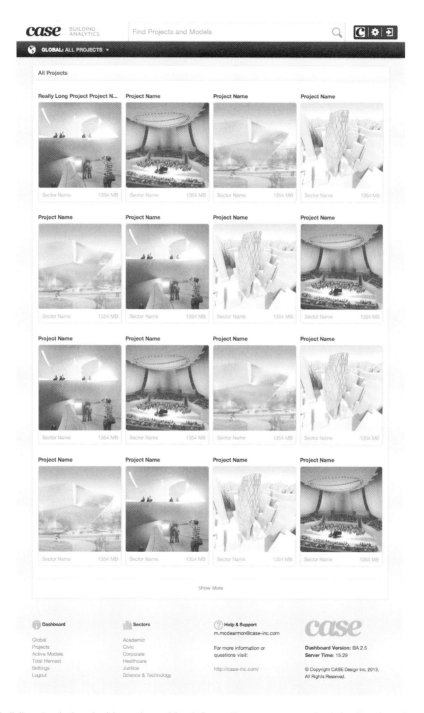

Figure 1.27:   The Building Analytics dashboard provides information on every project the firm has done. © *CASE*

(Continued)

SB: When data stays in one container for too long, it gets stale. It certainly loses its power. Data, like physical objects, can have momentum. If it sits for too long, it doesn't want to leave. If it's very agile and can be moved from tool to tool, without loss of structure or integrity, that data is much more valuable. Because you can analyze it more easily, append it, or modify it more easily. There's a lot of proprietary software that we use where the information that someone is looking for, like in a Revit model, is there. But the application may not have been designed in such a way that you can access it. A real simple example: floor area ratio (FAR) is a silly, stupid analysis that we should be able to do. But Revit can't compare two different things from two different categories. The building has mass and it has area, it has total floor area, but it knows nothing about the site that it sits on. So a tool like Dynamo can take those two objects and compare that to a formula and say, here's your FAR. You can also very easily hook up some visual feedback as you're designing. You don't need to have someone who is a Dynamo expert use Dynamo as a tool. It can be set up in advance and then minimized. A designer then could be working in Revit and they could be manipulating the massing model. And as soon as it goes out of compliance, it turns red. The whole model just turns red. Then they can push it back down again and it turns green. Just that simple act of connecting two pieces of data, that were already there, in a new way by using another tool is quite a revelation. We think of design computation as something that is about form-making and we're going to have double-curved surfaces. But really it's just a tool. You think of a problem like that where it requires someone manually taking a piece of data and putting it somewhere else. Once data exists in more than one place, it has a tendency of being wrong in both. When data can live in one place as the source of truth, and have connection back to the model, that's a better place to be. If you try to put all your data in one basket versus putting it where it makes the most sense.

A designer could be working in Revit and they could be manipulating the massing model. And as soon as it goes out of compliance, it turns red. The whole model just turns red. Then they can push it back down again and it turns green. Just that simple act of connecting two pieces of data, that were already there, in a new way by using another tool is quite a revelation.

—Sean D. Burke, NBBJ

What needs to be in place for this to happen?

SB: It could be an off-the-shelf tool. For us to be more successful in extending our capabilities and the reach of BIM, we need a little bit of a shift on the part of developers to give us direct access to our data, so we're able to query a Revit model from an external source. Data and geometry—the distinction is so fine. It's still data—it's just graphic data instead of non-graphic data. [See Figure 1.28.] They're both important. The computer doesn't care what's what. We just conceptually separate those two things because our profession is visually oriented. We can't see beauty in the Matrix. Most of us anyway.

The raw data behind the Revit user interface has a lot of secrets to reveal still. We just have to figure out ways we can get at it more quickly and easily. Maybe the file format needs to become open. Maybe its competitors need to take IFC more seriously and build an authoring tool on top of IFC so that there's no translation whatsoever. It's just there in an open schema that anyone can access from any tool. You just take the parts that you need and work at those.

People are getting the wrong impression where Revit's value lies. It's a database. We really need to start treating it like one.

—Sean D. Burke, NBBJ

Does style over substance present a danger in the development of thoughtful architects-in-the-making? Similar to algorithms for geometry versus for building performance. How do you anticipate data will fare?

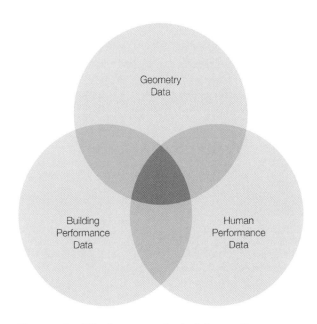

Figure 1.28:   Whether geometry, building performance, or human performance, it is all data. © *R Deutsch*

SB: Data will win when it is able to be validated. A concern of mine is how rapidly computation is expanding. I'm part of that expansion. I'm jumping into it, head first, because it has more potential value than BIM alone in how we work. The danger of that rapid expansion is people going in and grabbing algorithms from untrustworthy or unknown sources, putting them into their work, producing a result, showing the client and hanging your hat on that. It could have a severe backlash if we're not careful. I call it the snake oil salesman dilemma. You're standing up in front of the crowd with a flashy presentation, with all of these great graphics. If at the end of the day you give the wrong piece of data, or a piece of data that's interpreted in the wrong way to the client, and they latch on to only that—and that is wrong—the whole thing unravels.

There are two schools of thought when it comes to energy analysis in the industry. One, you're picking a baseline design and you're making it better or worse. It's like going to the eye doctor, and they flip the lenses: this one, or this one? You pick which one seems better. Here's the base, and out of the five different design studies we did, one in five [was] up to 30 percent better than the base. You're basing your decision on relative data. The other school of thought is hitting this exact number. Because that's what the software tells us. You're in early schematic design. You haven't thought of all the factors. You haven't thought of operations or occupancy. There are too many unknowns.

Take two presentations that are otherwise identical: one shows a number, while the other one shows a percentage, plus/minus. I would err on the side of loose interpretation of the results, rather than staking everything on the piece of software that generated it, whether commercial or an open-source algorithm; or the skill of the person who's driving this tool.

I've seen something that was presented that seemed totally out of whack with reality. Diving a little deeper, [I thought] oh, well, OK. This person had never done this analysis, or used this particular tool, before. We have to be really careful. The leadership at NBBJ is keenly aware of these things. And has done a lot of good due diligence with project teams to make sure they understand these risks. It's great to have their buy-in.

What about the sole proprietor? Or the small firm that wants to take advantage of all of these tools and methodologies, but they don't necessarily have the expertise? There's a lot of false confidence that can be gained from seeing a pretty graph that comes from a tool. When later examined, even commercial software can be completely unreliable.

You help facilitate change and transition in dynamic workplaces. Not everybody is comfortable with change. Technology is precarious. What do you advise?

SB: Pick something that you really love. Or something that aligns with your core values. And make that your profession. If your heart's not in it, it's a job. I get really pumped up every time I go to these industry conferences, not because of some new

(Continued)

feature that's available, but because I get to talk to all these other like-minded people that really have their heart in it and believe so strongly that this is meaningful work. When I was doing door schedules in AutoCAD that was not meaningful work. Someone could triple my salary and I would never work in 2D again. I want to create value, not suck it from the room.

Someone could triple my salary and I would never work in 2D again. I want to create value, not suck it from the room.

—Sean D. Burke, NBBJ

Back in 2011, you were one of the first people to describe real-time analysis working in a BIM environment. Can you describe real-time analysis—from a data standpoint?

SB: That's not even really real time. That's near real time. This isn't really energy analysis. This is just getting climate data, which to download from the NREL website is very painful, to make it useful. You then have to convert it into some file format that your energy modeling tool can read.

It's thirty times faster than traditional energy modeling because you're actually using your design model to generate the energy model tool. Then it's processed online, off of your computer, so you can continue working. If at the time you ran an Ecotect simulation or TRACE™ simulation, those things can take a long time to set up. And when they're running, it's occupying all of your computer's resources. You can't do anything else. You press a button, then walk away, because your machine is now useless until it's done.

Removing that from the equation is very liberating. You can do a lot more work while it's happening. You don't have to be as selective as you used to be about energy modeling. You never made changes, because you'd have to build a new model used by the engineer. But now, they can take the design model that's been processed in Green Building Studio and convert it back to gbXML, and brought into their energy model, enhanced with more intelligent data. Engineers that are able to work more closely with the architect are embracing this, and are a lot more successful at finding innovative solutions. Start with an optimized building design and add an optimized system design to complement that versus firms that aren't doing any energy analysis. They might be siting their building wrong, creating solar gain because it's facing slightly the wrong way. Using a poor design, then throwing it at the engineer, which is not collaborative. And you're saying, "make it better. Make it meet the minimum requirements." It's nearly impossible to meet the AIA 2030 Challenge by working that way. It has to be more collaborative. The systems integration folks, not necessarily the engineers—sometimes they're one and the same—are going to be better at this.

Moving from near real-time to actually real-time feedback on our work is very near. Our software can do it and our hardware can do it. It's just a matter of the vendors mobilizing to get all of that stuff created as a product and put in our hands. Autodesk may very quickly be challenged by some competitors in this space. There's Sefaira that's pretty close to real-time energy modeling. You're not working in a BIM world, you're still in this loose modeling tool. How do you transition from that to intelligent design data? When you have intelligent analysis data on top of a model you can't use in Revit? [See Figure 1.29.]

Building a BIM tool on top of a modeler is going to have the same challenges that building a BIM tool on top of a 2D CAD solution [had]. Revit's competitors—they're all mired in the fact that they are trying to be a general-purpose platform that has architectural tools on top. They're BIM. They're BIM tools. But they're not a database. And they're certainly not purpose built. Because in AutoCAD Architecture you can explode a wall, and now it's no longer BIM, is it? Just 3D faces and space that have no data attached to them whatsoever. You shouldn't have things that are that easy to cheat. Any editing should be nondestructive. Sure, SketchUp has the capability of creating BIM data. But you have to be so disciplined in how you do it.

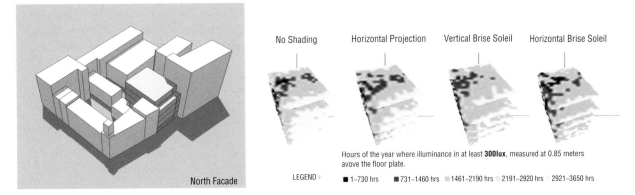

Figure 1.29:   Shading analysis using Sefaira's Daylighting Visualization. © *Sefaira*

Data versus Documents

Architects, of course, don't produce buildings. Unless they are working direct-to-fabrication, they produce instructions, in the form of design intent documents, for the making of buildings by others. This is an important distinction lost on many who have never worked with, or as, an architect. Architects have historically associated their value with the production of these documents, whether linen, paper, Mylar, vellum, or digital. As with documents, there are also many sources of data—sensors, BIM models, card swipes, barcode readings, and GPS, to name just a few—just as we have seen that there are many types of data—photos, video, and paper documents among them (these and other types of data are covered in Chapter 4).

But what about documents? Can't documents also be considered data? Or does everything have to become either digitized or datavized to become data? Perhaps the greatest leap forward in recent years has been our turn from being a document-centric industry to being a data-centric one. "Everything is data," says David Fano of CASE. "Our gripe is not with documents or with paper. Paper's fine. Paper serves a very valuable service." Fano gives an example:

Say that a 24 × 36 or 36 × 48 sheet size is the only way building information is conveyed. Why? That's an old thing that came from modes of production at that time. We have iPads now. We have laser printers that can go on the jobsite. Why shouldn't a drawing set be the size of a book? We can zoom in and zoom out now. Scale had to do with the size of a pencil and how much information you can put on paper. We need to recognize the opportunities that current mediums allow for.

"Documents are fine. If you look at the latest trends in databases, they're document-based databases rather than table or relational databases," adds Fano, and continues:

What we want to challenge is the presentation of the information. A lot of the thinking in the industry has been about CYA, document it so you can go back and say you did. If it's about giving the right amount of information to the right people at the right time, then we can challenge what all the principles are for what a drawing set is: the documents that are required to build a building. A document for me is a video file. Let's use video. Let's not confine ourselves to 2D abstraction.

Tyler Goss of CASE discusses the movement from architects producing documents to architects leveraging data and the implications for practice and education: "There's a fundamental shift from a document-centric to data-centric delivery methodology in our industry. With a few exceptions, the schools are not preparing people for this. That said, more and more graduates leave school with in-depth practical knowledge of Grasshopper, a parameter-based, rules-based design process. But that shift from a document-centric to data-centric approach, being the one who can lead a practice into making that shift themselves, is going to put themselves in a position of power more quickly than they would otherwise." (See Figure 1.30.)

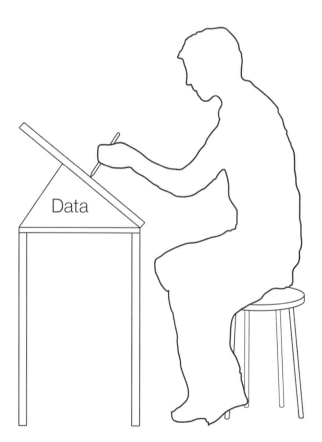

Figure 1.30:   Database: Ideas backed up with data is still why many people choose to work with architects. © R Deutsch

Goss provides an example of what he means by document-centric thinking in terms that will be familiar to anyone who has worked with Revit and BIM: "Revit can be used in one of two ways. It can be used to build a fundamental logic of a project. In terms of a logic of building. Or it can be used to expediently generate 2D documentation for contractual purposes. More often than not, it's the latter way that Revit is used."

Robert Yori cautions that there are different approaches and varying degrees of understanding and facility with the notion of "drawings as database." He compares the shift toward becoming data-centric with the fearful time when computers were first introduced into the architecture profession. "As a profession we struggled with the idea of tangibles versus intangibles, what's more difficult to embody digitally, and what can and should be embodied," says Yori. "Overall, we're all having to deal with increasing amounts of data. Those that are computationally inclined naturally would look to some sort of database solution. But I don't necessarily like to call it that from the start—it can scare people off."

To help explain this concept, the architect's instruments of service, the building documents, can be compared with data visualizations. "If you look at the rest of the world, data visualization has become this very powerful thing," says Fano. "The *New York Times* will spend a lot of money on the top data visualizer in the world because now you can understand very complex things in a very simple way. So for me, a drawing set is a data visualization. And it is time for that data visualization to evolve."

Architects have stacks of drawings—much of them archived. Should they consider this to be data they can access and use? Mani Golparvar-Fard, PhD, Assistant Professor of Civil and Environmental Engineering and Computer Science, University of Illinois at Urbana-Champaign, thinks so. "Yes, definitely. We can leverage [our proprietary] Mobile Augmented Reality System (MARS) platform to provide near real-time access to the PDFs of these drawings. We can use the interface to perform mark-ups." See Figure 1.31.

Figure 1.31: MARS web-based platform for crowd-sourcing construction activity analysis. Users provide annotations on the role, activities, and tools used by the craft workers and the platform extrapolates information to the video frames. © *Mani Golparvar-Fard Ph.D.*

The distinction between documents and data may soon become moot, due to the advent of BIM where conventional building plans, elevations, and sections can be seen as views of the model database. Zigmund Rubel of Aditazz speaks to this point when he says, "The documentation is an output of the (BIM) model. The model is what's going to get built." He continues,

> In our world today, documentation is what drives what gets built. What we're aiming for is we're going to virtually build whatever's going to get built. The documentation is just to support the regulatory and other aspects of the construction process. The data is what is actually getting built. Documentation is just a report from that. So it's a very different mindset than what is currently considered.

Case Study Interview with Jonatan Schumacher

Jonatan Schumacher is the Director of CORE studio, Thornton Tomasetti's firm-wide, virtual incubator of ideas, where he oversees research initiatives and strategic software development related to workflow automation for integrated building design, analysis, and fabrication methods. Having studied in the fields of product design, architecture, manufacturing, robotics, engineering, and computer science, Jonatan's versatile expertise includes digital fabrication, automatic model creation based on performance parameters, computational analysis, web development, and BIM workflow integration through custom automation. Jonatan lectures and consults on programming, interoperability, and parametric modeling at Stevens Institute of Technology, Columbia University, and the New York City Tech College.

You are the rare design professional who appears to be equally comfortable generating form and optimizing building performance.

Jonatan Schumacher (JS): It is very hard to find good people who are interested in, and able to do, both. There is Mostapha Roudsari, Integrations Applications Developer at Thornton Tomasetti (TT). He's one of those very rare individuals, an architect by training, who is focused on sustainability services and energy analysis. He develops Grasshopper plug-ins for weather data, daylight, and energy simulation. Given his design background, he understands what is important to firms, the process and method of analysis. I knew him originally from the (online) Grasshopper community. He is also very big on Twitter. It's funny how there is this second world where you see people you don't necessarily see at conferences. [See Figure 1.32.]

It is very hard to find a person who can understand automation but also the subject matter. Sometimes we think we should just hire computer scientists. Obviously, we can't pay them what Google pays them. But get somebody who

(Continued)

would otherwise work at Google. We had an intern last year who had two computer science degrees. It was very hard to work with him. He was so far removed from the reality that we are still dealing with paper and drawings—boring stuff. It didn't make any sense to him, coming from a different industry. But it is unfortunately the reality. There needs to be somebody who can at least understand how things are done here. Teaching concepts of computer science to architects and engineers helps us.

Everybody is at a point where algorithms are good at automating geometric model generation. That's one thing. The bigger thing is the data that comes with it.

—Jonatan Schumacher, Thornton Tomasetti

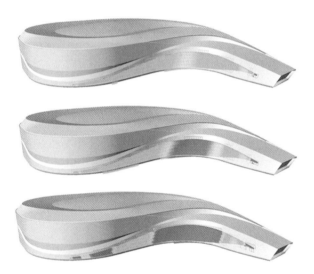

Figure 1.32: Thornton Tomasetti's CORE studio assisted 360 architects in the panelization of the Rogers Place Arena in Edmonton, Canada. A bottom-up approach was used to derive panel layout controlled by physics engine Kangaroo for Grasshopper. © *Thornton Tomasetti CORE studio*

Excel of course is just an everyday tool. Everybody can program with Excel. But it is limiting, when looking at the larger picture, where we want all project information to feed into a central repository. Take for example a big stadium project. Recently there was a deadline. Two people from our team were involved. They spent four

Is how a tool handles data ever a factor in you considering working with these tools?

JS: Certainly. Let's start at the other end. Look at 3Ds Max. It's basically rendering software. Even if you were to measure the areas of its meshes, they wouldn't be accurate. Certain software is incapable of, and not meant for, data extraction and data processing.

Once Grasshopper came out, we found that it was good for nearly everybody—especially engineers, who are good at thinking logically; they write Excel functions and macros every day. Grasshopper is like Excel coupled with AutoCAD. They knew AutoCAD, they knew Excel. So this was just another way to combine data with geometry. I would say that Grasshopper is our #1 tool right now. It's so easy to say, "show me all the beams in the building and give me the ones that are longer than 5 feet." It is so easy to do that kind of analysis. [See Figure 1.33.]

Figure 1.33: Thornton Tomasetti's in-house structural design suite: Thornton Tomasetti's CORE studio developed a number of tools for analysis of complex structures, and data visualization and mining thereof. © *Thornton Tomasetti CORE studio*

days working until 5:00 am in the office. Why couldn't we work smarter? They were like, this stair is being designed in that spreadsheet, and this part of the building is being designed over there. In the end, it's hard to combine everything into a single model. Everybody does their own separate thing. Nobody talks to the big repository of information. If used systematically, Grasshopper allows us to combine and mine information and data coming from different sources, such as spreadsheets and various BIM and analysis environments. But Grasshopper is still not a good database storage solution itself. This is why we developed TTX since Fall 2012. [See Figure 1.34.]

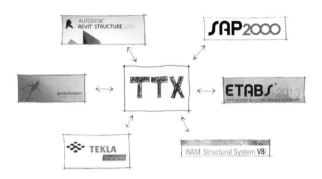

Figure 1.34: Thornton Tomasetti's CORE studio developed an in-house interoperability platform and BIM management suite: TTX. © *Thornton Tomasetti CORE studio*

Before deciding to develop our own interoperability platform, TTX, we were testing IFC file format on a large, fast-paced project. Certain companies, like Autodesk, are not motivated to work with IFC. We needed to get all this data from both Grasshopper and SAP into Revit, and it was not possible to do so in the workflow that the project required. If the input geometry changes, you lose track of which beams [in Revit] to replace with which beams [coming from Grasshopper]. IFC does not keep track of the unique identifiers that each program assigns to their BIM elements, so we can't use it well to make updates to existing models—especially if that model has changed, too. That is why we came up with TTX. It's an alternative to IFC. It's a file in the end, a database that contains all of the BIM information. It grows over time, and it can talk to all the different programs that we commonly use to model, analyze, document, and fabricate building structures. TTX is the common repository. We can now talk between the individual elements in all programs and keep updating our calculations. Over time we naturally keep growing this repository, as the project evolves.

In terms of finding talent, why would someone with a computer science background go to work in the AEC industry?

JS: Especially when it pays a third of what they were making in their respective industry… This person wanted to do some real, physical projects. We were lucky. There is obviously a large difference between creating software, or crunching numbers, and designing buildings that will live on for decades, which is attractive to some.

Do you see a need for exploring algorithms to further our capabilities and performance in design and construction over and above their capacity for generating form?

JS: In our R&D group, most people have a background in product design, engineering, or architecture, with a very strong interest in computer science. Very practically based. A couple of our people came from firms where they were working in Digital Project, or from a construction management or fabrication background. Computer science is important, as is an interest and expertise in a field related to our industry. It makes it hard for an engineering firm if the person only knows how to model well in BIM. That's not enough.

In terms of form-driven versus data-driven—both are nice challenges. On many interesting projects the architect doesn't necessarily think about data first and foremost. They're inspired by something formal. The data still represents a nice challenge and can be applied to any kind of design.

(Continued)

Some architects—big-name architects—don't care at all about the data. It is surprising. There are firms that tell us, we don't do 3D. It doesn't matter. Even then, as engineers we will do it for our own sake. We have to realize the geometry just as any engineer would. We just use different methods to get there.

We're very fortunate that our CEO Tom Scarangello made this conscious decision for Thornton Tomasetti to be the forerunner amongst engineering firms on the technology side. That's why we are investing heavily in R&D in our field. Tom understands that it will ultimately help the owner. We are often hired directly by owners, as opposed to architects or contractors.

We're focused on how buildings get built and what the complications will be on the construction side. This is why we want to run these kinds of studies during the design phase. Because there's a much greater likelihood that the building will get realized, compared to other high-end engineering firms that mainly work in the conceptual phases of a project.

Any other ways you can compress the process by using data or without losing the value of the data you already have?

JS: As engineers, long before all of this data talk, even before BIM was called BIM, we had 3D models with attributes. Data is always informing our designs. It is hard to address because I don't think of these as two different things. There is always geometry and data. The data is as important as the geometry is. The Petronas Towers in Kuala Lumpur, Malaysia, in the early nineties were analyzed in 3D. That's a BIM model. It's just that nobody had the term for it at the time. Data has always been a big part of what [structural] engineers do. [See Figures 1.35 and 1.36.]

Figure 1.35: Hurricane Sandy disaster visualization: CORE studio assisted the Property Loss Consulting Group at Thornton Tomasetti in visualizing data captured after investigations. © *Thornton Tomasetti CORE studio*

You work closely to integrate the building structure, building skin, and building performance. How and where does data come into play?

JS: On a current project, the Hudson Yards Culture Shed by Diller Scofidio + Renfro, we are the structural engineers as well as the façade engineers. It's a kinetic structure where the structure and the skin are one and the same. The skin sits inside of the structural frame. If you were to try to coordinate between two different firms, it would be a nightmare to manage. We're also helping to algorithmically design the frit pattern that is printed onto the ETFE skin panels, and as such integrating sustainability services into the design process.

The structural model and the skin model on this project are the same thing. It is a geometrically complex kinetic structure, which will sit on top of the Hudson Rail Yards. It is important to coordinate the information so that all the disciplines can work with them. We're designing the frit patterns, for example, not just as an image, but with a set goal for reduction of a predescribed amount of solar radiation. This is something that our skin group would not be able to

Figure 1.36:   Hurricane Sandy disaster visualization: CORE studio assisted the Property Loss Consulting Group at Thornton Tomasetti in visualizing data captured after investigations. © *Thornton Tomasetti CORE studio*

do. Because they don't have the computational power to model and mesh all of these details. Our sustainability group wouldn't be able to do this either by itself. We have to integrate the knowledge of the different disciplines—the knowledge of materials, and of solar performance—and automate the creation of frit pattern, as well as the radiation analysis—it is a very computationally heavy process. There are a lot of analyses being run just to figure out what kind of frit pattern to use. We are doing this with Grasshopper—so we can make real-time adjustments as we go, and as the building geometry evolves—using Ladybug and Honeybee, two Grasshopper plug-ins that Mostapha developed. It is all parametrically linked.

The real-time data, in these instances, helps you to make more assured decisions. How do you communicate the data that supported your decisions to the architect/client?

JS: I hope that we will soon be able to communicate issues and design recommendations to our client—the owner or architect—in real time. See that red area there in the model? That we still need to fix. So let's just fix it now, in the shared model, in the web browser.

In the past, you'd have to throw out your previous iterations.

JS: Exactly. Now we can work with the same model. Now we have a parametric model, so we can change the geometry and retrigger analysis to be run. Our motivation has been to find ways to help the architects early on, really early on, in the process. So they can understand their building: How much does it cost? How much does it weigh? How will it be fabricated? These we answer in the structural analysis program. Now, with these visualization methods, we can comfortably go to the owner, convey our findings, creating trust from the beginning.

Another concept we are actively developing is what we call remote solving. This started in a conversation with LMN Architects tech studio (LMNts.) Traditionally, there is a huge disconnect between engineers and architects—especially during the early design phases. Engineers tend to wait for architects to "freeze" their designs, before they will even take a look—and then they will just post-rationalize it. The motivation behind remote solving is to be able to proactively inform the architecture, while it's being designed, with engineering and constructibility constraints. [See Figures 1.37 and 1.38.]

Currently, there is no ideal workflow defined for file exchange between A and E. So often, we are given a surface model, and we have to spend significant time to find a way to extract the centerline geometry from that. By the time we give them back the results the design has changed, and we are not able to inform the design in the early phases. So we came up with this: We are hosting the analysis model on a server, and expose certain inputs and outputs to the architects (and to other collaborators). Then, every time that the architect makes a change, the analysis automatically runs and provides feedback necessary for the architect to make an informed decision for their next design iteration.

(Continued)

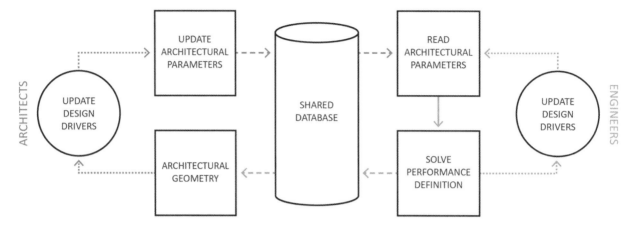

Figure 1.37:   Thornton Tomasetti joint research project with LMN Tech Studio. Remote Solving allows for automated analysis feedback by engineers at concept design phase. © *Thornton Tomasetti CORE studio*

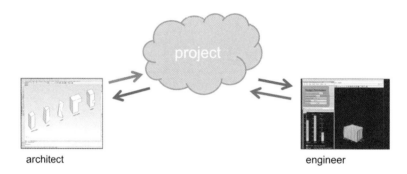

Figure 1.38:   Thornton Tomasetti joint research project with LMN Tech Studio. Remote Solving allows for automated analysis feedback by engineers at concept design phase. © *Thornton Tomasetti CORE studio*

In this example, the architect can control the massing and the grid lines. Every time they make a change, the architect's computer uploads the new geometry to the database on Amazon's cloud. Our computer downloads that, resizes everything in real time, and a minute or two later they have their updated tonnages, structural sizes, and carbon values.

There are some firms that want to hire employees with data visualization skills. At TT, this would be superfluous. Your data viz is built into your system.

JS: Here's an example where these are the drivers and the architects could drive them themselves. The architects were interested in panelizing a double-curved façade surface in a way where every panel would have the same exact geometry. We developed a script to help them do this. Moreover, the façade engineer advised that we should check for curvature of the panels, and make sure that they don't warp more than 20 mm. So, as part of our script we measured deflection in real time, and visualized it in color (red = too much warpage). In doing so, we gave that script back to the architects, so that they could investigate different design options. They could drive how long they wanted the façade edges to be and what angle they wanted them to be. Based on their drivers, the façade would essentially push and pull itself into place. The goal again is to have as little red as possible. This way, they can see which angles work and which don't work. We embedded fabrication intelligence into their design model. That way they have the data and can figure it out themselves. You can go with any design you like. But if there's too much red, for example, it's going to be very expensive. [See Figure 1.39.]

Does TT collect and warehouse its own data for use in projects or to improve performance?

JS: As part of our intranet solution, we have a private webpage for every project that features high-level project information: who is the key contact, services offered, construction date, etc. We can use this intranet to ask: what do we do in healthcare, what do we do on high-rise projects, what do we do in Dubai? Every project page also has inputs for structural system, average building weight per square foot, and for embodied carbon. I have been considering adding the TTX model for every project in there, too. So that in the future, we can always look back and extract BIM and analytical data. It's just a database, so we'll be able to open and read it. It won't get outdated, like a Revit model or a Grasshopper definition would. And it doesn't use up much storage capacity. We can open it in 10 years and run very detailed queries down to a single BIM element or structural analysis node.

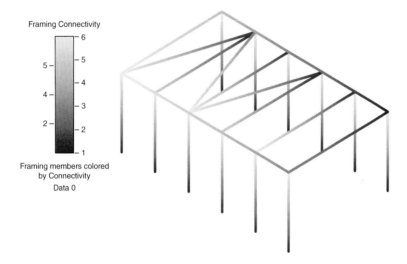

Figure 1.39:   Thornton Tomasetti in-house structural design suite: Thornton Tomasetti's CORE studio developed a number of tools for analysis of complex structures, and data visualization and mining thereof. © *Thornton Tomasetti CORE studio*

There is a need today for a thorough understanding of how data is being leveraged in architecture, engineering, and construction, and by owners and operators. The innovative use of data in design and construction has been enabled by recent advances in technology and workflows, but also by access to information and an improved appreciation of how data can positively inform a variety of processes in the profession and industry.

Notes

1. Unless otherwise indicated, quoted text through-out the book is from interviews with the author that took place between February and July 2014. http://techcrunch.com
2. David Fano, interview with author, March 10, 2014.
3. David Fano, "BIM in the cloud: Industry view," *AEC Magazine*, July 29, 2014; http://aecmag.com/59-features/627-bim-in-the-cloud
4. Mads Jensen, interview with author, May 13, 2014.
5. Quote from Marina Gorbis, Executive Director, Institute for the Future, at an NBBJ-hosted event called "Data and Delight," Bloomberg San Francisco, August 18, 2013.
6. Randy Deutsch, quoted in David Barista, "The Big Data revolution: How data-driven design is transforming project planning," *Building Design and Construction*, February 11, 2014; http://www.bdcnetwork.com/big-data-revolution-how-data-driven-design-transforming-project-planning
7. Ibid.
8. Sean D. Burke, "Autodesk University, a ReCap," *Paradigm Shift*, December 18, 2013; www.seand-burke.com/blog/2013/12/18/

2 A Data-Driven Design Approach for Buildings

Things get done only if the data we gather can inform and inspire those in a position to make a difference.
—Mike Schmoker

Our first questions concerning data-driven design are questions of status: Where is the AECO industry today on the data front? Where are designers, constructors, owners, and operators today in relation to data? Are they in denial? Are they accepting of the data that is available to them, or are they indifferent? Do they recognize the importance of leveraging data to create geometry, achieve increased building performance, track human performance, monitor business performance, and reach other goals? Do they recognize the value of leveraging data in their practices, but feel unprepared to do so? If so, what will it take for them to feel prepared to use data as a contributor in design and construction?

Five Trends Leading to the Rise of Data in the AECO Industry

Several trends that have come together explain the rise of data gathering and use by industry practitioners:

Instrumentation

One reality that explains the rise of data in the AECO industry, more than any other factor, is the fact that sensors are being added to almost everything.

Sometimes referred to as the Internet of Things (IoT), we ought to start calling it the Instrumentation of Everything. Tom Mulhern describes this trend: "A big impact of data on design right now is the instrumentation of everything. The instrumentation of building sensors and actuators. And the instrumentation of humans. Instrumentation will be the revolution. Instrumentation: our ability to measure what happens in buildings."

Zigmund Rubel defines big data in terms of instrumentation, as mechanized data. "Imagine if you have data being created by some sort of machine and that data stream was not going to stop ever," says Rubel. "Unstructured data to me is not big data. Big data is where you have streams of data coming out resulting in, through analysis, 'analytics' to look at. And when you look at a building, a building has tremendous opportunities to analyze big 'mechanized' data. Because there are all these gadgets in there that are mechanized already and need to be tapped for data collection and understanding." See Figure 2.1.

Datatization

Datatization concerns itself with turning everything into readable, sharable, comparable data, as distinguished from *digitization,* which involves converting pictures or sound into a digital form that can be processed by a computer. Whereas digitizing means simply capturing an analog signal in digital form, datavizing implies something more: that what is in

71

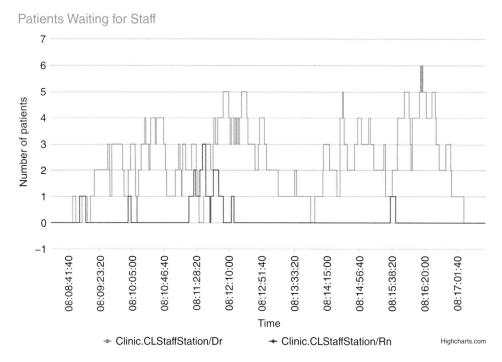

Showing for a typical day (day 8) over the course of the day the number of people waiting for either a doctor or their assigned nurse. From this graph we see that it might be worth adding a floater nurse or pool the nurses.

Figure 2.1:   Data indicates a need for intervention to reduce the time patients wait for staff. © *Aditazz*

the computer is intelligent, sharable, and made up of discrete data or functional data. An example is converting scanned documents into data. "For existing paper documents, we would need to datavize them, but not necessarily," says David Fano. "It depends on what you wanted to know." (See Figure 2.2.)

Productization

Productizing has close ties with fabrication. "One of our partners (ConXtech) makes steel beams and columns," Zigmund Rubel tells us. "If you look at the AISC steel catalog there's about 400 W-shapes. ConXtech narrowed it down to only 40. They work with 40 shapes. That's one of the reasons they're able to quickly design and assemble a steel structure. Because they've productized the process." Rubel continues,

It's an outcome of data analysis in the sense that they analyze the different steel profiles with the different beaming needs they would have and they're able to provide production efficiencies, as opposed to what we design professionals typically do: I'll look at this and tell you the ideal solution for your need. In reality, there really isn't an ideal solution. There's a choice. And if you reduce the number of choices, then you can get economies of scale from a process and delivery perspective.

Along with productization comes its opposite, de-productization: the AECO trend away from using out-of-the-box software products in exchange for add-ons, plug-ins, and hacking.

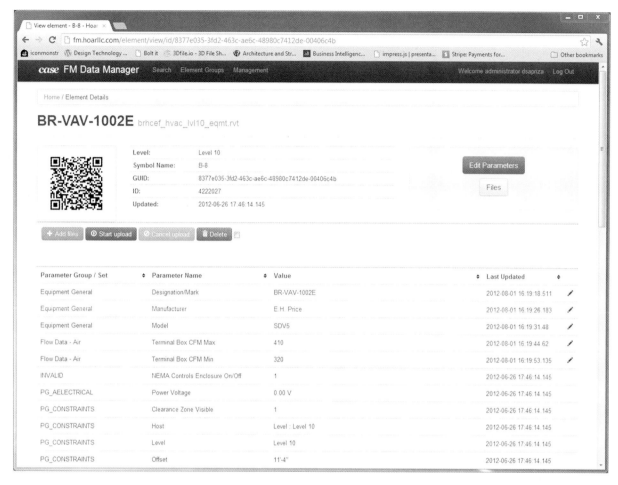

Figure 2.2:   Datavized information is searchable anywhere. Each asset has its own page, presenting data that has been extracted from the BIM model, allowing someone on site to access the data without needing to open up a BIM model. © *Hoar Construction and CASE Inc.*

Strategy No. 5: Eight Questions to Ask for Data Preparedness

Do we have:

- capacity?
- mind-space?
- the right culture?
- the right people on board?
- top-down/bottom-up support?

- a way of measuring results/outcomes?
- enough time and resources to take this on?
- the right attitudes and mindset to work with data?

Validation

One of the ways we validate is by legitimizing decisions through use of data. "How do you qualify design?" asks Zigmund Rubel. "I think the 20 percent is the creative process, where a particular decision point cannot be turned into rules. For example, the creation of a Parti is certainly creative and we do not see this ever going completely away from the human. But a computer can learn that certain shaped sites with certain zoning envelopes can have particular forms in them. The tools allow us to quickly get to a validated yes or no to a question if we can give it a set of rules."

Validation using data carries its own stigmas. David Fano sees validation as a challenge for a historically risk-averse industry. "We're scared to validate. All of the energy calculations on the building model said it is going to be this. Then they go back and measure it and

it is not anywhere near that. We can't be scared of that. We have to embrace those failures, learn from them."

Visualization

Lastly, data visualization (data viz) helps communicate complex information, insights, and abstractions to nonprofessionals, and makes data more accessible and understandable to more people. Data viz helps design professionals tell their stories in a compellingly graphical manner. (There is more on data visualization in Chapter 5.) (See Figure 2.3.)

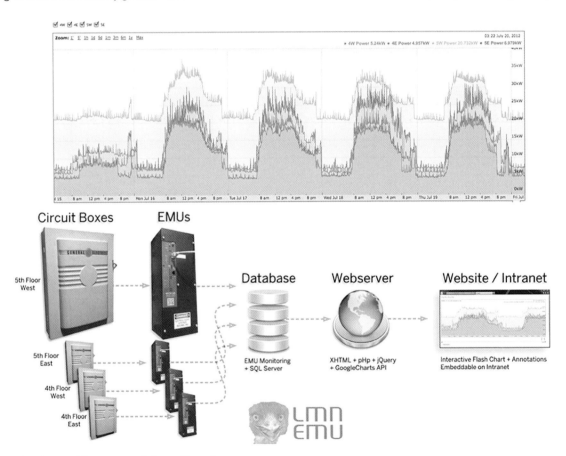

Office Energy Monitoring

Figure 2.3: LMN developed an energy monitoring system to quantify, record, and visualize the performance improvements of their office renovation. © *LMN Architects*

Case Study Interview with Zigmund Rubel

Zigmund (Zig) Rubel, AIA, is a co-founder of Aditazz, responsible for ensuring the performance and the quality delivery of all projects using data. Zig's efforts at Aditazz initially focused on creating a suite of building product parts to enable a "kit" approach to assembling buildings. He holds multiple U.S. and international patents, innovations that tie together the other building elements that Aditazz uses as its kit of parts through the use of data. Zig also leads several projects deploying data-driven design techniques; in particular, healthcare operators are experiencing the benefits of Aditazz's revolutionary data-driven approach.

Aditazz is a data-driven firm, a firm that goes beyond the status quo and boldly works with data to your betterment—not only your own competitive advantage, but also to take the industry further. Aditazz has taken this model further, in a very short period of time, than just about anyone else.

Zigmund Rubel (ZR): What I've always told my colleague, Deepak Aatresh—the person who founded the company, and a computer chip designer—is that our challenge isn't technology. It's culture. I think that's what you're trying to illuminate in your book.

You recognize that there are places in the planning process where the computer can make great gains. You also recognize that there are some parts of the process that will remain in the human domain. There are people who believe that architecture and construction will become a computer culture and robotic culture in the end. And that there won't be a place for them.

ZR: In all fairness, to some degree they're right. I don't want to minimize their fears but I think the reality, though, is that data-driven computer use in the industry will allow for a much more creative process for those who participate. We currently go through a certain process because we are given a certain set of tools—whether pencil or mouse—and can only react to the objects we create with those tools. Juxtapose this process if something is created based on a series of requirements, then we're having a very different experience. It's one thing to react to the drawing(s) we create. It's another thing to react to a catalog populated with solutions. I see a future where we're reacting to a catalog of predefined solutions. The reason I'm not intimidated is that humans are still making the decision, both in the requirements that populate the catalog and the decision of choice. I think the fear is that people think computers are going to make the decision and I don't see that happening any time soon. [See Figure 2.4.]

Some people, especially those coming from the fine arts, think that a blank canvas, blank page, blank slate, or blank Moleskine is the ideal versus defining creativity in terms of constraints.

ZR: I completely agree that a blank Moleskine is the beginning of art. And that will never go away. But in the creation of a building or architecture, it's so much more than that blank Moleskine. One of the cultural questions you might need to address is, is it irresponsible for us to hold on to the vision of the blank Moleskine, or can we separate pieces of the Moleskine, leave it in the book, and let the computer do the other parts? That's what we're trying to do at Aditazz.

Our business model is evolving. Nothing is concrete in our world. We want to create the catalog of components for our own use. The reason we want to do that is that we feel we'll be able to innovate more quickly if it is for our use

(Continued)

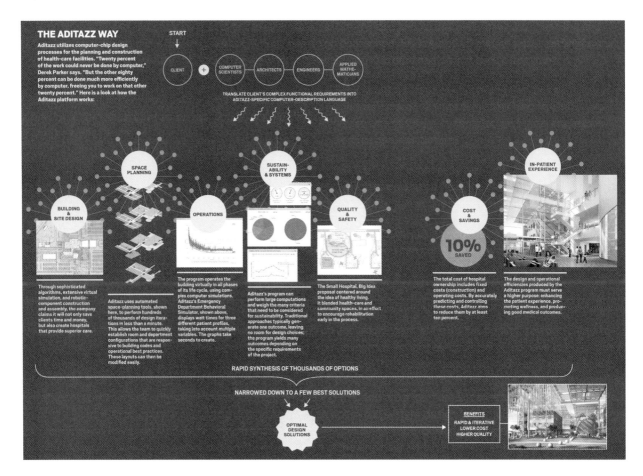

Figure 2.4: The Aditazz Way: An overview of how the software platform is set to revolutionize building design. © *Susan Szenasy,* Metropolis *magazine (first published in the October 2013 issue of* Metropolis *magazine).*

as opposed to everyone's use. What I've learned in the technology and software world is that it is far easier to create software for your own use than to create software to sell for everyone's use.

Does this mean that designers will need to compromise, having fewer choices?

ZR: Yes. They will have to choose what the compromises are. They will have to give up complete and universal freedom of design choices. They will have to give up their current state of freedoms to get a different kind of freedom that is based on outcomes, as opposed to design intent. They have to give up control at one level to get freedom of choice at another level. [See Figure 2.5.]

What the planning, design, and construction data will allow us to do in the AEC industry is create a simplifying technology. The first of Clayton Christenson's enablers.[1] Humans need to provide the creativity for the innovation.

Aditazz Building Products

Structural Frame	Concrete Deck Panel	Integrated Metal Wall Panels with Utilities	Multi-Trade Utility Frames
01	02	03	04
Field installation in 25% of traditional time	Field installation in 33% of traditional time	Field installation in 25% of traditional time	Field installation in of traditional time

Figure 2.5: Time savings brought about by utilizing Aditazz's catalog of building products © *Aditazz*

When you made the transition to Aditazz, were you concerned that working with data would be too abstract? Too far removed from the architecture you were educated and trained in?

ZR: I wasn't, but many or all of my colleagues initially were. The reason I am not afraid is because I felt I controlled what data to look for. Other people feel like they're being controlled by the data. If you created the tools and how the tools would work, you're actually controlling the outcome. If you're defining the process, it's actually working for you.

What mindsets do you suggest others will need to make a similar transition?

ZR: Willingness to make a difference; not afraid to fail; desirous to be bold and yet humble (Steve Jobs—*We're here to put a dent in the universe*). Otherwise, why else even be here? Per our investor—The three "I's" and one quote: Integrity; Intensity; Intellectual Honesty. Quote: *Be comfortable when you're naked*. Fed up with the status quo. Insatiable curiosity. Impatience.

(Continued)

Were these personal motivators for you?

ZR: Architects have been boxed in to provide a certain service and we can do so much more. I'm fed up with the status quo. When I first met Deepak, what I did was something that most people would not have done. I took a blind leap of faith and said let's go do it. It was a huge risk. What I weighed that on was: What if Deepak was right? Do you know Plato's Allegory of the Cave? Here's Deepak telling me that our reality is the shadows we see on the cave wall from a fire that we can't see, and by the way, there's a sun outside that's way more powerful. I took a chance of saying, you know what? I'm going to see if this guy is right. Most people would have just said, yeah, right.

Maybe what is needed for other firms to work with data is to hire people with curiosity; people who are not willing to accept the status quo.

Is the motivation for this approach about changing the architecture profession and AEC industry?

ZR: We want to transform the way buildings are conceived, realized, and operated. It is a completely bold idea. Our motivation is that our industry is broken and it needs to be fixed. The person who introduced my co-founder and I was Paul Teicholz, the Stanford professor that developed the productivity graphs of Construction and Non-Farm U.S. GDP from 1964 to today. Why has our industry not improved in productivity, and even regressed, while others have increased at a rate of 2.5 times? We should be ashamed that we've not taken this more seriously. [See Figure 2.6.]

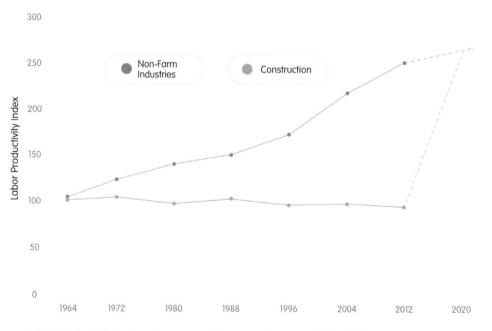

Labor Productivity in Construction and Non-Farm Industries 1964 - 2020
Source: Paul Teicholz, Aditazz Technical Advisory Board

Figure 2.6:   BIM alone won't improve labor productivity in the AEC industry, which, after more than 50 years of tracking, still lags other nonfarm industries. © *Aditazz*

My motivation to join my co-founder was that I was tired of selling hours instead of value. We all go to the interview and tell our prospective clients how amazing our firms are. We make it to the next hurdle, and we then have to justify our fees by the number of billable hours we have compared to the percentage of the construction cost. Is this right? I was amazed that there are industries that can automate mundane tasks, like locating fire extinguisher cabinets in a corridor, and we need a professional to do this.

What role does data play in enabling Aditazz to achieve this bold goal?

ZR: It's a medium for us to make decisions at each stage of the process. For us as designers to conceive the idea, validate the design, to ensure that whatever's built meets the design requirements. The basic premise is that you should operate your building prior to design, base the design on these requirements, build the building based on the design requirements, and operate your building based on your initial business model. Today, building occupants work around what is given to them.

Where on the three stages—planning, construction, operations—are you seeing the most interest?

ZR: The most interest is in the project conception phase. Our clients want to make sure we're building the right building. Today, a lot of decisions are based on spreadsheets. They are rules-based—based on data—at a very rough level of refinement. We're able to take it down to much more detail granularity and illuminate some of the nuances they wouldn't have otherwise seen.

A real-world example: We did a project for a healthcare system where we looked at an emergency room flows. They were planning to renovate the emergency room to increase their capacity. Based on our analysis, we demonstrated to them that when they did plan to renovate it, they didn't need to add as much space, and that they could delay the renovation for at least three years. They did make some operational changes in terms of workflow that resulted in changes in how they provided care. This study significantly reduced the money they were going to spend by over $20 million, and they delayed the timing of the renovation. That's not something we could have done with a spreadsheet. [See Figures 2.7 through 2.10.]

Is that what makes Aditazz a data-driven company?

ZR: It's one of the reasons. The most important thing we care about data is that it will give us more confidence in predicting our outcome. If we have all of these analyses showing us why a certain outcome will be provided, we'll have more confidence that a particular outcome will be achieved. If we just hope that it will work, then we are gambling, and unfortunately that's what many design practices do in their work product.

You've noted that healthcare professionals base their decisions on data. Do you believe this is true today for AEC professionals?

ZR: It is true in the individual silos, but not shared across disciplines.

My solutions are all nontechnical: 1. We need to focus on the end outcome and not what the individual parties are hoping to achieve; and 2. We should be compensated by the end outcome and not the individual deliverable. If I provide construction documents and the project is over budget, should I get paid for the whole thing? Are you providing value if the others aren't getting the objective that they want? Lastly, have an interest in the actual outcome of the project. If you say you're going to do a LEED building that consumes very little energy and it consumes a lot of energy, did you do a good job?

(Continued)

| Assessment & Formulating | Data Gathering & Analysis | Model Build & Validation | What-If Scenario Analysis | Final Report with Clear Recommendations for Improvement |

Figure 2.7:   Step 1: Assessment and Formulation and Step 2: Data Gathering and Analysis through Step 5: Recommendations for Improvement. © *Aditazz*

All of this is tied to data. Because the value decision points are all based on data. And we shouldn't be hung up on the data, we should be hung up on the value assignment to the data. We shouldn't get hung up whether we're exchanging data or not. If we think that the output of this spreadsheet is going to be the defining feature of the entire project, we should care about that. But if it's just a supporting bit of information, then who really cares?

I'm sure in your practice if you do the design and the contractor asked, "Can I get your CAD backgrounds?" you might have them sign a disclaimer, but in essence, he or she just wants data so that the outcome you have is aligned with the outcome that they have. And that's the kind of thinking we need. So I'm not hung up that this contractor is going to take my CAD background and distort it. They just want the data so they can do their job. If we have a desirable outcome and a happy client, that is what I think we all want.

Should the Aditazz model be the industry standard?

ZR: If we want to advance to the twenty-first century, it has to.

You are crunching a thousand variations in seconds.

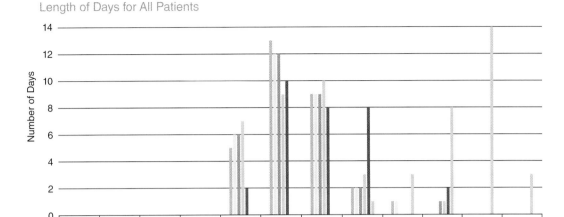

Length of Days for All Patients

Shows how the time to see 100 patients per day changes by adding more exam rooms. The y axis shows the number of days (out of 30) where it took the time, as indicated on the x axis to see the 100 patients. In all these scenarios, patients were scheduled every 20 minutes for an exam and 40 minutes for a procedure, with a 1 hour lunch break. As you can see, having less than 9 exam rooms reduces the efficiency greatly, while adding more has little effect. Note: If patients are scheduled every 15 minutes, that optimum number of exam rooms increases to 11, but it patients are scheduled every 25 minutes, then only 7 exam rooms are needed.

Figure 2.8: Impact of adding more exam rooms on number of patients seen per day. © Aditazz

Exam Room States

Showing on a typical day (the 4th) the number of exam rooms that are idle, the number that are used and the number that are wasted, that is rooms that are unavailable because for example a patient in the room is waiting for the doctor, or after a visit, the room is waiting to be cleaned by a medical assistant.

As you can see, as the day progresses, there is more waste, indicating that the patients are scheduled at a slightly higher rate than the doctors can handle. During the lunch break, the doctors catch up, but at the expense of their break.

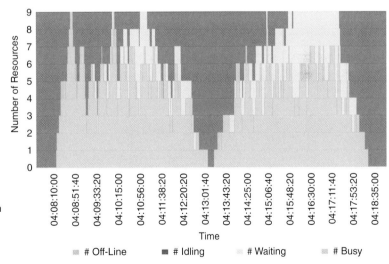

Figure 2.9: Exam Room States. Data visualization indicating the number of exam rooms that are idle, that are used, and those that are wasted. © Aditazz

(Continued)

Wait for Resources

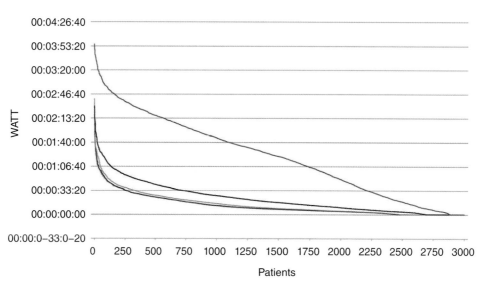

Showing for all 3000 patients the total amount of waiting time, either for a room or for a staff member. The patients are ranked by the time they had to wait. From this graph you can easily see the metrics or the various percentiles. The graphs shows the wait times for various numbers of exam rooms.

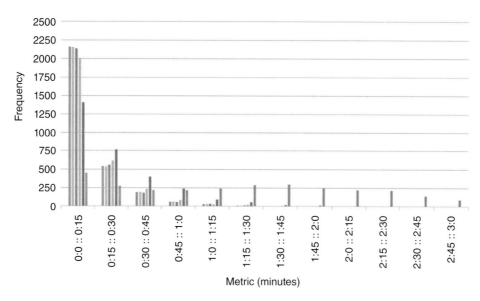

Showing the same information in a different way. For each amount of wait time (per 15 minute buckets), the graph shows the number of people that had to wait that amount.

Figure 2.10:   Data Scenarios. Two different means for visualizing data on exam-room wait times. © *Aditazz*

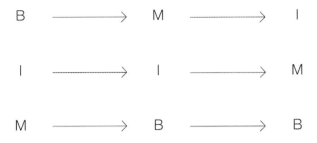

Figure 2.11: BIM, MIB, and IMB approaches. © R Deutsch

ZR: Right. We use cloud-based computing. That's one of the things that has allowed our company to exist. Before the late 1990s, only big companies had massive computing capabilities. Thanks to Azure, Amazon web services and the other companies that are out there, we can at a moment's notice call up a thousand computers to run some calculations. I don't think that our industry is ready to fully embrace this.

The infrastructure is out there to enable this to happen?

ZR: Absolutely. A firm of 20 people is spending $100,000 on software and $50,000 on hardware a year for something that they're not using all the time. What if they hired a software developer to customize some software for that same $150,000 that would run on the cloud only when they needed it? Those are the kind of decisions a firm in the future will have to make. Because many of the technology firms out there are using open source.

One of the things I learned in my Aditazz experience is, if I ever go back to traditional practice, which I assume one day I will, I wouldn't use Revit out of the box. I would use SketchUp—it's free—which would get me most of the way there. I would use Apache OpenOffice instead of buying Microsoft Office. There's an open-source equivalent for almost every software that architects use. There's something called Blender, which is equivalent to 3DS Max. In general, open source does about 90 percent of what the commercial versions do. We pay royally for that 10 percent. So if we're willing to live without the 10 percent that's where innovation could occur.

You've said: "Realize the building through computational efforts." Can you elaborate?

ZR: BIM is typically, Model the building, extract information from the model, and then build the building. I call this the MIB approach. What if you had information that generated the model, [from] which you then built the building? I call this the IMB approach. [See Figures 2.11 through 2.13.]

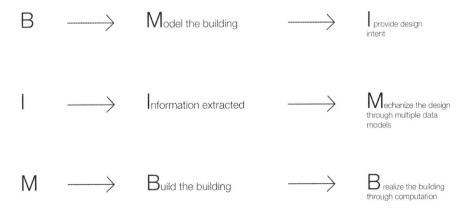

Figure 2.12: Variations on BIM approaches using data. © R Deutsch

(Continued)

Figure 2.13:   BIM. Where is your emphasis? On the building, information (data), or model? © *R Deutsch*

How does Aditazz utilize data? Where does Aditazz get its data? How can it be assured that the data is reliable?

ZR: We use data in all sorts of ways to test and create our solutions. We get our data from our clients, from industry sources, from building codes, from manufacturing specifications, from under rocks.

The most important aspect of the data discussion is that a human ultimately makes the decision. If we have the wrong data, it typically demonstrates its worth by not allowing what we would think is predictable. The point here is that we use the data-centric approach to quickly allow humans to make decisions.

Data-Centric Approaches

When speaking with individuals for this book, I asked each where they saw their organization falling along a continuum, with a basic awareness of data on one end, to data being their primary priority on the other. No value judgment was implied by this question. Some practitioners opted to create categories that fell outside or beyond the continuum. These practice types are also identified and explained below.

Practice Types

Before we can consider if there is as an ideal firm approach to data—whether one should strive to be a data-enabled, data-informed, data-driven practice, or perhaps somewhere between—we need to define the terms.

- *Data-enabled*: being aware of the data but not leveraging it.
- *Data-informed*: using data as a factor in the decision-making process.
- *Data-driven*: data is your primary priority.[2]

A Data-Enabled Approach

Some design professionals resist calling themselves data-driven because to them that term implies the elimination or absence of the human process. Evelyn Lee of MKThink voices such a concern: "We used to say we were data-driven but no longer like to say we're data-driven. Now we say we're data-enabled because data-driven eliminates the human process." She goes on to explain how the firm arrived at this decision:

> All of the clients we work with are organizations that really depend on facilities that support human productivity. Whether it's in a workplace or a learning environment. That's why we went away from data-driven to data-enabled because we use the data in support of the decision-making process but it's a

combination of bridging emotions, organizational vision and values, what they see as their future of the strategic outlook. Using data to understand the known quantities, then using the two together to make the decision.

Is there a sweet spot for a recommended role for data in the industry and where it is headed? For some, the choice between data-enabled, data-informed, and data-driven is situational. For Gehry Technology's Andrew Witt, the choice has to be based on the problem at hand and shouldn't be determined generically across all assignments or firms. "Each of these require an initial framing of a problem, separate and distinct from a particular heuristic." Witt adds,

> This framing and prioritization ultimately becomes the prerogative of the designer—the initial moment of creative decision. The more complex the framed problem, the more likely the heuristic will be on the data-enabled end of the scale. And ultimately, that is probably as it should be—design as a project to expand freedom of action, decision, and experience, not to limit it. [See Figure 2.14.]

A Data-Driven Approach

At the other extreme is the data-driven approach of this book's title, where data takes top priority. Of those firms that show a preference or inclination for being a data-driven practice—NBBJ, LMN, and KieranTimberlake come to mind—Aditazz can be considered to be in a data-driven class of its own.

Figure 2.14:   Data-driven design: The human/machine data spectrum. © *R Deutsch*

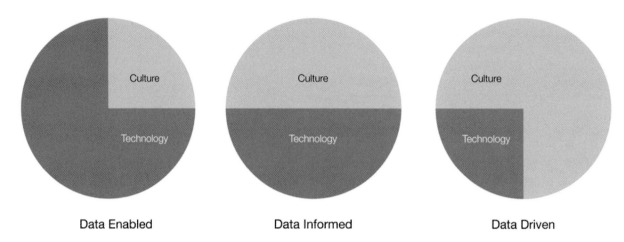

Figure 2.15: To become data-centric, the core of your efforts ought to be focused on firm culture, not technology. © R Deutsch

Data-driven firms go beyond the status quo and boldly address and work with data to their betterment: not only their own competitive advantage, and that of their clients, but also to deliberately take the industry further. These are firms that make use of the data, the technology, and the processes that are available to them, and allow the data to drive decisions on as much as an 80/20 basis—where 80 percent is data-determined with a scant 20 percent remaining for intuition override. In a very short period of time, Aditazz has taken this model further than just about any other firm. The question becomes whether there's a need for more data-driven organizations like Aditazz. Put another way, does Aditazz want to see others in the industry become more data-driven—with the accompanying increase in production, addition of value, and reduction of waste for owners, users, and the pub-

lic—at the expense of potentially reducing human input? Aditazz co-founder Zigmund Rubel encourages the competition. "We want others to embrace our vision, simply because when you don't have competition, you have no way to be compared to." See Figure 2.15.

Other firms, such as RTKL, hold the data-driven approach as a high bar to aspire to. "Our goal is data-driven," says Clayton Starr, Associate Vice President at RTKL. "We are looking at ways technology can help us make better design decisions and inform building performance through better understood metrics. Each project has different goals and we are looking into ways of standardization that language of goal-seeking for our clients and ourselves." It remains to be seen whether other firms will aspire to—and attain—the distinction of being data-driven organizations.

Case Study Interview with Andrew Heumann

As leader of NBBJ's Design Computation team, Andrew Heumann oversees strategy, development, and implementation of computational tools for a wide range of projects and applications. He has developed a suite of data-driven design tools for NBBJ's corporate and commercial practice, which aids in the management of project metrics, environmental and urban analysis, and façade design. Andrew is trained in both architecture and computer science, and has lectured and taught seminars at Cornell University, Yale University, California College of the Arts, and the University of Washington. His work has been *published in* Wallpaper* *magazine, CLOG journal, and at conferences, including ACADIA, the AEC Technology Symposium, Facades+, and SIMAUD.*

Who really needs to hear the message of data-driven design?

Andrew Heumann (AH): Designers first and foremost need to understand its potential. Not everyone in an organization needs to be a facile coder, but everyone needs to know the right kinds of questions to ask. A familiarity with the way algorithms and data "think" is critical—to being able to identify opportunities to employ them, to applying them effectively, and crucially, to not overpromising or overestimating what they do.

We are informed by data, and frequently use it to drive our designs. If an algorithm is driving the car, we've always got a hand on the wheel!

—Andrew Heumann, NBBJ

Is your firm a data-enabled, data-informed, or data-driven practice?

AH: I would say that NBBJ is a data-driven practice, but I am not so sure I'd draw a distinction between data-informed and data-driven. For us, it is critical that algorithms never make decisions—they just offer information and options. No dataset can possibly contain all the information necessary to make a good design decision, except in highly narrow domains. We turn to data plus simulation to evaluate many types of decisions—structural choices, energy performance, environmental impact, and even human factors like acoustics, views, thermal comfort, or travel times. However, we never let the optimum as dictated by the algorithm have the final say. Thus we are informed by data, and frequently use it to drive our designs. If an algorithm is driving the car, we've always got a hand on the wheel!

Strategy No. 6: Four Steps toward Making the Change to Be More Data-Centric

How can firms take the first steps toward applying data in their practices? How do you recommend firms make the change to be more data-centric? Where do they start? Can firms do this on their own?

1. Learn what others are doing. It's easier to recreate a capability someone else has than to come up with brand-new applications from scratch.
2. Hire an expert—who can write code and work with data.
3. Hire/train an evangelist—someone who "gets it" and can communicate its value internally and externally. Sometimes this is the same person as the expert, but not always.
4. Build "habits of mind" in the organization—the ability to identify problems that can be addressed with data, and a way of thinking about those problems to render them amenable to computational analysis.

—Andrew Heumann, NBBJ

Given the amounts of data being produced by the AECO industry, there is a huge opportunity here, but it is one that not many firms are yet pursuing. What will it take to get them to leverage data in their projects?

AH: It's a new way of thinking—data literacy, an awareness of the kinds of situations that can benefit from a computational approach—but more than anything it's a staffing problem: to receive the full value of data-rich design models, firms need to have employees—day-to-day designers and specialists alike—who know how to write code, be it in textual or graphical form.

(Continued)

How much of this is technology and how much is mindset?

AH: I'd probably call it a 50/50 split. Without one or the other, nothing new will happen. The key is that mindset has to spread through the organization more immediately than the technology itself, which can be—in the short term—handled by a few experts.

Strategy No. 7: Ask Good Questions

What qualities, mindsets, or attitudes would you recommend others develop in order to work with data?

These questions are good ones to practice applying to situations:

What can be measured, or quantified?

What can be made automatic?

What processes take little creative thought but lots of time?

What abstract structures present in the situation at hand are similar to structures in other situations/domains? That is, what ways of working with data can be adapted from other contexts?

What information about the task at hand is embedded into its digital representation (CAD, 3D, BIM, spreadsheets, etc.) and what isn't?

—Andrew Heumann, NBBJ

Can you describe a project where the use of data led to an improved decision or insight?

AH: At NBBJ we make an effort to ensure that no single dataset is an island. This reflects the reality of design: every decision affects every other decision in one way or another. A strong example of this is our Hangzhou Stadium project, currently under construction. Our parametric building model generated lots of data, but two kinds of information proved critical to the entire design. One was cost: we used the model to dynamically control the amount of steel in the structure while preserving the design intent. We were able to reduce the amount of steel by 67 percent compared to similar sports arenas. The other was human experience—the quality of the view. From every seat in the stadium, we could measure the distance, angle, and obstructions to the view of the playing field. Both cost and experience were critical pieces of information—as they are to any project—but the ability to make changes to the design and see the impacts to both factors simultaneously was a game changer. The project we delivered is cost-efficient and will offer superb views

of the field from every seat. We couldn't have arrived at the design we did without building the model as a data structure—rather than simply geometry—from the beginning. [See Figures 2.16 through 2.19.]

Do you have examples of how your firm uses computers in the capturing, mining, analysis, or application of data on a building project?

AH: On one design project, we tapped into the client's key card data from their existing facility to understand employee movement flows and facility occupation rates. Paired with directed on-site observation, this let us build up a rich picture of the way the company's employees behaved, and what parts of their facilities saw the most use at what times. This allowed us to make informed decisions in the design of their project, secure in the knowledge that the new facility would always meet or exceed current and projected need.

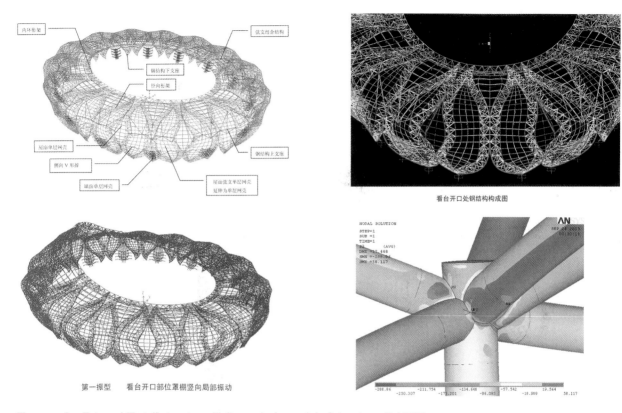

Figure 2.16:   External "Petal" structure: Finite analysis model of structure. © *NBBJ*

In another context, our healthcare practice, we've been able to leverage anonymized patient records and nursing log sheets to get a picture of how facilities are being used, and where doctors, nurses, patients, and specialists need to be and at what times. That same data was used to drive a sophisticated agent-based simulation model that we could use to evaluate our designs for their new spaces—and prove that the numbers and arrangement of patient rooms and other critical spaces would be efficient and adequate—and improve considerably on their existing facilities.

What is one way your firm has been capturing data?

AH: One example that comes to mind is a tool built by my colleague Nate Holland for early site analysis. For a selected site, the tool can tap into GIS data, 3D model archives, and internal records, alongside information scraped from public sources, like city and county websites. In this way we can bring together a site's geometry, its history, its zoning envelope, its contextual relationships—all at the press of a button. The tool has radically sped up our process of early site analysis, letting us move quickly on to design.

(Continued)

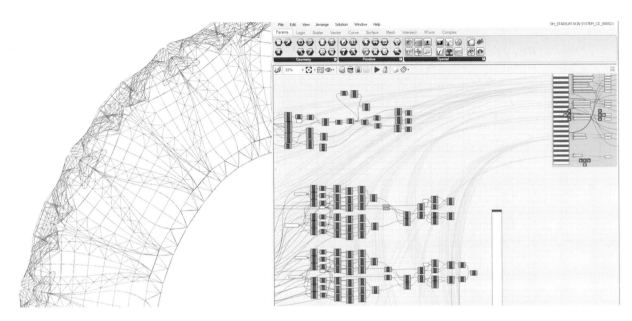

Figure 2.17:   External "Petal" structure: Grasshopper definition of structural skin system. © *NBBJ*

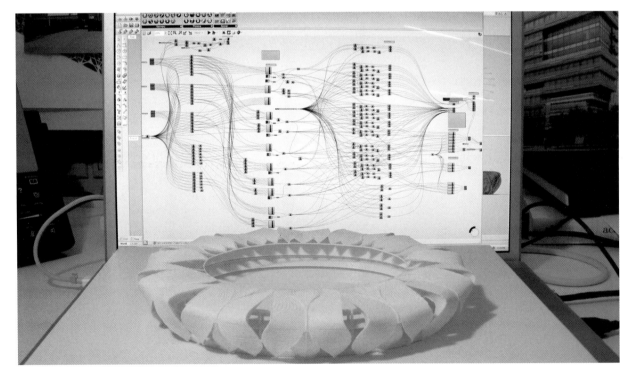

Figure 2.18:   External "Petal" structure: 3D print of concept design and the parametric model that generated it. © *NBBJ*

Figure 2.19:   External "Petal" structure: Hangzhou Sports Park rendering. © *NBBJ*

Have you or your firm utilized big data on any of your projects?

AH: The term "big data" is a difficult one, and tends to get abused. I tend to define it as datasets large enough to require specialized computational infrastructure—like cloud computing, or farms of machines like supercomputers—in order to process it. Under that definition I wouldn't say we're using big data. However, with a slightly more liberal definition, a server with hundreds of BIM models on it is big data—and in that case we use it every day, not just as individuals accessing specific projects, but with our tools that analyze and monitor the performance of all the projects in the firm, taking a look at all the models at once.

Ultimately data doesn't talk, or sing, or breathe, or draw, or even mean anything, until you DO something with it—process it, present it, interpret it—and algorithms are the means by which that happens.
—Andrew Heumann, NBBJ

Where are design professionals on the data front today?

AH: I can't speak for the design profession as a whole (though if I had to I'd probably categorize it as indifferent), but at NBBJ there's a high level of enthusiasm and understanding around the way data can increase the value we bring to our design work. [See Figures 2.20 through 2.23.]

Any last thoughts about data in design and construction?

AH: "Data" itself is actually beside the point. In my eyes, the important thing is algorithms—what you do with data and how you do it. Getting excited about data is like getting excited about letters (a, b, c) instead of literature. Data obviously

(Continued)

cannot be written out of the equation—it is the fluid through which everything flows, the common language that makes it all possible—but ultimately data doesn't talk, or sing, or breathe, or draw, or even mean anything, until you DO something with it—process it, present it, interpret it—and algorithms are the means by which that happens.

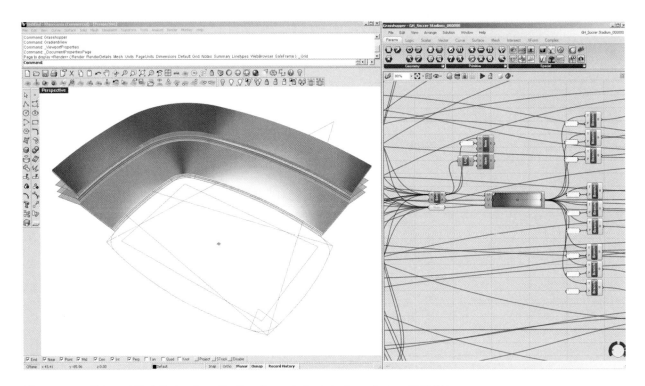

Figure 2.20:   External "Petal" structure: Section through final stadium design. © *NBBJ*

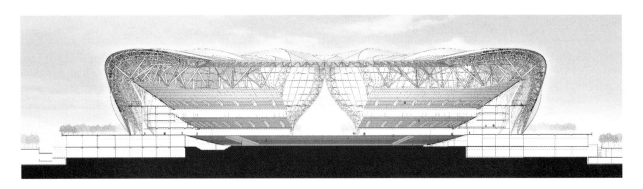

Figure 2.21:   External "Petal" structure: Successive geometric dependencies building up detail and complexity. © *NBBJ*

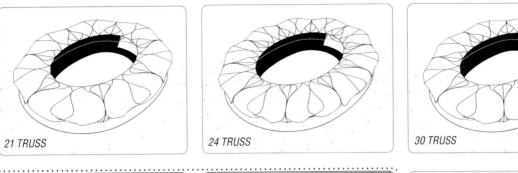

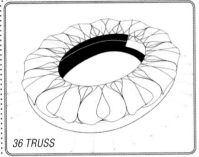

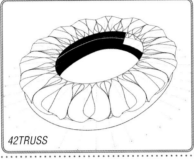

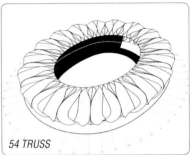

21 TRUSS

24 TRUSS

30 TRUSS

36 TRUSS

42TRUSS

54 TRUSS

Figure 2.22: External "Petal" structure: Geometric variations altering petal and truss count. © *NBBJ*

Figure 2.23: External "Petal" structure: Hangzhou Sports Park aerial rendering. © *NBBJ*

The Middle Ground: A Data-Informed Approach

Does a firm like SOM—a firm that helped launch AEC-APPs and regularly queries its BIM models for pertinent data—consider itself data driven? "I can't characterize the whole firm one way, but certainly aspects of what we do at SOM are data-driven," says Robert Yori, Senior Digital Design Manager at SOM, but then adds, "And some are data-informed." As with the data-enabled approach, the choice is situational. "There is some information that is better suited to being data-driven and some that is less so. So holistically, when we are approaching design, I would have to go with data-informed. Because there are some things that we do that are incredibly data-intensive. Some things that we do aren't so much."

Yori weighs the options, and sees the ideal approach for the industry as being data-informed,

> … although it is hard to generalize at that level. There are certain types of practice that are more data-driven. For example, my good friend has recently gone to work for a firm that focuses on healthcare …. A firm doing that kind of intensive work may be closer to data-driven. If you as a client want to go to a more sculptural architect, because you may be looking for something maybe a little less programmatically defined or rigorous, and want something that's more emblematic, perhaps you're closer to data-enabled. Being aware of data and understanding the role it can and should play in one's practice is very, very important.

One's stance in the face of data has implications for education as well. "In school, our professors often told us that architecture is about the problems you choose to solve; I would extend that and say, 'and how we choose to solve them.' As long as you are aware of the 'data factor,' and you're understanding when it might make sense to use it in your practice, and to what degree, that's key."

Brian Skripac contends that Astorino falls somewhere in the middle:

> We're not making post-rationalizations of decisions but neither are we solely using data to drive solutions. If data-driven is considered the ultimate utilization of data in design, we operate more on a validate-then-optimize basis. We try to capture what we know, design to it, test it out, then go back and forth. We're focused on sustainability and refinement/optimization through simulation. We might have a certain performance outcome we're trying to achieve. How do we get there? These four strategies are working, these three aren't working, let's focus on this option and refine it. This an area where we're starting to see how data can drive that design process, and respond to it, as opposed to relying on rules-of-thumb and institutional knowledge.

Sasaki Associates principal, Gregory Janks, concurs that a data-driven approach, where algorithms take top billing, may be too extreme:

> We are data-informed. During the last decade, we have spent much of our energy in thinking about creating strong analytic functions to support planning and design decisions, exploring both quantitative and qualitative variables. We have found the rigor of this approach necessary to create compelling high-value solutions for our clients. At the same time, we recognize that not every component of a problem is amenable to measurement, and that political, aesthetic, emotional, and other considerations can be critical. We are most proud of our ability to link analysis to design, and through the magic of this alchemy, to solve problems. So, yes, data is a (very important) factor in decision making, but not the only priority.

Grimshaw Architects is another firm that prefers to see more of a balance between data and input from experienced, talented individuals. Peter Liebsch, the firm's Global Head of Design Technology, says that they are data informed "where data is basically an add-on to make a better-informed decision." He still relies on data in the end:

> A big part of our decision making is still based on the experience of the individual. More and more, data is used to underpin what our gut feeling or initial response would have been. We see this especially in performance analysis. A good architect with years of experience can usually tell you whether the volume sits correctly in relation to the southern and northern hemisphere. But if you find your site surrounded by dense high-rises, with the shadows they cast and the compromised view corridor, you find that your gut feeling was not completely off but your façade performance will be different than you expected. We rely on data to give us a better product in the end.

For data-informed firms, data doesn't so much drive, but rather qualifies or enhances the decisions firms make. "I would say it informs decisions. Your mind thinks; information informs," says Solomon Cordwell Buenz's Managing Principal, Mark Frisch. As he elaborates:

> Say you are interested in detailing a door opening. Ultimately, someone is going to ask you 'What's the gauge of the hollow metal frame?' As long as you know exactly where to go and find out easily, you do not need to store that information in your head. You can focus on the most appropriate design solution and look up the appropriate gauge when required. Both are important, but the driver is the detail, not the gauge. In my view of the world of architecture and the process of solving technical problems, your head should to be able to think-drive

decisions the information warehouses are there to inform.

LMN Architects partner, Sam Miller, is another design professional who vies for data's middle ground. "Over the last couple years we've refined our thinking in that regard. We're somewhere in-between data-informed, or data-driven. The reason I say that is we are striving to access as much data as possible to inform our decision making. But we also don't want data to be the sole driver of our design process. There is a middle ground there." Miller explains the distinction—the need for a middle ground—in terms of architecture's less data-defined qualities: "The term data-driven tends to imply that the outcome is largely driven by the data. We're striving to make the best-informed decisions we can, but also knowing that there is only so much in design that you can capture with data. There's also a quality, an aesthetic, and other contextual issues that need to be woven into the solution in a way that data alone isn't going to achieve." See Figure 2.24.

How organizations choose to define themselves is not limited to design or construction firms. All companies that want to stay in business need to contend with data. Take the United States Green Building Council (USGBC). Chris Pyke explains that USGBC is in transition:

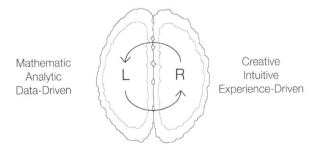

Figure 2.24: Data-driven design requires whole-brain thinking. © R Deutsch

For two decades, USGBC has been focused on building and empowering a movement to create buildings and communities that benefit people and the environment. Largely as a by-product of this work, USGBC has created a unique stream of information about a growing fraction of the building industry in the U.S. and around the world. Today, USGBC recognizes that these data—when effectively combined with others—can fuel a new era of market transformation. Overall, these changes suggest an organization that is currently "data-informed" is rapidly evolving toward one that is "data-driven" or even "data-centric."

Hybrid Approaches: Data-Ready to Data-Nimble

To some extent, labels such as data-enabled, data-informed, and even data-driven are arbitrary. There are many other similar terms that could have been used to define both individuals' and firms' approaches to using data in their design and construction projects. That said, firms took to them and responded in relation to one or another of these labels. Exceptions to this could be seen as ways firms differentiate themselves in relation to data-informed firms. Two such examples follow that exemplify these traits. See Figure 2.25.

Figure 2.25: We need to do a better job of balancing our tools with our processes. © R Deutsch

Jill Bergman, Healthcare Principal and Vice President at HDR, believes that there will be firms taking on each of those directions, and a few may be thriving in all three areas. She believes that "the best approach is to be data ready." KieranTimberlake's Research Director, Billie Faircloth, takes a different tack when describing her firm's approach to data:

> We are data-nimble. Data-nimble means that we are first conscious that data is infrastructural to all of our efforts—it is latent in our actions, intrinsic in our selections, keystrokes and forms, it is implicit or explicit in our simulations. Such consciousness is extended to the practice position of being able to accept data produced by others, to question and query data, augment, and expand it. It is likewise extended to our position that architects should produce, not merely consume, knowledge. Data-nimbleness is an essential first principle because design is a multivariate endeavor. When one designs, his or her power lies in the inscription of a boundary around that "data" that will and will not participate in the design process.

Case Study Interview with Jonathon Broughton

Jonathon Broughton is an architect turned design data specialist working in London, UK, developing an emphasis in the use of data in design and also analyzing the outputs of the design process. This work began while he was with Alsop Architects, then expanded while working for Allies and Morrison Architects, where he shifted his role to Data Wrangler and Specialist Modeler.

As a data wrangler, how do you interact with the rest of the office?

Jonathon Broughton (JB): I sit in the corner of the office with the BIM team. There are two streams of the work that I do. It's technology-focused, information-driven, and mostly about human education. Sometimes I find I am most helpful sitting next to someone explaining how to get an answer from the information they already have. Watching middle-aged men with childlike wonder in their eyes when they're getting information out of something that is super basic is quite satisfying. There are other times when the thing for me to do is to listen, go away, build something, and say here, just use this. [See Figure 2.26.]

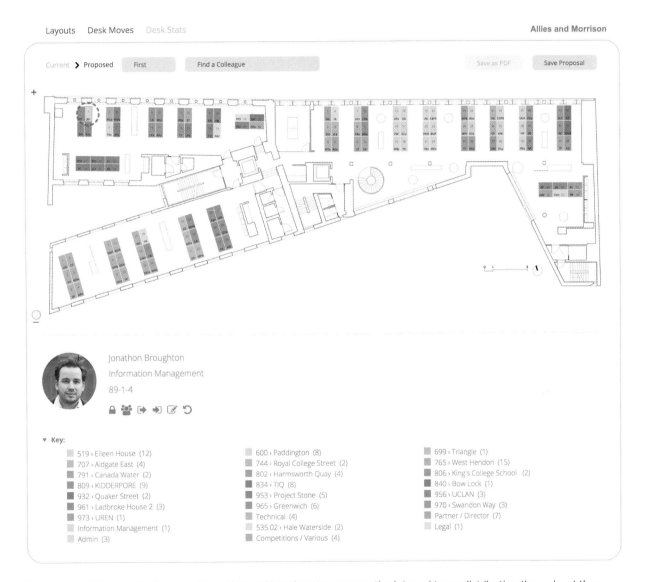

Figure 2.26:   Web application used by Allies and Morrison to manage the internal team distribution throughout the practice's studios and floors. Linking data to project resourcing, IT equipment, and staff profiles allows management oversight of many metrics in a simple tool also used by staff to find colleagues. © *Jonathon Broughton*

(Continued)

Describe your role and your title.

JB: Design Technologist has the most resonance outside of Allies and Morrison. That is why I have that as my title. My official title is Data Wrangler and Specialist Modeler. I'm trained as an architect but quite deliberately don't describe myself as one. Technologist can mean working out where the grommets are and how not to let water into the building. Inside the office I don't use that word.

Big data once required crunching—but it can be ungainly and unstructured. Is wrangling a better metaphor?

JB: It is. Big data hasn't been properly assessed within our part of the industry. It isn't about live, real-time monitoring and social streams. Big data is grappling with the fact that people are, whether they know it or not, generating information and generating data. The reason why it is "big," it is not huge quantities as such, but it is massively unstructured. That's because so many times it's depending entirely on who has generated it. While we technically all have the same means of production, we all theoretically have the same sort of deliverables. Ultimately every single person in my organization as well as others I am exposed to, including clients, will make ad hoc, bespoke data models that briefly fit the purpose. Just because they are unstructured, and just because they are disparate and bespoke, doesn't mean they don't all have meaning. The wrangling side is about knowing where to look and knowing how to filter and offer insight. It's very easy, incredibly easy, with the tools that we have to build really, really, really data-rich haystacks. What we need—and what's missing in our industry—there's a real need for those people who know, maybe instinctively or have a hunch, where the needles may be. And it's those sorts of people that need to apply rigorous algorithmic analyses using analytical tools. Go find me those needles, but what we don't need is people who are just really good at making very good haystacks.

The most baseline imperative—the BIM imperative—currently is being driven by people who don't understand what it is they want out of it in the end. In the UK it is a quite bureaucratic drive toward a means of production or delivery. There isn't really yet an understanding of why—they know roughly why, they think it will be more efficient and measurable—[but] they don't understand the mechanism by which it can be transformative or make people or the industry more effective. All we know is that it can make really big haystacks. In that environment work needs to be done, not solely by those in production, but clients need to be educated more than anybody else. Right now they are paying for this information. We are being paid to produce it, but they are paying to receive it. I can help architects make slightly better dog shampoo or help people extract value out of the information that they have paid for. An architect—with the right skills and motivation—should be in a good position to do that. As a traditional design team leader and single point of contact for a client, we should be the ones who are saying we can do this.

An architect with 20, 25, 30 years of experience ought to be able to do what you describe. Is there something in the approach you take that can enable others to do this sooner?

JB: The most basic learning that anyone can do is to as quickly as possible get to where they can visualize information in nontraditional means. Whether that is learning processing or learning Tableau or D3 or Grasshopper making information turned into volumes and shapes and patterns. There's something interesting about visualized data. Unless you're trained and interested in running things through an R algorithm, where you can apply algorithmic insight, there's something beautiful about experimentation, play, where you don't know what's going to happen if you try this. The freedom of experimentation that a traditional architect in training has lends itself massively to being able to intuit information out of datasets by the power of visualization. [See Figures 2.27 through 2.29.]

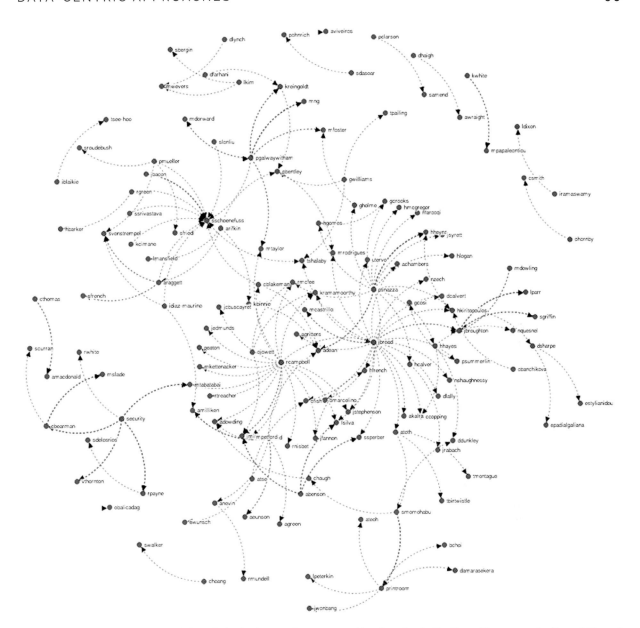

Figure 2.27:   Analysis of a typical day of who in the studio was searching for who. Indication of frequency by line width and directionality by arrow. © *Allies and Morrison*

We built an intranet of project data—knowledge-based management. Recently, I looked into what was the most used part of our intranet? If we were to refresh it, where should we spend our effort? It turns out 90 percent of the staff 100 percent of the time just use it to look up internal phone numbers. There's a huge amount of information collected

(Continued)

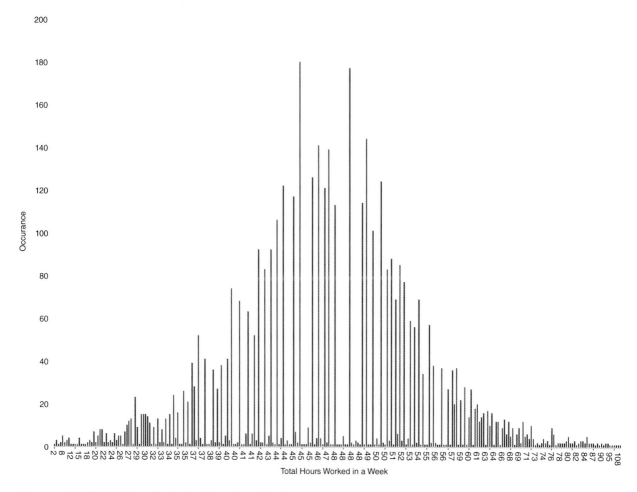

Figure 2.28:   Distribution of submitted total working hours per week over a five-year period. © *Allies and Morrison*

over 15 years. We know that they're using the phone list as the portal for all other information. I found the reason they use the phone page as their way in is that people like looking up people in lists of people. I built a tool so that every time you clicked on someone, it would record who clicked, and who they were looking for. What I produced instead was a network graph, plotting who looked at who, the lines would get thicker if someone looked at someone multiple times. We find in these really interesting visual patterns that the same people would look each other up multiple times each week. You would see these instances where someone would run someone up for information, had been unsuccessful, put the phone down, and would look someone else up. You could visually see the thought processes that were going on just from what people had clicked. It was an interesting way to observe how people might engage with information. We were also able to gain insights into the fabric of this society of our office by doing this visualization. We didn't have this purpose in mind when we built it. I don't think it takes a great deal of learning to learn these very basic visualization tools. The traditional education of an architect is one where you are encouraged to play, experiment, take risks, and not necessarily know the answer. People shouldn't lose sight of the fact that

Figure 2.29: Return on capital: Interactive analysis of time worked and overtime distributed by date by architects. Presented information can be filtered and cross-correlated by individuals, sector, individual project, and director in charge. © *Allies and Morrison*

intuition has a part to play in design as much as it does in data analysis. I see a lot of the education of designers of the twisty towers, despite having huge capability in this means of production, there's a tendency to learn by rote that which should offer infinitely variable possibility. If anything, passion should be making architects freer to make decisions that haven't been made before.

You also describe yourself as an application programming interface (API) shepherd.

There isn't a good word to describe what it is what I'm doing. Data scientist isn't it. I'm not trained as a data scientist. There are people who are coming out of universities trained in it. Data scientists are being hired by architecture firms—but I don't think that's where the opportunity is. What I can bring—maybe because I'm an architecturally trained person—is different. We shouldn't be spending a great deal of time on people who can deliver us pure analytics because all they're going to give us is the answer to the question we give them. We need to be putting emphasis in those people who will give us the right questions. One of the things I think I can do is intuit the right questions for people.

Do you view working in data as an opportunity for someone to differentiate themselves in this competitive field?

JB: I don't think so. We should be doing a much better job of describing this sort of activity as an additional service and value-add. If we don't, it will be the differentiating factor. I think we should be a lot more bullish about this and say, no. It's more work than we would normally do, so you should pay us for that.

I don't think it's a ship that's sailed. There's additional services and there are some things we should legitimately be describing as value-add. Your new means of production is something that you should be charged more for. When you've been promising all along that you've been delivering coordinated buildings is questionable. We may have been kidding ourselves

(Continued)

for the last three decades that CAD has been allowing us to coordinate buildings. It certainly hasn't. What it has been doing is allow us to do, at best, is coordinate a set of drawings. It is philosophically difficult to ask for more money for delivering the same service. The opportunity for anyone who is moving toward a BIM process is to use the opportunity to make the means of production hugely more effective. Gain the benefits internally to make yourself more profitable, or happier, whatever it is they can get out of it.

Do you find that others understand what you do?

JB: No. I try my hardest not to explain myself because if I try to explain what it is I do, it is so far from what people understand that it is counterproductive. Because they're thinking, he's occupying a desk, I'm occupying a desk; I'm working all hours getting these drawings out, he's just having fun in the corner. It's much better for me to ask: Do you have something that's causing you a particular problem? Is there something in the way that you are working right now that—even if you don't know why or how—could probably be better? Then it's a much easier conversation to describe what I would do if I were in your position. If they have time to try it, they realize it is saving them X hours/week. That may be the thing that makes him go home and see his kids on a Friday night. That's when they suddenly understand what it is that I do. Demonstrating works. Explaining doesn't.

At first glance at Allies and Morrison's work, data seems like the antithesis of what it is about: the work has such warmth, depth, variety, and presence. How can data help achieve these ends?

JB: I think it's possible to be two things at once. To be better informed can only be a good thing. We have now the best opportunity to be as well informed about what it is we are doing. That's the transformative effect we have right now. We can always be learning more about how we're doing things, how we can be doing things. I don't think your means of analysis and production should be manifest in what it is you do. I don't think that what you do should belie the way that you achieved it. Just because you've applied smart ways of working to achieve that end shouldn't necessarily be in what you look at when you occupy a space. I don't believe you have to assume that data-driven design should be fancy curtain wall patterns, because our biggest opportunity is improving everything that we do. There are a lot of opportunities for using analysis and data for making what we do better. It doesn't necessarily change what the design looks like.

Is there an instance where you allowed intuition to override the data on a project?

JB: We worked on a car park project. It looks like it might have been the output of an algorithm. The effect at night, when the car park is occupied and the lights are on, is this very interesting ethereal aura to the building that looks very deliberate. It was probably very random. The car park project is one someone intuitively came up with—they were tasked to come up with a random distribution and that's what they managed. If you objectively analyze it, they got it right. It was done by intuition and that's probably enough. Someone making a calculated decision, where the calculation exists, is enough. [See Figures 2.30 through 2.33.]

People fear that technology and data will mean the end of delight in architecture and place-making. Data and delight: Do you think the two can live compatibly together?

JB: I don't know if I would say they are contradictory. It depends on your attitude. If you could imagine that you could boil the world down to a set of algorithms, then the role of the craftsman is probably dead. If that isn't one's position—it

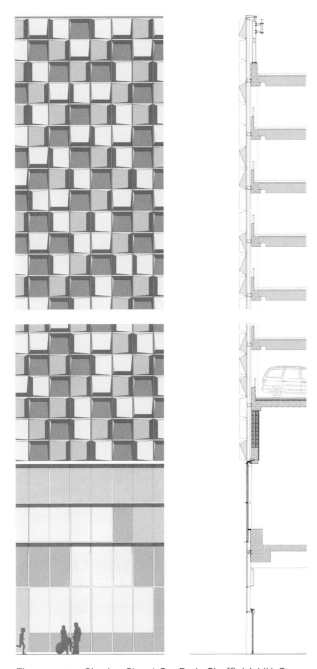

Figure 2.30: Charles Street Car Park, Sheffield, UK: Over-clad facade to a new car park composed of a single angled module with "random" distribution. Work was made both to make the population of the pattern random, and then to correct it to *appear* more random. © *Allies and Morrison*

isn't mine—algorithmic design, data analysis, is a means to an end. To make our lives better. To empower the architect to make his or her intuitions.

Algorithmic design, data analysis, is a means to an end. To make our lives better. To empower the architect to make his or her intuitions.
—Jonathon Broughton, Data Wrangler

What exactly does data do for you in your projects that craft and knowledge, intuition, and experience, can't accomplish?

JB: I hope you don't mind me hesitating a moment while I dismiss my whole purpose in life [laughs]. Data allows you to do that much more of it. Data allows you to be that much better. You can be more efficient. Wouldn't it be good if you could learn so much observing yourself doing something, that the next time you do it you can do it better. Or quicker. Or cheaper. Or more effectively or sustainably. We couldn't do that before—exploiting technology. We don't need to do active time-and-motion studies. We can apply exactly the same motivation, thought, and application to anything that we do but we can do it completely passively. The more we can do passively, and be able to interpret and offer insight into what it is that it is telling us, the better we will be as designers. It's not something that, in and of itself, will radically make people better designers. You can't create a workflow or an API that will allow people to have better taste. You can't influence fashion or the foibles of your client. No matter how hard you try, the world can't be boiled down into an algorithm. We're all humans. At one level, the foibles of human interaction are much more interesting than anything data can do. [See Figure 2.34.]

No matter how hard you try, the world can't be boiled down into an algorithm. We're all humans. At one level, the foibles of human interaction are much more interesting than anything data can do.
—Jonathon Broughton, Data Wrangler

(Continued)

Figure 2.31: Charles Street Car Park, Sheffield, UK. ©
Allies and Morrison

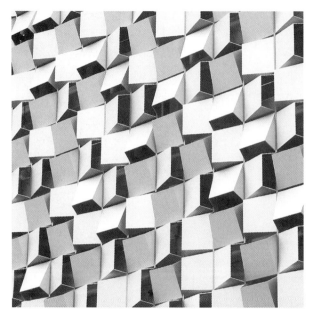

Figure 2.32: Charles Street Car Park, Sheffield, UK. ©
Allies and Morrison

If someone is wedded to being a data-driven designer,
more power to them. But it's not the thing that will

Backing up our ideas with data—it is still why people
come to architects. To come up with that which they
couldn't come up with themselves. Data and technology
allow us to have another tool we can master or
experiment with to assist us in portraying, constructing,
or delivering that thing that the client is paying us to do.
Looking at the flipside, no client's going to come to an
architect and say what I want is a data-driven design. We
can, in the best interest of everyone, exploit whatever
tools we can to make our lives better and more effective,
and deliver better buildings and experiences for our
clients. We should exploit whatever tools we can. But it
doesn't replace intuition.

Figure 2.33: Charles Street Car Park, Sheffield, UK. ©
Allies and Morrison

Figure 2.34   King's Cross Central Master Plan regenerates 67 acres of central London from a former railyard into a mixed-use development covering residential, commercial, cultural, and retail use connected by a robust framework of streets and spaces. Automated output of an analytical tool (not shown) measures the proportion of an urban condition achieving a benchmark degree of visible sky. © *Miller Hare Limited, used courtesy of King's Cross Central Limited Partnership*

motivate someone to pay them. It might be if it produces something really cool and innovative. Then great, there's space for everything.

What is it exactly that data does for you—and your projects—that standard knowledge or experience or intuition can't?

JB: Sherlock Holmes was highly intuitive, but only after he had collected sufficient data to eliminate the false positives.

What Would Google Do?

One's approach to data is not always a choice. There are times when the approach is driven by a firm's culture, or based on the market sectors or project types that the firm pursues. Some clients have data-driven cultures—think tech firms such as Google or Apple. If you are working in design or construction in certain sectors—on certain building types such as technology headquarters—you're expected to be a data-driven firm with a data-driven approach.

How important is it to Google that the firm they work with is data-driven? What do you look for in a firm that's going to design and build one of your data centers? "It is an absolute must-have to be data driven," confirms Peter Pellerzi, Manager on the Data Center Global Engineering Team at Google. He explains the role data plays when selecting firms to partner with:

> One of the first few interview questions asked is "why did you do it that way?" The wrong

answers are "because that is the way we always do it" or "the client told me to do it that way." In my mind, the way we always did it really doesn't help to move innovation forward, and the client telling you to do it that way is also not helpful because I, personally, have been dead wrong on major items. Having a partner that can come back and say to the client "Look, I know that is what you want but let me show you the data on what that means versus these other options" is absolutely vital.

Beyond data centers and technology headquarters, healthcare projects readily lend themselves to a data-driven approach. Aditazz chose to focus on healthcare projects because they are rules-based and would benefit from a data-driven approach. Are there other building types or market sectors that would lend themselves to a data-driven approach? "The clients we want to pursue are owner builders and operators," says Zigmund Rubel. "They need to get the capex and opex [capital expenditure and operating expense] tradeoffs, so we can have a dialogue with them. We have recognized our approach can be easily be used for airports, commercial complexes, schools, and urban planning."

Some firms are data driven and recognize the value and benefits of using—capturing, analyzing, and applying—data in projects. Many others are on the fence or are slow to adopt and to adapt, which can be dangerous when it comes to working with technology as well as data. "In the technology industry we work with fairly traditional technology adoption curves," says Mads Jensen, CEO of Sefaira.

There is always a part of the market that likes to try things early, and others that prefer to wait and see. There is debate as to how much of this is driven by our environment, and how much is biology. One might imagine that some of these traits (e.g., being first with technology gives you competitive advantages, whilst taking a wait-and-see approach can be less risky) are closely linked to evolutionary biology—i.e., different means of survival. I'd posit that in the history of the world, more groups have faced extinction because they were late to adapt than those that adapted quickly.

Notes

Unless otherwise indicated, quoted text throughout the book is from interviews with the author that took place between February and July of 2014.

1. See Clayton Christenson, "The innovator's dilemma," *HarperBusiness*, 2011.
2. Definitions provided by Robert Yori, interview with author, July 7, 2014.

chapter 3 Learning from Data

Disciplines aren't just separate subjects you pick out of a course catalogue. They involve infrastructures comprised of people, artifacts, and institutions that generate, share, and maintain specific knowledge in complex and interconnected ways.

—Lisa Gitelman

The fact that you are reading this book means you are taking a first step to better understand the scope of how one works with data in the AECO industry. Bringing attention to the topic of data ought to stimulate educators to tackle this topic in school, which does not happen often enough today. Students today may be exposed to both hands-on and computer simulation techniques through which they explore the impact of design on building performance, where building design solutions influence energy consumption, thermal comfort, and daylighting performance from the early stages of design. However, these students are nonetheless often unaware of issues related to the leveraging of the data that drives these simulations. This understanding about advanced use of data comes down to not only how, but also when, one becomes prepared to do so.

Five Factors Ensuring Data Preparedness

The primary influences on data preparedness are time and readiness. However, other factors, including people, metrics, and industry conditions (the "radar" factor), also play significant roles.

The Time Factor

Design and construction professionals feel pressured for time. Between pressures brought about by the economy, new technologies, and work processes, they have more to deal with than they feel they can handle. "I don't think anyone is in denial," says Brian Ringley, Fuse Lab Technology Coordinator at CUNY. "But it's a time of almost overwhelming change and people are busy." Many firms are seeking support by looking outside their organizations to building technology consultants. Ringley adds, "This is why it will be up to entrepreneurs and consultants with a real stake in innovation to essentially institutionalize and prepackage big data for AEC. AEC's got enough on its plate to be expected to go at this alone."

Firms want to keep up with the competition and are feeling pressure either to train their current employees to work with data, to hire talent from outside, or both. "I believe that design professionals see the need to address these issues on the horizon," says Chris Pyke of USGBC. "Probably not today or tomorrow, but relatively soon."[1]

The Readiness Factor

Our familiarity and readiness to work with data will have a strong impact on and implications for the

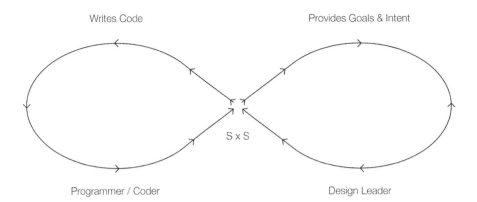

Figure 3.1: Investment in multidisciplinary project teams and new graduates with emergent technological specializations will be key in managing this change. This diagram depicts working side by side (S x S) to collaboratively develop how algorithms are going to work. © *R Deutsch*

AECO industry. It's a question of preparedness: How prepared is your organization to start to work with data, or to take your use of current technology tools to the next level?

However, preparedness implies more than training and talent: it's also a mindset. "I think they recognize it but are still unsure on how to utilize it and, more importantly, how it improves design," says Clayton Starr of RTKL. "It will require new attitudes, workflows, and expertise in a tradition that has struggles with change." Starr continues:

> I personally believe that many feel poorly equipped to incorporate data and associated technologies into their work. They are concerned about impacts of their professional practice, including cost and liability. In part, their interest in data will hinge on how information about "performance" comes to be understood with respect to specific AECO roles and responsibilities.

The People Factor

Having the right people on board is critical, especially those who are predisposed or motivated to work with data and see the value in doing so. Ringley again: "Investment in multidisciplinary project teams and new graduates with emergent technological specializations will be key in managing this change." Interest in, and appreciation for, what data can accomplish has to be both a top-down and a bottom-up effort. Leadership on the data front must start at both ends, and requires equal dosages of enthusiasm and understanding of how data can add value in the organization and on project work. (See Figure 3.1.)

The Metrics Factor

When working with data, design professionals need to become aware of the outcomes from a quantitative standpoint. They need to be able to answer two questions:

1. What is the value for our firm in implementing data into our processes?

2. How do we measure that result in a way that others can immediately understand?

Not everybody in the AECO industry recognizes the importance of leveraging data in design. The thought of describing or justifying one's design in terms of numbers, rather than more subjective qualities such as the senses or emotions, still makes some design professionals uncomfortable. The culture of design runs deep. And yet, the ability to point to specific metrics will go a long way to convince others of the value and potential impact of a project in terms of the very sensations and emotions the project elicits. Think of this as collecting the data on data.

While our industry is still playing catch-up, design professionals outside of architecture have already caught on. "A lot of design practices are data driven," says David Fano of CASE, "because there's a much tighter connection to the market." He explains:

> A website is trying to drive a certain funnel of interactions so that they buy this thing or click on this thing. If my design does not enable that, then it's bad. It's not qualitative anymore, it's quantitative. So I need to quantify it. There's eye tracking and click-through rates. We don't do that with architecture.

The time has come for architecture to do this as well.

The Radar Factor

Firms are becoming aware that they need to reduce waste and increase productivity. They need to provide proof for their design intentions, and back up their building performance claims.

This awareness is what drives their interest in incorporating data into their workflows and processes. Mads Jensen, CEO of Sefaira, concurs: "The industry is increasingly becoming attuned to the need for good analysis through a design process. And there is obviously no analysis without data to analyze. The industry has access to more data than ever, and we see a stronger and stronger trend towards incorporating analysis at all stages."

Whether a firm will make use of the data it has available to it can be determined based on something as simple as whether data even shows up on its radar. Many firms and organizations remain indifferent to data, and to the positive impacts it can have on building and planning projects. Marco Hemmerling disagrees with this assessment: "The major part of professionals is more insecure than indifferent, which has to do with lack of information and ability to deal with Big Data."

How do we address this insecurity? Thought leaders and advocates for data in architecture and construction are helping to fill a knowledge gap, and are starting to remove any insecurity based on unfamiliarity with data. I asked London-based data wrangler Jonathon Broughton whether he thought data was now showing up on organizations' radars. "In architecture not as much as I think there should be. There is a lot of emphasis right now on the outputs from BIM and there are dedicated design studios in universities investing intellectual rigor into 'press the design-me-a-building' button." Broughton describes these firms' data use as a value-added proposition as opposed to a simple means to an end: "However, there is good work being done across AEC sectors in systems and processes now and has been before the UK BIM Mandate. Unfair to say they are alone, but CASE in NYC and Arup and Studio Klashka in London stand out for advocacy. New cost consultancy firms such as Alinea are springing up, which are investing in human and intellectual capital to best position themselves as data-fluent BIM-centric." He adds:

> Knight Frank as Property Agents is offering sector-leading research both as a general knowledge USP and also a bespoke consultancy. With a global scope covering regeneration projects in Detroit, Russia, and the Middle East, Happold Consulting leverage data analysis as both the driver behind the strategies they recommend and also lean toward public

engagement through visualization and inter-action with the research they undertake and the findings they conclude—and of course clients such as Argent and Stanhope taking seriously the exposure of information as assets and the learning they can make from their own built capital.

Brian Skripac of Astorino, a 100-plus-person single-source AEC firm with offices in Pittsburgh, Pennsylvania, USA; Abu Dhabi, UAE; and Palermo, Italy, also cites CASE as a leader in these efforts: "You see thought leaders like the team at CASE work with data, and they're able to get into a BIM and drill into things, it is so detailed and refined. They're mining all kinds of relevant information from building information models for future use. It makes you wonder how did they do that? What need triggered that information to be captured?" (See Figure 3.2.)

The use of data hasn't fully penetrated the AECO industry, according to Skripac: "It's still at a high level where it's somewhat theoretical for so many people and firms. I think the point of comparison for Big Data in the building industry today is understanding more of what you see with large firms like SOM and HOK who are taking advantage of data which is often used for generative and performative design." He adds, "From a mainstream design side, it seems a little off to the future as there are many firms still trying to implement BIM. I have to admit, it really makes me think about it and try to wrap my head around what to apply it to for my firm's everyday use because it can be so powerful."

So, how does a design professional such as Brian Skripac find an entry point—an "in"—for himself and his firm? "For me personally," says Skripac, "I look at it from an analysis and simulation standpoint, where data becomes readily available and something tangible, but that real deep dive straight into data, and how to communicate it, still seems further down the road to make it informative and manageable."

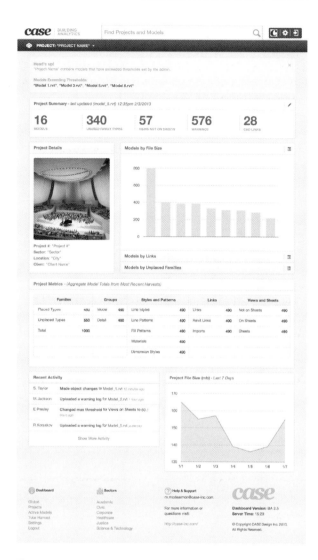

Figure 3.2:   By analyzing BIM models associated with the project, project overview reveals current status of the project, highlighting outstanding problems within the model while providing data on recent activity within the model. © CASE

Training, Learning, and Working with Data

Questions concerning learning to work with data are legion: How does one learn to work with data? When is it best to learn to work with data? Is it better to be exposed to it in school, or wait until one is working in a practice? Who will teach architects to leverage data to further their designs? Who will assure that contractors are up to speed on the multiple ways data informs performance on the jobsite?

The experts I spoke with for this book are all comfortable working with data. How did they get this way? Is it something they were born with, or something they were exposed to when growing up? Was there something in particular in their education, training, or background that prepared them for working in a data-led practice? What, if anything, in their education prepared them for a career working in data and taking an algorithmic approach to the work they do? When did they first realize that they were comfortable working with data? When did they realize the importance—or potential impact—of working with data? Was one of your a parents an engineer who brought home a computer for you to take apart? Later in this chapter, we will explore what in their education prepared these design professionals for careers in the AECO industry where they are working with and in data and taking an algorithmic approach to the work they do.

Quite frankly there's a need in the profession for people trained in this process. I think that higher education should be developing this specialized skill set.

—Mark Frisch, SCB

MKThink recently advertised to fill an environmental technologist position to join the Innovation Studio. Among the new hire's responsibilities, they included: "Researching, implementing and overseeing building technologies to measure and verify building performance. Exploring potential applications of the Building Information Models and other parametric data to project building performance—

including but not exclusive to predicted energy use and generation, region-specific daylight models, acoustic levels, material impacts. Technical analysis in support of project teams including calculations that support proof of concept."

Where will candidates to fill this position come from? Are schools graduating designers with these capabilities? Will companies be expected to train people on the job? What can schools be doing to better prepare professionals for the future that positions like the one at MKThink portend? Currently they are somewhat rare, so when you find the right people, you want to clone them—and repeat the process it took for them to arrive where they are.

Control the Tools, Control the Data

Learning technology and tools is important—but one message stands out: *It is not enough anymore to learn existing tools.* Design and construction professionals need to feel comfortable either shaping existing tools to fit their needs, or otherwise creating their own tools. Most acknowledge that digital natives—the Gen Y or Millennial workforce—are extremely comfortable taking on new tools and work processes, including those involving building data, especially when compared with earlier generations.

According to CASE's David Fano, there's a grassroots effort happening at the student level, where they feel empowered by their ability to make their own tools. "I'm really excited to see the generational shift in the building industry. There is a generational understanding of our relationship with knowledge, skill, and tools where we mastered them. We invested a very long time building a relationship with a piece of technology, whether physical or digital. The new mindset is about catching the light and the tools just participate in the way in which they need to. The objective is the driver, not the tools." See Figure 3.3.

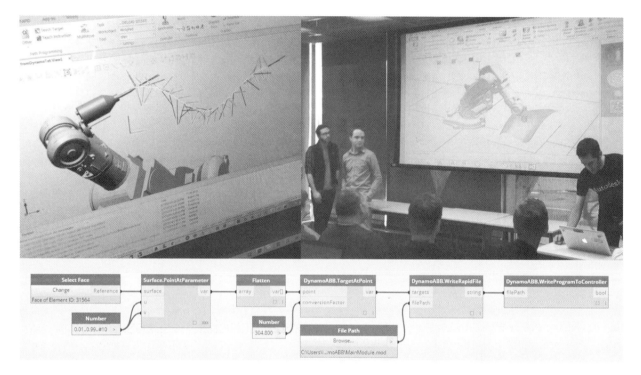

Figure 3.3: Proof of concept for direct model-to-fabrication using BIM data. DynaRobo visual programming environment for Revit Dynamo and robotics. Pictured (left to right): Brian Ringley, Colin McCrone, Ian Keough. © *Brian Ringley, Colin McCrone, Ian Keough*

The value lies less in learning any one tool than in having the confidence and wherewithal to pick up new tools for the task at hand. Being proficient is no longer sufficient.[2] "The tools are going to change every year," says Fano. "They're not worried about having to learn a new interface. At my age—I'm in my mid-thirties—I don't want to get an Android because I don't want to learn a new interface. The younger kids aren't like that. They're not scared they're going to break it. My generation and up feels like they're going to break it. The younger generation feels like if they break it they'll get a new one or they'll fix it. I'm really excited about that."

While it may be at best ill-advised, or at worst impossible, to generalize for an entire generation, as with most things, it depends on the specific circumstances. How comfortable are a university professor's students with using and adjusting to new tools and technologies? "It depends on the student and their academic context," says Brian Ringley. "I have taught similar classes at three different architecture programs and seen vastly different attitudes and abilities. Some students are good at using new tools and others are not. I would say the same about the population at large." Ringley reinforced the notion that it is no longer enough to be proficient at any one tool; rather, one must be comfortable applying what one learns to multiple circumstances and problems:

Many professors are very good at learning how to learn. That's the hardest thing to convey to the students. I don't need to teach you every single button and command and macro in Rhino. I need to teach you the basic concepts of NURBS modeling and what the workflows are. And then you can apply that knowledge quite broadly. Once you pick up a few of the packages, it's not about learning the software. It's about using what tool you need for the job. Then the process becomes pretty abbreviated at that point.

Working with data in the curriculum raises more questions that can currently be answered. How will we prepare the next generation to work with data in a curriculum where we will be asked to crunch numbers, when the NAAB accreditation board already has overloaded our curricula? Are we now going to require a quantitative statistics or economics course on top of the qualitative marketing and business courses that—for years now—we have been recommending design professionals take? Is it more important for would-be architects to ensure that water is kept out of the building than to know how to deal with data?

The current generation is comfortable working with new tools and data. What about the earlier generations—Gen Xers and Boomers? In the introduction, we described many of the challenges in working with data, one of which—especially for architects—is that data is too abstract. I asked Zig

Rubel whether he was concerned that working with data would be too abstract when he made a career transition from Anshen+Allen to Aditazz. Is it possible that data is just too far removed for some from the architecture one is educated and trained in? Rubel said he wasn't concerned, but "many of my colleagues initially were." He continued:

> The reason I am not afraid is because I felt I controlled what data to look for. Other people feel like they're being controlled by the data. If you created the tools and how the tools would work, you're actually controlling the outcome. It's like the adage: give someone a meal, they'll be hungry the next day. Teach them how to fish, and they'll eat for a lifetime. If you're defining the process, it's actually working for you.

Rubel explained his comfort regarding work with new tools and data in terms of his background as an electrician. "If your light at home isn't working, you're trying to figure out is it the bulb, is it the switch, is it the wire? There's a process one goes through to figure that out. Imagine a much more complex piece of equipment that you had to troubleshoot. I learned that process when I was an electrician. So I felt comfortable knowing that if I controlled the process to create the machine, then it will create what I want. And I wouldn't have to worry about being controlled by a machine."

Case Study Interview with Brian Ringley

Brian Ringley is on the Global Design Technology Team at Woods Bagot, where he leads efforts around Rhino, Grasshopper, fabrication, and analysis workflows; curates and develops custom digital toolsets; and provides intensive project assistance for globally significant projects with high degrees of complexity. He teaches at City Tech (CUNY) and Pratt Institute's GAUD, where he focuses on the use of a data-centric approach within parametric building models to directly drive and automate architectural manufacturing. Before going to Woods Bagot, he was the Fuse Lab Technology Coordinator at City Tech and worked in the architectural offices of KPF in New York and London, Dellekamp Arquitectos in Mexico City, and R&Sie(n) in Paris.

(Continued)

Your focus has been on the technology and tools. Are there particular tools/technologies that are better at handling project data? Is this ever a factor in your considering working with these tools?

Brian Ringley (BR): Yes, some software manages data better and yes, this is always part of the consideration when researching new software to incorporate into City Tech's Fuse Lab.

CAD packages featuring nondestructive parameterization (Grasshopper), history (Maya), or associativity (SolidWorks) are preferable for a better understanding and utilization of geometrical data, as opposed to working with Rhino sans-Grasshopper or a low-level CAD modeler such as SketchUp, though it's worth mentioning that almost all CAD packages are being actively developed toward such capability. [See Figure 3.4.]

Being able to manage data is not the only consideration here, as the issue of data interoperability is ever-present in AEC software workflows. In addition to the all-powerful Excel, it's important to have interoperability tools on tap such as Chameleon, the Geometry Gym suite, and the subscription-based CASE Pro Apps. This is an area that is very much in flux and we're seeing design technologists develop custom in-house solutions such as TTX by Thornton Tomasetti's CORE Studio/ACM Team and Lyrebird developed cooperatively by LMN Architects' tech studio "LMNts" and Dan Belcher, a developer at Robert McNeel & Associates.

Do you see a need to explore the implications of human behavior to further our capabilities and performance in design and construction?

BR: Yes, certainly the implications of the built environment on human behavior and comfort are central to this conversation, and to AEC as a whole, so therefore the ability to model such things should be at the forefront of the data conversation. However, it's likely that we'll continue to see a form- and image-centric approach to data (how can data form a massing, shape a space, or define the manufacturing of a building

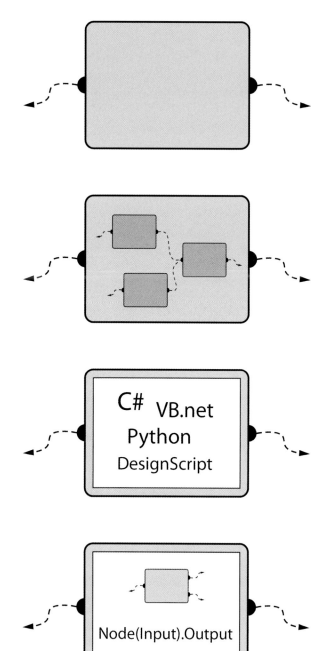

Figure 3.4: The Node-ification of Everything: Visual programming has become *de rigueur* for designers interested in leveraging computation in their modeling processes. © *Brian Ringley*

component) and data-as-economic-justification (false-color diagrams as indicators of high-performance, cost-saving, environmentally marketable architecture) before firms seriously delve into sociological and psychological incorporations of data into the built environment.

For many design students and professionals, the subject of data isn't nearly as compelling as the generation of interesting form. Do you see this as an impediment to data use in the AECO industry?

BR: Yes. The industry is centered on the image when budget allows, and otherwise is consumed with satisfying economic constraints, so this is not only an impediment to the use of data in architecture, but (and perhaps correspondingly) a danger to the future of the profession itself.

Depending on how you look at it, the perceived value of architecture has been in continual erosion for decades and new technologies (computation, BIM, data, etc.), if used "properly," offer a post-recession opportunity to reverse this path. It will take a lot of risk, and I think that architecture-at-large has been historically risk-averse, particularly those firms and individuals still stinging from the bad economy. So I suppose more so than a preoccupation with form, a preoccupation with risk mitigation will impede the integration of data into AEC.

Regardless, I truly believe that now is the time for firms to invest in emerging technologies, R&D, and a human resources strategy that stops punishing candidates for youth and inexperience and instead focuses on the unique skills and ability to innovate that our newest generation of AEC professionals have to offer, lest we lose them to more agile industries. [See Figures 3.5 and 3.6.]

Who really needs to hear the message in favor of leveraging Big Data in the AECO industry?

BR: Students and educators—let this be a grassroots movement. Students have the most energy and are least resistant to change (because they're not changing anything if the new paradigms are all they've ever known). I also think that AEC technology and BIM consultants, who base their businesses on adding value through technology, can help spread the data gospel, as they've added value through recent BIM, performance, computation, and fabrication/manufacturing technologies.

It seems like a "trickle-up" effect would be the best approach here—an in-the-know new hire proves value to a project leader or an in-the-know consultancy proves value to a firm, and everyone works together to prove value to the clients. This isn't to exclude proactive firms, clients, and operators, but historically they're in the minority. They have too much experience and too much to lose.

What will it take to get AECO industry firms to leverage data in their projects?

BR: I actually think that sourcing or mining data is much more of a challenge than integrating data into design. I think that the establishment of collective and dependable AEC data sources and corresponding improvements to AEC software's intuitive ability to tap into said sources are the key to getting buy-in from the industry.

You can't expect a firm to scour and qualify massive, disorganized banks of data from the far reaches of the Internet—it needs to be more user friendly both in terms of accessibility and reliability.

The other side of the coin is developing a critical attitude toward data—the more accessible the data is, the more likely that professionals will begin to trust it blindly.

(Continued)

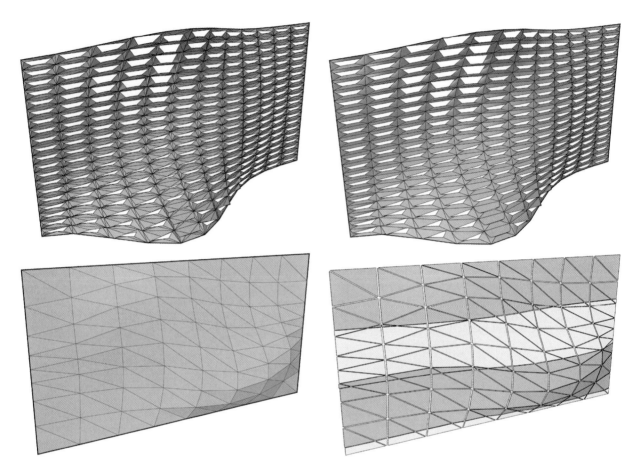

Figure 3.5:   Using proxy models to satisfy a variety of deliverables with a single dataset. Parametric platforms allow users to create multiple versions of a model based upon a shared dataset. © *Brian Ringley*

Can you describe a project where use of data led to an improved decision, insight, or outcome?

BR: An easy example would be the solar insolation example—one could use rules of thumb, common sense, and experience to determine the arrangement of a façade-shading screen to maximize energy performance and program-determined daylighting, but throw in computationally designed freeform geometry on the front end, and the ability to daisy-chain data downstream all the way to the manufacturing of said screen on the back end, and you have your full justification for utilizing data.

What tools do you use in working with data? When it comes to working with data, what recommendations would you make concerning these tools?

BR: Again I would point to the problem of sourcing data as the largest hurdle. It's no problem for me to use DIVA or Ladybug within a Rhino/Grasshopper workflow to directly reference certain elements of environmental data, or Elk or

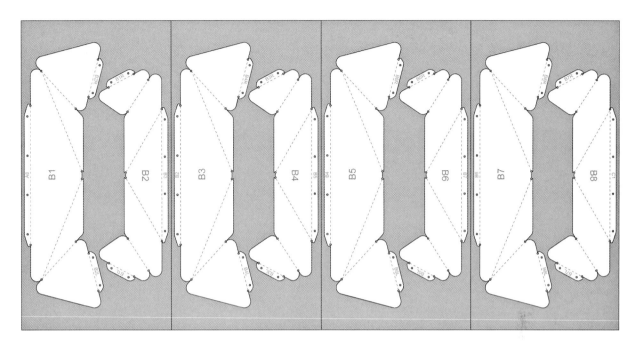

Figure 3.6: Sheet layouts for fabrication can be derived from the same dataset using proxy models within a parametric definition, making this an effective strategy for a virtual design and construction (VDC) workflow. © *Brian Ringley*

Meerkat for GIS data, but what if I want city data on acoustics at a given intersection, or foot traffic data to determine siting or egress, or anything really?

So you've got at least two problems as concerns data tools. One is do I have someone who is knowledgeable of existing tools and can curate these tools for project teams based on each project's individual data needs, and two, data can be just about anything from mundane geometrical properties to sociological datasets harvested over the last century, so how can something so large and practically unknowable (without curation and visualization) be wrangled and systematized for efficient use?

And we haven't even mentioned designers' relatively new capability to collect their own data through microprocessors and other physical computing hardware such as the multitude of input/sensing devices available for Arduino boards (which can be linked directly to CAD through tools such as Firefly), or through industrial robotic arms and drones hooked up with 3D scanning devices and other sensory end effectors. The possibilities are really quite stunning and largely untapped. [See Figure 3.7.]

Can you give an example of how you use technology in the capturing, mining, analysis, and application of data on a building project?

BR: We've looked heavily into DIVA workflows for high-performance façades, as well as downstream interoperability so that the initial data can automatically generate corresponding BIM data for construction documentation and

(Continued)

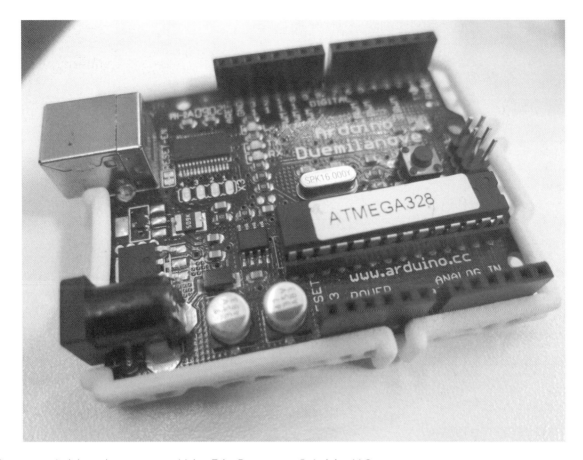

Figure 3.7:   Arduino microprocessor. Maker Faire Rome 2013. © *Arduino LLC*

corresponding toolpathing, bending, and cutting data for architectural component manufacturing. We've also acquired a few AR.Drones that will be used to collect audio, video, and photographic data to help augment existing GIS data for the purposes of site analysis.

In the future the Fuse Lab is interested in developing an inventor/hacker course where students will propose their own AEC hacks/theses and then propose and implement a workflow that moves from data collection/integration to design to manufacturing. The product could be anything ranging from software to innovative manufacturing workflows to responsive façade panels, but it will all be generated and actuated through data.

What is it important for students to know—or be familiar with—before graduating, in order to succeed in a data-enabled/data-driven profession? What are some of the things you're teaching?

BR: Well, this is pretty specific, but we talk at length about "remapping" data as it's used to help generate architectural design. For example, a student may not have direct access to the last century of tidal changes along the Brooklyn waterfront, but may desire to parametrically link this data to their design. If they make a researched speculation as to the minimum and maximum range that this data could be, say in feet above sea level, they can then remap this data to correspond to a 0 to 100 percent scaling of an aperture or opening relative to a building panel, or a 0- to 10-foot parcel setback or elevated distance on a waterfront site. [See Figure 3.8.]

This basic understanding of how to remap one set of numbers (whether it's through an Excel formula, a Grasshopper node, or otherwise), a data range, to another set of numbers, an effect range, is an important concept to understand even before students learn how to harvest, curate, and integrate Big Data into their projects.

People who are most comfortable working with algorithms and data science come from outside our industry. Architecture students aren't being taught to work with data. Or, if they are, it isn't being called that.

BR: Right. They may have accidentally touched some data. It's very hard to attract people with these skills from outside. It's really becoming almost disastrous from a human resources level. We should really be working harder to attract people from the NYU Tisch School of the Arts or other programs where they aren't traditionally educated in architecture. But they have visual skills. The issue is, we probably don't have time even if we could integrate it into a program. Like new technology, it's always on top of everything we're already doing. It's not necessarily always replacing older technologies, but sometimes that is the case.

There's not a lot of time. It would be great to take advantage of the fact that these people are now going to work with data. We know how to work with visualizations—we're visual people. Let's let the data viz people come into the office and translate the language of data into a language that's actually usable for us in a way we understand. There are computational designers who can take datasets and use that to drive geometry. That's one part of the puzzle. For everyone to see the value—clients, the firm as a whole, society, the

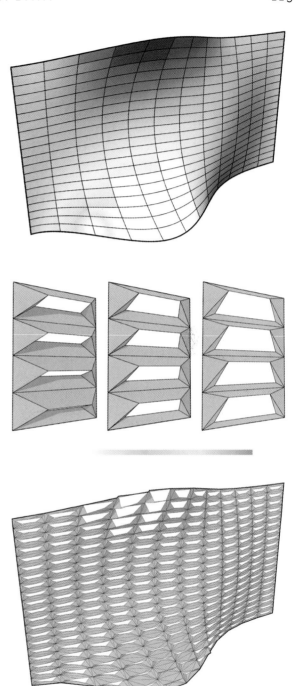

Figure 3.8: Remapping data allows for any dataset to be proportionally scaled within a numerical range for a given geometric transformation. © *Brian Ringley*

(Continued)

industry—by being able to provide provocative, digestible, understandable visualizations. I see words like data-curation. The problem with it is it's so big and messy. What is it?

You've alluded to the risk involved when firms choose to work with data to help make more assured decisions versus rationalizations after the fact.

BR: In the early stages of data-as-justification—we think of data-as-design-generator but also as justification of something to a client, public, or team—there's justification of stuff we already know. We see this so often with students: the sun is always in the same spot this time of year. OK, we got that. At one point, when teaching DIVA, I realized we needed to build a physical model, and that I needed to give them a crayon and have them color in where the insolation is occurring. Because it is as if once the data is there, common sense just falls to the wayside. We need to understand where the sun is relative to the building—go to the planetarium—before we get into this. A danger of introducing software at too early a stage in their education is that they were doing all the steps right—the workflow, the Grasshopper nodules were plugged in where they were supposed to go—but they had inverted the logic. So that the building was shading where there was no sun, windows were opening up where there was way too much sun. But they did all the steps right. That is a huge danger of data—I'm speaking here beyond the students and to the firm as a whole—there is trust in data that removes our critical thinking. We need to be careful about that and have ways to validate rules of thumb we already know.

We also have new kinds of data and nuanced data. An example might be if we wanted to cross-check multiple datasets. The sun is in this location. Let's bring in some GIS, especially in an urban environment, to see where the sun is occluded by buildings. Also we might be doing daylighting—but cross-referencing daylighting doesn't mean anything if I'm not looking at daylighting per task, per programming. There are also types of data you brought up when you mentioned the quantified self, of health and well-being. Do health-trackers have some sort of interface with how we run our building system control? There is all of a sudden all of these crazy networks that can start to happen when the building is communicating to the power grid; there is an owner invested in how energy is being used wisely, in an automated manner within a building. That's cross-referenced with programming, individual health and behavior; all of a sudden I have a few IP addresses on my body. Those are going with the thermostat and the sun shading. So there are all of these cross-referencing of datasets. We're not quite there yet.

It's our job to implement data, but I do think we need some entrepreneurship from the AEC industry, as well as educators, to spur curiosity, talk about possibilities, and AEC to integrate the technology.

Impact of School Culture on Learning Data

Should it be up to schools to implement data, to expose future design and construction professionals to working with data? Is school the right place for this to happen? Or would something be lost? "When I was in school, Michael Mcinturf, working with Peter Eisenman for a while, then with his own office, was teaching this Maya course," explains Ringley. "It was insane how popular it was. People would sign in after the course was capped. You'd have a computer lab full of students, then you'd have two rows of students holding laptops in the back. Because this knowledge was so precious, rare, and exciting."

Comparing the situation then with today: "Now, I get the sense that people will have this kind of CV checklist. 'I know 3D printing, I know CNC, I know Grasshopper.' It's not about how amazing those softwares are. It's, 'I better fill my CV so I'm eligible for the jobs I want to have.'"

How many studios in architecture school build on a previous studio? Almost none. You start from scratch.

—David Fano, CASE

"We've built technology that makes it easier," explains Fano. "But it's really just a mindset. You'll go to some firms and see some guy tucked away in the corner who keeps a spreadsheet with metrics of every project they've ever done. It's really just a way of thinking. Excel is fine. A notepad would be fine. It's more thinking of information as this resource that you can go back and reference. Our mindset is very much like, next project, next project, and next project."

What is it about education that leads to this behavior? "School encourages that," continues Fano. "How often in design studio do you see a critic tell a student after the first week, you nailed it. Done. That's counter to the whole idea. I've got to tell this kid to do something different. It's ingrained in our thinking. Always do better, always challenge what you've done. Our thinking has to shift to what we've done is a resource to do better. How many studios in architecture school build on a previous studio? Almost none. You start from scratch. It's really just a shift in thinking. The tools or technology are whatever. Some will help you do it better than others."

Our job as educators is not only to transfer information, but also to inspire, spur curiosity, and talk about possibilities. Working with data does not preclude the latter from happening, whether it is learning to work in robotics, virtual reality, and/or augmented reality. "We just need to be really good as educators about showing the way to those things to keep people excited about that," says Ringley. "That's what our responsibility is. Is it really up to us to train someone and can you really do that outside of office standards? Probably not."

Peter Liebsch, Global Head of Design Technology at Grimshaw Architects, agrees. "Should schools teach software? Should students come out of universities knowing Revit or AutoCAD? I would say no, because it would limit them so dramatically. They would go down the completely wrong path." Liebsch explains:

> If you take this into account, you're going to end up with very good designers with good ways to express their ideas visually, whether a hand sketch, Rhino model, a rendering, or a physical model. What you need is the ability to analyze the brief and come up with a solution how to go from A to B. That's what I'm after. From those who will be working in computational design, they get into it very quickly—they've probably used it in one or two studios at university. We still have to adjust them to the Grimshaw workflow, standards, templates, and so on. The majority of candidates probably don't learn the software tools in school, but instead they teach themselves.

Part of the problem can be attributed to students allowing the software to dictate their outcomes. Ringley addresses this: "In a capstone studio . . . they may be taking parametric façade data through something like IFC, bringing it in as adaptive components, and specifying for construction. That's a beautiful thing and totally makes sense. We should have those competencies coming out of our program. But as a sophomore student in studio making a box, because that is just what the tool is suggesting? That can be a bit problematic. I think

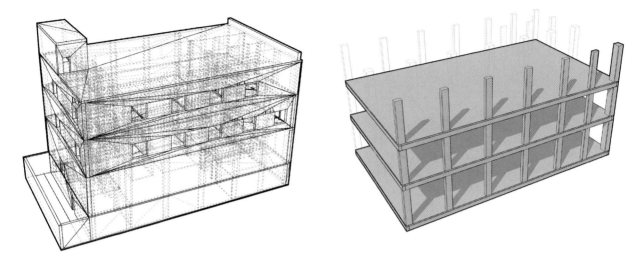

Figure 3.9:   Challenges of interoperability are not purely concerned with geometric fidelity from one platform to another. The model on the right is a direct reference of the one on the left, each existing concurrently in separate platforms. © *Brian Ringley*

it is equally problematic if they have uncontrolled NURBS surfaces or models out of Maya that are self-intersecting, a bunch of garbage floating in space." (See Figure 3.9.)

As with implementing technology tools such as BIM, so too with data. It will require the combined effort of academics and practitioners to ensure that the next generation is adept at leveraging data in their projects. "It's our job to implement data, but I do think we need some entrepreneurship from the AEC industry," concludes Ringley, "as well as educators to spur curiosity, talk about possibilities, and AEC to integrate the technology."

Data Visualization as a Gateway to Working with Data

For someone who is interested in learning to work with data, an excellent first step would be to learn how to visualize existing data. Data wrangler

Jonathon Broughton provided an example of how the nondesigners on the team learned to work with data within an existing large-scale project:

> On the King's Cross project, one of the things I have been working with them on is to move their internal processes to a common point of reference for all of their project managers (PMs), design managers—everyone across the hierarchy of the business—to using a GIS portal to all of their project-specific knowledge. Everything now is tagged and spatially located. They are being taught how to do spatial queries on their own project. That's been a fascinating process. People who aren't A-architects, they aren't designers, they're business people. I've been teaching them how to use spatial analysis tools to better understand their own business product: we're mapping leases, and historical data, archaeology, utilities. Everything all in one space. [See Figure 3.10].

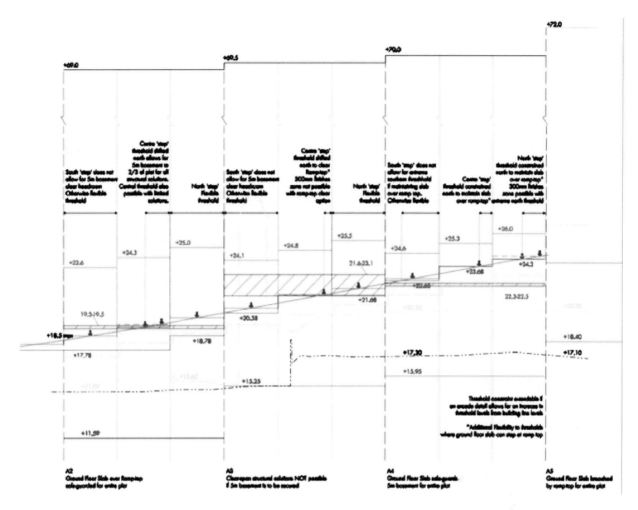

Figure 3.10: King's Cross Central Regeneration master plan: Parametric analysis to optimize for a retail subdivision, floor-to-floor heights, and main entry points. © *Allies and Morrison*

Strategy No. 8: Play with Data

Messing around with data lends itself to the work habits of architectural interns and other emerging professionals.

People who experiment and bring software home at night "just to mess with it" will feel more comfortable taking on new tools and processes in the office. "There's something interesting about visualized data," says Broughton. "Unless you're trained and interested in running things through an R algorithm, where you can apply algorithmic insight, there's something beautiful about experimentation, play, where you don't know what's going to happen if you try this. The freedom of experimentation that a traditional architect-in-training has lends itself massively to being able to intuit information out of datasets by the power of visualization."

(Continued)

"I've always been sort of a data guy," explains Michael Kilkelly, a principal at Space Command. "Right out of grad school I worked for a start-up. I started playing around with databases. Got comfortable working with raw data in that format. I haven't shied away from that. When I worked for Gehry's office I would build databases for them. For construction observation, various things where you'd do room data. We would have to do room data sheets for very big projects, it was just easier to do in a database than in something like Excel. Having had some exposure to that, I wasn't afraid of Big Data in that capacity."

The Background Question

Some architects, engineers, contractors, and others in the AECO industry just seem to have a knack for working with data. One explanation for their comfort with data and new technologies may be their upbringing—what they were exposed to when growing up, and attitudes toward technology in the home. Reasons for their data aptitude—and attitude—can be teased out by asking: Is there something in a person's background that predisposes that person to be able to work in data in the AECO industry? What in their education, training, or background prepared them for working in a data practice? This I call the *background* question, where you have to first look back to move forward.

For some, their first exposure to data was at home, and so the questions become more targeted: Was there some seminal event that happened in their childhood or tutelage? Did they, for example, take apart a Commodore computer that they got for Christmas when they were eight and immediately know what they wanted to do with their life? Where were they first exposed to data? What in their education prepared them for a career working in data and taking an algorithmic approach to the work that they do? When did they first realize that they were comfortable working with data? When did they first realize the importance or potential impact of working with data?

Data wrangler Jonathon Broughton's response is typical of many in the AECO industry who have taken the data route. "My father brought home a home computer when I was eight years old," says Broughton. "I grew up on a farm and he was convinced by some salesman that this was going to solve his farm accounting. From the age of eight I was fascinated by, at the time, ViziCalc. This is not your typical childhood hobby, but I would spend huge amounts of time helping my father work out spreadsheets to figure out which breed of duck to invest in and how we are going to measure milk yield. The germ was set early." Broughton arrived at a career in data by learning to asking excellent questions:

> When I went through school I didn't ever focus on computer science, information technology, or anything like that. It was always a hobby. I got involved at my high school teaching lateral thinking and the work of Edward DeBono. It was keeping me out of trouble and keeping other kids more interested in learning than traditional learning was allowing them to be. From this I got the teaching bug and ended up teaching other things I was interested in. So I taught a class in computer programming. This was at a time when if you were doing information technology in school, you were being taught how to do Word, word processing, and data entry. What I was really interested in was how to infuse people to think and ask—similar to lateral thinking—how might I use this tool to answer a question [when] I don't yet know what the question is, let alone what the

answer is? That's what I'm interested in now. And that was what I was interested in then.

Andrew Witt, Director of Research at Gehry Technologies, also had an early-adopter parent. "I was always fascinated by computation," explains Witt. "My dad worked as an engineer. He would bring home computer spare parts. My brother and I built computers as kids. We were always fascinated by Pascal and programming. I was 10 or 11 years old at that time. From there we were interested in fractal geometry, programming fractal generators."

Sometimes you don't have to take the computer apart and put it back together again for it to have an untold influence on your future career. "You mean, as in, what's your formula for having those great ideas?" said Toru Hasegawa, of Columbia University GSAPP's Cloud Lab, Proxy, and Morpholio, when asked about what in his background might explain his interest in data. "My parents weren't necessarily tech heavy, but my dad did buy the first IBM PC. He was an early adopter. While I didn't touch the computer until much later, one could say that just having it around the household could have made a difference. It wasn't like I was programming at age eight. I literally learned programming in my third year at Columbia University. I was already 20 years old at that point."

Not every design professional who works with data feels comfortable talking about what inspires them or about their backgrounds. When I asked SOM Senior Digital Design Manager Robert Yori how he explains his interest in data, he responded in terms of what data can do. "My interest in data stems from its use as an enabling tool to help with design decisions. Computation has the potential to greatly increase efficiency. That's part of it. More inspirationally, data can be used as the genesis of a design thought, which is perhaps less quantifiable." Then, when pushed a little harder, Yori offered:

I got here as a result of having an interest in systems. My father was an engineer. Growing up, we were always taking stuff apart, putting things back together, learning the mechanics of things and how they worked. Our first computer was a TRS-80, and I started learning how to write programs with it. It was a lot of fun, and I continued through school. Increasingly, mechanical interests, including working on cars, occupied my thoughts. I was an avid musician, absolutely fascinated by the systems that drove music theory—the structure of music.

This led to a breakthrough that in part explains Yori's success within an esteemed firm such as SOM:

Going to architecture school, like many, my first studio was a graphics studio. We learned to understand different media. What it meant—or what you could get it to mean—when you used ink on Mylar versus pastel on watercolor paper. Or the difference between hot and cold pressed watercolor paper, or what newsprint could do. I was equipping my toolbox to enable me to convey what I wanted to convey, to describe my thoughts and ideas most effectively.

This interest in media led to progressively more complex tools. "As I progressed in school, and then out into the working world, my tools were increasingly computational. I wanted to understand how those tools worked—from an intellectual standpoint and also from a pragmatic standpoint. Since I was the low man on the totem pole, I was the guy who was responsible for printing all the drawings, among other things. I didn't want to stay there until three o'clock in the morning trying to figure out why the drawings didn't print out the way we wanted them to. Naturally, because that's just how I am, I started looking into my toolset. Taking things apart. Trying to understand why things were the way they were. So I could understand it better and be better at using the tools that I had available to me."

Case Study Interview with Toru Hasegawa

Toru Hasegawa has focused his interest on the impact of programming on design process. He is currently a co-director at Proxy Design Studio, co-director of Columbia University GSAPP Cloud Lab, and a co-creator of the Morpholio Project. From these distinct vantage points he explores the multifaceted nature of computation. Proxy Design Studio explores potentials within the computational paradigm for a range of clients, providing expertise in both design and realization. With Mark Collins, Toru founded the Cloud Lab at the Graduate School of Architecture, Planning & Preservation, Columbia University. The Cloud Lab researches ways in which the proliferation of device culture, the development of the cloud, and the ubiquity of social networking are collectively shaping the creative process. Toru is a co-creator of the Morpholio Project, which seeks to create a new platform for presentation, dialogue, and collaboration.

You wear many hats. Help me understand which I am speaking to.

Toru Hasegawa (TH): I currently wear three hats. I teach at Columbia University where I am co-founder and co-director of the Cloud Lab. I also have my design practice, Proxy Design Studio. I also have a company called Morpholio. While all unique, the research all happens at Columbia University; the design implementation of algorithms and computation with Proxy. Morpholio focuses in software development on mobile platforms such as iPhone and iPad, and how that is changing the creative professions.

Are you trained as an architect?

TH: I am 100 percent trained as an architect. [At my] graduation in 2006 from Columbia University GSAPP I was bridging drafting, T-square, and eraser—and radically shifting into computational platforms. When I started to monkey around with the computer, AutoCAD wasn't in my reservoir of software. I was more messing around with a software called Shade 3D. This was early NURBS modeling.

The introduction of the Internet opened the floodgate for software. This was around the tail-end of the paperless studio culture at Columbia University. That's where I picked up programming by myself. As paperless studios were dying out, because everyone started to use computers, it wasn't anything novel anymore. The thought of using your own software to deal with your own design inquiry or toolsets lives on to this day. On the one hand, do you just buy this commercial software and just use it? Or do you take the computer as a general-purpose machine that technically could do anything? I was self-taught, no training whatsoever.

Working on Proxy residential design projects—for example, the Sangenjaya residence, with N Maeda Atelier, in Tokyo—our role was seeking out the unique private solar situation of the site. For a site that was surrounded on four sides by adjacent lofts, we wrote this algorithmic process to find the best way to pour in light from above: a window opening vertically to the sky. One of the diagrams describes the propagation of light from the roof down to the ground floor. We were asked to set up the custom software to determine that.

For the Stabile Center, with Marble Fairbanks Architects, we were asked to design this cloudlike perforation pattern. This was an example of what is now called multi-objective optimization. Our charge was to optimize acoustics, so we ran an acoustics simulation of pre-perforation airborne geometry. We analyzed the spatial conditions to see where it reverberated the most. The space has a funny function as a student center room—like a reading room—that serves as a lecture hall. It wants to be a lecture room, but it also wants to be a reading room. In a lecture hall you don't want echoing or buffering of sound. [The challenge was] designing something that we like aesthetically, but at the same time, making sure we're not compromising the performance.

We developed the software to develop the perforation patterns. The perforation pattern data that we wrote out went directly to a CNC fabricator. We had to simulate that pattern first. Then we had the algorithm make the drawings. The final algorithm is the drawing of the right amount of point constellations per line. The CNC fabricator we were dealing with gave us detail feedback, like: we really don't like polylines because it takes longer; we like elliptical geometry but not circular geometry. All this detail of how they wanted the geometry.

On the Proxy website you talk about design as search.

TH: To designers, it is culturally accepted that a designer has an idea and boom—it comes out. The reality is never like that. You're searching for something. That's a core principle—we don't know what we're looking for. The process doesn't constitute a method.

To search for, say, two parameters. To explore the two-dimensional plane you do rely on algorithms for that search. That it resulted in a novel form was an early approach for Proxy. A beginning.

More and more that we deal with it, day in and day out, you realize that the human assessments are extremely complex, powerful measures. A human can look at an image and instantly know what it is about. Its compositional qualities, etcetera. Whereas an algorithm can take a large amount of computational resources and still not know what that image is about. This is where the Cloud Lab started to tap into biometric intelligence.

Now I'm going to go into the Cloud Lab research that we've been doing at Columbia University. If you use computational means to look into data and figure out an optimal solution, or a better pro forma, you get all of this side of engineering flooding into architecture. What is the optimal solar exposure on the side of a building? Or what is the most efficient structural layout of beams in a building? They all lead to unfortunate yet optimal solutions for engineering problems that are all mathematical. What is the most optimal shape structurally? It's a sphere. Spheres are extremely strong in compression from all points. Time has proven it is the most optimal shape on earth. So an optimal-, or performance-driven, solution in a numeric sense, using computational means, doesn't necessarily lead to novel discoveries.

The actual hint of that was the brain. The brain recomposes our experiences into dreams and thoughts. It is almost like the natural randomizer. We came across the research of a biomedical engineer, Paul Sajda, who does research in neurocomputational modeling and neuroengineering at Columbia University. He was working on a blink of an eye assessment called RSVP for Rapid Serial Visual Presentation. He has a Big Data problem because he has lots of data in the form of years' worth of video footage. What does he do with that? A soldier isn't going to watch years and years of video. The computer vision software wouldn't be able to make any assessment that is useful. On the computer side, they would rapidly show 5-10 images to a human subject wearing a device that reads the brainwave data coming from his head. They synchronized the data looking for a clear signature brain wave pattern called a P300—indicating when a human has an "aha" moment. Because they are showing the images so quickly, humans can't possibly think about solving a problem. They ask the subject to look for something: a watch or truck tracks. All the subject needs to do is look. If one of the images spikes their P300, they know exactly which image it was. They can correlate on a very high level. Meanwhile, the machine is learning the person's P300. In other words, the machine gets better and better at capturing the person's attention.

(Continued)

We took this system and ran a studio called Brain Hacking studio. We had students ask questions that aren't numerically definable. For example, what feels comfortable? What is love? Trying to solve these complex problems numerically is near impossible. We worked with the idea that we could take the data directly from the brain, rather than relying on formulas and mathematical equations to run through globs of data in a geometric or structural environment to assess that. The enlightened moment for us was realizing we could cut that away. We knew it was one set of data analysis. But as designers we're interested in what lies beyond that.

On the one hand, do you have to write programs to generate a lot of options? So we took the images of what the students made of options and then had them inquire a question of interest. One student made a landscape of boxes. One of the professors asked, can you walk through it? The results were really interesting. We discovered for some circumstances we could use this technology to address design inquiries. This is where the research we did in Cloud Lab led in terms of search.

Can you speak to the issues surrounding the collection of cognitive data in terms of how we sense and process space to be used toward the production of architecture that cognitively engages us more directly?

TH: The collection of cognitive data—currently the EEG [electroencephalography or EEG is the recording of the brain's electrical activity by sensors placed on the scalp] is the data pipe by which people are collecting in the world of neuroscience. We also have MRIs. We have two types of data collecting. EEG is almost real-time data collection where you can figure out the data streaming in on the spot. MRI is more like the photography of your brain. One of the scientists I have been in touch with in Japan over the past three years is Yukiyasu Kamitani. He researches what you are seeing via the data he collects from the MRI. Say he shows you a black-and-white image of a plus sign, circle, or triangle. The MRI does a scan of your brain. Based on that data, they can make out the image of what you are looking at. What you see is what we get. If we can take your MRI data, we can technically view what it is you are dreaming.

How does that relate to architecture? He is correlating the brain patterns that are just like radically different datasets. MRIs are much more microscopic in that you can pinpoint certain things, whereas EEG is data that is made up of electrical currents that leak out of your brain. They are very weak signals. So you are tapping into data that is hard to capture to begin with. On top of that, you are trying to figure out what it means. Which is much more difficult than capturing data where you know exactly what you are looking at.

He is researching spatial stuff. A lot of the EEG experiments are done in static-free rooms to avoid capturing noise or bad data. You really can't do research on architecture if your environment is so structured. It will come soon. There are probably spatial experiences that can be understood better from a neuroscience standpoint.

Learning to Work with Data in School

So, is it up to those in higher education to ensure that students graduate with the ability to work effectively with data in their building projects? Tyler Goss, Director of Construction Solutions at CASE, an AEC technology consultancy, believes it is. "There is not enough emphasis on the data-centric design approach in education," says Goss.

> We still think of education as object-based. Object-based as additive, rather than rules-based. Understanding a rules-based design process is probably the most valuable thing

you can take out of an architectural education. If you can find it. There are a lot of schools that are not teaching that. I didn't get that in school. I got a very good schooling in that while I was with SHoP Architects, in performance-driven design, both on the economics side and on the design side. That was for me what shifted me away from a historical, academic architectural approach.

"I realized that many problems we face have information-driven solutions and being able to access information increased the speed and quality of solutions," Mark Frisch, FAIA, Managing Principal at Solomon Cordwell Buenz, says about his own interest in data and information. "That leads to an interest in the process of knowledge sharing. Quite frankly there's a need in the profession for people trained in this process. Higher education should be developing this specialized skill set."

Challenges of Teaching Data-Driven Design

Just as architects of prior generations would take pride in mastery over pencil, trace, pen, and vellum, architects today must embrace mastery over data.
—Andrew Heumann, NBBJ

One of the challenges regarding data, mentioned earlier, is that data is not perceived by all faculty members as an architectural topic in a traditional sense. Exposing students to the many ways they can leverage data in building design, for example, does not necessarily require a course dedicated to the subject of data in building design and construction. Learning technology in school can be seen as a gateway to understanding how to work with data. If higher education can get more students thinking in terms of data in architecture and construction, learning to work with computational tools and digital technologies can be one potential first step. "I learned parametric modeling in Grasshopper fairly early on in the course of my education," says Andrew Heumann, Leader of NBBJ's Design Computation team, "which shaped my interest and ability in computation and data at large. I jumped at the opportunity to take programming classes, and have been passionate about it ever since." Heumann cautions about overemphasizing geometric data over and above other types of data, such as performance data:

> Educational programs in architecture need to stop thinking about data and computation as a means to generate novel forms, or pursue a particular style of design. All design today makes use of the computer at some point, and therefore data is a part of the process, whether you're aware of it or not. Learning code—the language of data—is critical to being able to do work, both creative and technical, on a digital platform. Just as architects of prior generations would take pride in mastery over pencil, trace, pen, and vellum, architects today must embrace mastery over data, which is the new means of representation underlying all work being done today in one way or another. [See Figure 3.11.]

One missed opportunity in education is BIM in general, and Revit specifically, having been relegated to a documentation tool, as opposed to a data-rich design tool. Digital Practice Leader at NBBJ, Sean D. Burke, agrees. "I like to call that a misunderstanding of the nature of the tool," he explains.

> Once an opinion like that is formed, it takes a long time to unravel it. It exists in the professional community as well. It's a level of comfort that folks have as well as what they were exposed to and when. If someone first learned Revit six years ago, yes, the conceptual tools were terrible. It has come a long way. You want to give people a chance to revisit that assumption or performance memory, and show them some cool stuff. Until you can get

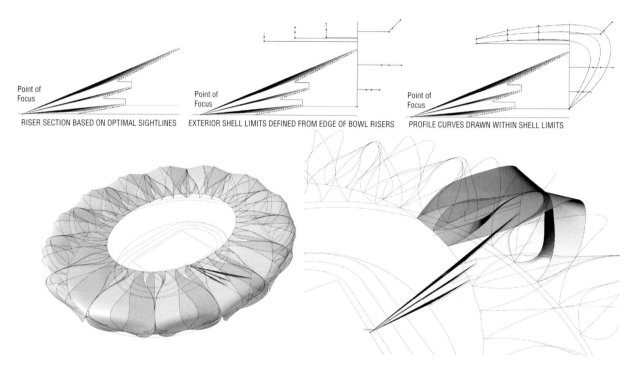

Figure 3.11: Hangzhou: Geometric construction of stadium risers and external "Petal" structure. © *NBBJ*

them to adopt it and start using it, they'll go back to the tools that they know.

Another challenge in teaching data in school is that data isn't nearly as compelling as the generation of interesting form. We see this as an impediment to data use in the AEC industry, and this habit and misperception begin in academia. It is a relevant concern for students and educators, who are both often fixated on form. But there are signs that the current generation is moving away from the strictures of a formalistic approach to building design—they're more concerned about performance and impacts on the planet—leaving the door wide open for implementing data in their designs. If there is one downside of learning data in school, it's that graduates become attractive to other industries, sectors, markets, and fields. "The most promising outcome is that

they become the future leaders of the firm," warns Ringley. "My fear is that these recent graduates are going to work for places like Google. The closest they might come to architecture is working for Autodesk. Right now, there's not really a lot of incentive to go into architecture. You have to go to school for a long time. School is really hard. It's really expensive. You can barely get a job. The job's not fun. The job doesn't pay well. You have no free time. What part of this is worthwhile?" (See Figures 3.12 through 3.15.)

Learning outside of Architecture

One alternative to learning data in a traditional architectural program is to have exposure in another major or field of study. More and more architecture students are pursuing double majors in college, with an opportunity to learn how to work with data in the second major—for

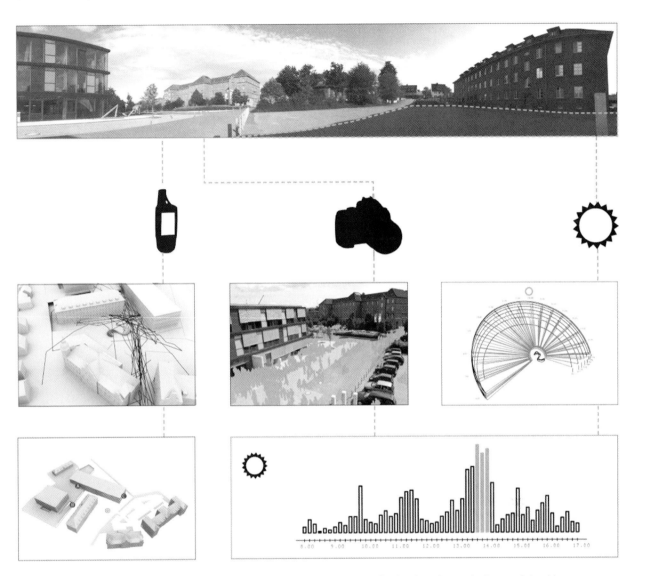

Figure 3.12: Marco Hemmerling's former student Jens Böke based his final university project on a data-driven process, investigating the movement of students on campus to define the best location for the design of summer pavilion SunSys.
© Marco Hemmerling MA, Jens Böke

example, in an MBA program, or in construction management. Andrew Witt, Director of Research at Gehry Technologies, was trained as both an architect and a mathematician. "Around the data/noise question, having a mathematics background gives you very structured, methodical ways to transform noise into data and ultimately information," says Witt.

It gives you some specific ways to signal process. What a lot of people interpret as

Figure 3.13:   The structure itself reacts to the solar radiation so that the orientation of the building follows the sun path, which was taken from the specific weather data. © *Marco Hemmerling MA, Jens Böke*

data mining is really an evolution of signal processing, something that grew out of military tactics in World War II. What's the most effective way to respond to a particular kind of system behavior documented through data? Without a mathematical background, it's more difficult to understand the ways in which data might inflect information or the way in which the underlying behavior can be variously interpreted. Among the things that I apply from my mathematics background in architecture are statistical methods, which are ways of understanding what data and datasets are actually relevant and telling a story.

It helps classify what kind of data is relevant and which is distracting. The shape optimization techniques that we developed are really about interpreting the signals. Particularly when a large or undifferentiated amount of data is produced, that sort of statistical or signal-processing expertise may be necessary to create meaning around data. This may happen across a single project or multiple projects. There's probably more opportunity to extrapolate information from behavior across dozens or hundreds of projects, or even at an industry scale. With a single project there may not be enough data to make generalizable

Figure 3.14: SunSys Pavilion was driven by a computational design approach aiming at an early integration of relevant data to build up a robust and flexible design model. © *Marco Hemmerling MA, Jens Böke*

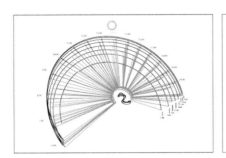  

Figure 3.15: The SunSys Pavilion project's sun gradients. © *Marco Hemmerling MA, Jens Böke*

Case Study Interview with Aimee Buccellato

Aimee Buccellato is an assistant professor in the School of Architecture at the University of Notre Dame and co-founder of University of Notre Dame's Sustainable Data Community.

Where are you now in your efforts on the data front?

Aimee Buccellato (AB): It's still very strong. I am only one part of a team. Working with engineers, computational scientists, framework and information systems specialists, decision theorists, and sociologists at Notre Dame, we are trying to solve a large problem in terms of my domain—architecture, engineering, and construction. It's a challenge that a lot of domains and industries are facing right now with this huge influx of data and information. It doesn't mean that we have great access to that information, but it is proliferating. We're all working along parallel paths; our work is to identify and find examples and connect bits of information that different stakeholders in the AECO industry have. And see how we can use things like machine learning and decision theory to help us look through and connect that data without it being so manually intensive. There's a lot of uncertainty out there, right? There's a lot of data and you can book- or Google-search everything you want. But you have no real way of knowing what the quality of that data is. We suffer from that in some ways, too, with our simulation and analysis tools. We put a lot of confidence in the tools we use and the design and operation decisions that we make based on the analysis of the simulation data. There is still a liability issue. We've identified the problem. We've identified a core of the people who have witnessed and experienced the problem in research and practice across the domains. Now we have shifted from looking at probing the problem into how we're going to solve this problem. A lot of the effort that we're spending right now is in creating a material transformation pattern—an ontology or machine-understandable vocabulary—which could help map, for example, a generalized way that building materials make their way to a construction site: a life cycle map/pattern. Working with web experts and spatial ontologists to understand how we can create a pattern that will allow us to connect heterogeneous data together, to course through that data, data that is currently in many different locations and formats, and sometimes defined in different ways. So we're working with folks across the country who are leaders in the spatial ontology field and the semantic web.

Why isn't there a vendor-neutral, platform-agnostic, easy-to-access clearinghouse to capture, gather, and disseminate sustainable building data?

AB: It would just be very expensive for somebody to be that clearinghouse. Would it be subscription-based? What would the incentive be to get involved? What we're hoping is that it can be an open source, and that is what we're making an effort towards and getting funding to construct, similar to what you see in the sciences. There are a lot of institutions playing host to this information. They're all good sites, but their data is localized. There are a lot of places that are repositories of data. It's living there, posted to these databases and these sites, and somebody or some organization is responsible for updating them, bringing information in and validating it. All of that is very time-consuming and expensive. [We want to] take it one step further, to add structure to our AECO data, and generate ways for the data to be correlated and associated, without undermining the fact that there are these databases. They're just in a lot of other places. A lot of this work is really the domain of the experts who create design patterns for data. In the work we're doing right now, we've shifted a lot of focus in that direction.

The tool I have been developing for the last several years, The GreenScale Tool, will be a better, more useful, tool for architects in the design process. It's not out yet. There are many reasons for developing it. We got to a certain stage in its development and realized it will certainly pull together crucial pieces of information at certain periods of time in the design process better than any of the available tools today. However, one of the biggest challenges to this—or any tool, frankly—is just data. And the reliability of data. In some ways we have to work around ourselves and say, we can develop this tool using data that is currently available to all. We can try to make it more efficient in the collection and analysis of that data. But ultimately, what we all really need is access to better, more accurate and reliable data—and tools that anticipate the sheer magnitude of data that is being generated, by architects, engineers, and the very buildings they've designed, each and every day. Data is really the overarching problem and one that won't go away.

In the design of our buildings, each of us, at our desktop, in our computers, in the BIM, are creating loads and loads of data. It's usable internally. Sharing it is risky. On the other hand, we keep doing a lot of this work redundantly. The technologies change. The materials change. Where they come from change. Energy sources that produce them change and get more efficient. It's a big problem. But it's one that we would all benefit from more advanced thinking, about how we handle the data in the design process. And inevitably the data our buildings will generate and hopefully feed back into a model. So we can all, whether internally or in a shared capacity, learn from the buildings that are being executed and performing.

We're beyond saying we know there's this problem. The data and stakeholders all live in different places. We're working, in some ways, more collaboratively than ever. But still we have not yet found a way to make access to the usability of the data easier.

Those interested in collecting and sharing data in the AEC industry seem to be made up of disparate, stand-alone individuals in academia and practice. What made you recognize that there was a need for a community of these like-minded experts?

AB: Based on my education, I have certain philosophies and methods of practice. I had an instinctive belief in, and in some ways an empirical belief in, certain design principles, and materials and methods, as well. What I initially set out to do is add more ammunition to a current argument about sustainable design and construction, using numbers and paper, versus what tends to happen, which is basic, polemical arguments. So I set out to teach how buildings, which purport to do one thing, which is be highly sustainable, high-performance, extraordinary and exceptional in many ways, and cut them up and ask: how, exactly, are you meeting those claims of exceptional performance? For example, if you're a building that's 70 percent glass and have terrible exposure to the sun. That forced me to look at the tools that we have at our disposal to do this high-level analysis. I saw there was a gap in the tools and data to really understand how our buildings perform. Not just when the lights turn on. But if we have to aggregate all those material decisions along with those operating energy decisions, what is the bigger picture? What is the bottom line? Finding that there was no one tool that I could use to do the kind of research that I do, I thought: surely somebody could build me this little thing, right? I really just wanted something to help me do my research faster and more accurately. That's when I began to realize that this is a much bigger problem and issue. How is it that we have not solved it yet? Buildings are the largest-scale experiment you can conduct. And we do it once. In science, it's not enough to have two replicated experiments. You can't even produce a scientific paper if you have only done something twice. You need three—three is a minimum. I still feel very responsible as an architect for whatever I take from the earth, to put something new on the earth—and feel that responsibility, especially since we haven't (yet) found a source to produce better tools and methods for evaluating the broader impacts of what we do. As a practitioner, teacher, and researcher, I recognize that there are way more voices out there. I need to get people who are doing post-occupancy work in the room. To find out where their data gaps are. Living in a city like South Bend, knowing the struggles we have to make our physical plant operate more efficiently. To make

(Continued)

improvements to our infrastructure when there is no money to make it (happen). It was that kind of thinking that led me to say I have this one specific perspective. I think it's a strong and informed one. But I certainly don't want to be ignoring the fact that there are a lot of people out there who are probably wondering about many of the same things, based on gaps they observe in data, and gaps in simulated versus actual building performance. That's when my work transitioned beyond what I wanted to conduct in my own lab. And begin to think about: We should be thinking bigger. We should be thinking like scientists. We should be thinking about data—building data, building information—as an asset. Data that we really need to share, if we're going to make any impact and influence on the environment and people.

Where does this need to connect people in the data space come from?

AB: Call it stewardship, I guess. I'll credit some of it to my foundational education as an architect, to be extremely rigorous and thoughtful about how all the pieces of your building come together. This caused me to be pretty methodical in my approaches.

Why the focus and application of data for building performance and not for building geometry?

AB: Buildings aren't machines. They're structures that are created to facilitate, support, and foster human habitation, collaboration, and happy, wonderful lives. Durability and sustainability go beyond what they're made out of. There are optimal solutions that can be met if we look beyond buildings as just operating devices. If they're not as high performing in cultural, social, and human ways, then nobody's going to take care of them. And those buildings will not sustain, they will not survive. So they won't be durable or sustainable no matter what they're clad in, or whether their systems are passive or active to support our comfort in them.

We call it sustainability data because what I hope these technologies will do is effect greater change, across the industry, in how buildings are made. A lot of that is just awareness. From the very beginning I thought if I could just pull some numbers together, little exposés of buildings that purport to be very sustainable, I thought that this would raise awareness: people just cannot ignore numbers. But, what if you had a tool that's on your desktop that's adding up the broader impacts of what you're doing as you're designing it? You can't not stare at that number and wonder—wow, I've got to change what I'm doing here. We don't have tools in front of us that really influence our design decision making. We're certainly not data-enabled in our decision making. And if we are, it's usually too late. We really need to lower the bar to access the usability of this data to a greater swath of the professional community as students as well.

You're an academic and researcher as well as a practitioner. How—if at all—to you apply data in your own practice?

AB: To be frank and honest, we don't. There's a project we have right now that's affiliated with the university that we intend to use the tool technology on. For a small firm, I would equate it with hunting and pecking. As a practitioner, you dip into your palette of materials in your toolkit, where you can, to be efficient. This is a huge problem. Even if you're a firm that doesn't care about sustainability, even on a level of efficiency. It's how you database it. It's how you internally manage the information that goes into your building. We are still operating from our drawings as repositories. Because we're small. And not able to capitalize. There's no tool out there that can do what I know I need to do.

We will all benefit from greater access to data that is usable and validatable, where the uncertainty of the data can be made obvious to the user. We are not yet able to do that in our small practice. But that's where I see the potential.

inferences about what the data means. In statistics you have samples, but you have to take a variety of samples before those inferences can be significant and accurate. There's this problem called the Founders Effect, where if you sample only a very restricted population, then your inferences about the general population are going to be super skewed. Maybe there is some call for deep analytic work, but probably more at the industry level than the project level.

Data in Transition: Between School and Practice

The alternative to learning to work with data in school is to rely on picking it up once you are out of school, in practice. Here, the onus is on the firm either to ensure proper training or, for example, to hire staff to address computational design tools from a performance perspective; or it is up to the employee to self-train outside of office hours. Again, familiarity with digital tools and technologies serves as a segue to a career where one predominantly works with data. "When I graduated from college, the economy was pretty bad," explains Sean D. Burke. "There weren't a lot of jobs. Eventually, I got a call—someone had recalled I was good at AutoCAD. Soon after getting the job, I put on the hat of CAD manager, tinkering, and writing AutoLISP. Today, with Dynamo, and more modern programming languages like Python, it's making it a lot easier for people to start to adopt new ways of working off of their existing tools without having to recreate everything from scratch."

Noncompensated Learning

When there isn't a curriculum where one can learn to work with data in design and construction, where can one turn? Brian Ringley talks about a

form of self-directed learning he calls *noncompensated learning*, "which is a pretty foreign concept for some people and for some of my students." He explains:

> The idea being if you want to learn something you go out and learn it. There's not necessarily a course to take or to purchase to gain or access that knowledge. The consequence of that is that you will do things your own way, which may not necessarily be the right way. When you synthesize your kind of self-learning with more formal means you end up being quite knowledgeable about a subject. A good example of this is DIVA, which is absolutely great software for integrating things like solar analysis into a design process. That is something where myself and other professors at City Tech, like Anne Leonhardt who founded and is the director of the fabrication lab there, we just have this mentality that you just go in there and figure it out. It's really not that hard. Which is an important mentality to have. At the same time, we were able to teach it with enough competency to start to get the results we wanted with the students. Later, CASE did one of their workshops and I wondered what it would be like to learn from Nathan Miller. It was amazing to [be able to] cross-check my own understanding of that. I have done almost everything that way.

Learning to Work with Data in the Workplace

The people who are most comfortable working with algorithms and data science have come from outside the AECO industry, when firms have been fortunate enough to attract and retain them. It's hard to attract people with these skills from outside. Architecture students, by and large, aren't being taught to work with data. Or, if they are, it isn't being called that. Brian Ringley agrees: "They may have accidentally touched some data." He continues: "It's really becoming almost disastrous from a human resources level. We should really be working harder to attract people from the NYU Tisch School of the Arts or other programs where they aren't traditionally educated in architecture. But they have visual skills. The issue is, we probably don't have time even if we could integrate it into a program. Like new technology, it's always on top of everything we're already doing." This is an instance of the little-time, few-resources challenge discussed in the introduction to this book.

To implement working with data, Ringley envisions a workplace where architects work alongside data visualization experts:

> It would be great to take advantage of the fact that these people are now going to work with data. We know how to work with visualizations—we're visual people. Let's let the data viz people come into the office and translate the language of data into a language that's actually usable for us in a way we understand. There are computational designers who can take datasets and use that to drive geometry. That's one part of the puzzle. For everyone to see the value—clients, the firm as a whole, society, the industry—by being able to provide provocative, digestible, understandable visualizations.

"The stuff you learn in school you're not going to learn elsewhere," argues Robert Yori.

> And the stuff you learn in practice, you can pick up in practice. There's enough you have to learn in school. You can't put it all into 4-5 years. You'd have a 10-year degree cycle if you did that. Plus, some amount of the "practical" information is perishable, as it

is in medicine. That's why we have continuing education. So oftentimes, practice is a better place to learn technology in terms of execution and production. But if you think of technology as an approach, and a means to an end, and if you're using it as part of your design problem-solving skills, that's a really important component of the academic experience.

Yori continues:

> Back when I was in school, nobody wanted to look at anything produced by a computer. Maybe my critics and professors didn't think it was graphically compelling enough, maybe they felt they couldn't react to it in the same way that they could react to the hand-produced work. But understanding it as a tool and a means to an end was really important to me. It positions technology as the beginning of a design idea—along with many other ideas, experiences, and such. If you're motivated to approach technology that way, you will naturally learn whatever tools that happen to be in use at the time. When you get into practice, you'll pick new tools up.

This is why being proficient at any one tool is not sufficient either to garner a coveted position at a desirable firm or to be effective once in an organization. "That deep knowledge of any one piece of software is probably not the way to go," says Yori.

> Software changes so fast. Companies change hands. How many people still have the same rendering tool they used a decade ago? It's not about the program, but what the program is doing. I often use a language analogy. English is my primary language, but in elementary school I started learning Spanish. I began to understand the structure of language far

better than I did when I was learning English, because I had two frames of reference. I began to understand the framework in which languages work. That can be applied to technology, and it can be applied to tools. Gaining a level of fluency in a particular tool should mean that you not just know that tool, but that you understand the framework in which that tool operates, and how it could operate. That's when it gets into your brain. That's when you can use it as a genesis point, and make it an integral part of your thought process. That's the difference between being able to think and dream in a language, as opposed to just knowing how to translate a phrase from one language to another.

Notes

Unless otherwise indicated, quoted text throughout the book is from interviews with the author that took place between February and July of 2014.

1. See C. R. Pyke, "Frontiers of Engineering Symposium: Using information technology to transform the green building market," *The Bridge 42*(1), 33-40. (Washington, DC: National Academy of Engineering, 2012); https://www.nae.edu/Publications/Bridge/57865/58569.aspx
2. Randy Deutsch, "Why being proficient is not sufficient," *BIM + Integrated Design*, November 27, 2013; http://bimandintegrateddesign.com/2013/11/27/why-being-proficient-is-not-sufficient/

part II Capturing, Analyzing and Applying Building Data

Data are familiarly "collected," "entered," "compiled," "stored," "processed," "mined," and "interpreted."
—Lisa Gitelman

Where Data Is Found, How and When Data Is Used, and Who Uses It

Just as design professionals have tools in their arsenal for developing designs into building models and plans, they also have a tool at their disposal for justifying and explaining decisions in a way that will convince and persuade. We capture, analyze, and apply data to be prepared for occasions when we need to defend a particular course of action. Design professionals may be comfortable with ambiguity and uncertainty, but recipients of their decisions may not be.

To justify, we ask *why*? *Why* is your building circular? *Why* is its orientation E-W and not N-S? *Why* did you build here and not closer to the city center with in-place amenities and infrastructure?

But the question "why" seems like a luxury—like something extraneous—implying academic curiosity but not necessity. The question "why" is not action-oriented. To ask it requires stopping action. To respond to it requires one to backtrack, to cover old ground.

Design professionals' actions are expected to be purposeful, even when they aren't or aren't explainable to the lay public. Especially in a country where one is innocent until proven guilty, one does not normally need to justify until something goes awry. One's decisions need not be constantly defended. Rather, challenges to them are what require defense.

For this reason, design professionals keep responses to the question "why" in their back pocket, in case they need to be pulled out and recited. Their proofs are both subjective and objective, artistic and scientific, intuitive and factual. When asked "why," they answer with "how."

chapter **4** Capturing and Mining Project Data

In God we trust. All others must bring data.

—W. Edwards Deming

Before one can mine data, there has to be a source to mine. The source can be a public one, such as open data, or a private one, such as a client's database. There also has to be a means by which the data is mined. This can take place using sensors, swipe cards, mobile devices, or any number of methodologies. Evelyn Lee, a strategist at MKThink, uses data in a number of different formats: "anything from a card swipe upon entering a building, to understanding how far students are traveling to determine if there are enough schools in a school district, to how many offices are occupied by a major constituency on a regular equipment basis—or do each of them need private offices? All different types of data." She continues, "[T]he other thing we do—in terms of our data sources, and where we are comfortable getting our data—we mine public data; we get data from our clients; and in many cases we go out and collect our own data in the field." In this chapter we look at public and private sources of data, and the multivariate means by which data is captured in the AECO industry.

Public Sources of Data

The Holy Grails of public data sources are vendor-neutral, platform-agnostic, easy-to-access clearinghouses to capture, gather, and disseminate data. And like the Grail, is there evidence that they even exist? Thankfully, the U.S. government has done a fairly good job of doing exactly this on a variety of fronts. For a sample concerning sustainable building data, see the following links:[1]

www.eia.gov/consumption/commercial/

www.eia.gov/consumption/residential/

www.energystar.gov/

http://eere.buildinggreen.com/

http://energy.gov/

And there are others. Chris Pyke calls his employer, USGBC, a little organization with a big IT footprint. Today, this notably includes:

LEEDOnline.com

GBIG.org

LEED Dynamic Plaque, http://www.leedon.io

"LEEDOnline is a serious piece of mature information technology that reflects over a decade of continuous development," says Pyke. "It handles certification processes for over 1.5 million square feet of real estate per year. LEEDOnline is a 24/7 operational resource for thousands of professionals working in over 150 countries. This SAP-based enterprise system manages workflows between AECO professionals and project reviewers." He continues:

> GBIG.org is an integrative information plat form powered by the Ruby on Rails web frame work. GBIG.org consumes and aggregates information from a variety of sources, including LEEDOnline, the U.S. EPA, and hundreds of secondary sources. GBIG.org uses an increasingly sophisticated set of processes to combine, organize, and integrate these data to provide rich, multi-faceted information about projects, buildings, and places around the world. Late in 2013, we surpassed 1,000,000 green building activities, and we continue to grow quickly. For context, only 20,000 of these activities are a completed LEED certification. In GBIG, every LEED project has an individual dashboard, buildings have timelines, and places have dynamically generated reports. Most database elements are exposed through Application Programming Interfaces.

In terms of more general public data sources, Tom Mulhern notes:

> We began at Gensler to use economic market data in the design process in a more intentional way in terms of workplace planning, looking at entry and exit data for workers on large campuses to understand the building use. In urban planning there has always been data collection. We were looking at typographic segmentation data from economic databases, laying it out against property tax records and property ownership records. Trying to get some insight as to what the city needs. What to do with the public housing stock.

He continues: "Look at site selection decisions. The real estate data is their data. They're looking at market analyses. They're looking at branch data.

At resale value. Their business is built around the mastery of that data. Their ability to process that data on behalf of their client."

How important is the use of specific, local data—as opposed to more general sources of public data—when developing potential strategies with clients, architects, engineers, and other consultants? It depends on a number of factors; for example, climate and situations where there's very little local climatic variation versus significant variation. (See Figure 4.1.)

What a lot of people interpret as data mining is really an evolution of signal processing, something that grew out of military tactics in World War II.
—Andrew Witt, Gehry Technologies

Another resource for data is building documents. Where do these documents come from? How is the data compiled? For example, are web crawlers used to gather information? "We have a research team here at Reed Construction Data and what they do is spend their time talking to architects, owners, contractors, and engineers, and procuring those plans and specifications from them," says Jennifer Johnson, Senior Director of Product Development.

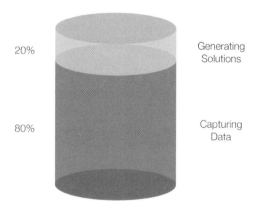

Figure 4.1: The 80/20 rule of generating solutions from captured data. © R Deutsch

"When they're posted online (like most government agencies do), and we know they are, we use technology to scrape those sites and download the software. We have architects, engineers, sometimes general contractors, that will email us plans and specs, or provide us with paper copies of them. So we get them from the industry."

Johnson continues: "We get our plans and specs through our relationships in the AEC industry. Through our strategic partnership with AIA, architects are pretty friendly to us, and in turn we give them some pretty nice benefits. We have engineers, GCs, and owners as sources, and we work to publicize their projects." She adds, "We absolutely use technology wherever it makes sense. And for us, that makes sense in the public sector for those documents we know are publicly available. . . . We configure our technology to go after specific sites with specific information on them. We don't just say, hey, there's the web out there, find something interesting. A really good site for us is the DOT.[2] So we have created our processes to go out and pick up that data."

Open Data

Mathematicians, statisticians, computer scientists, marketers, and hackers are using a global network of sensors, software programs, information collection devices, and apps to reveal in ever-greater detail the effects of our perpetual reform on the world around us.

—Patrick Tucker[3]

Open data[4] is data that can be freely used, reused, and redistributed by anyone—subject only, at most, to the requirement to attribute and share alike. The open data movement has, in particular, had an impact on urban policy and how data can transform city living. "I'm very excited about all these new ordinances coming on everywhere requiring sharing of energy use data because that's a real key for getting market transformation until people understand how much energy their buildings are using compared to others," says Erik Olsen of Transsolar.

Would design professionals make use of an all-encompassing database if made available? "Absolutely," says Jonatan Schumacher, Director of CORE studio at Thornton Tomasetti. "We are starting to work with data available from the NYC Open Data initiative. In the case of [project] cQ,[5] we can use publicly available data to help us make informed decisions of which building owner to address to schedule the next Local Law 11 façade investigation."

Case Study Interview with Ryan Mullenix

Ryan Mullenix is a design partner at NBBJ and is a strong advocate for data-driven design, a process that uses custom algorithms to link geometry with data to augment both human and building performance. Ryan has led the design of numerous award-winning projects both nationally and internationally, including the design of Google's new Bay View campus in Mountain View, California. His work and expertise have been featured in the Wall Street Journal*, Fast Company, the* San Jose Mercury News*, Newsweek, Quartz, Bloomberg News, CNBC, and* National Public Radio.

NBBJ Board Chairman Scott Wyatt, FAIA, sits on a panel at one data event, firm principal Duncan Griffin participates in another. NBBJ's Design Computation leader Andrew Heumann speaks at conferences on data-driven design. You have a lot of people in the office on top of this subject. Many design principals don't know their firm's data capabilities—the talent, the technology, the processes and workflows; you do. What is it about NBBJ that enables this awareness?

(Continued)

Ryan Mullenix (RM): I have been working within design computation for quite some time, getting a first introduction through parametric modeling and generative components. Many years ago, we were considering how technology could assist us on the fabrication end of the profession, but I became fully invested in design computation while working on a project in Taiwan. We were considering how CFD modeling could help us design collaborative spaces that would draw people together. We were attempting to pull physicians out of their physically enclosed work environment into a position where they were seen and visible, and where the work they were doing was readily available to other physicians. That's where I first sensed how powerful these tools could be. [See Figures 4.2 and 4.3.]

For the last 2½ years of my career, I have been the lead designer for the Google Bay View Campus in Mountain View, California, where we have taken design computation to the next level. And that is to a level where computation addresses not only building performance, but human performance as well.

As you can imagine, a company like Google has loads of resources and loads of data—they're a data-driven company, so data comes first. A big part of our first venture was to prove our initial concepts were right, that the thinking from the outset was ideal for their method of working. We wanted to provoke them in the right way, to create the proper collegial and collaborative environments that delivered well on both building performance and human performance. We have done a number of studies with Google that really get to the core of what they desire in terms of encouraging creativity, stimulation, and productivity across their staff.

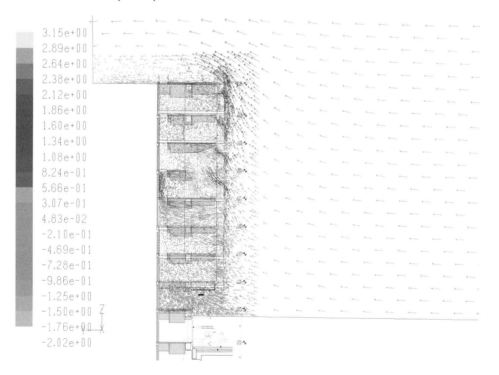

Section view of S22 (x=30m).

Figure 4.2:   Interior rendering: Computational fluid dynamics analysis of building section. © *NBBJ*

Plan view of L03 (z=1m, relative height from floor).

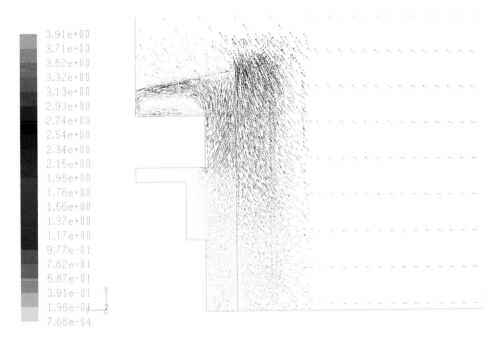

Figure 4.3: Computational fluid dynamics analysis of building plan. © *NBBJ*

We're now exploring this approach in the commercial sector. We're looking at urbanization, the way cities are evolving, and trying to better understand human experiences. We're now applying what we've learned in the corporate realm to the urban sector. [See Figure 4.4.]

Since Google is the premier data-driven company, did you and NBBJ feel compelled to use data, both the building performance and human performance side of it, in your design approach and your decision making?

RM: It was a really symbiotic, synergistic relationship. We learned quite a bit from Google throughout the process. We proposed to them before even being hired that design computation could allow more time for creativity. I wrote a blog post that speaks to both my belief and our firm's belief on how design computation provides more room for creativity because quick iterations and rapid prototyping determine ideals faster. When you find better outcomes faster, you provide more time to spend in the creative phases with your client.

That was certainly where we were headed with Google. What was interesting was finding an even broader spectrum of human conditions that can be explored and tested through design computation.

When your project team uses computational design to get you the best views, do you trust the tools? Do you override them with intuition and common sense?

RM: There's certainly a trust factor. Part of that trust is in the individual you are working with, understanding their depth of knowledge and experience. Part of your trust is based on having time to test the outcomes. We test our algorithms

(Continued)

Figure 4.4:   Google Bay View campus in Mountain View, California. © *NBBJ*

on a variety of cases. We even test them on ourselves sometimes in our office. The third part of this trust is related to intuition. I can say that intuition factors in a lot. We'll look at a daylighting analysis, for example, and your gut will tell you if the outcome is in line with what you should be seeing. And if it's not, it's actually a fun opportunity to explore deeper. Is my intuition off? Is the algorithm off?

Relative to the Google project, one moment that was really fascinating came as the team—both us and the client—honed in on quantitative data. It was at that point that we began to understand the importance of the qualitative as well. What started off as—I don't want to call it prescriptive, but it certainly was to an extent—data-driven, developed into a big conversation on the importance of experience, and the importance of the qualitative successes in a campus.

NBBJ at one point added five outdoor rooms to the Google campus design. Can you explain how the design of these rooms was driven by data?

RM: There were a series of analyses we performed—we looked at time of year, we looked at sun; we wanted to make sure that we were providing shade for an individual in the summer but sun for them in the winter; we looked at wind passing through the courtyard over the course of the year; we wanted to ensure each courtyard addressed the users' comfort. Those were some of our environmental criteria. We looked at view; how do you see in so you can understand who is in the courtyard. For example, we had a room called the Quad, harkening back to an academic setting in terms of activity, openness, and visibility. It's a place to be seen, and you want people to be drawn to it. We also did a series of in-depth analyses on successful academic and corporate courtyards across the world. We looked at height; height has a big impact on how you feel in a place. We looked at the width of those courtyards. On how they opened up at the end. We looked at paths; we developed an algorithm that explored how paths might cross. We constantly discussed the importance of intersections and their resulting serendipity. But also how you can begin to construct a network path across the campus based on entries and amenities; and how you can encourage those interactions to happen more frequently.

Data doesn't answer a question. Data is just information. Its importance is in how you take that data and use it to address the problem you are trying to solve.
—Ryan Mullenix, NBBJ

How has your experience working on this project impacted how you use data?

RM: This project used a lot of data, so we're much smarter coming out of it on how to decipher such information. Smarter in terms of understanding the techniques, the way we craft our tools. We always look at our algorithms as a tool that we hand-craft. So how we make or write that tool is incredibly important—the old adage of garbage in, garbage out still holds true. One of the most intriguing comments I've heard recently, from a San Francisco futurist, is that data is just data. Data doesn't answer a question. Data is just information. Its importance is in how you take that data and use it to address the problem you are trying to solve. That's been a big focus of ours.

The reason we call it data-driven design is because now we know how to manage that data. That's not to say we didn't know how to manage it before, but it was a much more arduous process. It wasn't instantaneous. It wasn't something we got immediate feedback on.

So in Taiwan, we were working with Carnegie Mellon University to develop CFD modeling of collaborative spaces. It took some time. And it still takes a little bit of time for CFD modeling. But now we have more of a finger on the pulse of that data so we can be smarter and more proactive in our modeling and our testing. [See Figure 4.5.]

You have said "Buildings date themselves in their inability to be flexible or inability to serve future tenants."[6] What role, if any, can data play in helping to create projects that are more flexible and adaptable?

Figure 4.5: Koo Foundation exterior rendering. © *NBBJ*

(Continued)

RM: This was alluding to a larger philosophy of learning buildings:[7] The ability of buildings to adapt, evolve, and be flexible over time according to their users' needs. We build a building that's meant to be there for a hundred years. The challenge with data is that data is often too specific. When we talk about learning, evolving buildings, they tend to be more general. They need to address a number of uses and number of users. They need to be able to respond to trends you may not be able to perceive.

We are currently looking at the future of flexibility, of single tenant versus multitenant efficiency on floors, daylight, visibility across floors, and floor to ceiling heights. There are a number of aspects we intuitively know about these attributes. Now we're putting them into a composite variable system, tying them to a pro forma, and assessing how to create buildings that give short- and long-term returns on investment for owners and occupiers. That to me is how data can influence the right approach for building longevity.

NBBJ has stated that the next step in its technological evolution is the use of design computation, software programs that use algorithms to link geometry with data to address specific problems. How is NBBJ utilizing these tools: to create geometry, for better building performance, or for both?

RM: It's all intertwined. The evolution of design computation has had moments of focus. Computation really started with building geometry. Part of it was as a cool tool with intriguing results. Part of it was, hey, this could lead to new means of fabrication; it could lead to efficiencies in the field. Then we got into building performance and the analyses we could perform to understand how a building was going to work within an environment. Then geometry and building performance were tied together. Now we're understanding human performance, human experience, how to link that to data and research. So now we have a three-part system. I don't think they're separable. They all should be tied together. Additionally, just as important as performance is beauty. We strive to create outcomes that are a balance of the two. A design that performs exceedingly well, that meets all of the owner and tenant needs but also is beautiful and memorable, a design that serves humankind.

My first experience with design computation was on a project in Kazakhstan where we were trying to understand the best way to achieve a form the client desired, which emulated the surrounding topography. Among the questions we asked was how to take this complex form we have drawn digitally and make it real? How do we build that? So we developed a number of tools that look at the planarity of glass; we looked at how mullions would sit next to each other; we looked at insulation; and thermal breaks. That was one of many first steps. Then we looked at slab edges and structural systems to tie the façade together, to detail it as a fully integrated approach. [See Figures 4.6 through 4.9.]

Many firm principals and partners abdicate the design technology—the algorithms, the computational design tools, the analysis—to others. How important is it for you to keep up with this stuff? Why not just leave it to the recent graduates?

RM: I don't think of it as something that can be written in a vacuum. I don't write the codes—as I have progressed in my career, I unfortunately have less and less time for that. However, I still enjoy hands-on engagement throughout the design process. What I think is wonderful and encouraging to anyone, regardless of experience or age, is that you can sit down with someone who knows how to write code and collaboratively develop on paper how an algorithm is going to work. For me, it draws both sides of the brain together: the mathematical, analytic side and the creative, experience-driven side. That's where I feel the most successful algorithms are, ones that explore the quantitative and the qualitative.

Figure 4.6:   Samsung: Samsung courtyard rendering. © *NBBJ*

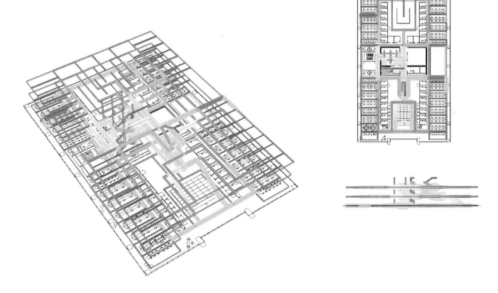

Build up Map of Most- and Least-Traversed Zones

Figure 4.7:   Samsung: Travel distance + calories. © *NBBJ*   (Continued)

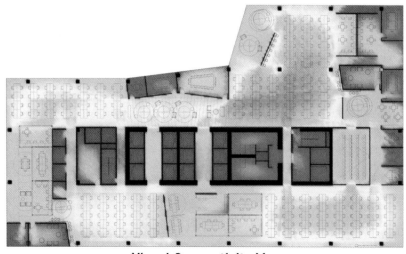

Visual Connectivity Map

Figure 4.8:   Samsung: Travel distance + calories. © *NBBJ*

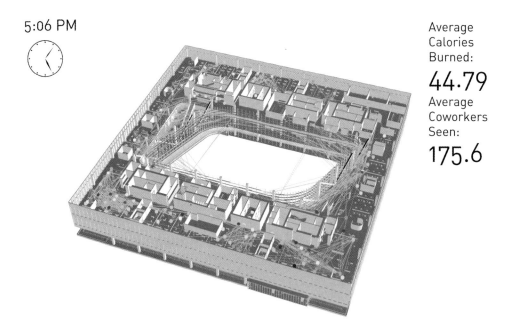

5:06 PM

Average
Calories
Burned:

44.79

Average
Coworkers
Seen:

175.6

Figure 4.9:   Samsung: Screenshot of Agent-based model analyzing calorie expenditure, distance traveled, and cross-floor visibility. © *NBBJ*

One of the algorithms we developed for Google from the very outset involved me working in a graphics program saying, OK, how do I connect all of these dots? Building height, size, proportion, orientation, spacing … all on a blank slate. Then sitting down with one of our really talented computational designers and asking, does this have merit? Does this have value? If so, how do we make it better? For me, it's a lot more about that type of collaborative effort. You need to have enough understanding of how formulas can uncover what information you seek and where you want to go with that information. Other than that, everyone has the opportunity to contribute.

Private Data Sources

Private data can be collected from many sources: clients, the field, existing BIM records, and other proprietary and industry sources and databases. As with all sources, the data has to be captured from a reliable source.

Client Data

Firms typically draw on a number of sources for their data, including public information that is available online, but in some cases they also draw on proprietary databases, particularly for demographic information. Often the source of this data is the building clients themselves. "First, there's collecting the data—the objective data that surrounds the project—and bringing it to bear," explains Tom Mulhern. "Data about the client's organization. How many people, what departments, how do they interact with each other? Professor Alex 'Sandy' Pentland's[8] corporation is Sociometrics.[9] They're putting trackers on people as they go through their workday. They use that data to monitor the flow of people in their current state." He continues:

It's not like you'd model that and then design around it. The potential there is to model, to

understand it, and find the difference you want to create. It's about making the boundary objects between modeling or drawing what's called in communication theory boundary objects. To an architect it's a model of a building that will stand up, look good, and fulfill its function. Clients place themselves into it. They imagine walking through it. It's a very concrete thing. They're not evaluating it in the same way. That boundary object sits on the boundary of the conversation. You can talk about the thing and the architect can derive knowledge and purpose from that conversation, and the client can too. Having data allows you to create much more interesting boundary objects between the architect and client.

Where does Aditazz—a data-driven company that uses data in all sorts of ways to test and create solutions—get its private data? "We get our data from our clients, from industry sources, from building codes, from manufacturing specifications, from under rocks," says Zig Rubel. "The most important aspect of the data discussion is that a human ultimately makes the decision. If we have the wrong data, it typically demonstrates its worth by not allowing what we would think is predictable. The point here is to use the data-centric approach to quickly allow humans to make decisions."(See Figure 4.10.)

Collect data → Run analyses → Ask smart questions → Derive insights → Make informed decisions → Act on decision

Figure 4.10:   Collecting data is just the first step in how data leads to action and how decisions are derived from data. © R Deutsch

Collecting Field Data

Design professionals will also capture data directly from sources—including sensors, scanning devices, and many, many others—in the field. "We use a lot of data in a lot of different formats—anything from a card swipe upon entering a building, to understanding how far students are traveling to determine if there are enough schools in a school district, to how many offices are occupied by a major constituency on a regular equipment basis—or do each of them need private offices? All different types of data," says Evelyn Lee.

Challenges to mining and collecting one's own data are twofold, according to Brian Ringley. "You've got at least two problems as concerns data tools—one is do I have someone who is knowledgeable of existing tools and can curate these tools for project teams based on each project's individual data needs," says Ringley, "and two is that data can be just about anything from mundane geometrical properties to sociological datasets harvested over the last century, so how can something so large and practically unknowable (without curation and visualization) be wrangled and systematized for efficient use?" Ringley continues:

> And we haven't even mentioned designers' relatively new capability to collect their own data through microprocessors and other physical computing hardware, such as the multitude of input/sensing devices available for Arduino boards (which can be linked directly to CAD through tools such as Firefly), or through industrial robotic arms and drones hooked up with 3D scanning devices and other sensory end effectors. The possibilities are really quite stunning and largely untapped. [See Figure 4.11.]

Figure 4.11:   Arduino Starter Kit in Italian. © *Arduino LLC*

Sensors and Mobile Devices

Sensors monitor the built environment, capturing data on air quality, acoustics, noise, and climate, among other things. A company called Heat Seek is even using temperature sensors to expose complaints and heating violations in New York City.[10] Sensors are also used to capture huge amounts of field data.

Firms such as RTKL have experience working with sensor data, having dealt with existing-condition 3D scans and photogrammetry. "Harvesting public data is something we have begun looking into to help feed internal performance databases," says Clayton Starr.

"The other thing we do—in terms of our data sources, and where we are comfortable getting our data—we mine public data; we get data from our clients; and in many cases we go out and collect our own data in the field," say Evelyn Lee. MKThink's Innovation group is incubating a new technology firm called Roundhouse One, named after the building they currently occupy. They're developing a proprietary software platform called 4Adaptive based on something that MKThink's

Strategy group has been doing for a number of years. "The other thing Roundhouse One does is they send technicians out into the field to implement sensors," explains Lee. "The sensors can track everything from environmental conditions down to air quality and acoustics—how loud systems are during the day. We also have a technology that tracks—the wi-fi sniffer— which is more accurate than the old way of standing there and counting how many people are going through a space. We can track movement and chart repeat visits from an individual with the same phone. We collect data from clients and mine data from public sources and, when necessary, we go out and gather our own data." (See Figure 4.12a–d.)

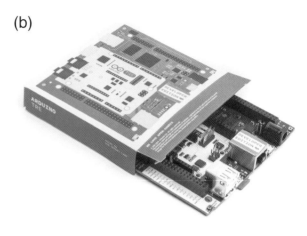

Figure 4.12: (a) *Arduino e la luce*. Sensors are simple little things that measure and report on change, and in so doing they emulate the five human senses: (b) Arduino microprocessor. Sensors are attached to all sorts of living and inert objects so they can share what they observe. (c) Arduino microprocessor with cover (Maker Faire Rome 2013). Sensors work tirelessly, never needing sleep and never demanding a raise. They notice changes where humans miss them. (d) Arduino Robot unboxed. Sensors already know what building you are in. Not too far into the future, your mobile device will also know what floor you are on, what room you are in, and in which direction you are moving. (Robert Scoble and Shel Israel, *Age of Context: Mobile, Sensors, Data and the Future of Privacy*. Patrick Brewster Press, 2014.) © *Arduino LLC*

The Quantified Self

Looking at the Quantified Self movement, David Fano of CASE notes that "people like metrics because they like to benchmark where they are. The reason people weigh themselves is because they want to know the way they were the day before. There's an opportunity to expose that. In terms of sustainability, most people don't actively want to hurt the environment. They just have no idea of the impact that they have. If we could do this with buildings—expose people to the data—this could have a better impact than any of these sustainability and energy movements. Every time you leave your light on, you just cost yourself $5." (See Figure 4.13.)

"My wife, Kim Erwin, has been working with big personal data" at the IIT Institute of Design, explains Tom Mulhern. "The data people get from observing their own behavior as it is digitally recorded. Through a Nike Fuel band or other means, and these in the not-so-good work groups. What work groups do well today and which will do well tomorrow? We look at the data analysis. We see these kinds of social patterns in the good work groups."

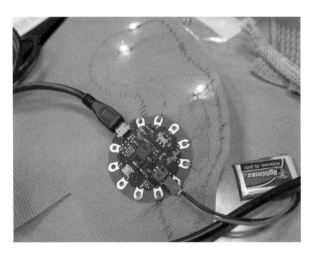

Figure 4.13:   Arduino microprocessor. Arduino Meets Wearables Workshop. © Arduino LLC

Are firms sitting on data that they aren't even aware of? David Fano sees this as a missed opportunity. "Yes. Any firm that is working in BIM. Their own internal enterprise resource planning (ERP) to better understand how they work. The traffic on their websites. Timesheets, calendar schedules for clients. There's lots of data that's going unused or not considered as useful information."

Card-Swipe Readers

Often used in conjunction with other means of mining field data, card swipes can often provide data that cannot be captured by other means. "Probably the most interesting thing we've done recently is, we're working on this dorm at the University of Chicago," says Erik Olsen. "We're trying to better understand the occupancy pattern of the dorm better because it's actually quite strange, right—when students are there or not in their dorm rooms? The university gave us card-swipe data for their existing dorms, so we can use that as a data source to try to understand how they use the building." Though, as Olsen discovered, there can be a downside to overreliance on card-swipe data: "They only swipe in, not out, so we only have half the picture. It's better than nothing."

"On one design project, we tapped into the client's key card data from their existing facility to understand employee movement flows and facility occupation rates," says NBBJ's Andrew Heumann, who also uses data from card swipes in conjunctions with other means of capturing of field data, including that of the naked eye. "Paired with directed on-site observation, this let us build up a rich picture of the way the company's employees behaved, and what parts of their facilities saw the most use at what times. This allowed us to make informed decisions in the design of their project, secure in the knowledge that the new facility would always meet or exceed current and projected need." (See Figure 4.14.)

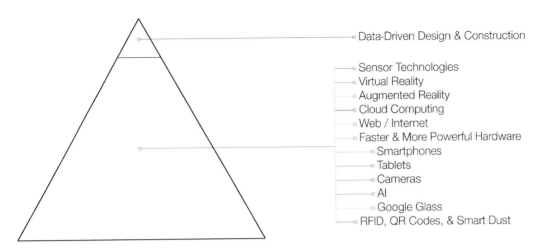

Figure 4.14:   Data-driven design and construction rely on the capture of reliable data from a variety of sources. © R Deutsch

Social Media

Social media is yet another potential source for valuable data and information for architects and planners. What does data from social media have to do with buildings? "Anything from FitBits to FourSquare to Instagram—it's all geo-located," says David Fano. "If I'm an architect and I'm doing a building in midtown, let me see what the people in midtown are doing. Where do they go eat? What kind of food do they eat? What are they tweeting about? One day doesn't matter, but if I look over the course of a year, it does. How many people use Citi Bike? Citi Bike made all of their data public." Data from social media can in fact be of more immediate use to designers, especially in comparison with more traditional means of gathering demographic data. "Census is every ten years. It's out of date the day it comes out," says Fano.

Case Study Interview with Sam Miller

Sam Miller is a partner at LMN Architects, where his work encompasses a diversity of civic, education, and cultural projects. He has led many of the firm's most prominent projects, including the Seattle Central Library, the Seattle Art Museum Downtown Expansion, the Museum of History and Industry, and a new School of Music for the University of Iowa. In addition to his project responsibilities, he heads LMN's Green Group, focused on advancing sustainable design knowledge, resources, and approach. He is also a leader of LMN tech studio (LMNts), which performs research and development of design technology, including simulation, parametric modeling, digital fabrication, and human-computer interaction.

You have written that LMN tech studio has advanced your research-based, data-driven design approach to work. What do you mean when you describe your approach as data-driven?

Sam Miller (SM): Over the last couple years we've refined our thinking in that regard. We're somewhere in between data-informed or data-driven. The reason I say that is we are striving to access as much data as possible to inform

(Continued)

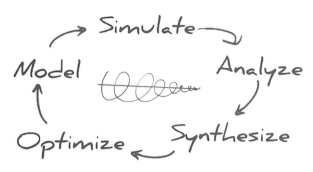

Figure 4.15: LMN's use of technology affords a highly iterative design process informed by simulation and analysis of critical project parameters. © *LMN Architects*

our decision making. But we also don't want data to be the sole driver of our design process. There is a middle ground there.

One of the important roles that LMNts (tech studio) has evolved into is not just enabling design technologies within the office, but customizing design technologies to work with our design process. So that the tool is adapted to what it is we are trying to achieve and the way we are trying to achieve it. And not the other way around. [See Figure 4.15.]

The term *data-driven* tends to imply that the outcome is largely driven by the data. We're striving to make the best-informed decisions we can, but also knowing that there is only so much in design that you can capture with data. There's also a quality, an aesthetic, and other contextual issues that need to be woven into the solution in a way that data alone isn't going to achieve.

Is the implication with a data-driven approach that intuition is downplayed?

SM: Yes, that's fair to say. Intuition is backed up by data—and getting better—because we are learning as we are getting this data, doing this modeling and doing these simulations. We're learning about what factors are most important in terms of affecting outcomes. Then the next time around we're starting at a more informed place. I would say that our position is evolving and improving.

There is only so much an algorithm can do. In the end it's really important to maintain a human touch on directing the outcome.

—Sam Miller, LMN

You're written about your own personal transformation—working in carpentry, engineering, and construction. Can you talk a bit about the transformation that LMN went through in becoming data-driven, and what role data played in the transformation?

SM: We always considered ourselves to be a research-based firm in that every project was a unique opportunity to explore new solutions. What has significantly changed over the last seven to eight years is the role of data in that. For example, we have always done a lot of physical modeling. Taken the modeling and done daylighting labs, sun studies, and light characteristics. But now we're doing it in an order of magnitude more sophisticated way. It is allowing us to explore different ideas more quickly. The biggest change for us is the iterative approach. Having the data at our fingertips so we can test lots of different ideas, learn from that, and move the design in a direction that takes advantage of what that has to offer. [See Figures 4.16, 4.17, and 4.18.]

As a firm, we recognize the value of this from a design standpoint. We also recognize the power of it, the opportunity that the technology is presenting, and we are actively trying to leverage that.

Have you found that the iterative cycle has been reduced from a matter of days to a matter of hours or even in real time?

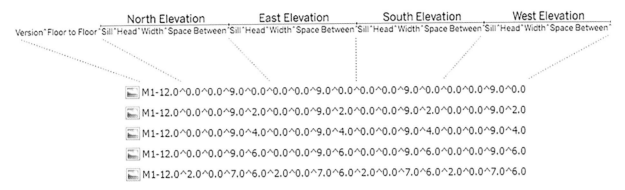

Figure 4.16: Visualizations of design iterations are named according to the controlling parameters, which allows for later regeneration of a particular iteration. © *LMN Architects*

Fenestration Studies

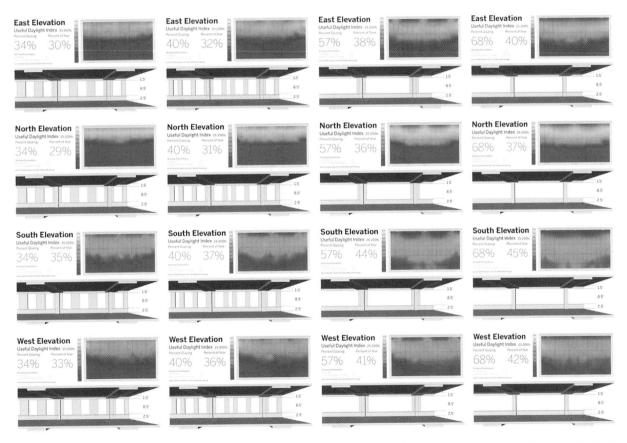

Figure 4.17: A matrix of iterations compares the effectiveness of increasing the glazing percentage to increase daylight coverage. © *LMN Architects*

(Continued)

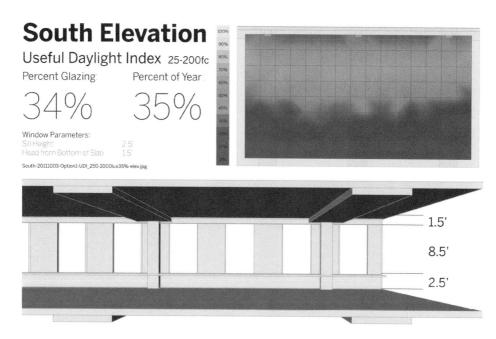

Figure 4.18:   Example of a typical shoebox daylight study comparing percent glazing to percent of year that desired lighting levels are achieved. © *LMN Architects*

SM: Yes, it is. And that's because the interoperability has really changed our workflow for the better. The industry has moved in the direction of better interoperability. But also our tech studio has helped to facilitate interoperability between platforms. We've been able to share modeling from one platform to the next. With the parametric modeling and other tools at our disposal, the cycle time is getting smaller and smaller. It's down to hours, not days anymore.

LMNts came about in part with a focus on design technology. How much of working with data would you attribute to technology and how much is mindset?

SM: This goes back to the idea where we are looking for somewhat of a middle ground. Where we have the data to inform our decisions, but also want to still maintain a design process that goes beyond an algorithm-based output. We want to study many different options. But in the end, we want to filter that through our design aesthetic and design approach to make sure that the outcome isn't just algorithmic.

To be realistic, there is only so much an algorithm can do. In terms of coming up with a solution that meets all the different criteria that are established, it's very difficult to quantify a solution. In the end it's really important to maintain a human touch on directing the outcome.

What tools do you use in working with data and what recommendations would you make concerning these tools?

SM: We're interfacing a lot with our SQL databases. As an example, we are doing in-house energy monitoring where we installed energy monitors on our electrical consumption in the office. We're grabbing hold of that and dumping it into a SQL database and then accessing data for visibility. LMNts is using programs for analyzing and daylighting.

This predates the recent renovation of our office. We wanted to get baseline data for the performance of the office. So we installed energy monitors a couple years ago and collected the data—plug loads in lighting, server loads, etc.—and now are continuing to gather data. We'll soon publish how things are going. Lighting loads, for example, are about 60 percent less than where they were, which is pretty exciting.

Maybe if we had IBM's Watson in our office, maybe we'd start getting where algorithms could account for a greater percentage of our design outcomes. And we're quickly getting there. It's incredible, the power that algorithms have brought. But in the current state of technology, it is still very important for designers to exert a role in the outcome of the design process.

One of the challenges that we face is in the iterative design process where we are now generating hundreds of design solutions, potentially using parametrics; the challenge becomes not generating the solutions but evaluating the solutions. How do you keep track of and evaluate the output? How do you optimize it? That is, in and of itself, its own significant challenge. Because there is so much information and you need to begin to evaluate: is it more important that we have daylighting across the floorplate? Or enhancing the views? How do you start to prioritize the opportunities? And, if you have a hundred outputs, how do you expediently dive into that, evaluate them, and determine which are the most successful? There's only so much you can do to evaluate hundreds of options. If not a great solution, there's the possibility that a kernel of a great idea might be left buried in there somewhere.

Can you define the criteria precisely enough that it embodies all of the design aspirations for the project? In a small study for a shoebox where you want to optimize daylight and views versus glare and thermal performance of the glazing, you could define the criteria very closely. If you are looking at a whole building design that needs to fit into a neighborhood context, where there are design review issues, and constructability issues—all the other myriad of issues that start to come into play—at this time we don't have the level of sophistication to write an algorithm that can optimize a solution that addresses all of these different issues. Over time, maybe. Large, complex building projects are very sophisticated and challenging. If you could define the goals and the desired solution precisely enough, you could write an algorithm that could get you there. But I would challenge anybody to say they can do that up front.

The architectural design process is one of exploration. You don't often know what you are looking for until you have explored many options and then start to see where the opportunities are. The challenge in defining the end goal and writing an algorithm to achieve it is we don't know what the end goal is at the beginning. And it is only through the design process that we learn where the opportunities are and that informs the approach. It's not to say it can't be done. Given the size and complexity of these projects, and the current state of design technology, we're a ways off before we're able to do that. There are certainly some in the profession who will say that we will never entirely be able to do that. There are components that can do this. There are parametric software tools—like Galopogos and other evolutionary computing software—that are heading in a direction where there is a machine-learning component. But as designers, we're learning as we go. LMN, as a research-based firm, we've always believed strongly in the value of design exploration. It takes time and iterations to really hone in on opportunities that will solve the problem.

Our groups are doing some very interesting things with data visualization to try to graph output in a way so we can quickly assess performance and identify a promising subset for further exploration. It even goes down into the file-naming protocol. One of the ways we are going at that is the files are being generated, and the performance is being determined, we're embedding coding literally in the name of the file. So you don't even need to open the file to get a sense of how the performance is working. If you get a list of a hundred files in the morning when you come in, after running it overnight, you can quickly sort through those and identify which ones are the most promising ones for further exploration.

(Continued)

I'm starting to see an uptick in the interest of firms in the role of data in design…. It's a potential problem for the profession in that there is a kind of the haves and have-nots situation developing.

—Sam Miller, LMN

You were one of the first in our industry to write and post on a data-driven approach to design and construction. How would you describe where our industry is, in terms of accepting and working with data?

SM: I'm starting to see an uptick in the interest of firms in the role of data in design. The technology is moving in the direction of broader adoption of analytics into the design process. It's a potential problem for the profession in that there is a kind of the haves and have-nots situation developing. There are resources required to take this on. Some of the smaller firms are going to struggle. They've struggled with Revit adoption, let alone all of the other pieces we've been talking about and are utilizing. It's a challenge, particularly for smaller firms, to get into this in a meaningful way. Whereas the larger firms generally have the resources and some form of an R&D wing that can explore it. The challenge for bigger firms is broader adoption across their office because they may have a skunkworks off in the corner. But if they have dozens of offices around the country, how do you encourage a broader adoption of all of this? That is one thing LMN has working in our favor. We're a big enough firm that we have the resources to do this exploration. But we're a small enough firm to be nimble enough to adopt it fairly widely about the office. [See Figure 4.19.]

Figure 4.19:   LMN is using parametric modeling and iterative simulations to compare bridge alignments and structural configurations in an effort to limit cost and maximize design potential. © *LMN Architects*

There is starting to be a greater recognition across the profession of the importance of working with data. There are a number of factors that are coming into play. Higher energy performance in buildings is going to be a big driver because it is going to require simulation and analytics. And there are other influences pushing the industry in that way.

Has LMN or LMNts utilized big data on any of your projects?

SM: If by big data you mean grabbing hold of the larger dataset that's out there, the primary way in which we have been using big data has been by using GIS information. That's been a really terrific benefit for us. The publication of a lot of GIS information in the public domain. For almost every project, we're grabbing GIS information and utilizing it. We have an urban design group within LMN, and that's been a nice entry for us to become familiar with it and to think about the broader dataset in terms of what it represents. In terms of context, and how do we leverage information that's in the GIS.

You have written that "[d]ata-driven design has transformed the iterative loop to model, simulate, analyze, synthesize, optimize, and repeat." How has this digital process improved—if at all—upon the old analog approach of Make It Break It Fix It?

SM: It goes back to design being pre-digital in the iterative process. Where it's an exploration and the learning is happening. And the design outcome cannot be pre-identified at the beginning. It is only through that design process that you can determine where the opportunities are, and where the successful solution lies. And only define the best solution after diving into it. I do think they are related. In the old analog version, in the process of breaking it you were analyzing, and the fixing it is synthesizing that back together. There is a close relationship. It's grounded in the fact that the design—pre-data, pre-digital—was an iterative process in its best form. Digital hasn't changed that. It's enhanced it.

In terms of data, can you describe an example where LMN ran a simulation that led to a surprising result?

SM: Recently we designed an acoustic reflector in a concert hall in Iowa. [See Figure 4.20.] At first our acoustical consultant was a little nervous because he had never had that level of manipulation of the form that he had. Nobody quite knew where that was going to go in terms of what the shaping of it was going to be. We did a lot of back-and-forth on that, and by the end the acoustical consultant was very excited. Because he had this level of manipulation and refinement that he's never had before. He could really dial into the design from an acoustical standpoint.

In terms of interoperability, we got a copy of the acoustic analysis software that our consultant was using. Not so that we could run the software. But just so that we could confirm that we could output models and geometry in the native format for that software. So that the consultant didn't even need to think about it. He could just take the file and open it up in his software, and that made it much easier and efficient for him. As a result, he was willing to do a lot more of the analysis because he wasn't generating geometry. He was just taking his file and running it.

The outcome was a shape and a geometry that was unexpected. There were surprises as we were defining the geometry. The acoustical consultant really learned something. And even though he is a seasoned veteran, and was doing this for many years, he's never analyzed the geometry and had the ability to manipulate geometry to the level he had. In that process, he learned quite a bit about what is going to be effective. It's not built yet, so we can't say it is effective yet, but according to the model, it's going to be a terrific space.   *(Continued)*

Figure 4.20:   The form and patterning of the University of Iowa School of Music acoustic reflector was iteratively developed based on the acoustical requirements, location of audiovisual equipment, theatrical lighting, and fabrication constraints. © *LMN Architects*

The data-driven approach appears to offer speed. What impact, if any, does this approach have on project quality?

SM: It is an age-old problem that predates technology. It's like: When do you put the pencil down? We pride ourselves on doing really significant design and high-performance buildings, whether by high-performance one means energy or acoustics, etc. We believe that we need to use these tools to enhance the design quality of the work we're doing. Our hope is that we can differentiate ourselves in the marketplace not by doing things faster and cheaper but by creating buildings that really take it to the next level in terms of performance. And that will allow us to get more work from clients who are interested in doing that sort of thing.

I don't think it's the same old, same old. I really do believe there is a brave new world out there that we're heading towards.

—Sam Miller, LMN

How likely is it that we in the industry are fetishizing data? That these aren't really data-related questions?

SM: It's fair to say that we are in the midst of a revolution in terms of how we work. I don't think we're fetishizing it. It's fair to say it's not the same old thing but with different tools. The tools are radically transforming how we work and, more importantly, the outcome of our work. There's urgency in how we address issues surrounding climate change, energy performance, and other important issues: people living in cities, and how do we create environments that are responsive and appropriate. There's the urgency and the opportunity from the tools standpoint to radically change how it is that we're approaching the design—and construction with digital fabrication—that is really transformative. So, no, I don't think it's the same old, same old. I really do believe there is a brave new world out there that we're heading towards. The profession must change or we're going to get bypassed. We're going to become archaic if we don't grab hold of this.

The question is: How do we do that? How do we maintain the right level of design authority so that it doesn't become algorithmic, or the contractors don't just take it over and start building stuff without thinking about these things? For us, it means grabbing hold of these tools, and leveraging these tools, to demonstrate value.

Mining Data in the BIM

BIM is often thought of primarily as a documentation tool. But those who hew to this definition are missing out on the fact that BIM is also a rich source of data, where plans, elevations, sections, and schedules are particular views not only of the model, but of the underlying database.

The BIM database, as has already been alluded to, can be queried and mined for project data. This has implications not only for the project team members who query the model for data that is going to help make decisions, but also for management and leadership, and for business development and marketing of a firm's services based on past experience that is captured—and now mined—in the BIM.

In one example of data mining in BIM, CASE has helped firms identify what content should make it into a content library. "Go and explore 50 projects that were done in BIM, then extract all the data, then do a data mining effort to understand what doors are used the most across the firm," suggests David Fano. (See Figure 4.21.)

Data from past projects can be a valuable resource for firms, one that remains relatively untapped.

"There are at least two types of data we work with: building/project data and office data. What I call office data—how our process works from a business perspective—in my opinion is more mature," says Mark Frisch, FAIA, Managing Principal at Solomon Cordwell Buenz. "Interestingly, our profession knows more about the business side than we do about the building/project side. While the office data is relatively sophisticated it would seem to follow that the building data would be at a similar level, but my experience is that it is not. Better understanding the relationship between the two is in its infancy and, in my opinion, ripe for attention." (See Figure 4.22.)

The planning, design, construction, and operations of data centers are one example where data from past projects plays an especially large—even vital—role. "Any large owner operator should collect, or start collecting, historical records of how reliable, efficient, costly, sustainable, and other lessons-learned data points from past construction and operations," says Peter Pellerzi, Manager of Data Center Global Engineering Team at Google. "It would be to their advantage to consider these and any new information, such as present market conditions, in the next project. Why would you use the same roofing system if you have data that shows it performs poorly?"

Figure 4.21: Through data analysis, the Model Overview can track the objects within a model and how they change over time, giving managers insight into how the model is progressing and where problematic areas may lie. © CASE

Other Data Sources

Other sources of data, such as those for health-care projects and building façade performance, can be captured by means as mundane as log sheets or tracking employees and as far afield as drones. "Our healthcare practice, we've been able to leverage anonymized patient records and nursing log sheets to get a picture of how facilities are being used, and where doctors, nurses, patients, and specialists need to be and at what times," says NBBJ's Andrew Heumann. "That same data was used to drive a sophisticated agent-based simulation model that we could use to evaluate our designs for their new spaces—and prove that the numbers and arrangement of patient rooms and other critical spaces would be efficient and adequate—and improve considerably on their existing facilities." (See Figures 4.23, 4.24, and 4.25.)

Another example is provided by Brendon Levitt of LOISOS + UBBELOHDE: "We've looked heavily into DIVA workflows for high-performance façades, as well as downstream interoperability so that the initial data can automatically generate corresponding BIM data for construction documentation and corresponding toolpathing, bending, and cutting data for architectural component manufacturing." Levitt has also used drones to collect data for projects. "We've also acquired a few AR.Drones, which will be used to collect audio, video, and photographic data to help augment existing GIS data for the purposes of site analysis."

"Our Healthcare studio once led an evaluation of the usage of space that required pinning trackers on staff, patients, and equipment, and monitored the data for six months before making design recommendations," says RTKL's Clayton Starr. A team of internal analysts then took that data visualized to the client. The result? Improving efficiencies of current resources would negate the need for expansion.

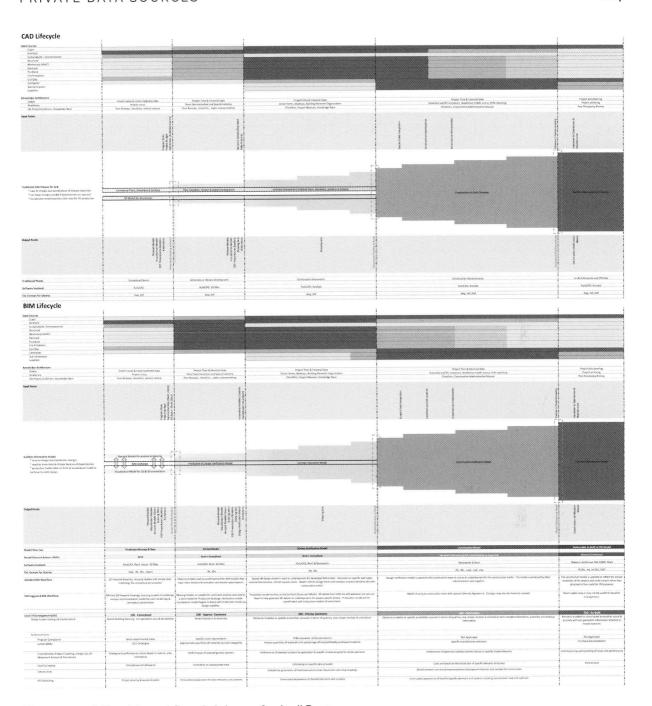

Figure 4.22: Office data workflow. © *Solomon Cordwell Buenz*

Figure 4.23:   Koo Foundation. © *NBBJ*

Figure 4.24: Interior rendering: Koo Foundation interior kitchenette rendering. © *NBBJ*

Figure 4.25:   Interior rendering: Koo Foundation auditorium rendering. © *NBBJ*

Having a Data Collection Strategy

To turn information into insights, don't just go out and collect data. Start with a data collection strategy. Start by asking: Where will the data come from? How will we compile our data? For example, will you use sensors or card swipes to gather information? Is technology even necessary for the sort and size of data you are trying to collect? You have to ask yourself: What makes sense for you and your team in this particular situation? "We absolutely use technology wherever it makes sense," says Jennifer Johnson, Senior Director of Product Development at Reed Construction Data. "And for us, that makes sense in the public sector for those documents we know are publicly available. We configure our technology to go after specific sites with specific information on them." Johnson continues:

> We don't just say, hey, there's the web out there, find something interesting. A really good site for us is the DOT [Department of Transportation]. So we have created our processes to go out and pick up that data. It doesn't make sense for us to use our resources to have someone calling on that when the government is telling us we have to put everything out there. Please come and get it! So we do. It makes sense that we do. When we're going after private work we have a network of our own researchers that are forming these AEC relationships. They're calling, emailing, meeting with our sources to access those plans, specifications and project details.

Strategy No. 9: Create a Data Collection Strategy

Don't just go out and collect data. Start with a data collection strategy.

Start by asking:

Where will the data come from?

How will you compile your data?

Is technology necessary for the type and size of data you are collecting?

What makes sense for you and your team in this particular situation?

In our experience, successful data collection begins with clear intentions and a commitment to a systematic, robust process for data capture, coding, and management. Unfortunately, it is relatively rare to see all of these elements come together in practice, and, in the real world, the best, large-scale examples of enterprise data collection in our industry rely on old-fashioned manual data collection (e.g., CoStar).

—Chris Pyke, USGBC

In our experience, successful data collection begins with clear intentions and a commitment to a systematic, robust process for data capture, coding, and management," says USGBC's Chris Pyke. "Unfor-tunately, it is relatively rare to see all of these elements come together in practice, and, in the real world, the best, large-scale examples of enterprise data collection in our industry rely on old-fashioned manual data collection (e.g., CoStar).

What specific means will be used to gather project data? Here are the technologies USGBC uses: "Moving forward, we are particularly excited about the prospect of indoor sensors and location-based analytics to transform the collection and analysis of information about occupant experience and space utilization," says Pyke. "This is one of the most game-changing sets of technologies on the near horizon." Location-based analytics are used to gain information about users while inside their premises and can be categorized into two types: static and dynamic (i.e., movement data). "Static data includes census-related data, satellite photography and maps, business listings, and so on. Dynamic data includes events that occur and are registered as consumers move around in their daily lives. The most important source of dynamic information is the data generated by mobile devices."[11]

Brian Ringley offers alternative means for gathering pertinent project data. "With the rise of photogrammetry we've actually seen a lot of scan data collected through tablets and phones rather than through more arduous techniques such as CMM arm digitizing or laser light scanning." Ringley adds: "We're also looking into low-cost handheld 3D scanning devices such as the Fuel3D which look to compete with existing, higher-cost and arguably less user-friendly (at least in terms of software workflow) handheld scanners such as the Artec Eva."

Benefits of Collecting Your Own Data

There are a number of benefits to collecting one's own project data. Here we explore an example: providing owners and design teams with an early reality check on the design direction chosen to implement client goals and objectives.

Again and again, throughout the interviews conducted for this book, design professionals told stories of how having the opportunity to collect data on a project not only served as a reality check for client goals and assumptions, but in many cases also led to unexpected outcomes. "We're working for one school district that everyone is moving into," reported Evelyn Lee. "One high school is anticipating growth from 1200 to 2000 students in 5 years. The school district was interested in building out the adjacent site that they owned next to the high school as another middle school." Lee continued:

The high school said no, we are over capacity and need to build an extension. They brought us in. We could have done this without visiting the school. We did a visualization and occupancy study that showed that over 80 percent of the classrooms that were scheduled were over capacity but, during almost every period during the day, because each teacher was assigned one classroom, 40 percent of the classrooms were empty. There we used the data to say yes, we understand why you feel like you are over capacity but, if you change some administrative rules on how you run the school, you'll be able to get a higher utilization rate out of it. The PTA had been surveyed. The principals had been surveyed. The faculty and administrative staff had been surveyed. They all agree they're over capacity. Then they saw the data and saw that they were not over capacity.

Lee provided another example of data's ability to course-correct client hunches before moving forward with a design direction: "With The Nature Conservancy, they were all screaming 'we need our own offices.' Classroom size was just one data point," says Lee. "We pulled many other data points. We did a lot of observation data points: e.g., 30 percent of you aren't in your offices 3 days per week. Rent is going up by this much. If we can shrink the floor plate by sharing office space—and you can break down your silos by talking to one another—not having your own office can make for better research outcomes." And the outcome? "Nobody has their own office now," says Lee.

Case Study Interview with Gregory Janks

Gregory Janks is a principal at Sasaki Associates, where he leads the firm's strategic planning practice. He blends academic, financial, and physical considerations in holistic problem-solving through rigorous data-driven analysis and design excellence. His expertise includes campus master planning, strategic planning, financial-planning and resource allocation models, data mining and data management, academic planning, space use analysis and programming, academic medical centers, student and residential life, and the development of technology-rich interactive graphical decision support systems. He has a PhD in mathematics.

How would you describe Sasaki's approach in relation to data?

Gregory Janks (GJ): We are data-informed. During the last decade, we have spent much of our energy in thinking about creating strong analytic functions to support planning and design decisions, exploring both quantitative and qualitative variables. We have found the rigor of this approach necessary to create compelling high-value solutions for our clients. At the same time, we recognize that not every component of a problem is amenable to measurement, and that political, aesthetic, emotional, and other considerations can be critical. We are most proud of our ability to link analysis to design, and through the magic of this alchemy, to solve problems. So, yes, data is a very important factor in decision making, but not the only priority.

Where in the integrated mix does data fit into strategy at Sasaki?

GJ: The heart of our data-driven approach is to analyze and understand the world and our clients' conditions, and through this deep dive, to understand what is fixed and what is malleable. In this sense, constraints are not the enemy of good planning, but rather its friend: unconstrained solutions spaces are vast and impossible to navigate. Constraints provide the constellations that guide us to good answers. Our innovations are therefore exactly about how best to develop organic solutions. Where possible, we then model change, and create dynamic feedback loops that can inform ongoing decision making.

Our goal, in planning, is to ensure mission drives the physical environment. We believe successful planning represents ideas, and we therefore combine mission, organizational, financial, and physical considerations to create stunning urban design and architectural ideas that focus less on the development of a static plan that runs the risk of immediate obsolescence, and more on a process that is able to respond nimbly to changing circumstances. In practice, this means developing a long-term vision, based on key principles, ensuring that future options are not foreclosed, and that every move builds incrementally towards a larger goal; identifying priority projects that launch us toward this long-term vision in a realistic and meaningful way; and the reinforcement of an effective planning process, driven by principles and data, that integrates multiple variables, so that new scenarios can emerge as needed. We strive to create a strategic posture, and to equip our clients with the building blocks needed to respond rapidly to changing circumstances. The ongoing use of data is fundamental to this process.

This philosophy has deeply influenced our planning work—in a truly integrated fashion, bringing together planners, designers, landscape architects, architects, economists, etc. In the last two years, we have begun to see how impactful it can be in our built work, as we have begun exploring new possibilities. [See Figure 4.26.]

Can you provide an example of how analysis informs decision making at Sasaki?

GJ: A recent great example is our work with Brown University [where] the university's strategic objectives require significant investment in its school of engineering. [See Strategy No. 14 in Chapter 5.] [See Figure 4.27.]

(Continued)

Figure 4.26:   Sasaki's integrated approach relies on the interaction of many hands. © *Sasaki Associates*

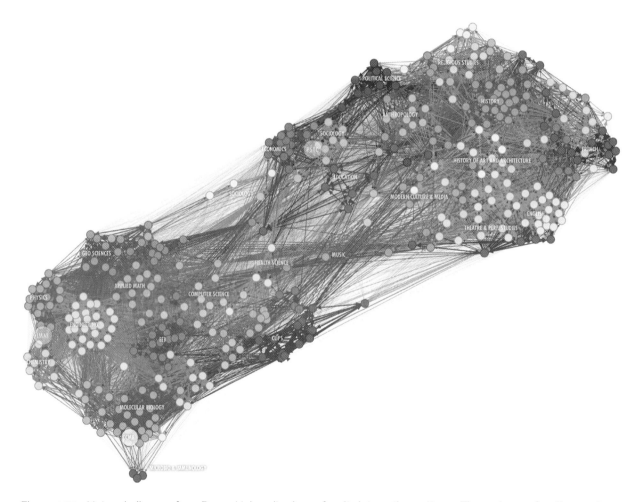

Figure 4.27:   Network diagram from Brown University shows faculty interaction patterns. The nodes are faculty members, the colors are departments. Nodes that are close together want to collaborate; nodes that are further apart less so. © *Sasaki Associates + Brown University*

As director of Sasaki Strategies, you juggle multiple forms of data—geometry, building performance, human performance. Where does organizational data (i.e., strategic planning, financial planning, and resource allocation) come into play?

GJ: First and foremost, we believe in solving problems. If the only tool in your toolkit is a hammer, then every problem looks like a nail. We therefore do not approach our clients' challenges with formula-based answers. We seek to understand, to truly understand, the nature of their problems, and from within that understanding, to identify the critical variables for success. This means following the rabbit hole wherever it may lead: strategy, finance, mission, design, ecology, politics, wherever. What good is a renovation strategy if it is unaffordable? What good is a new kind of classroom if it doesn't reflect desired pedagogical innovations? What good are energy reduction targets derived absent from a growth plan? Solutions are not solutions if they do not cover the relevant spectrum, so we create no artificial boundaries within our own thinking between physical and organizational variables. It is about the problems.

There are so many individuals performing hands-on work with data in the AEC and planning space. Is there a need for hands-off management or leadership to help connect the dots? How would you describe the role of the leader of data-centric efforts?

GJ: It is an interesting question. In a former life, I was (oh so briefly) an academic, and most of my work today is with colleges and universities. That experience certainly colors my viewpoint, perhaps more than it should. With that disclaimer, I believe strongly in project-based thinking. That's where ideas and methods are best derived, tested, refined, and executed. Abstract exercises often lack authenticity, at least with respect to real-world decision making. I am also leery of "management," especially when it leads to conformity, formulas, and orthodoxy. Orthodoxy can only be right for a brief moment in time, and then must have the capacity to renew itself. This is a very difficult process to manage (centrally). So, for me, a great leader of data-centric efforts is a person who is constantly seeking out new problems, expanding their toolkit, sharing their knowledge, and advancing ideas that change the world—this last meant quite literally: that result in actual and effective change in the world. Let the Darwinian forces of success then allow these techniques to aggregate into a formal body of practice.

How would you—in your multifaceted leadership role—describe your contribution as it relates to data?

GJ: It is for others to judge my contribution. In my own head, I strive to understand what kinds of things can be measured, and which cannot, and how both groups can contribute to decision making. I work hard to allow data to speak qualitatively when it can't speak quantitatively, and above all, to make data accessible through visualization techniques and to express itself through storytelling. This last is fundamental. We've all been through those endless presentations of number after number that amounts to not very much. If the data is meaningless, keep it to yourself. Find the meaning. Tell its story.

Sasaki Strategies is described as an internal, interdisciplinary think tank dedicated to incorporating new methods of analysis and data visualization into practice. Does this group operate as a separate entity within the organization? Or would you say it is generally integrated into project teams?

GJ: Integrated. Integrated, integrated, integrated. It must be. We've learned through bitter experience that it is most prone to failure when it is separate. It shines when it is incorporated soup-to-nuts into every aspect of the project.

(Continued)

Strategy No. 10: First Steps to Becoming Data-Centric

How can firms take the first steps toward applying data in their practices? How do you recommend firms make the change to be more data-centric? Where do they start? Can firms do this on their own?

Ask:

> Who is impacted by the decisions resulting from the practice?
>
> How can I measure or visualize the experience of those affected?
>
> Does this lead me to think about a particular dataset?

Don't try to collect every piece of data in existence. Don't create a metric so you can say you have a metric. Don't be afraid to say you don't know.

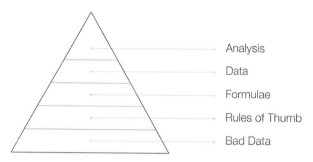

Bad data is worse than no data. Formulae are bad. Emphasize analysis over data. [See Figure 4.28.]

Figure 4.28:   Bad data is worse than no data. Formulae are bad. Emphasize analysis over data. © R Deutsch

Where to start? With the analytically minded people you already have (analytically minded is not the same as pedantic!). With a problem-centered world view. With an appetite to do things differently. With fearlessness, and good intentions, and a recognition that you won't know the answer at the beginning; that's why you are going on the journey.

Experiment. Iterate. The goal isn't to get it right the first time. If you're not seeing progress by the Nth time, get help from outside.

—Gregory Janks, Sasaki

Who—in terms of role—on the project team is most receptive to decisions backed by data? Any role less receptive to data-backed decisions?

GJ: We have not experienced huge differentiation in internal project team receptiveness by role or discipline. It is much more a personality thing. The meme of "analyst versus designer" is likely as old as time, and is not, for us, particularly meaningful. Analysis is part of design (or is it vice versa?), and the best folks quickly understand this. Of course, there are always traditionalists who are less receptive; and of course, there are business consequences—think, for example, when the recommendation is not to build—which can cause understandable resistance.

As I've previously mentioned, much of my work is in the academy, and from that perspective working with scientists and thinkers is terrific. They understand the methodology and are prepared to change their minds when merited by the evidence. Those have been hugely positive experiences. Of course, there are always political considerations, and external project team members with a political agenda not served by the facts will ignore that which is not convenient.

Planning appears to have made the greatest gains in the AEC industry using big data via GIS, iPhones, and so on. What do you think this can be attributed to?

GJ: Large-scale stakeholder engagement has always been challenging. Town hall meetings are dominated by the loudest voice in a self-selecting population. The ability to crowd-source planning problems is truly democratizing. We are now able to get large-scale input, and to have everyone's input count equally. That is fundamentally changing the planning process. It has been wonderful for us, because now we can say, it's not us, your fancy East Coast consultants saying X, it is your own people.

Is it the size, the unstructured nature, or the quality of the result that Sasaki finds most useful working with big data?

GJ: The quality of the result. It is our job to bring the structure, and the size is helpful because that's what makes it meaningful, but ultimately the data must say something, must speak to a problem, and it is in the quality of that result that the magic resides.

What would you want others to know about Sasaki's myCampus interactive mapping tool as it relates to data?

GJ: myCampus is an interactive online mapping application that allows us to engage stakeholders like never before. We've used it at multiple scales: myCampus, myCommunity, myBuilding (with a focus on post-occupancy). This web-based tool enables individuals to comment on how they use a campus (or building) and surrounding neighborhoods today and how they would like to use it/them the future. Within the university example, students, faculty, and staff can provide feedback on favorite classrooms and social spaces, preferred study areas, research spaces, perceptions of safe or unsafe areas, preferred retail locations, food and recreation, open spaces, and key vehicular, bike, and pedestrian travel routes. Recent instances of myCampus at Johns Hopkins University, Brown University, and Georgetown University have generated tremendous participation with well over 2000 respondents placing over 40,000 icons for each institution.

What other tools do you use in working with data? Generally, when it comes to working with data, what recommendations would you make concerning these tools?

GJ: We cannot sufficiently emphasize that tools do not solve problems in and of themselves. Thinking solves problems. In 2014, the most efficient way to express that thinking is often through technology, but there is no magic button for resolving complex planning and design challenges. We believe in the necessity of data-driven decision making, of making that data accessible, and then using that data to fuel the creative leap in a design process that expands the possible and, through its rigor, finds simplicity in complexity.

Rather than having specific tools, we often think of ourselves as having a toolkit from which we can combine various parts to create something that will address the specifics of the problem with which we are confronted.

With all of those caveats, our tools generally fall into three buckets. The first are our crowd-sourcing tools for stakeholder engagement. The research collaboration survey from the Brown example and myCampus are in this category. Next we have a series of tools that are essentially GIS in nature, linking data to geospatial realities, and allowing for modeling and measurement of physical scenarios. Finally, we have a series of models with interactive dashboards that allow for the identification of critical variables, and for the exploration of their changes in value. These are often financial in nature, but can cover the gamut, from traffic modeling to prioritization exercises to building programming.

We can only do this because we are blessed to have some seriously mad technologists in-house who are always cooking up new gadgets. So my only recommendation would be to get great people, and to focus on the thinking. If you do that, the tools take care of themselves.

(Continued)

Get great people, and focus on the thinking. If you do that, the tools take care of themselves.
—Gregory Janks, Sasaki

What are some of the ways Sasaki has been capturing public and private data?

GJ: Like everyone else, we have done some experimentation with mobile devices, although I wouldn't say we are leaders in that field. We certainly draw on whatever public information is available online, and in some cases have used proprietary databases, particularly for demographic information. We are interested in sensors, and where our clients have them deployed, we have used that information, but we have not yet done a premeditated installation. For most of our clients, though, it's a case of going to war [using] the data we have, rather than the data we wished we had. In many cases, these are rich and compelling. Of course, that isn't always true. But it is amazing how much data is out there, just waiting to be tapped.

What will it take to get design professionals and firms to pursue and leverage data in their projects?

GJ: This is certainly an idea whose time has come. Many firms are becoming interested, and of course, our great leading firms have long been pushing the envelope. The biggest question for me is how broad we, as an industry, are prepared to be in our thinking. Is this just about energy? Materiality? Physical variables? The truly big opportunity is for holistic thinking, and that, I would agree, not many firms are pursuing. But there are market mechanisms at work. If these new methods provide value for our clients, then we will all be forced to follow. We have, of course, seen technology revolutions in the industry before with CAD and BIM. This is a little different in some ways, because ultimately it is more about a way of thinking than a way of producing, but the adoption process may be similar.

Challenges of Data Collection

Not Every Firm Can Do This on Their Own

Some firms discover, especially when starting out on a data implementation program, that they can do this on their own. "I actually think that sourcing or mining data is much more of a challenge than integrating data into design," says Brian Ringley. Often when facing the challenge of mining data, firms will seek help, by working with a consultant or partnering with another company. One firm, dsk architects, took the latter route, opting to partner with IMMERSIVx for total facility design data and management solutions. IMMERSIVx is a technology, process, and software development firm providing consulting services and solutions that transform isolated business and financial data into useful and actionable insights. The firm works with companies in all industries, but specializes in the architecture, construction, and owner/operator markets that utilize BIM, GIS and facilities/asset management

tools.[12] "We find that as architects and designers, although we have the knowledge to discuss the data and value the data, it is incredibly complex to gather the data," explains Jill Bergman, Director of Healthcare and Knowledge Management at dsk architects. "IMMERSIVx has the technology and understanding of how to connect, validate, and leverage data into useful and needed information."

One More Thing

Data gathering is not always easy, and even when it is, the process of collecting data can be tedious and time-consuming. This is as true when gathering data for design as it is when mining project data to help improve construction workflows. Tedious data-gathering capacities and practices, according to Tyler Goss of CASE, inhibit teams from developing integrated approaches to business processes like estimating, sequencing, or facilities management. "Trying to mount a new data capture is typically going to fail because it's an additional piece of work," says Goss. "This is going to cross all parts of the building lifecycle, not just construction, the value proposition of a tap, a swipe, a click, or a data sample, or whatever it is that takes you time. And the value is not immediately apparent to you." Goss explains the consequences: "While you may do it because you understand the grander vision of the building lifecycle, you're going to miss it more often than not. Which means you're going to end up with data that is fuzzy, data that is inconsistent, you won't have well-structured data if it's not drawing off of the immediate value proposition of the people who are creating it."

Goss has seen this happen a number of times on projects that have lofty visions and complex processes. "The task of collecting productivity data falls to a field engineer who doesn't understand what they are doing, with a field superintendent, and they start testing—and that data is captured in a quali-

tative way," says Goss. "It gets very fuzzy. And gets very hard to standardize and normalize that data across a certain number of people. And because the data collection is tedious, arduous, and stops being done, you have incomplete data, and you cannot mount anything on top of it."

"Mani Golparvar-Fard built a whole career off of that," explains Goss, "off of the fact that that data collection is tedious and annoying." (See Figure 4.29.)

"My primary interest is to use photos and videos plus BIM because they are easy to use, because they are already available and don't need training," says Mani Golparvar-Fard, PhD, Assistant Professor of Civil and Environmental Engineering and Computer Science at the University of Illinois at Urbana-Champaign. "I am also getting more interested in leveraging commodity smartphones, as they are becoming more ubiquitous on jobsites. My core focus is to contribute to the body of knowledge in computer vision,

Figure 4.29: The vision of automated video-based assessment on construction sites. By detecting, tracking, and analyzing jobsite activities of equipment and workers in real time, performance metrics can be automatically assessed. © *Mani Golparvar-Fard, Ph.D.*

by creating model-based methods for photo/video analysis, and to contribute to the body of knowledge in construction management, through automated performance monitoring." The key for Golparvar-Fard, as it also is for Tyler Goss, is for data-mining efforts to be built on top of—not in addition to—existing technologies, processes, and workflows. For data gathering, collection, and mining to succeed, they have to be perceived by users as an integral part of one's existing process, not as "one more thing."

Notes

Unless otherwise indicated, quoted text throughout the book is from interviews with the author that took place between February and July 2014.

1. Links provided to the author by Brendon Levitt of LOISOS + UBBELOHDE
2. http://www.dot.gov
3. Patrick Tucker, *The Naked Future: What Happens in a World That Anticipates Your Every Move?* Penguin Group US, 2014, p. xiii.
4. The Open Definition; http://opendefinition.org
5. http://core.thorntontomasetti.com/aec-technology-hackathon-2014-project-cq/
6. Carrie Ghose, "Architectural styles through decades didn't always heed needs of workers within," *Columbus Business First*, October 9, 2008; http://www.bizjournals.com/columbus/stories/2008/10/06/focus1.html?page=2
7. Stewart Brand, *How Buildings Learn: What Happens After They're Built.* Penguin Books, 1995.
8. http://web.media.mit.edu/~sandy/
9. http://www.socio.com
10. http://hubs.ly/y0b5v50
11. Juan Herta, "Towards location-based analytics: Making data meaningful," March 6, 2014; http://makingdatameaningful.com/2014/03/06/towards-location-based-analytics/
12. http://www.immersivx.com

5 Analyzing Data

Maybe stories are just data with a soul.

—Brené Brown

Storytelling makes data digestible. It gives data meaning.

—Virginia Backaitis

Innovative firms, large and small, are using data to advance their practices, enable better insights, and yield more assured decisions; to reduce risk, manage complexity, and visualize results; to gain confidence and defend their design direction, learn more quickly, and consider impacts of multiple factors simultaneously. They're mining their experience and past projects as a searchable database, to improve their intuition and to move the design along.

Once data is mined, it has to be analyzed if you are to gain any benefits from it. There is no analysis without data to analyze. Analysis can be thought of as a series of questions you ask the data. CASE, for example, developed dashboards that reveal space usage in master plans that break down post-occupancy usage, that analyze energy requirements, and apply predictive interaction analysis to office environments. These analyses seek to answer: To what extent can building data predict future outcomes or behavior?

As a process, analysis can be incorporated at all stages of the building life cycle, whether for energy/building performance, daylighting, costs and schedule, market analysis for site selection decisions, social patterns in work groups, labor productivity, or waste utilization—to name just a few possible areas. For the sake of clarity, though, let's start out by defining a few terms.

Analysis versus Analytics

In an effort to clarify the distinction between *analysis* and *analytics*—terms that are often (incorrectly) used interchangeably—we must recognize that each term conveys a different meaning. As Mads Jensen of Sefaira explains, "For me, analysis is a perhaps more rigorous process that starts from first principles and uses a compressive model to analyze an issue."

At Sefaira we use first-principles physics to analyze almost everything, so the things we do are rigorously based on physics down to the granular detail. Contrast this with analytics, which is sometimes used as a more shorthand statistics-based analysis which we use to find patterns in situations where we either don't understand or can't fully explain the underlying principles. For instance, we might want to find buildings with a high potential for retrofit in a large portfolio, and not have sufficient data available to do a rigorous physics-based analysis of every building. We might then use, for example, utility bill data and statistics to benchmark which buildings offer the greater opportunity, without actually modeling what happens in each building using physics.[1]

Strategy No. 11: First Steps in Applying Data Analysis

How can firms take the first steps toward applying data analysis methodologies in their AEC practices?

Where to start?

With the analytically minded people you already have (*analytically minded* is not the same as pedantic!).

With a problem-centered worldview. With an appetite to do things differently.

With fearlessness, and good intentions, and a recognition that you won't know the answer at the beginning; that's why you are going on the journey.

Experiment. Iterate. The goal isn't to get it right the first time. If you're not seeing progress by the Nth time, get help from outside.

Ask: Who is impacted by the decisions resulting from the practice? How can I measure or visualize the experience of those affected? Does this lead me to think about a particular dataset?

Don't try to collect every piece of data in existence. Don't create a metric so you can say you have a metric. Don't be afraid to say you don't know.

Bad data is worse than no data. Formulae are bad. Emphasize analysis over data.

—Gregory Janks, Sasaki Associates

Predictive Analytics

We saw how CASE's dashboards not only analyze energy requirements, but also apply *predictive* analysis to office environments, to determine to what extent building data can predict future outcomes or behavior. According to David L. Morgareidge, Predictive Analytics Director at Page, predictive analytics uses discrete event simulation software and statistical analysis tools, among other techniques, methods, and processes, "to test the operational efficiency of existing or proposed facilities, applying the science of analytics to provide quantitative, objective, data-driven focus to the entire design process."

In a virtual, digital-design environment, predictive analytics identifies targeted solutions—saving clients time, space, resources, and money. "Predictive analytics is not just a set of tools, or folks with degrees in industrial engineering, statistics, and finance, that get bolted on to a traditional delivery model," explains Morgareidge. "Predictive analytics is instead a project design methodology that has different inputs, different schedules and task sequences, different types of client interaction, different deliverables, different costs, and different ROIs."

One would expect that teams will benefit from the rational, logical approach that predictive analytics offers. But can predictive analytics foster a consensus-building environment for the duration of a design project? "Predictive analytics helps to more rapidly build a stronger, more durable consensus among all members of the project team better than any other design methodology," says Morgareidge. "It is a transparent, data-driven process that eliminates the damaging effects, including schedule delays and the revisiting of decisions, which are often caused by firmly held emotional and subjective opinions."

It is just this level of certainty that predictive analytics enables that explains its appeal and Morgareidge's career-long dedication to the process. "I want to be able to say to each and every client that within their unique set of spatial, temporal, and financial constraints, I have found the optimal solution that delivers all of the organization's stipulated performance benchmarks and fulfills every aspect of their program in the most cost-effective and least disruptive manner possible. Working toward that goal is the only professional objective I've ever had." Morgareidge provides an example illustrating the benefits of predictive analytics:

> One of the most important benefits of predictive analytics is its ability to thoroughly evaluate a very complex, multifaceted solution space while calculating the interdependent performance impact of all relevant variables. In healthcare, for example, the administration can't say that it has successfully cut staffing costs if simulation shows that in the proposed solution patient queues are too long, left-before-treatment-complete percentages increase, and the staff is overworked. Predictive analytics properly done, is, by definition, the design method which is most likely to yield a balanced perspective....
>
> Any of six key elements can drive clinical and financial performance in healthcare: architectural space, medical equipment, IT and communication technologies, staffing models, scheduling protocol, and clinical processes. When we start an assignment, we don't make any assumptions about which one will have the biggest effect, which will have no effect, or whether there will be capital costs required. Almost every project ends up being a surprise to someone on the client side. It's a pleasant surprise if "pleasant" means cheaper, smaller, better, or faster. Of the 40 projects that I've done, 39 have been just that. However, the key thing about this approach is that its intent is not to make things cheaper, smaller, better, or faster. The intent is to make them right. On one of those 40 projects, simulation revealed that the proposed design was actually undersized,

and more space would be necessary. The client had been developing their operational concepts around this undersized floor plan for over one year. Their assumption was that the floor plan worked. Predictive analytics told us otherwise, and as is usually the case, because of the transparent and objective nature of the process, the client had no qualms about authorizing the increased space; they were confident in the accuracy of the analysis.

> Predictive analytics and simulation technology allows us to scenario-plan. It is a low-cost, low-risk, and very rapid way to "exhaust the solution space" and test hundreds or even thousands of alternatives until you find the optimal one that fits within the financial, spatial, and temporal constraints of the client while still achieving their operational and financial performance objectives. Every industry makes forecasts and the firms that stay in business revise them often and are thorough in their study of risks and mitigation strategies. That is what predictive analytics helps our client do.

Morgareidge's description of predictive analytics calls to mind the approach discussed earlier by Zigmund Rubel of Aditazz. "Our crystal ball is no better than the tarot card reader down the block, when it comes to human behavior," explains Rubel.

> But when functional behavior can be characterized into quantifiable associations with rules, we can be very accurate in our behavior. For example, when we modeled one Emergency Room, we were not able to initially get the model to perform the way the actual Emergency Room worked. It turned out that we were missing workflow data of having some of the patients waiting in the corridor to either be discharged or be admitted. Once we captured this behavior, we were able to match our model to reality. In this case, we were able to provide predictive analytics.

Brendon Levitt's interest in using computational tools stems from his interest in predicting building performance and anticipating the experience of a place, not only in terms of what it looks like or how light might propagate, but in terms of what it feels like. "Simulation is a powerful means to this end but, importantly, it is not the only one," says Levitt. His practice emphasizes the validation of simulation results, which means that they want to know that they are simulating phenomena that exist in the real world.

CASE has developed dashboards that reveal space usage in master plans that break down post-occupancy usage, that analyze energy requirements, and that apply predictive interaction analysis to office environments. "What we've observed over the past six years at CASE is an explosion in the amount of data being captured about the people, buildings, and cities that make up our everyday experience," says Tyler Goss. "Increasingly, this data is limited only by the sensitivity of our sensors, our ability to capture it, and the capacity to analyze the results." Goss provides an example:

> The near-ubiquity of wifi and smartphones helps us understand occupancy and utilization with exacting real-time detail—and this data is as applicable to the construction phase as it is to post-occupancy analysis. Likewise, holistic performance data harvested from Building Management Systems has been used to identify significant events such as fires—providing another measure of automated risk mitigation. Even something as simple as harvesting dynamic demographic information from social platforms like Foursquare and Twitter can give building owners and designers better information about the needs and desires of people in a given urban environment. All of these trends have put the industry right on the cusp of an explosion of predictive analysis.

Goss adds:

> The great thing is that the vast majority of this data is already at our fingertips. And while harvesting it today can be frustrated by inconsistent or incompatible data schemas across enterprise-level building systems, these traditional barriers are being disrupted by improved sensor capacity, novel analysis methods, and more than anything by highly connected and extensible systems (like the Nest thermostat). While this disruption is happening today in the consumer space, it's only a matter of time before these technologies and approaches work their way into enterprise-level systems.

Case Study Interview with Mads Jensen

Mads Jensen is a visionary in the use of cloud computing for high-performance building design. He founded Sefaira in 2009 with a mission to transform the way buildings are created, and he passionately champions the use of deep computing to put real-time performance analysis in the hands of all designers. Today Sefaira provides the leading software for performance-based design, and the company has won numerous awards, including the 2013 Sustainability Leaders Innovation Award and the 2013 Green Data Award. Prior to founding Sefaira, Mads was a business executive at IBM in Paris and London. He holds a BSc in International Business from Copenhagen Business School and an MBA from INSEAD.

You said, in an interview, that "we set out to create a new type of web-based design tool that would allow green buildings to become the norm." Where does Sefaira find itself today on the path to achieve this goal?

	MASSING OPTION	SHADING DEPTH	ANNUAL ENERGY	EUI	sDA	ASE	HEATING	COOLING	CO2	UTILITY COST
	BASELINE	0m	161448 kWh	99	65%	18%	13183 kWh	47255 kWh	84207 kgCO$_2$	£35,674
	OPTIMISED ENVELOPE	0.50m	122458 kWh	61	65%	18%	14641 kWh	12326 kWh	61657 kgCO$_2$	£26,011
	% DIFFERENTIAL		▼ 24%	▼ 38%	-	-	▲ 11%	▼ 74%	▼ 27%	▼ 27%

Annual Energy Use | Energy Use Intensity | Spatial Daylight Autonomy | Annual Sunlight Exposure | Heating | Cooling | Carbon | C Operating Cost

Figure 5.1:   A "strategies and bundles" framework helps identify design strategies with the biggest impact on performance, and find the combinations ("bundles") that deliver breakthrough performance. © *Sefaira*

Mads Jensen (MJ): To some extent we have come a long way, and in other ways we are just getting started. Sefaira today offers the only platform capable of doing a full dynamic energy and daylighting analysis of a building design in real time. This means that every time a designer makes a change to their 3D CAD/BIM model, we perform a full hour-by-hour analysis of all daylight and energy flows (covering the 8760 hours over the year) and return the results to the designer within seconds. Armed with such insight, designers can make better design decisions, ultimately leading to better building designs.

At the same time, we are only getting started. We work with 260 of the world's leading design firms [as of April 2014], and whilst that's great, it still means that most of the world's firms are not benefiting from the power of real-time performance-based design. We are working hard to change that! [See Figure 5.1.]

Looking at your staff, we see mathematicians, physicists, and software developers. Do you think this approximates the model for design teams in the AEC industry?

MJ: We have a strong conviction in the ability of cross-functional teams to solve difficult challenges. We therefore have a diverse staff, both functionally and culturally. We have several architects and mechanical engineers on our team, in addition to our computer scientists, mathematicians, etc. I would think that our team is quite different from the typical building design team, as we work to design and build software rather than to design and build buildings. But many of the disciplines that are required to design a building are found within our team, as we need those skills in residence to build good software for the industry.

You have said that effective green building design requires data-driven decision making. Why use data to get your ideas across?

(Continued)

MJ: It is hard to think of performance in the absence of data. How do you know whether your building design will work? The data will tell you. So performance data is central to our thinking and to what we try to bring to our users.

You have indicated that "Sefaira's innovation in cloud-based data-driven design brings a whole new level of analysis to the industry." Please elaborate.

MJ: The vast amounts of design data we have available today give us a whole new opportunity to design for performance, but two barriers have been standing in the way of this:

- Most traditional analysis was desktop based, and desktops do not have the computational power required to analyze all the data in real time, which really is what is required to incorporate analysis fully into the highly iterative nature of design.
- Even some of the historical attempts at using web application for building analysis have lacked the ability to convert design models (as they exist on the designer's desktop) to models that can be analyzed in real time, and so users would have to go through a laborious conversion and uploading process every time they'd made a small change to their model. This could mean that it would take hours to analyze a design change that in itself had just taken 10 seconds to make on the model, which is fundamentally at odds with the notion of performance-based design.

At Sefaira we have introduced true real-time analysis, meaning that every design change is analyzed and visualized to the designer in seconds. That is what we mean by "a whole new level of analysis." [See Figure 5.2.]

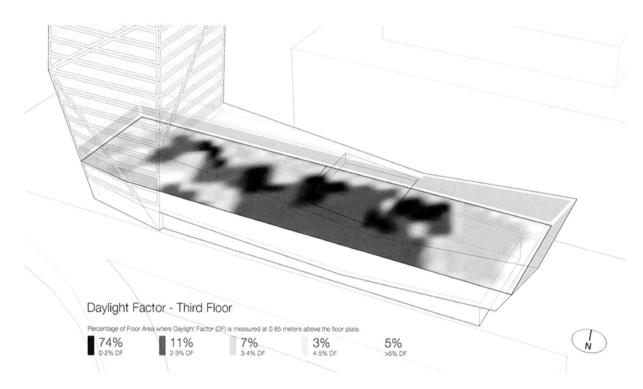

Daylight Factor - Third Floor

Percentage of Floor Area where Daylight Factor (DF) is measured at 0.85 meters above the floor plate.

74%	11%	7%	3%	5%
0-2% DF	2-3% DF	3-4% DF	4-5% DF	>5% DF

Figure 5.2:   Daylight factor visualization in Sefaira's plug-in. © *Sefaira*

Cloud technology is the only platform that can deliver the necessary design iterations required for zero carbon. Your software couldn't have existed 10 to 15 years ago?

MJ: Precisely. Full dynamic simulation is computationally very intensive. Ten to fifteen years ago designers would set a single analysis to run overnight, expecting the result to be back the next morning. We deliver the same analysis in a few seconds, enabling the designer to react to the information from the analysis and use that to drive the next iteration of their design.

With Sefaira, users can optimize their building portfolio and designs based on data-driven analysis. Can you explain how Sefaira utilizes data-driven analysis? Where does the data come from? How is it gathered? How is it communicated to the users to help them make decisions?

MJ: Sefaira uses first-principles physics to analyze all aspects of a design's performance, and every time a change is made, the full implications of that change are analyzed and visualized to the designer inside their CAD/BIM environment. The data is mainly coming from the designer's CAD/BIM model, and we then augment that with climate data, solar ray-tracing, etc. Data is as much as possible communicated visually to provide an information-rich platform on which designers can optimize their designs.

How do you explain the appeal of Sefaira to the investment community and subsequently to the AEC community?

MJ: Performance-based design promises to change the way buildings are designed, which will impact all of the construction value chain. Investors often look for trends and technologies with the ability to fundamentally change an industry, and they see Sefaira as a company with a potential to do just this. [See Figure 5.3.]

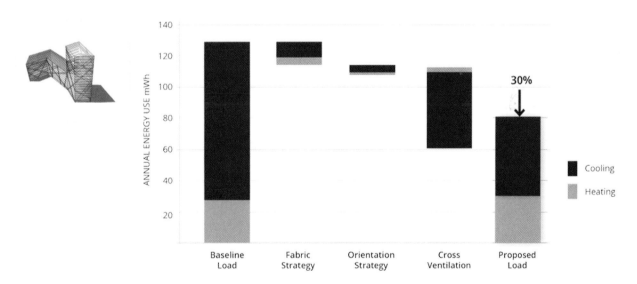

Figure 5.3: Flowchart showing the incremental impact of environmental strategies on a building. © *Sefaira*

(Continued)

What are the roots for Sefaira's reliance on data-driven design?

MJ: I grew up in the construction industry and have had a delight for buildings and architecture all my life. At the same time, I grew up in the '80s in parallel with personal computers, and I've always been fascinated with the real-time nature of man-machine interaction. Good software can give you intuitive, real-time answers to incredibly complicated questions, which in turn allows you (the user) to make much better decisions. We have derived inspiration from this. We have also derived inspiration from games design. In many ways, computer games have pioneered models for data-driven decision making. Games like Sim City were way ahead of business software in terms of giving users a data-rich and immersive environment in which to make decisions, and a continuous feedback loop enabling more iterations and ultimately better decisions. That's the long answer.

The short answer is that we are really just standing on the shoulders of the phenomenal advances we've seen in computer science in the last three decades. We live in an incredible age.

Data, technology, and software are often seen as fairly rational tools. I recently saw a tweet: "@Sefaira enables architects to design high performance buildings by providing intuitive real-time feedback as part of their design environment." Elsewhere, someone wrote that Sefaira "not only changed the way I design but also tested my intuition: assumptions that had seemed intuitive were actually wrong."[2] One often sees the word *intuition* used in relation to your software: "Through intuitive software, we aim to put the most powerful analysis in the hands of designers and decision makers everywhere…." Why an emphasis on intuition?

MJ: Human intuition is so unbelievably powerful, and it shapes every moment of our lives and every part of our history. We have been greatly inspired by Kahneman's and Tversky's incredibly powerful research on human psychology (popularized in Kahneman's *Thinking, Fast and Slow*), and it seems clear to us that our intuition is always with us—sometimes for good and sometimes for bad, but always there. Building physics is a complicated discipline. Sometimes it gives counterintuitive answers (such as: reducing the size of your windows might make your building consume more energy), sometimes just answers which our intuition could have never figured out on its own (such as: the optimal shading length is 1.3 feet—anything shorter or longer will mean higher energy use and lower daylight quality over the course of a year). The intuitive qualities of architects are what we find in the very best of the arts—those ephemeral qualities that computers just can't replace. So what we try to do at Sefaira is to make all the hard scientific analysis very accessible, very intuitive, if you will, so as to augment the great intuition good designers already possess. We simply see that interaction between man and machine as a great way to leverage the things humans are great at and delegating the things we are less great at to computers.

How important is it for design professionals to be able to test assumptions quickly in the early design phases?

MJ: Design is an exploratory process. Humans are visual beings, and we can relatively quickly assess the visual implications of a change in our design—especially with great 3D visualization and rendering software. Assessing the performance implications—on the other hand—is nearly impossible without analysis. I'd like to put floor-to-ceiling windows on the western façade to provide better views of the Empire State Building. What does this mean for my energy use, compared to windows that go up 80 percent of the way? Without a full analysis—who knows? But with analysis we know, and that gives us a much better basis on which to pursue (or reject) a given path. [See Figure 5.4.]

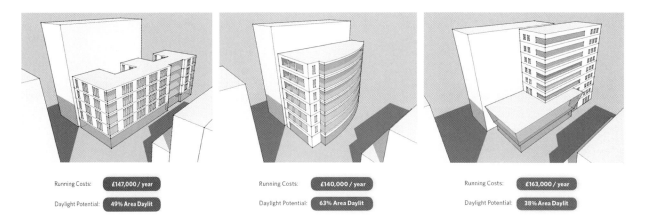

| Running Costs: | £147,000 / year | | Running Costs: | £140,000 / year | | Running Costs: | £163,000 / year |
| Daylight Potential: | 49% Area Daylit | | Daylight Potential: | 63% Area Daylit | | Daylight Potential: | 38% Area Daylit |

Figure 5.4:   Architects can compare design options and measure their performance using chosen parameters. © *Sefaira*

Are there particular technologies that are better at handling project data?

MJ: Cloud technology has opened up whole new ways of storing and accessing data, opening new ways to collaborate. We try to be tool agnostic, preferring to work with the tools our users like to work with. We don't really see it as our mission to tell people which platform to design on; for us it is mainly a question of helping them be as productive and creative as possible.

Do you see a difference among the firms that you interact with—that engage with your software—between those that are data driven and data averse? Does one have an advantage over the other?

MJ: In the technology industry we work with fairly traditional technology adoption curves.[3] There is always a part of the market that likes to try things early, and others that prefer to wait and see. There is debate as to how much of this is driven by our environment, and how much is biology. One might imagine that some of these traits (e.g., being first with technology gives you competitive advantages, whilst taking a wait-and-see approach can be less risky) are closely linked to evolutionary biology—[that is,] different means of survival. I'd posit that in the history of the world, more groups have faced extinction because they were late to adapt than those that adapted quickly, and therefore we think those that are quick to embrace the technology evolution stand a better chance of getting ahead from a competitive standpoint. This goes for performance-based design and cloud technology as it has done for many other technologies before it. [See Figure 5.5.]

What do you perceive the primary barriers are to gathering and sharing data in organizations and/or in the industry?

MJ: It is still too hard to gather and share data effectively, because the AEC software industry hasn't provided the AEC industry with sufficiently good software. If someone had told us 20 years ago that we could access almost all of the world's information with a few keystrokes and a click, we might have thought them deluded. Then Google came. Now the world is in a fundamentally different place. The AEC industry will see the same change once the right tools are in place (note: it won't be Google—it will be a different technology more suited to the nature of work in the AEC industry.)

(Continued)

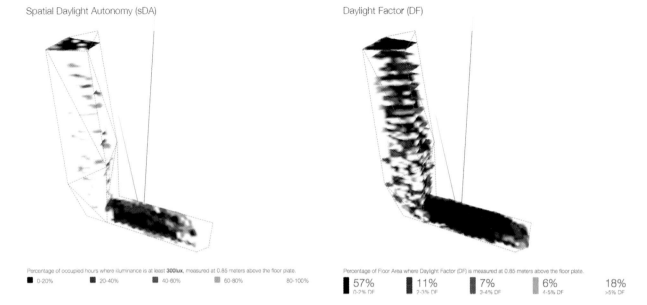

Spatial Daylight Autonomy (sDA)   Daylight Factor (DF)

Percentage of occupied hours where illuminance is at least **300lux**, measured at 0.85 meters above the floor plate.

| 0-20% | 20-40% | 40-60% | 60-80% | 80-100% |

Percentage of Floor Area where Daylight Factor (DF) is measured at 0.85 meters above the floor plate.

| **57%** | **11%** | **7%** | **6%** | **18%** |
| 0-2% DF | 2-3% DF | 3-4% DF | 4-5% DF | >5% DF |

Figure 5.5:   Architects can toggle between two daylight metrics: Spatial Daylight Autonomy and Daylight Factor. © *Sefaira*

For many design professionals, the subject of data isn't nearly as compelling as the generation of interesting form. Do you see this as an impediment to data use in organizations and the AEC industry?

MJ: We don't really see a difference between geometry data, performance data, or any other kind of data. At the end of the day, it is all data that goes into creating a great building design, and the more of it we can provide easy access to (for authoring, interrogation, manipulation etc.), the more powerful we can make designers. Buildings are obviously all about the visual form. But how does the changing of the visual form impact the daylighting quality for the occupants? How does the shadow from the neighboring building (or glare on your desk!) impact the quality of your work? We know that most architects care immensely about producing great buildings for their occupants. Good data helps them get there. [See Figures 5.6 and 5.7.]

Have you witnessed growth on the data front?

MJ: The industry is increasingly becoming attuned to the need for good analysis through a design process. And there is obviously no analysis without data to analyze. The industry has access to more data than ever, and we see a stronger and stronger trend towards incorporating analysis at all stages. [See Figure 5.8.]

Working with data: How much of this is technology and how much is mindset?

MJ: To succeed with performance-based design, we have to focus on performance. We have to focus on more than just "does it look good, does it have the square feet my developer needs?" It is also a question of: "Does the building perform in a way that is positive for the ultimate owner/occupier and the environment/context they live in?" Analysis will tell us how well we are doing. And that is where the competitive spirit sets in. If I am competitive and feel that I'd only

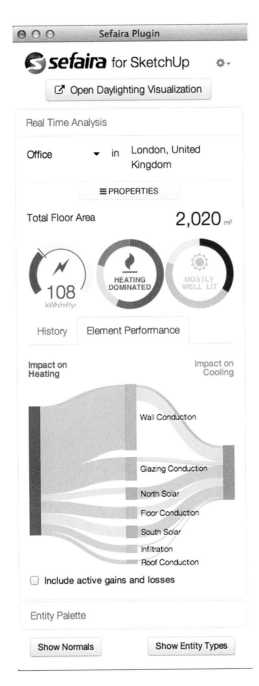

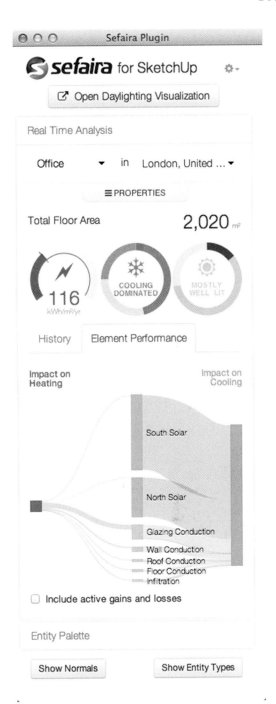

Figure 5.6: The Sefaira for SketchUp plug-in communicates a building's performance in an intuitive, easy-to-understand way, showing a breakdown of factors actively affecting the design's performance. © *Sefaira*

Figure 5.7: Sefaira for SketchUp plug-in Bad Performance result. © *Sefaira*

(Continued)

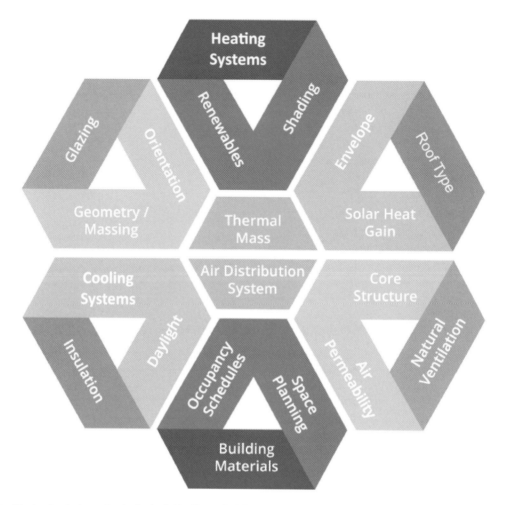

Figure 5.8:   Strategies to investigate for holistically optimizing the built environment. © *Sefaira*

want to design buildings that are great, because they perform great, then my competitive spirit will drive me to ever better performance stemming from ever better design. That—and some curiosity—are probably the only two mindsets that are really key. The rest is really just the hard work that goes into all good building design.

Analysis Tools

NBBJ has stated that next step in its technological evolution is the use of *design computation*, software programs that use algorithms to link geometry with data to address specific problems. I asked Ryan Mullenix how NBBJ utilizes these tools: to create geometry, for better building performance, or both? "It's all intertwined," says Mullenix.

The evolution of design computation has had moments of focus. Computation really started with building geometry. Part of it was as a cool tool with intriguing results. Part of it was, hey, this could lead to new means of fabrication; it could lead to efficiencies in the field. Then we got into building performance and the analyses we could perform to understand how a building was going to work within an environment.

Sean D. Burke concurs: the integration of building, human, and organizational performance is key no matter what the building type. "We've done a lot of projects for healthcare and some high technology companies," says Burke.

Mostly in the analysis space, things like combining multiple factors to help make a decision. The Bay View project we did for Google, we did sight-line analysis to nature and different views; combined with daylight harvesting combined with producing heat gain. We were able to optimize all of them and show the different solutions based on the design criteria using computation in a very rapid way.

Building Simulation

Some of NBBJ's clients, explains Burke, asked them to do real-world analysis and capture to put it into their projects. He provides a healthcare example, where NBBJ was asked to identify how well a waiting room design would work with the flow of patients and staff, while inputting different criteria, such as the number of staff or the patient rooms. "We've done both real-world simulations, where we're capturing the data manually," says Burke. "We're now looking at ways where we might be able to do this visually. We might have people wear a little badge throughout the day and see where they go, where they spend most of their time, when they pause. We also have digital tools that do the same thing. There's a product, FlexSim Healthcare, that helps us simulate those same conditions. And we can validate the tool against reality and vice versa."

Strategy No. 12: Two Ways to Think about Energy Analysis

There are two schools of thought when it comes to energy analysis in the industry.

One, you're picking a baseline design and you're making it better or worse. It's like going to the eye doctor, and they flip the lenses: this one, or this one? You pick which one seems better. Here's the base, and out of the five different design studies we did, one in five had up to 30 percent better than the base. You're basing your decision on relative data.

The other school of thought is hitting this exact number. Because that's what the software tells us. You're in early schematic design. You haven't thought of all the factors. You haven't thought of operations or occupancy. There are too many unknowns.

—Sean D. Burke, NBBJ

Performance Analysis

Beyond building geometry, design and construction professionals use data to analyze building performance—energy, sustainability, commissioning, life cycle—and human performance, as firms leverage data to analyze organization performance.

Analysis for Sustainable Design

What is the value in being able to cross-check analysis data across projects over time? "We were the first structural engineering firm to join the AIA 2030 Challenge," explains Jonatan Schumacher, Director of CORE studio at Thornton Tomasetti.

As part of our commitment we developed the carbon calculator in Grasshopper, as well as carbon query tools for Revit and Tekla. From our completed BIM models we extract embodied carbon quantities. So over time we understand [what] the baselines for embodied carbon quantities per square foot are for buildings of a certain size, type, and location. We keep track of, and grow these datasets over time. The goal is that over time, we can hopefully lower the average values per square footage."

Strategy No. 13: Analysis for Sustainable Design

What sort of analysis goes into the development of a team's sustainable design concept?

We always like to start with the climate analysis and look at what are the potentials for the climate independent of architecture. Temperature, humidity, wind direction, solar radiation, integration of natural ventilation, how much shading we might need in this climate, humidity control. And site analysis, especially of the wind situation, what massing is involved, on what side, especially in an urban area, how that might result in solar shading. Those are what we would do for a general analysis. Sometimes we might do energy predictions of typical programming, making basic assumptions to get a general idea about what the energy consumption of the building might be.

We'll do the same thing, exploring a little more detail, to see if the climate could work for just natural ventilation. We'll take a generic shoebox space, without any architectural design, test the parameters in which we could maintain comfort in that space. Beyond that, all of this leads to then not doing simulation for simulation's sake. Which I am very much concerned about, because it is very much in vogue these days. We would rather ask specific questions. Based on that initial contextual analysis, understanding what is going on with the program, what design ideas are evolving, certain questions start to arise. That's an interesting idea, but does it even work? Or comparing two options, these are interesting options, but which one performs better? We always do the analysis with the intent of answering specific questions rather than doing the analysis hoping something interesting might come out of it.

—Erik Olsen, Transsolar

Understanding baselines for energy analysis for buildings is key. In Strategy No. 12 (earlier in this chapter), Sean D. Burke presents two schools of thought when it comes to energy analysis. How does he decide which to side with? "I would err on the side of loose interpretation of the results," advises Burke, "rather than staking everything on the piece of software that generated it, whether commercial or an open-source algorithm, or the skill of the person who's driving this tool."

Case Study Interview with Erik Olsen, PE

Erik Olsen is a mechanical engineer and expert in integration of architectural and low-energy indoor comfort solutions. As director of Transsolar Climate Engineering's New York office, he works collaboratively with clients, architects, and other engineers worldwide to develop and validate low-energy, architecturally integrated indoor climate and energy concepts. Erik has been lecturer and guest critic at Harvard University, MIT, University of Pennsylvania, and Columbia University. In addition to his specialist work at Transsolar, he has worked as a consulting mechanical engineer on a wide variety of building types and launched and directed the city of Chicago's Green Permit Program.

Transsolar is a leading climate engineering firm whose scope is to ensure the highest possible comfort for people with the lowest possible impact on the environment. What role, if any, does data play in ensuring that you hit and maintain this sweet spot between highest possible comfort for people with the lowest possible impact on the environment?

Erik Olsen (EO): Looking at existing data, we're benchmarking both for energy and comfort. Having clear targets for design—or what is our definition for a low-energy design—what are we trying to achieve absolute energy use-wise. The same thing for comfort. We have been using and exploring so many new comfort metrics in a more expanded way of defining comfort, where people might traditionally just use temperature. These are both very important ways of evaluating the performance of a design. In the design process, we're generating our own data in order to understand how different designs perform. What the trade-off between them might be.

How do you go about generating your own data?

EO: That's really the core of our practice and is probably what makes Transsolar a little unique. Even the name of the company, Transsolar, comes from TRNSYS—one of the main thermal simulation softwares that we use. The practice is founded upon the idea that what we are here for is generating integrated climate concepts, which is about an idea and how that idea works physically with the architecture itself, and the systems in the building. Then to explore those ideas, we have to do simulation. We do a huge variety of simulation depending upon the task at hand. The most used tool is TRNSYS for dynamic thermal simulation—what most people call energy simulation. It is a little bit of a European and German perspective to use the term *dynamic thermal simulation*, but I really like that because it emphasizes the point that what these simulations are actually modeling is the computer model, a computational model of thermal behavior in the building. Energy consumption is just an output of the model, it's not simulating energy directly. We're doing daylight modeling. We're doing computational fluid dynamics for detail airflow patterns. We do a lot of custom, detailed, hand-built sets of equations to represent whatever problem we have at hand.

In the vocabulary for this discussion, I increasingly realized when we get into modeling, the question of simulation or modeling, what does that mean—especially for an architectural audience? I'm sure it is a big disconnect, because the word *model* to an architect is a physical or digital representation of geometry—of points in space. Which is not at all what we mean when we say *model*. For us, a model is a set of equations to represent a physical phenomenon. Which is the normal engineering and science term for model, as in, we're going to model this behavior.

(Continued)

What tools do you utilize in developing and validating climate and energy concepts?

EO: Among other things, we use TRNSYS. We're part of a consortium that developed and sells TRNSYS. It's a completely modular simulation software that can be used for simulating dynamics, hourly or sub-hourly, annual behavior for all sorts of dynamic systems. It can model a thermal solar power plant, not even a building. We write the largest single module of that, which is the model for simulating the building physics of a multi-zone building. There's a French company that writes the graphical interface for it. It's sold and used around the world. A handful of American engineers use it, very unusual in the U.S. Very heavily used, the dominant software, for dynamic thermal simulation in Europe. We're the German distributor for the software. Our level of using it, and the way we use it, is a little different than anybody else. It's only one of many other tools that we use depending on the assignment.

The idea of what a simulation tool should do, and how you use it, is very different from TRNSYS. It's not like eQUEST where you plug and chug. The learning curve is long and steep. It really requires an expert user. You can't just say I want an answer, plug in a number, you have to understand what you are simulating.

Can you be a climate engineer today without mastering the technologies you're describing?

EO: If you want to use very conventional and known strategies, then possibly. If you're not going to try something new, if you're not trying to advance the practice, but just do what's been done before—it's a vanilla climate, a vanilla program, vanilla everything—then you can repeat what's been done before. But if you're trying to advance, try new things, improve performance, create new space types, new architectural experiences, then no.

How important is the use of specific, local data when developing potential strategies with clients, architects, mechanical engineers, and other consultants?

EO: It depends on a number of factors. A starting point for us is always climate data. If you're in a situation where there's very little local climatic variation, then the generally available weather data—TMY data—is usually pretty valid. There's no reason to be more specific. However, if you're in an area where the typography is extremely varied, the generally available weather data is probably incorrect, because of the elevation changes, or you're in a valley but the weather station is not. Then, more local data becomes extremely important. If you're in a situation where there's urban heat island and the weather data is not from the downtown area. It also depends on how important the precision of the data is. If you're doing a natural ventilation concept, and the concept is completely wind-driven—and you're assuming a certain wind direction, you're not going to be providing the mechanical cooling, and the building totally relies on that wind-driven ventilation— then pretty specific, local, accurate wind data is very important. If you're doing a concept where natural ventilation is a bonus, not something you design for, and there is a mechanical cooling mode, then it may not be so important to invest the kind of money to try and get that data. That same thinking carries on for other types of data, such as energy benchmarking. A lot of times you only have to have regional or national data for energy benchmarking. If you have a very unusual use type where a broad benchmark number is inappropriate, it's probably better to get a few sample projects to benchmark to. Or it depends on the client. If you have a client who is not so interested in what others are doing, but they want to prepare it themselves, then you're going to have to get their personal data in order to be convincing to them.

How does working with data enable Transsolar to go beyond the conventional, limited idea of energy conservation?

EO: The key is considering the climate and really digging in to understand what are the variations in the climate, what are the opportunities of this climate. When you think about typical energy conservation strategies, you might not think about how they actually vary from one climate to another. Especially with more variations in climate.

Any observations you can make about the open data movement, urban policy, and how data can transform city living?

EO: I'm very excited about all these new ordinances coming on everywhere requiring sharing of energy use data, because that's a real key for getting market transformation until people understand how much energy their buildings are using compared to others. Ordinances now here in New York and in Chicago are taking the first critical steps. I don't think it has done that much yet because it takes time to reach people.

Big Data presents not only challenges but also the potential to improve what governments do. Brett Goldstein is the former Chief Data Officer for the city of Chicago. I believe New York City's CDO is Rachel Haot. Can you talk about the importance or necessity for a city such as New York to have a data portal that the public can access and for a point person such a Chief Data Officer to manage the information?

EO: As a user of that data, especially when benchmarking in large cities, to have that information available in a more organized fashion would be so valuable. We've used the published energy data from the New York ordinance and that was quite helpful. When I was at the city of Chicago, back in 2008, trying to even think about that sort of thing, we didn't get anywhere. It just wasn't ready for that then. It was a little bit decentralized as well.

Do you have an example of tapping into data that you are not familiar with?

EO: In some cases we have had the luxury of setting up a weather station and collected a year of weather data from it, to make sure the data we are operating from are correct. When we're working in all of these different locations, how do you balance between using the data and saying OK, this is what the data tells us, this is enough, and understanding the local concerns, the construction culture, the cultural expectations for buildings. The weather data doesn't tell you that. When you have to deal with facilities people, no matter how much data you give them, they'll only go on their previous experience.

From this, it sounds like you collect data, run analyses, you ask questions ... the results of which lead to insights from which you make informed decisions?

EO: That's right. The main challenge, and the most difficult part, lies in asking smart questions. Yes, we can model things other people probably can't. But the first value is, can we ask questions that other people don't ask?

Based on the climate change we have been experiencing, at what point do you question the reliability of using historical data? You're designing a building that today may be comfortable, but how about 20 years from now? Does some of it need to become more predictive?

EO: This definitely has come up in conversation, and it is an interesting question. For energy prediction, so far it hasn't seemed so critical. If it is 2 or 3 degrees Fahrenheit warmer on average, it is not going to influence the energy consumption so much. Similarly, even for equipment sizing for mechanical engineers, the question comes up. If you're going to have mechanical cooling, whether or not it is going to be 2 to 3 degrees higher doesn't really affect the equipment sizing. Peak loads are so much more solar driven in buildings than due to outside temperature. The place where it would come up is if you do not have mechanical cooling, but are relying entirely on natural ventilation for cooling, you really have to address that. It would be worth looking at what's the worst-case scenario of what the climate

(Continued)

might be like 20 or 30 years from now. Will the spaces in the building be comfortable then? I can imagine doing that, I just haven't had to do that yet. The other big discussion in this whole climate change, a hot topic particularly in New York after [Hurricane] Sandy, is resilience. All of the arguments for resilience in buildings helps to reinforce the need for good passive design. Because a good passive design building after a power outage will remain more comfortable than a mechanically cooled building.

It's interesting how you are using extremely sophisticated tools and processes to arrive at what will essentially result in a passive design for a resilient city. Transsolar performs highly sophisticated computational simulations (e.g., thermal, lighting) for concept validations. When seeking proof for a recommendation for an innovative but otherwise untested technical system, can you describe your computational simulation workflows?

EO: The most interesting or surprising thing to many audiences would be that we don't necessarily launch into a full-blown detailed simulation using TRNSYS or whatever the tool is. The most new and novel approaches usually require starting with something simpler to understand it. Basic engineering hand calculations, we might literally do by hand or by spreadsheet, and ask what the behavior is going to be. After that we would put it into software intended for that sort of analysis, what we call EES: Engineering Equation Solver. Then, as it becomes clearer and we understand the problem, we have to look at it a little more accurately with more detail. We might move it into a simulation such as TRNSYS. Lastly, especially for something very novel, at a certain point we test with some sort of performance mock-up, to verify that the performance is as we expect it to be.

Even for very complex systems, you can develop a very confident hand calculation representation of it, which gives you an upper bound and lower bound. Here's a worst-case basis for what the true answer might be. And here's what a best-case representation might be. They might be 50 percent apart, but for a first blush of trying to understand the problem, that's totally sufficient. Much better to spend one day doing that than to mock up something that might give you the wrong answer.

Transsolar is immersed in simulation technology and computational tools. For many design professionals, the subject of data isn't nearly as compelling as the generation of interesting form. Do you see this as an impediment to data use in the AEC industry?

EO: I feel that this fascination with form is changing somehow. In the younger generation of architects, the fascination with form is not what it was for the older generation of architects practicing today. It's already changing. From my own perspective, I want to help architects make spaces that are unique, delightful, and comfortable so you can accomplish what you're supposed to accomplish in it, if you're supposed to accomplish anything, inside those spaces. So you have to be able to understand what the experience is inside those spaces, from all aspects, in order to be able to do that. That's very much about human experience.

Energy consumption matters as well, and comes down to real numbers. People's understanding of that kind of data is starting to change, which is helpful. More informed architects today are starting to understand not to talk about some percent energy savings over some arbitrary baseline, but just what the energy consumption is. They ask what is good and what is bad for energy, in the same way they ask what is good and what is bad for comfort.

Now they're asking: how can my form be novel and interesting but also work with some kind of performance idea, or at least not hinder the performance idea?

There will always be the kind of architects who want to develop an interesting, pure concept and see how it works. Others who are very interested in a concept that is very integrated with the performance idea from the beginning. Both are OK. I'm happy to work with both. I'm not sure every building has to be the result of a performance idea. The first approach is OK as long as it is eventually integrated.

When you're working with that first type of architect who already has a specific idea for aspects other than building performance, when discussing performance, we'll point out why certain parts of their project are problematic. The constructive answer isn't, no, I'm not interested in that. The answer needs to be, that doesn't work for me and this is why. I am trying to accomplish X and the idea you have is against achieving X. If we understand something else the architect is trying to accomplish, maybe we'll propose a different idea that works with that. Or maybe by talking through it, they'll have another idea. But if they're not willing to have a conversation, that's a no-go.

Anything to add concerning computational design and influencing or predicting human behavior?

EO: That's a big interest of ours as well. I personally am interested in: how do we in North America lap off this culture of engaging physically and taking responsibility for your own comfort? For example, opening or closing windows or shades. How do you make a design that performs, but also its aesthetic encourages people to interact with the building, because it visually reminds them that they're supposed to, and it's also visually interesting so they're encouraged to. Part of that is understanding what people's behavior is. How do people actually interact with buildings. Which there's very limited research on. This started as a thermal comfort survey in our office where we monitored window positions and temperatures. Talk about being data-driven! We collected data on our own office so we understood what's going on in our office at any time. There's a survey that we sent out at the same time that pops up on our computers three times a day and asks: Are you comfortable right now? We set this up so we can prove to clients that we can accept higher temperatures. This was interesting for understanding user behavior. People open and close windows, things like that. We're also starting to look at how you minimize plug loads through the use of dashboards. There's a lot of research that shows that you can't just use a energy dashboard that shows energy use and that's it. You have to give people feedback, whether they should turn their light off. It's more effective if you give them a switch right there.

Analysis Tells You How Close You Are to Your Targeted Goals

The emphasis in the design professions has historically been on using algorithms to create interesting geometry and form. Recently, there has been a change in the use of algorithms for building performance and other impacts of building design, including human performance. "There has been a greater and greater interest on the performance side of things," argues Andrew Witt. "That's been facilitated by the fact that there's more formal flexibility in the building geometry. Would it be possible to talk about an impactful building performance if there wasn't some generative or parametric logic to the building itself? They're two sides of the same coin. This is something that has been evolving since at least the 1960s or 1970s, when computational models also had this performative, generative aspect."

Data, in whatever form it's presented, is only as useful as the people who understand it and can apply it.
—Brendon Levitt

Analysis of Human Performance and Behavior

In addition to building performance, there is advanced software for simulating pedestrians and analyzing crowds. There's a tremendous amount of data about the sun and air temperature," explains Tom Mulhern, Senior Vice President and Chief Innovation Officer of Dātu Health.

What other data could become accessible to the designer? The flow of people through space? There's a great tool that I always wanted to use because I thought it would make the conversation with clients so much more rich, called Oasys MassMotion. It's a sign of things to come. Building agent-based modeling of people in buildings is not just about knowing where to place the fire exits. Instead, we can say this is the kind of behavior we want to stimulate. We want people going to the conference rooms. MassMotion's objective is very simple. They just want to get from point A to point B, and they have some kinds of parameters around what they will and won't do to get there. We build more sophis-ticated behavior models. The only reason we would do that is to create a data model of people. You can start to ask yourself: I want to put a social space here and a social space here. Now I'm going to run that and see what happens when a thousand people come into campus. What do they do?

People don't have speculative conversations about whether the sun is going to hit the roof at a particular angle. There is no speculation about that. The sun is the sun. Given such latitude on June 17th, if there is no cloud cover, it's going to hit that roof. With the design of spaces to support social activities, it's just a big black box. Nobody knows. Everyone has their stories. Everyone's going to love being in this atrium. OK. Except you and I both have been in atriums that we don't love being in. It will be embarrassing to the company when they spend all of this money on a space that nobody uses. It's a multi-variable problem. A lot of decisions happen because people believe one scenario or another about how people will use that space socially.

Case Study Interview with Chris Pyke, PhD

Dr. Chris Pyke is Vice President of Research for the U.S. Green Building Council. His recent work includes research on green building finance, human health, greenhouse gas emissions, and resilience. He directs the development of the Green Building Information Gateway (www.gbig.org), a unique global data platform for the green building industry. Dr. Pyke serves in a number of technical advisory roles, including representing the United States on greenhouse gas mitigation issues related to residential and commercial buildings on the United Nation's Intergovernmental Panel on Climate Change. He is a faculty member at George Washington University, teaching in the graduate Sustainable Urban Planning Program.

Who really needs to hear the message of data-driven design?

Chris Pyke (CP): Personally, I think that the entire industry will be shaped by data and, increasingly, the evidence-based practice that it supports. I believe that this imperative will flow down from the expectations of owners, investors, and other stakeholders—entities that have experience with data and analytics from other industries. Traditional AEC participants will ultimately respond to these opportunities and, in some cases, requirements.

For this to happen, how much in your estimation is technology and how much is mindset?

CP: First and foremost, this is an issue of cultural change. I am trained as a scientist, and I see a world full of testable hypotheses. I crave the data needed to provide objective evaluations of all aspects of our built environments. For me, every building system, design element, whole building, neighborhood, and community is an experiment waiting to be realized by linking intent to outcome with the appropriate data. This is a common cultural mindset for scientists, much less so for AECO professionals.

Design is an artistic expression and uncertainty is not a challenge but an existential risk for most AECO professionals. AECO professionals will need to decide if data-driven decision making is something they want to embrace. Personally, I think the world will ultimately require a fundamental shift in mindset, but individual professionals and institutions will ultimately mediate the pace of change and its impact on practice.

What attitudes would you recommend others develop in order to work with data that would lead to greener buildings?

CP: Data linking design intent with operational outcomes turns buildings into natural experiments. Understanding [that] buildings are real-world experiments opens the door to data-driven analysis, systematic evaluation, and, ultimately, dramatic improvements in outcomes. Realizing this opportunity requires fundamental changes in prevailing attitudes among AECO professionals.

As one example, most professional publications in the AECO industry place a strong emphasis on celebrating success. For example, *ASHRAE Journal* provides monthly features on exceptionally high-performing buildings. Yet, these publications provide relatively little coverage of failures and underperformance. Contrast this emphasis with journals for professional pilots; these publications focus overwhelmingly on failures. "Plane lands safely ..." is not a story.

"Building performs as designed" shouldn't be a story. We should want to talk about underperformance and failure. We need to find ways to talk about these issues in ways that address the real, practical circumstances in the AECO industry (e.g., our litigious culture). Clearly, if the aviation industry can find a way, so can we.

Can you describe a project where the use of data led to an improved decision or insight?

CP: Over the past several years, USGBC has developed a global data platform called the Green Building Information Gateway (www.gbig.org). The platform seeks to dramatically improve project transparency, provide market context, and create rich, federated timelines of building performance from multiple sources. Today, we see GBIG users asking critical questions about why a project or building is "green." They are "unpacking" the LEED plaque to see which credits were achieved and how patterns of achievement relate to specific policy goals. They are using this data to inform project decisions, such as pushing for higher levels of certification or helping convince clients that specific strategies can be done in their circumstances. Increasingly, we are also able to link LEED certifications with data from municipal benchmarking programs. This is beginning to provide long timelines of asset performance. Sometimes this information allows us to recognize exceptional design and management (e.g., One Potomac Yard in Arlington, Virginia, or NREL Research Support Facility in Golden, Colorado). In other instances, it raises questions about operational performance or data quality (e.g., Stoddert Elementary in Washington, DC).

(Continued)

What are some of the ways USGBC has been capturing data that have been particularly effective?

CP: In our experience, successful data collection begins with clear intentions and a commitment to a systematic, robust process for data capture, coding, and management. Unfortunately, it is relatively rare to see all of these elements come together in practice, and, in the real world, the best, large-scale examples of enterprise data collection in our industry rely on old-fashioned manual data collection (e.g., CoStar).

Moving forward, we are particularly excited about the prospect of indoor sensors and location-based analytics to transform the collection and analysis of information about occupant experience and space utilization. This is one of the most game-changing sets of technologies on the near horizon.

Where are design professionals on the data front today?

CP: I believe that design professionals see the need to address these issues on the horizon: probably not today or tomorrow, but relatively soon. I personally believe that many feel poorly equipped to incorporate data and associated technologies into their work. They are concerned about impacts on their professional practice, including cost and liability. In part, their interest in data will hinge on how information about "performance" comes to be understood with respect to specific AECO roles and responsibilities.

Using Analysis Data to Make Decisions

Analysis of data goes beyond the optimized design solution to look at how the solution comprehensively performs, often requiring human input. Daniel Davis of CASE describes how Snohetta's Oslo office wanted louvers on a project to perform to meet certain criteria. "The Grasshopper definition in this project worked by trying every louver orientation, running the analysis, and presenting the results on a spreadsheet," explains Davis.

> A designer could then go back to the spreadsheet and say "at this orientation I get this performance." So the Grasshopper definition wasn't giving a designer an optimized solution, it was rather giving the designer the data about the performance potentials. The designer can then look at that data and use their judgment to evaluate the options. They might go with the theoretical optimum, or they might decide to use a configuration that is slightly less than the theoretical optimum but more aesthetically satisfying. This is a type of reasoning computers are terrible at. It's the best of both worlds: the computer is doing the analysis the designer would find far too tedious; and the designer is using that analysis data to make a decision that is far more sophisticated than anything the computer could make.

Before data can be used to make decisions, collected metrics and data sources must first be aligned. Using the 2030 Challenge as an example, where firms keep track of the reporting for projected energy use, NBBJ's Sean D. Burke points out that every project does this analysis in its own way, or may not be using the same tools. "Some may be using Green Building Studio, IES, or a consulting engineer to do energy modeling for us," explains Burke. "We're getting data back, but it's all in these disconnected reports. We're trying to figure out, how do we aggregate all of that? And put it in a place where it can be reported on, where the data can be sliced and diced in different ways, so you can make better decisions when starting a project? It's very manual right now, and we want to eliminate that by getting as much data as we can directly into the model. And if we can't do this, we have to ask ourselves *why*?"

Strategy No. 14: How Analysis Informs Decision Making

Brown University serves as an excellent example of how analysis informs decision making. "The university's strategic objectives require significant investment in its School of Engineering. Multiple 'obvious' factors suggested that new space should be constructed over a mile from the academic core. Recognizing the decision's importance, the university paused. While Brown believes in evidence-based planning, the challenge was finding relevant data. The university is famous for its open curriculum in which undergraduates have great freedom of choice. We undertook a novel network analysis of the interrelationships of course enrollments and academic departments to better understand how students exercised this freedom, and conducted a similar exercise for faculty by mapping their research collaboration patterns across academic and partner units, and core research facilities. We also built a financial model to better understand resource constraints and to define the impacts of likely available funding. These academic and financial considerations combined with our traditional design strengths—we compiled datasets tracking mobility patterns, and related them to important activities like learning, studying, and collaborating; we measured the suitability of the existing building stock to support laboratory research; we analyzed how peer universities are physically arranged, focusing on which functions belong in the academic cores; we measured square footage capacity by identifying sites and adjusting for political realities and neighborhood considerations; and we investigated Brown's presence in the Jewelry District to see how key program and urban design moves could revitalize this urban neighborhood and act as an economic engine for the city. As a result of the work, the university reversed course, and decided to keep engineering integrated within College Hill."

—Gregory Janks, Sasaki Associates

Analysis Turns Buildings into Real World Experiments

Data linking design intent with operational outcomes turns buildings into natural experiments. "Understanding that buildings are real-world experiments opens the door to data-driven analysis, systematic evaluation, and, ultimately, dramatic improvements in outcomes," explains Chris Pyke of USGBC. "Realizing this opportunity requires fundamental changes in prevailing attitudes among AECO professionals."

There are a lot of opportunities for using analysis and data for making what we do better. It doesn't necessarily change what the design looks like.

—Jonathon Broughton

With Analysis, the Means Doesn't Belie the Ends

A first glance at Allies and Morrison's work—such warmth, depth, variety, and presence!—data seems like the antithesis of what it is about. Jonathon Broughton says that he values high-quality, efficient, joyous place-making. How can data analysis help achieve these ends? "I think it's possible to be two things at once," says Broughton.

> To be better informed can only be a good thing. We have now the best opportunity to be as well informed about what it is we are doing [as possible]. That's the transformative effect we have right now. We can always be learning more about how we're doing things, how we can be doing things. I don't think your means of analysis and production should be manifest in what it is you do. I don't think that what you do should belie the way that you achieved it. Just because you've applied smart ways of working to achieve that end shouldn't necessarily be in what you look at when you occupy a space. I

don't believe you have to assume that data-driven design should be fancy curtain wall patterns, because our biggest opportunity is improving everything that we do. There are a lot of opportunities for using analysis and data for making what we do better. It doesn't necessarily change what the design looks like."

Strategy No. 15: Start Simple, Technology Optional

We don't necessarily launch into a full-blown detailed simulation using TRNSYS or whatever the tool is. The most new and novel approaches usually require starting with something simpler to understand it.

1. Basic engineering hand calculations, we might literally do by hand or by spreadsheet, and ask what the behavior is going to be.
2. After that we would put it into software intended for that sort of analysis, what we call EES: Engineering Equation Solver.
3. Then, as it becomes clearer and we understand the problem, we have to look at it a little more accurately with more detail. We might move it into a simulation such as TRNSYS.
4. Lastly, especially for something very novel, at a certain point we test with some sort of performance mock-up, to verify that the performance is as we expect it to be.

—Erik Olsen, Transsolar

What Analytics Helps Accomplish

Brian Skripac of Astorino provides an example of what can be accomplished with analytics. "If everyone is able to look at analytics, they can then define their own processes for leveraging it," explains Skripac, "but when you bring the owner on top of that and the owner has analytics it's even more powerful."

Take a healthcare facility, for example, that might have data about how patients are being treated, how doctors and nurses are engaging them from central or decentralized nursing stations, same hand versus opposite hand rooms and other considerations. There's so much about evidence-based design (EBD) that can be integrated with these facts that you can start to see beyond big-picture trends, and drive solutions that can be benchmarked with the numbers.

Providing Analysis on Top of Data versus Just Providing Data

Jennifer Johnson, Senior Director of Product Development at Reed Construction Data, spends a lot of time with customers understanding what some of their current market dynamics and challenges are, and what it is they'd like to do but can't figure out how to do. "Then we create products that meet their needs and bring solutions to market," says Johnson. "Where we've been primarily designing lately is analytics on top of data instead of just displaying data." Johnson continues:

We had a CEO who retired last year. He encouraged the change of data to information. One of the key thinking points for him was providing additional intelligence on top of data. We have a partner that we work with who developed an analytic offering and asked if they could use our data within it. We started doing that and started exposing these micro-trends over our data to our customers. It was love at first sight. Imagine a Google-like search box and instead of giving you all the best restaurants in your city you're getting a list of how your products stack up against the industry over time over geography by project categories. So we started there and just kept going. This developed into an in-house analytic offering which allows us to tie in with all of our other products.

Strategy No. 16: Leverage Data as Means to an End

For Sefaira, the logic flows a bit like this:

- We all need to think about performance, because we all need to think about how we can deliver better outputs from our work.
- For the AECO industry this means thinking about building performance and incorporating it into everything we do.
- The way to get better performance is to integrate analysis into a tight feedback loop so that when we iterate on our work, we get rapid feedback on where our iterations are taking us.
- Analysis requires data, so we need access to data, and we need data integrity. We should all care about this. Otherwise our analysis becomes flawed and we won't deliver high performance.
- So, if I am a contractor and I am considering replacing window type A with window type B—what are the implications? I'll only know if I analyze the data.
- This goes for everyone else in the value chain who makes decisions, which is ... *everyone*.

—Mads Jensen, Sefaira

Take a Tip from a Data Compiler

It is not just the data, but contextualizing the data, that makes it more valuable. "Everyone knows there's a lot of data," admits Johnson. "The hardest thing is to show you the right amount of data—and the right kind—in a way that makes sense to you." She continues:

> Enough information for you to make a decision off of. It's really easy to paralyze people with data. There's an unlimited amount of information you can aggregate and pull together, but try to put in a dashboard without it being 12 pages long! That's not usable. The hardest thing is to really boil it down to the three to five factors that are really going to make a difference in your business. You need to know what the construction activity is. What the forecast is. What are the handful of things you need to know? How do I expose that view so the trends become very clear? Once those trends are clear, go and dive deep into the data and do any kind of analysis that you need to. Let's not miss the forest for the trees. I need to hone in on just a few key pieces of information that are exposed to you that are most relevant to your business.

Case Study Interview with Brendon Levitt

Brendon Levitt is a licensed architect and holds architecture degrees from Yale University and the University of California, Berkeley. Mr. Levitt is an associate at Loisos + Ubbelohde, where he has served for more than a decade as project manager, modeler, and designer for a wide range of buildings. With proficiency in diverse software tools from Therm and EnergyPlus to Athena and Radiance, he has contributed to cutting-edge research on thermal comfort and energy modeling, life cycle analysis, daylighting design, lighting design, and data visualization. Mr. Levitt writes and lectures on sustainable design and the synthesis of contemporary culture, human comfort, and new technology, and serves as adjunct faculty at UC Berkeley and California College of the Arts, where he teaches design studios and building technology courses related to sustainable design.

(Continued)

You work with a prototyping visualization toolkit, developed for the Grasshopper visual programming environment, which enables the situational development of information graphics. Can you provide a bit of background on this tool?

Brendon Levitt (BL): We sought to create a graphically based data visualization tool that could provide rapid feedback in the same environment in which geometric and performance simulation could be accomplished. Our goal was to create an integrated dashboard from which to conduct simulation so that we could speed the feedback loop from creation to analysis to synthesis. As the tool developed, it was honed so that specific data input formats could be more readily accessed and manipulated.

By enabling more nuanced and customizable views of complex data, Dhour offers designers an exploratory framework in contrast to the highly directed tools currently available. How important is this flexibility and freedom to experiment to design professionals when analyzing and visualizing data?

BL: Flexibility is important to help the designer ask and answer the appropriate question for the job. Many existing platforms have pre-baked visualizations which pigeon-hole the designer into asking the wrong question. For instance, it's common to see designers show energy graphs as evidence that the building is comfortable. While energy consumption is certainly related to thermal comfort, it is often not an adequate proxy for it. [See Figure 5.9.]

It is sometimes said that the same algorithmic tools that are used for building performance are used for developing innovative building form. The latter gets most of the attention in the media and arguably from students and designers. Why an interest and focus in using computational tools for working with and visualizing building performance data?

BL: The first statement in this question is a crucial one at the crux of the BIM issue. The same algorithmic tools are not typically used for building performance and for form-making. It is a common fallacy that advanced BIM more readily enables both form-making and building performance analysis. In practice, however, the two disciplines require such different types of information and expertise that an "integrated" building information model is unrealistic and usually unnecessary.

Two examples: one as an architect and the second as a building performance specialist. As an architect, when I want to show a client what a building might look like, I will construct a model of the exterior. If I then want to show what a conference room might look like, I would construct a different model that focuses on fleshing out the interiors. Each model has different types as well as granularity of information. This "scene design" approach is a common method of cutting down on the time it takes to construct a model as well as the rendering overhead and file size. By focusing only on the information that is needed, we increase speed and accuracy.

The same approach is true for performance modeling. If I am interested in daylight penetration, I will construct one type of information model that includes material reflectances and sky conditions. I will focus my modeling efforts on the elements that contribute most to the daylight in the scene, like the mullions or ceiling geometry. In contrast, if I'm interested in modeling thermal comfort, I would concentrate instead on the area and thermal conductivity of the mullion. If I construct a daylight model that is used as an energy model I will get incorrect results, because the information contained in the model will not be the appropriate type or granularity. [See Figure 5.10.]

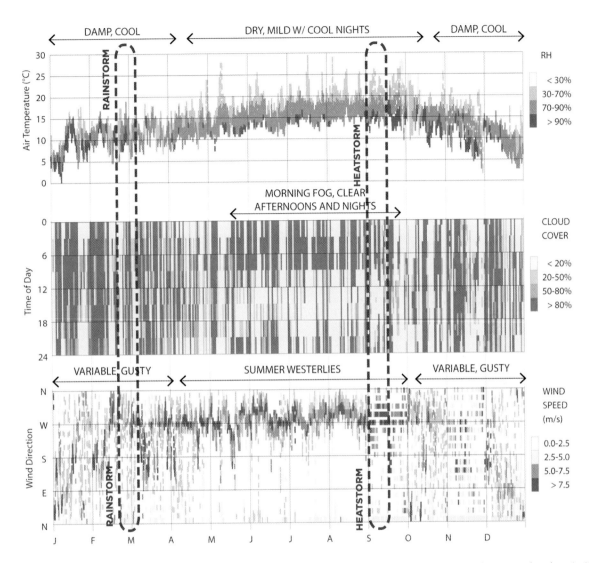

Figure 5.9: A snapshot of Oakland, California's climate using typical meteorological year (TMY) data to make clear to the client what Loisos + Ubbelohde is doing when using the climate file as an input to energy simulation. © *Loisos + Ubbelohde*

My interest in using computational tools stems from my interest in predicting building performance and anticipating the experience of a place, not only in terms of what it looks like or how light might propagate, but in terms of what it feels like. Simulation is a powerful means to this end but, importantly, it is not the only one. Our practice emphasizes the validation of simulation results, which means that we want to know that we are simulating phenomena that exist in the real world. We have validated both our daylighting and thermal predictions to within very narrow bands. This increases our confidence in our simulation methods and allows us to get into cutting-edge regimes of performance—because we understand the underlying physics and can trace results from fundamental principles.

(Continued)

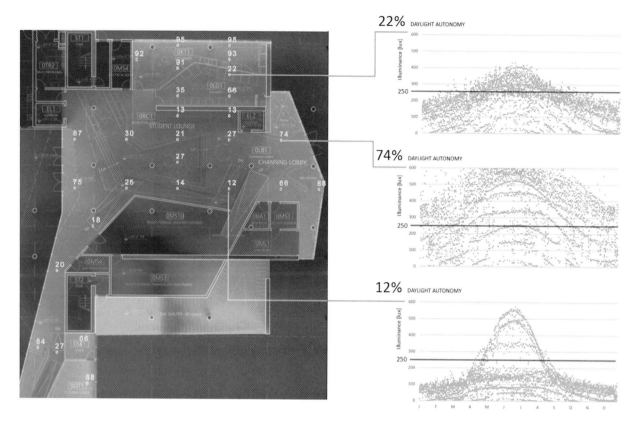

Figure 5.10: A graphic technique created by Loisos + Ubbelohde for a dormitory in Berkeley, California, for electrical lighting design and daylighting. Image shows a value engineering proposition. © *Loisos + Ubbelohde*

Why is data visualization important and to whom is it important?

BL: Good data visualization is a means to better understanding the underlying patterns in large amounts of data. This is important to anyone who cares about understanding data. Our brains have a hard time processing more than about seven numbers at a time. However, we can see patterns in an image that represents millions of numbers. Who is this important to? Anyone who is curious about the world. [See Figure 5.11.]

There are many ways to visualize data. Why use computational tools for data visualization?

BL: In many ways, computer-based visualizations are a poor way of visualizing data. They tend to be homogenous and boring. One of the goals of Dhour was to bring back some of the art of visualization that comes with hand drawing. When you draw by hand you have more control over line weight, hierarchy, and composition. In addition, you have a greater propensity to edit out what is less important. Many of the problems of modern-day data visualization stems from the use of computational tools.

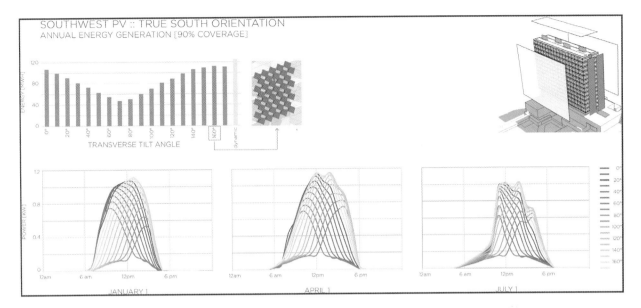

Figure 5.11: A visualization looking at the potential for building integrated photovoltaic (BIPV) systems that would shade the building as well as generate energy. The visualization asks: What would be a good angle for the PV versus investing in dynamic PVs? © *Loisos + Ubbelohde*

Of course, there are advantages to the computer processor, namely the ability to deal with very large amounts of information and the ability to mass-produce visualizations. The problem we set for ourselves was to combine the best of both methods by bringing our training as graphic designers, architects, and analysts together. [See Figure 5.12.]

The message about data-driven design has to be that experts are required for their expertise and that a digital model does not hold the expertise, the experts do.
—Brendon Levitt, Loisos + Ubbelohde

Who really needs to hear the message of data-driven design?

BL: For too long, architects have been hearing that they need to be experts in everything, from climatology to structural engineering to materials science to financial modeling. This is not realistic and it's not desirable. The result is often misinformed and lacking in suitable complexity. BIM has come along and promised to resolve this. Now, architects are relying on software companies to supply expertise. This is even worse.

The message about data-driven design has to be that experts are required for their expertise and that a digital model does not hold the expertise, the experts do. Data, in whatever form it's presented, is only as useful as the people who understand it and can apply it. [See Figure 5.13.]

Can you describe a project where use of data led to an improved decision or insight?

BL: We have thousands of examples in our practice. We did some work on a school where the architects and engineers had anticipated that the classrooms would need a substantial HVAC system to handle overheating. Using a detailed

(Continued)

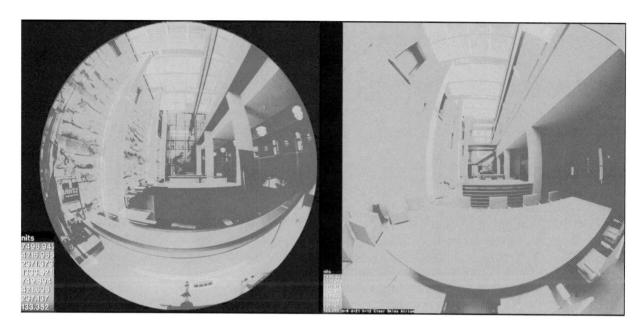

Figure 5.12:   The image on the left is a photograph using high dynamic range (HDR) photography. The image on the right is a simulation using software for predicting daylight performance. The impressive thing about them is that they correlate so well. © *Loisos + Ubbelohde*

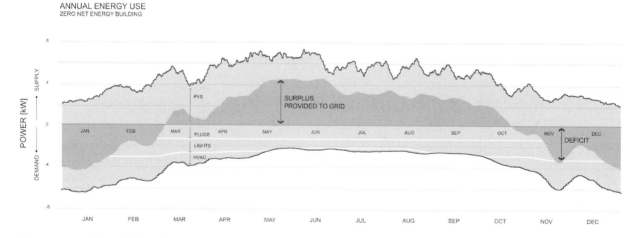

Figure 5.13:   A description of energy generation versus consumption. Below the middle line plots how much energy will be used for various uses versus how much energy can be generated using PV panels. © *Loisos + Ubbelohde*

thermal model, we assumed that the building would have no heating or cooling systems and we simulated the resultant indoor temperatures over the course of a year. We found that by increasing natural ventilation, installing ceiling fans, and shading the windows, indoor temperatures stayed in a comfortable range. This not only saved money for the school district, but it improved comfort conditions for the students.

This is a success story that illustrates why BIM can be dangerous without the correct expertise. The architects and engineers used the tools available to them and came to their conclusions based on a combination of their experience and the data-driven results from those tools. As experts in high-performance buildings, we came with an entirely different approach—one that valued the building envelope as a primary filter for comfort. We used a purpose-built building information model to help us prioritize envelope improvements and subsequently to quantify the expected performance. In addition, we used custom data visualizations that emphasized the role of thermal comfort to help us communicate the results to the client. The difference in approach may be subtle, but it is crucial.

Dhour Case Study

Brendon Levitt and Kyle Steinfeld taught a class called Building Performance and Visualization, where they encouraged students to use Dhour to discover how the performance of a case-study building might be improved. One student group looked at the potential for increasing occupant comfort during the summer through cross-ventilation and night flushing of a studio art building in New Haven. The resulting drawing is shown in Figure 5.14. The team searched for a graphical method that would help them to understand the potential for reducing the number of hours of mechanical cooling. They used conditional logic in Python and graphical overlay techniques to arrive at an answer.

First, a wind map was created showing the magnitude of hourly wind speed through each day (*y*-axis) and year (*x*-axis). Then, using a post-processing script for adaptive thermal comfort, hours that were too cold were masked out while hours of comfort were muted. Hours warmer than comfort were color-coded to show the magnitude of wind speed. These hours then became the focus of subsequent studies focused on natural ventilation strategies.

Once the team understood that wind would be available and accessible for cross-ventilation, they simulated and visualized the resultant comfort conditions. These heatmaps chart the degrees from comfort for each hour of the day (*y*-axis) and year (*x*-axis). Blue values are degree-hours too cold, yellow-red values are too hot, and light gray indicates comfort. A summary histogram reports the number of hours at each degree from comfort. The progression from "Base Case" to "Daytime Cross" shows the decrease in overheating hours. Overheating is decreased further by considering evaporation off the skin due to increased air movement when cross-ventilation is present. The data was post-processed with a script that increases the upper threshold for comfort by 2°C for any hour with cross-ventilation.

Above each comfort graph is a simple line graph that reports the volumetric airflow rate for the analysis zone. This line graph explicitly shows the increased airflow with cross-ventilation, and, importantly, allows for the correlation between airflow and thermal comfort. It also served as a diagnostic check to ensure the simulation was running correctly.

By allowing cross-ventilation during occupied hours and night flushing during unoccupied hours, the number of overheated hours was reduced by 78 percent (from 2462 to 557 hours). Both the graphical methods and conditional logic enabled by Dhour were key to this exploration. The team was able to mask out extraneous information and then superimpose an overlay rich with the information most pertinent to their exploration.

They were also able to post-process the raw data with a conditional logic that expanded the scope and specificity of the energy simulation results. Through a juxtaposition of graphics, both in sequence and in type, the team was able to see direct correlations between a given strategy and the effect on occupant comfort.[4]

(Continued)

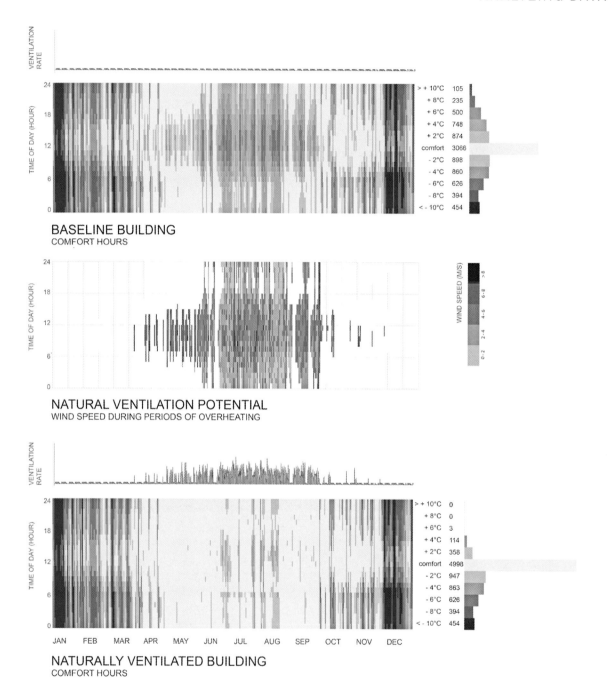

BASELINE BUILDING
COMFORT HOURS

NATURAL VENTILATION POTENTIAL
WIND SPEED DURING PERIODS OF OVERHEATING

NATURALLY VENTILATED BUILDING
COMFORT HOURS

Figure 5.14:   Natural ventilation diagram from a class called "Building Performance and Visualization" in which students were encouraged to use Dhour to discover how the performance of a case-study building might be improved. © *Joyce Kim and Oscar Diaz*

Analysis versus Synthesis

Producers of Knowledge, Consumers of Data

"As brokers of the built environment, architects are dealing with data continuously," says Billie Faircloth of KieranTimberlake. "And many times that data is veiled as practices. When it's given to us in the form of building product specs, it means that someone is doing an experiment on our behalf. And it has generated data that comes to us as information about having to use something." She continues:

> The position I am taking with data in this question is: architects should be producers of knowledge, and not merely consumers of knowledge. We can actually be in the position to produce knowledge. Meaning that we not only have to measure things, quantitatively and qualitatively, but we also have to be in the position of synthesizing and analyzing those things, producing knowledge from the data that we collect. We passively receive bits of data throughout the process chain. We receive it. We consume it. We can be much more conscious about what we're working with, how we're working with it, where it came from—the provenance of the data, so to speak—and whether or not it is really what we need. We can also be much more conscious of the questions that that data answers versus the questions that we are actually asking.

Bad data is worse than no data. Formulae are bad. Emphasize analysis over data.

—Gregory Janks, Sasaki Associates

Analysis Is a Central, Integral Part of Working with Data—and with Design

Who—in terms of role—on the project team is most receptive to decisions backed by data? Is any role less receptive to data-backed decisions? Do firms experience differentiation in internal project team receptiveness by role or discipline? "It is much more a personality thing," says Gregory Janks. "The meme of 'analyst versus designer' is likely as old as time, and is not, for us, particularly meaningful. Analysis is part of design (or is it vice versa?), and the best folks quickly understand this. Of course, there are always traditionalists who are less receptive; and of course, there are business consequences—think, for example, when the recommendation is *not* to build—which can cause understandable resistance." Analysis is a necessary step, in other words—but synthesis is not complete without the act of applying the data, which is the subject of Chapter 6.

Notes

Unless otherwise indicated, quoted text throughout the book is from interviews with the author that took place between February and July of 2014.

1. Mads Jensen, "Preamble: On the use of data and data driven design and performance-based design in the design of high-performance buildings," as provided to author, May 2014 (unpublished).
2. www.aecbytes.com/viewpoint/2014/issue_69.html
3. http://readwrite.com/files/files/files/images/tech-adoption-lifecycle.jpg
4. Brendon Levitt, excerpted from "Dhour, a bioclimatic information design prototyping toolkit," conference proceedings from ACADIA 2013, Adaptive Architecture.

chapter **6** Applying Data

Data-driven design is about presenting options, not answers. And some options are all about making people happier.

—NBBJ's Computational Design Team

So far we've mined and analyzed the data. Now it is time to apply it. This chapter explores first steps and best practices for applying data, and suggests who in an organization best works with and leverages the data they have available to them. (See Figure 6.1.)

First Steps

How can firms take the first steps toward applying data in their practices? How is it recommended that firms make the change to become more data-

Figure 6.1: Application of data is action-oriented, arriving after data has been identified, mined, analyzed, and visualized. © R Deutsch

centric? Where, in other words, do they start? How much is technology and how much is mindset? Can firms do this on their own?

Firm Size and Project Size as Factors

How do firms take the first steps toward applying data in their practices? Brian Ringley suggests that firm and project size are factors in how firms take first steps with data. "Firms have a variety of approaches to the integration of big data into their practice based on the size of their practice and the scope of their work," says Ringley.

"It's likely that larger firms will develop in-house expertise and disseminate through a central tech studio, or via decentralized tech leaders within large project teams, whereas smaller firms will look to external resources and consultants." Ringley acknowledges that how data is applied raises challenges beyond firm and project size:

> It's a bit tricky though, as the precedent for this approach, found in the integration of computational and BIM technologies, has been largely software or tool-based. A data strategy, on the other hand, can lie both within software workflows and completely outside of them. Not only do firms face the challenge of developing a general culture of data awareness,

they also have to be concerned with the practicalities of its mining, integration, and, eventually, its proof of value to the client.

Strategy No. 17: First Steps before Applying Data

1. The first steps a design practice can take are to educate its workforce on the existence of and reasons for the performance gap while communicating the benefits the practice and industry at large can receive by sharing data.
2. Secondly, firms should take steps to record design, management, and performance data—for medium to large projects, this process may be made more efficient with the uptake of BIM.
3. Finally, the practice should put steps in place to share their data.

—Gregory Janks, Sasaki Associates

Start with a Problem

To recommend how to get started in applying data, Clayton Starr of RTKL uses the recovery program analogy. "The first step in treatment is admitting you have a problem. Some firms can do this on their own, but not many," advises Starr. "There are highly intelligent people out there who run very effective consulting services that are beginning to address, at least, the technological needs of the team. There also needs to be a commitment at the top levels of your company and a real investment into personnel that can help teams achieve the project goals."

Brian Skripac of Astorino agrees that firms can do this on their own. "You just need to realize that big data is everywhere; it's not something that's inaccessible," says Skripac. "The more you learn about it, the easier it is to grasp this idea. To get started you to have a problem or question that needs to be solved and realize that big data can help provide the answer. It's about transforming the mindset or culture of how to use technology and merge that with the capabilities in your organization. Once you're able to do this, the expertise will cultivate internally since its value will become immediately apparent."

Some suggest that teams seek assistance when first starting out. "In the broadest sense, I have always been amazed by sole proprietors—those who work by themselves," says Robert Yori of SOM. "I've always needed to bounce my ideas off of somebody. From the earliest days of architecture school, it was always about communicating and understanding and getting feedback and criticism. No matter your situation, I would recommend at least talking with somebody about it. It's always good to have somebody to talk to about it."

Get Particular: Address Concrete Problems

Once the mindset of those who will be working with the data and capabilities in your organization have been determined, the next step is to pinpoint what problem specifically you will be addressing—and what specific data will help you arrive at a solution. "If we sit down and think about how we design," says Ringley, "there are specific subsets that are of particular importance." He provides two concrete examples:

> Urban data—not just GIS but noise and crowd behavior—environmental data—not just solar data but also data on hurricanes, on flooding. There are concrete examples and that is the obvious starting point. That gets us conversant in the use of data in the AEC industry. Then, as new datasets become relevant, or as innovators make them relevant to the benefit of the industry, that can happen more and more quickly.

Strategy No. 18: Plan for the Data

Clients and building owners will be the first drivers of this step. It can be a big impact for a firm to take, in time, staff, software, training, and process changes. Having a successful client delivery will help AECs think about the owner's data in a new way.

Owners' need for data varies greatly, both in what they need and how they want to use it. For a team to successfully see the data live through a project and come out on the far side can be very eye-opening. Seeing and finding the path that information needs to follow through the life of a project, all the software changes, team changes, design and scope changes, will help better shape how the firm can change their practice.

I typically see firms trying to solve this as a software choice. Framing this as a process change and structuring your teams around the change is a better way to look at making a change.

Change should start small, and with a project that has data in mind. The end result of being data-centric is to plan for the data.

As an example, think about doors. Almost every design project has a door, or many or several thousand. And yet, each project has a different set of doors, different kinds, different schedules, different way of numbering, and different codes or standards to uphold. Being data-centric is not having a Revit door library, nor is it sheet standards for door templates, details, hardware, and schedules. When used well, those help. This is also the kind of data most firms have, but may not all fully leverage for individual projects, or across the firm.

Being data-centric for a design firm is setting your digital tools and libraries to be visual representations and repositories for data. What information does the digital image of a door hold? Are there links and paths from the door to schedules? How connected is your software to a single database? How many places would you need to make a change to a door number? Can you query the data? Is the data held separately from the visual image of the door (if you delete the door, does the data go with it)? The framework remains while the data and information may change. Having many fields to hold future data is important as well. How many names and numbers will one door have? Room number link, door number during design, door number during construction, door number for the building owner, door name and number for the local department, door number for facilities management team. They all point to the same door. The data needs to live throughout the project, still point to that door. Post construction, some information will need to live on, while some may not need to be carried forward.

—Jill Bergman, Healthcare Principal and
Vice President at HDR

The Right Tool for the Right Problem

Many of the individuals interviewed for this book continue to work with Excel in their application of data on building projects. Depending on the project scale and scope, Excel may be the right tool to use at the right time. "Understanding how and when to use the potential of Excel is important," says Robert Yori.

And once you use it—you want to be motivated to do so. Understanding the informational components behind the graphic output that you are getting, even if you are just doing 2D or 3D CAD. Revit, or any building information modeling (BIM) tool, is a barely concealed database. If you begin to get the sense of that—that they are all very structured databases and good starting points—you're off to a great start. Unfortunately, the tools are normalizing the data through a rigorous input process, which is the cause of many frustrations. But they do normalize it, and they do offer a level of consistency, which is great— especially if you're not quite sure what you want to do with that data. At least you have a clean, useful dataset and can begin to analyze it, start to ask it things. Then you begin to see the benefits. From there, you can progress further in a less guided, less restrained fashion.

Case Study Interview with Billie Faircloth

Billie Faircloth, AIA, LEED AP BD+C, is the Research Director and an assòciate at KieranTimberlake, where she leads a transdisciplinary group of professionals leveraging research, design, and problem-solving processes from fields as diverse as environmental management, chemical physics, materials science, and architecture. She fosters collaboration among disciplines, trades, academies, and industries in order to define a relevant problem-solving boundary for the built environment. Billie was the keynote speaker at AIA Seattle's Data-Driven Design Forum (2013.)

Describe KieranTimberlake's approach to working with data.

Billie Faircloth (BF): We are data-nimble. *Data-nimble* means that we are first conscious that data is infrastructural to all of our efforts—it is latent in our actions; intrinsic in our selections, keystrokes, and forms; it is implicit or explicit in our simulations. Such consciousness is extended to the practice position of being able to accept data produced by others, to question and query data, augment, and expand it. It is likewise extended to our position that architects should produce, not merely consume, knowledge. Data-nimbleness is an essential first principle because design is a multivariate endeavor. When one designs, his or her power lies in the inscription of a boundary around that "data" that will and will not participate in the design process.

What role does data play in the answer to the question, "Why do we build the way we do?" and is the emphasis on geometry, building performance, human performance, or organizational performance?

BF: The emphasis in the question "Why do we build the way we do?" is on all of those things. The question is provocatively and perhaps productively broad. While I might want to constrain its emphasis to, for instance, how pieces and parts of a building go together, or to the logic of their assembly, or to their resultant form, this question when approached broadly allows us to challenge the range of the boundary we inscribe. The question might also provide a glimpse of the entire design endeavor as we begin to realize that as we design, we broker. I for one immediately begin to think about materials, the mass flow of materials—where they come from and where they are going. I wrestle with our role as "customer" in the building products supply chain, as my mind begins to search out an alternate relationship to the transformation of matter. And time—the definition of "real time," a working definition for "time," is pressing. "Why do we build the way we do?" positions us to dissect not only our role and where we situate ourselves in the act of "building," but it also challenges how we engage design as much as it challenges us to consider what might participate in and constitute the act of design.

As data is infrastructural to how we practice design, it is thus intrinsic to exploring an answer to the question, "Why do we build the way we do?" Architects manipulate data continuously. Often data is veiled in "practices," or simply the rituals to which we are habituated. We passively receive bits of data throughout the process chain. We receive it. We consume it. We can be much more conscious about the data we're working with, how we're working with it, where it comes from—the provenance of data—and whether or not it is really the data that we need. Does analysis of it actually help us answer the questions we are asking? And, when we take up the position to produce knowledge, we might just become authors of datasets and thus challenge our "practices." We begin to measure and survey—quantitatively and qualitatively—and to analyze and synthesize to produce knowledge from the data that we collect, and we do all of this as part of the design process. [See Figure 6.2.]

Research has been described as the core enterprise that drives the production of KieranTimberlake. Does your research group operate as a separate entity within the organization? Or is it integrated into project teams?

BF: Searching and searching again is integral to our whole organization. We constantly move and assess our practices to ensure that this is the case. We've built practices that permit, for instance, a materials engineer to sit alongside

Option 1 - Corrugated Shingle Cladding   Option 2 - Translucent Panel Cladding (Selected)

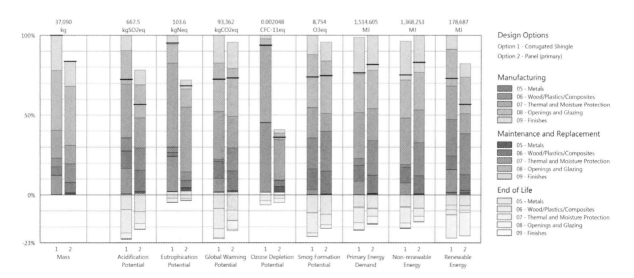

Results Per Life Cycle Stage, Itemized by CSI Division   © KT INNOVATIONS

Figure 6.2:   Options explored using Tally with results per life cycle stage itemized by CSI division. © *KT Innovations*

(Continued)

an architect and for both to engage design. We remain suspicious of any tendency to treat each other as consultants, or the tendency to solely provide expert advice. We put the question that we're asking, and the problem we're trying to solve, or the design that we're pursuing, in the middle of the table and let these differently knowledged minds at it, let them play with it. Fundamental to this approach is the belief that the methods and knowledge bound to these other skill sets are absolutely applicable to the products of the design process. Fundamental as well is the belief that designers are not exclusively trained as architects. A wireless sensor network, a software tool, a building envelope, or a whole building—in our estimation each one of these requires holistic thinking and thus a transdisciplinary approach in order to overcome some bad practice habits. [See Figures 6.3 and 6.4.]

Figure 6.3:   Wireless sensor network. © *KieranTimberlake*

How do you recommend firms make the change to be more data-centric? Where do they start?

BF: Because we are a research-driven design firm, and our projects can be defined in many ways, we've come to understand the question mark as infrastructural to our practice. Each individual at KieranTimberlake has the agency to use it. A firm might begin by legitimizing the question mark and dedicating resources to pursue a thriving question-asking culture. The application of data is inseparable from the presence of "infrastructural question marks" in the sense that we have the agency to advantageously query data.

We might then proceed to inventory the data that we practice with daily. Where is it? Who authored it? Why was it collected? One of the most surprising and straightforward datasets resides in our energy models in the form of a TMY3 dataset (Typical Meteorological Year, version 3), which describes the climate of a place using the past 30 years of data. Engineers routinely model and simulate our designs in the context of this dataset. But which site/space/place does this dataset describe? Is it our building site, is it the regional airport, or was the data collected in a valley while our concern is a ridge? Should we accept this numerical climatological description of our "site," or should we pursue practices that might allow us to become more certain of the data? Recognizing that TMY3 data embodies time, should we play with it so that we might engage prediction across other time scales? An energy model is predictive, and is poised to generate design feedback—right here our opportunity to pursue data consciousness and to design with data resides. Just as the TMY3 dataset already impacts products of design, so do other datasets.

Our design culture is equally process driven, data driven, and research driven. When asked "how," I decidedly come down on the side of mindset.
—Billie Faircloth, KieranTimberlake

What mindsets do you recommend others develop in order to work with data?

BF: In a management sense, a firm might ask, "If I begin to think this way, what are the risks? How much will this cost, financially and otherwise?" Yet, I find it difficult to speak in this "sense" and on the behalf of other

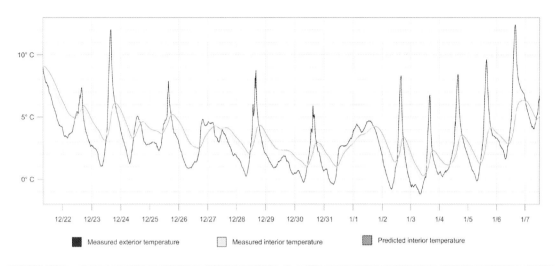

Figure 6.4: Wireless sensor network. © *KieranTimberlake*

(Continued)

designers—design includes the design of process. Stephen Kieran and James Timberlake design processes as much as they design buildings. They orient themselves to design through question-asking. They are the original sleuths in this firm—they are the original question askers. I would not be here, directing searching and searching again, if it weren't for their disposition to orient themselves to the design process and data in this way. Data is synonymous with question-asking. As a result, our design culture is equally process driven, data driven, and research driven. When asked "how," I decidedly come down on the side of mindset.

What in your background prepared you for working in a data-driven practice?

BF: I didn't take a computer apart. My dad is a contractor. I started working with construction document sets around the age of 11 or 12, unrolling them and marveling at their bulk. I rifled through the sheets and tried to decipher the abbreviations and the instructions, even as I helped to produce as-built sets. I spent the ages of 14 through 18 working directly in his construction firm, which was our family's business. Early on I had to dissect specifications in order to ensure that we procured the proper material or product, and as I engaged architectural education I became increasingly suspicious of the provenance of materials information, especially those that were mash-ups of acronyms and numbers. To sleuth is part of my genetic make-up. I can't help but ask, why do we do the things that we do?

Is there a KieranTimberlake project where the application of data yielded insights or results that the project otherwise might not have had?

BF: In order to answer your question, I will define *application* broadly because I interpret this question linearly and prescriptively, as in "apply data and voila!"—surprise, discovery, serendipity—perfect architecture.
I will provide an example where the application of other "practices" resulted in the creation of a dataset, which when analyzed, provided insight into the true nature of the design at hand, and a reminder of that boundary we are prone to inscribe around the "data" that will and will not participate in the design process. [See Figures 6.5 and 6.6.]

I refer to our green roof vegetation study, which began with the simple question: "What's going on up there?" This question erupted from the mind of a colleague trained in environmental management and ecological thinking when he happed to spy what appeared to be a mass of "volunteer vegetation" on a green roof that had been installed some years previously. He hypothesized that given what appeared to be unmaintained growth coupled with new species, the roof performance had likely changed. Other colleagues, one trained in both architecture and environmental management, and one trained exclusively in environmental management, but both with studies in urban ecology, took up the challenge to determine how the performance of the roof had changed. They were equally desirous to demonstrate an ecological/architectural approach to the roof, as ecology has a way of bringing thinking over time to the fore more readily.

They proceeded to devise a novel survey method, and to "practice" that method for this roof as well as all of the other roofs we had installed previously, explicitly mapping where vegetation occurred and what type it

Figure 6.5:   Green roof vegetation study. © *KieranTimberlake*

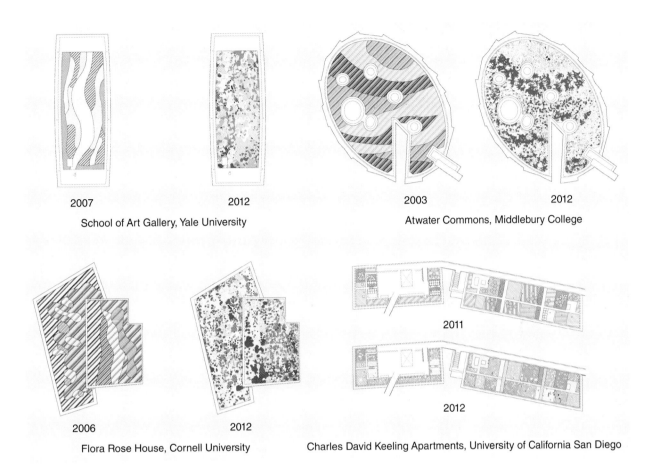

2007   2012

School of Art Gallery, Yale University

2003   2012

Atwater Commons, Middlebury College

2006   2012

Flora Rose House, Cornell University

2011

2012

Charles David Keeling Apartments, University of California San Diego

Figure 6.6:   Green roof vegetation study. © *KieranTimberlake*

was. We did this for two years in the same or nearly the same season each year. As they began to analyze the collected data and to compare the pattern of vegetation to the original planting plan, they could easily observe the formal differences, and they could number the new "volunteer" vegetation. But they were surprised to find evidence of a richer story about the intersection between ecology and the act of design. For instance, they could make direct correlations between species density and roof form, as the roof had a way of trapping water in certain areas. They could likewise make correlations between light regimes—overshadowing, for instance—and species density.

In other words, what they discovered was a more thorough description of the variables at play in the design of a roof that supports a layer of vegetation. These maps helped reveal to us the system of relationships between the form of the roof, vegetation species and density, roof hydrology, climatological factors such as temperature, humidity, and precipitation, and roof maintenance regimes. Engaging practices this way—be they characterized as data intensive or not—might just position the act of design to become that much more meaningful.

Data-Enabled Project Teams

What does a data-enabled project team that can benefit from the data available to them today look like? Is it very much like the team a firm currently has in place? Are there missing players? Are architects going to sit side by side with hackers and algorithm builders? Data-driven Aditazz, for example, employs computer scientists, architects, engineers, and applied mathematicians. How close is this make-up to what the industry's future integrated project teams will be as we enter the data-driven age?

"We think we're on the right path," says Aditazz's Zig Rubel. "We also know we have a long road ahead of us and know that as a project requires unique experience, our team will morph and change."

What about for self-described data-informed firms? "More and more, we, as an industry, are seeing computer scientists working with architects and architects pursuing computer science postgraduate degrees," says Greig Paterson of AHR (formerly Aedas). "The Adaptive Architecture and Computation (AAC) masters at The Bartlett, UCL, is an example of a course that caters to a broad range of disciplines who are interested in architecture, computation, and data." Paterson continues:

> In my time at AHR, I have worked with architects, computer scientists, engineers, energy analysts, and physicists. Collaboration between industry and academia has also been central to many of the R&D projects at AHR—a relationship that I am very much part of as I am undertaking a doctorate at The Bartlett, UCL. Multidiscipline groups have been successful at AHR and I see it as the future in medium to large architectural firms. [See Figure 6.7 and 6.8.]

KieranTimberlake is another firm that relies on multidisciplinary groups to achieve their data ends and benefit from the data that is available to them today.

"We have built and will continue to build a trans-disciplinary team inclusive of skill sets and ways of thinking from, for instance, architecture, design, sculpture, environmental management, urban ecology, green infrastructure, materials engineering, chemical physics, electrical engineering, or digital signal processing—as we pursue a process that surrounds our projects with the information, data, knowledge, and methods that they require," says KieranTimberlake Research Director and Associate Billie Faircloth.

"Right now in our office we have architects sitting side by side with individuals who are prone towards scripting, coding, computer science, and digital signal processing. The overlap or subset of knowledge that exists between myself (trained solely as an architect) and these individuals is a wonderful subset, and I am still in the position of understanding the differences and compatibilities between my 'design brain' and, say, the 'computer science/coding brain.'" She continues:

> Some of these individuals have dedicated their education exclusively to these skills, and some of them are trained as architects. We might call them "hackers" or "algorithm builders." But I can equally observe that as our office leverages iterative processes, optioning, and collective intelligence, we also leverage a quality of design education that often remains unnamed, mapped, or explicitly taught. Design education immerses us in the enjoyment of multivariate problem solving. This begins with the first design studio. We might not be aware of the process by which our design brain emerges as our neurons are remapped to engage this type of problem solving. Overtime, we increase our capacity to hold many things in relationship to each other at once. Intrinsic to our education, to design, is "hacking" and "algorithm building." There's a wonderful pedagogical and curricular shift

Digital Middlemen

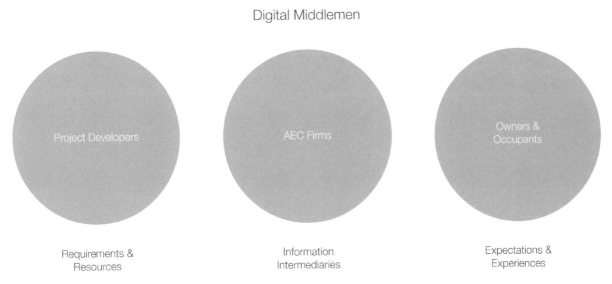

Figure 6.7: Information intermediaries act like digital middlemen between project developers and owners and operators. © R Deutsch

Digital Middlemen

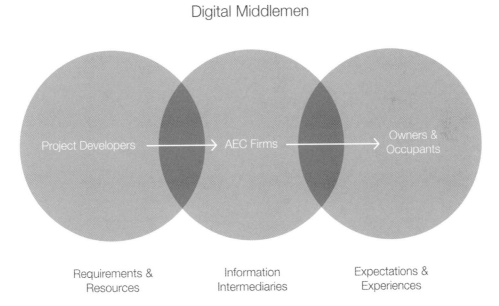

Figure 6.8: Information intermediaries serve as digital middlemen integrating and linking data throughout the project life cycle. © R Deutsch

that is happening in many schools of architecture that recognizes and formalizes this intrinsic attribute of the design act in a number of ways.

I asked Andrew Heumann, Leader of NBBJ's Design Computation team, if we will recognize the design team of tomorrow. "Absolutely, teams look different, at least in the short term," says Heumann. "New, data-empowered teams need programmers and specialists in the kinds of data being generated/analyzed. That means statisticians, computer scientists, environmental scientists, but increasingly also social scientists who can help make the link between data and lived, human experience." Heumann goes on to describe the team member of the future:

> In the long term, I think—at least from the standpoint of the technical ability to code—it will become less of a specialization and more of an expectation of all players in the game. Just as today any productive member of a team is expected to know how to use the Internet, productivity applications, email, relevant CAD software, and so on, the team member of the future can easily manipulate large datasets and write automation routines with some form of code. The line between using an application and scripting for that application is only going to get blurrier. Designers, engineers, project managers, administrators will all benefit from being able to manipulate information in the form of data.

Data Specialists vs. Data Generalists

The collection and analysis of data can be taken on by more generalist team members, though there are advantages to using data specialists when applying that data. "It's not just about getting the data in. It's about scrubbing it, preparing it, getting it ready," explains Sean D. Burke. "Normalizing data

in a way that it is predictable is very challenging. The people who are responsible for this don't do it on a regular basis, so it's probably taking them a lot longer to do. End designers who are wearing multiple hats." Burke considers the make-up of future teams:

> We'll probably need some folks who are data management specialists, who can quickly transform the data we get from the client, in whatever form it might be. Sometimes you get spreadsheets, sometimes you get databases, sometimes you get text in a PDF that came from Word. It's very hard to work with a lot of that stuff. Even when it is in Excel, they're using Excel as a report card rather than as a database where each row is a unique record. Where they're setting it up for presentations, it's very hard to course through. Having a database architecture manager in an architecture firm that is doing things that are part of the project vs. people in IT who do that by connecting to accounting. Nobody is doing it for the design work. It's just a matter of time, a very short time, before that becomes an absolute necessity.

[See Figures 6.9 and 6.10.]

Gregory Janks of Sasaki says their team includes mathematicians, computer scientists, English majors, economists and business folks, social workers… and planners and architects. "Unfortunately, there is no school for what we do," explains Janks, "so we have had to be creative in our hiring practices, and to dream up tests we can give to people from a myriad of backgrounds. We care about what you can do, not what your degree says." In considering the make-up of future teams, Clayton Starr of RTKL believes "it's a different team, or at least an augmented version of our current structure." He lists the missing players, emphasizing the need for specialists:

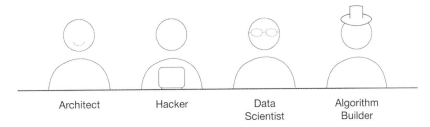

Figure 6.9: Architects today increasingly work alongside specialists: hackers, data scientists, and algorithm builders. © *R Deutsch*

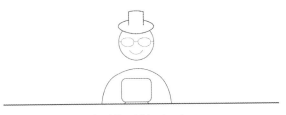

Figure 6.10: Data-informed architects think like hackers, data scientists, and algorithm builders. © *R Deutsch*

Computer programmers, customizers, scripters, and analysts. So often, designers are confronted with what would be a data-driven problem to solve, and proceed to solve it with methodologies that cannot begin address the problem. Or, at least they understand what it would take to solve, but haven't the knowledge or expertise on how to solve it.

Chris Pyke of USGBC anticipates that teams will change due to the fact that "buildings will increasingly be asked to perform in operation across their entire life cycle." Pyke continues:

This performance will need to be demonstrated with data, increasingly collected in real time from sensors and individuals (e.g., citizen scientists). Traditional, AECO teams will need new skills to create, manage, and interpret these increasingly diverse and per-

vasive data streams. Architects will maintain a central role on these teams only if they adapt their practice to demonstrate results that are reflected in real-world data. Consequently, AECO teams will evolve to look more like those used in Agile software development: lean, dynamic, ephemeral. However, there will always be limits to this analogy. Construction is a risky business with strong path dependencies. This is different from software.

Strategy No. 19: Should the Data Team Be Integrated or Stationed in the Corner?

In Chapter 2 we met Jonathon Broughton, a data wrangler situated in the corner at Allies and Morrison. When people in the firm want to engage him, they go to him as they would any nonintegrated resource within the office. Is this the best setup to ensure that data is successfully applied on projects?

"You have to go under cover in an office," says Brian Ringley, squarely on the side of embedding data individuals on teams:

The unfortunate truth is, I could start slinging my guns about computational design, fabrication, all these amazing weird-looking things I've done. That's not going to get you where you need to go. You just have to play the game which is, at every

(Continued)

firm, the people who are in charge of hiring, money, and being responsible to the firm, the future, and to the client, I want someone with infinity years of experience, who knows BIM, and drafting. Because that's really safe. So, know those things just enough to get by. Within project teams, the opportunities for technology are everywhere. There are inefficiencies within traditional design processes. There are certainly inefficiencies within BIM and Revit itself. Then start innovating just on the project level. That's going to be a more long-term benefit. Because the problem is that the firms that don't use consultants, who have in-house teams, can always be seen as frippery. These people can be hidden moles, secret agents within project teams. They're innovating on that level. This shouldn't be a high-tech team. This should be architecture. This *is* architecture.

In favor of the data expert in the corner is David Fano of CASE. "We've built technology that makes it easier. But it's really just a mindset," explains Fano. "You'll go to some firms and see some guy tucked away in the corner who keeps a spreadsheet with metrics of every project they've ever done. It's really just a way of thinking. Excel is fine. A notepad would be fine. It's more thinking of information as this resource that you can go back and reference."

Benefiting from Team Diversity

Firms benefit creatively from having a diverse cross-section of individuals. Team diversity can also have a positive impact on outcomes when working with data. "One of the things that we need to do a better job of on our website, especially as we go after RFQs,

are the various degrees we hold," says Evelyn Lee of MKThink. "We have a rocket scientist, we have a lot of analysts, we have a psychologist, we have a cultural anthropologist and mathematicians. It is truly a diverse firm and I believe more firms would benefit greatly if they brought in other individuals from different backgrounds." Lee expanded on this line of thinking: "If architects want to be at the table, when it comes to sustainability or what is happening to the future of our cities, they'll need to find themselves partnering with people from other backgrounds. There will be more models where all of the partners of the firm will not be architects. They may be sociologists or biologists or economists as partners in the firm. That will enable them to think a little more broadly about things that are of value to the client. That's where I feel things are headed."

Zig Rubel concurs. "Diversity in team composition is especially the case at technology firms," says Rubel. "Because they're constantly asking the question, what is needed? They need to have a wide range of perspectives to know what is required."

If designed well, suggests Sefaira's Mads Jensen, software ought to do away with the need for across-the-board diversity from the earliest stages onward. "Cross-functional teams are powerful, but every building project cannot have five specialists involved from the get-go. The good news is that—if the software industry does its job—the AEC industry won't have to try to fill the gaps we've left. The objective is to create software that is so good that architects can create great buildings without needing to become computer scientists."

Case Study Interview with Andrew Witt

Trained as both an architect and a mathematician, Andrew Witt is a designer whose work explores the interrelationship between perception and topology, as well as the relationship of architecture to deductive and convergent methods encapsulated in digital processes. He is Research Advisor at Gehry Technologies (GT was acquired by Trimble in 2014) and Assistant Professor in Practice in Architecture at Harvard University, where he teaches geometry and digital design. He was previously a director at GT's Paris, France, office, where he consulted on parametric design, geometric approaches, new technologies, and integrated practice for clients including Gehry Partners, Ateliers Jean Nouvel, UN Studio, and Coop Himmelb(l)au.

What role, if any, does data—and the ability to share data—play in the success of GTeam and your other efforts?

Andrew Witt (AW): Data has to be made intelligible before it can be shared, and data which is intelligible for one use may be noise for another. I do think the amount of raw data produced as collateral to a project is not a bounded quantity. You can be producing 1 terabyte of data, 50 petabytes of data, 6000 terabytes of data. Unless it's made intelligible, data is really nothing but noise. Part of the challenge in the AEC industry is that data should be filtered and interpreted in the context of specific actions. As much as anyone, we can fall into the trap of thinking that data is information in the sense of being informed and shaping decisions. But without a framework for whether that data is relevant for a particular action, it becomes noise. There's an important duality of data noise in our information culture.

What in your background contributed to your having the unique skill set and mindset to work at a high level in both design and technology?

AW: Around the data/noise question, having a mathematics background gives you very structured, methodical ways to transform noise into data and ultimately information. It gives you some specific ways to signal-process. What a lot of people interpret as data mining is really an evolution of signal processing, something that grew out of military tactics in World War II. What's the most effective way to respond to a particular kind of system behavior documented through data? Without a mathematical background, it's more difficult to understand the ways in which data might inflect information or the way in which the underlying behavior can be variously interpreted. Among the things that I apply from my mathematics background in architecture are statistical methods, which are ways of understanding what data and datasets are actually relevant and telling a story. It helps classify what kind of data is relevant and which is distracting. The shape optimization techniques that we developed are really about interpreting the signals. Particularly when a large or undifferentiated amount of data is produced, that sort of statistical or signal-processing expertise may be necessary to create meaning around data. This may happen across a single project or multiple projects. There's probably more opportunity to extrapolate information from behavior across dozens or hundreds of projects, or even at an industry scale. With a single project there may not be enough data to make generalizable inferences about what the data means.

In statistics you have samples, but you have to take a variety of samples before those inferences can be significant and accurate. There's this problem called the Founders Effect, where if you sample only a very restricted population, then your inferences about the general population are going to be super skewed. Maybe there is some call for deep analytic work, but probably more at the industry level than the project level.

I was always fascinated by computation. My dad worked as an engineer. He would bring home computer spare parts. My brother and I built computers as kids. We were always fascinated by Pascal and programming. I was 10 or 11 years old at that time. From there we were interested in fractal geometry, programming fractal generators.

What are some of the companies that can structure unstructured big data?

AW: Probably the best examples are the most impactful examples, the ones that come closest to aggregating huge but homogenous datasets. Companies like Zillow, or Redfin, people working in the real estate industry. These are super-homogenous datasets. They're a big and an impactful way to analyze data in terms of very specific financial

(Continued)

positions. One of the challenges of building information is that there is so much of it that is not relevant to any specific strategic decision about a project. It's a little hard to separate the forest from the trees. There are some opportunities for companies that can begin to sift through and remove the extraneous data around the project relative to a specific decision. This helps support those decisions in a very light and insightful way. I guess I would rather have a building insight model as opposed to a building information model. Building information models don't really support decisions as much as they just support the production cycle of the project, which is also valuable. It could be that all of the information is relevant for some decision. But most of it is irrelevant to most decisions. It is a challenge to begin to facilitate decisions with the right information.

Big data's not a surgical tool. It's a blunt instrument.
—Andrew Witt, Gehry Technologies

What are your thoughts about today's emphasis on data and big data in AEC?

AW: Just because things are momentarily at the forefront of our consciousness doesn't mean that they're necessarily a fad. But we may not yet understand what the impact of those things is, big or small. Time will tell. One of the things I always think about in terms of big data, especially as it is relevant to the building industry, are statistics I saw a while ago about the relative efficacy of smart cities. The study suggested that many city systems could be improved up to 5 percent with smart monitoring. Five percent is not nothing, but maybe you're not restructuring the way everybody is doing things and framing whole new industries. That is way less impactful than I would have thought. Big data is an incremental way to give broad information around genericized datasets. Big data's not a surgical tool. It's a blunt instrument. My intuition around big data and the construction industry is it's something that will be helpful, but I don't think it is going to be some new Theory of Relativity. There will be a more objective way of thinking about those large-scaled trends. It's going to talk about trends. It's not going to talk about the specifics of a particular project. It will give us a more informed framework in which to make generalized decisions. It's a step toward a more objective understanding of the building industry.

My intuition around big data and the construction industry is it's something that will be helpful, but I don't think it is going to be some new Theory of Relativity.
—Andrew Witt, Gehry Technologies

Will architects be asked to do more coordination of data and information?

AW: The coordination of information in a general sense—drawings, schedules—is not new, but the variety of representations of information is definitely new. There's been a huge explosion in the way information has been represented. So there has to be some facility in the media of information. But it is easy to overstate the value of information management on the building process. We're maybe asked to manage or produce more information than is necessary for the execution of the project. There's a negative correlation between the amount of information that's produced for a project and our ability to understand that information. All things being equal, I don't think anyone wants to be coordinating more information. But having information that's digitized means that the coordination can be more automated. Most of that coordination can become machine-enabled. That's more attractive than the role of the architect as an information coordinator.

Before information coordination can be automated, [the information] has to be standardized and homogenized. In effect, it has to be made into big data. You have to take information from all of those sources and regularize them in such a way that it's automatable. This is where platforms like GTeam play a role: They make the information mutually interoperable, so that automation is possible. Ultimately, our goal should be to automate as much of this as possible, and in fact minimize the active role we need to play in the information management process.

You've mentioned that GT acts as a digital-data referee. How so?

AW: In concert with clients, we would establish the rules for data transactions. We'd also regularize the process of data exchange. We assured that data was pure, that it had the proper integrity, that it was exposed to the right parties. There's some aspect of persuasion that's in play there. That was a human dimension to what we are doing.

You said that in 10 years people will be sharing vastly more information than they are now. What primarily will this be attributed to?

AW: It's the opportunistic availability of both data and the means to share it. It's not necessarily based on some new requirement to share. There's a greater and greater expectation of higher and higher fidelity communication. People will have the means to execute high-resolution communication. People won't necessarily be communicating more frequently. But the resolution of that communication will be much higher.

Have you seen a change in the use of algorithms for building performance or other impacts of building design, such as human performance?

AW: There has been a greater and greater interest on the performance side of things. That's been facilitated by the fact that there's more formal flexibility in the building geometry. Would it be possible to talk about an impactful building performance if there wasn't some generative or parametric logic to the building itself? They're two sides of the same coin. This is something that has been evolving since at least the 1960s or 1970s, when computational models also had these performative, generative aspects. Performance always impacts geometry. And geometry is rarely explored as a pure indulgence in itself.

Given the choice, would you rather talk geometry than performance?

AW: Owners are human and they're motivated by a range of objectives. Data facilitates a better understanding of the implications of pursing those objectives. There's definitely a danger that decisions based on data can feel a little inhuman. But in the end humans are always making those decisions, so there's always the prerogative to override the data. Information is another thing on the table. In few cases is it the sole arbiter of decisions. [See Figure 6.11.]

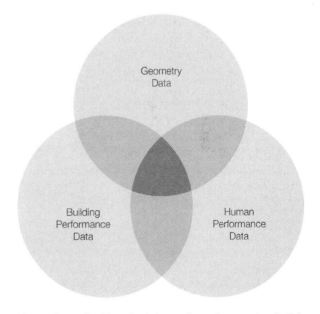

Figure 6.11:   Seeking the intersection of geometry, building performance, and human performance. © *R Deutsch*

Data-Intensive Roles

Most of those interviewed for this book believe that building project teams will include programmers, coders, computer scientists, and data scientists, in addition to—or in lieu of—the occasional data wrangler. This will have implications not only for human resource departments, but also for education and training, because design and construction professionals will need to learn how to work on integrated teams with data and computer experts.

Andrew Heumann of NBBJ is of the mind that the place to start is with understanding. "Designers first and foremost need to understand [data's] potential," says Heumann. "Not everyone in an organization needs to be a facile coder—but everyone needs to know the right kinds of questions to ask. A familiarity with the way algorithms and data 'think' is critical—to being able to identify opportunities to employ them, to apply them effectively, and crucially, to not over-promise or over-estimate what they do."

Programmers, Coders, Computer Scientists, and Data Scientists

Some confusion has already been brought about by the prevalent use of the title *architect*: data architects vs. architects who use data. Michael Kilkelly is one architect who has always liked the *information architect* moniker. "In a lot of ways that's what architects do," explains Kilkelly. "We manage information and the flow of information and the distribution of it. It's too bad the web guys got to it first. It wouldn't necessarily be a full-on coup to take it back." He continues:

> Working at Gehry's office, the position I was hired for was Information Architect. They were looking for somebody who had a technology background but who was also an architect. Someone who could in essence manage the flow of information for this one particular proj-

ect. That was what drew my eye when I saw the opening. This is a little between both.

Architects will need to learn how to code in order to bridge role gaps, believes Marco Hemmerling, Professor at Detmold School of Architecture. "Indeed, the profession of the architect is changing rapidly," says Hemmerling. "New partners/advisors come in play that bridge the gap between design and construction using latest technologies. Programming will become a core competence in our field since it enables the connection and integration of various data/information, independent from the given software platforms."

NBBJ's Sean D. Burke sides with hiring someone who has a computer science background "because the way that they need to interface with the data is quite limited. We just need to outline the strategy for what we need to do. They'll learn more about design as is necessary," says Burke. "It's a rare individual who's going to be able to be a trained designer or licensed architect and also be a database administrator and do that effectively, because there are so many other pressures on their time."

But is it an advantage or disadvantage to hire a data person from the data science/analytics realm over an architect with analytics skills? Mark Frisch, FAIA, Managing Principal at Solomon Cordwell Buenz, describes the ideal data-driven candidate. "Some of what I am talking about are skills that everyone should be familiar with," says Frisch. "Project information needs are constant; in order to gather it, store it, and access it every architect should have a fundamental understanding of information processes." He adds:

> Further, in many offices there is the need for an information specialist. Ideally they would have a thorough background in information management and the associated tools. In order to be strategic, they need to understand how to apply the information, which requires

that they understand the architectural needs; that is, they should be very familiar with the architectural working process. I think that this position lives outside of the traditional information management group and is more closely allied with the library. I might have a harder sell (with my partners) on creating a totally new position—not because it's overhead but because nobody understands its value. The people in the more traditional data-intensive silos such as our CFO are understood. On the other hand, project data management has not been around long enough for offices to understand where or whether it fits in."

I might have a harder sell with my partners on creating a totally new position—not because it's overhead but because nobody understands its value.

—Mark Frisch, FAIA, Solomon Cordwell Buenz

Frisch continues:

The same question could be asked about what is the best background for a visualization specialist; are they architects trained in graphics or are they graphic specialists working on architecture? We have one of each. The truth is that the one with no architectural background approaches the work with a graphic sensibility and the one with an architectural background tends to be interested in the newest technology. They're both good. They work very well together and with their complementary skill sets produce a very rich and ever-evolving product. In the case of data, I don't know if it's an architect who understands all the things that we do and has a real affinity for data, or someone who understands analytics and applies it to architecture. If I could only have one, I would probably start with the former.

Strategy No. 20: Computer Scientist vs. Emerging Professional

There are going to be situations where firms have that computer science person on board. Is the three-person firm going to do that? Probably not. It's going to be more the role of the "emerging professional." Look at what technology capabilities emerging professionals have, especially coming out of school. That is what the value of a BIM leader is, too. It's not just somebody who is technical, both the BIM leaders and emerging professionals need to embrace their T-shaped personalities. It's a continued reflection on the profession's transformation from a traditional CAD manager role to today's BIM leader position. A CAD manager was someone who taught you AutoCAD and focused on things from only a software/technical standpoint, but they could have been positioned in an architecture firm, an engineering firm, or a civil firm. It wouldn't have mattered. Today we see individuals who have a much deeper understanding of the practice of architecture and know how to apply technology to that practice. That needs to continue to evolve with how we can apply technology and translate data from one spot to another. That's where emerging professionals are completely savvy and able to do that. That's where the opportunity is going to be. That allows the industry to take advantage of it. It doesn't matter if you're a small or big firm. Emerging professionals have that knowledge or expertise which needs to be harnessed and taken advantage of.

—Brian Skripac, Astorino

Jonathon Broughton of Allies and Morrison wrestled with the data person's title for a while. "Data architect," after all, is already taken. "There isn't a good word to describe what it is what I'm doing," admits Broughton.

Data scientist isn't it. I'm not trained as a data scientist. There are people who are coming out of universities trained in it. Data scientists are being hired by architecture firms—but I don't think that's where the opportunity is. What I can bring—maybe because I'm an architecturally trained person—is different. We shouldn't be spending a great deal of time on people who can deliver us pure analytics because all they're going to give us is the answer to the question we give them. We need to be putting emphasis on those people who will give us the right questions. One of the things I think I can do is intuit the right questions for people.

The Data Wrangler

Allies and Morrison is made up of qualified architects working with urban designers, and furniture, product, and interior designers, as well as technical specialists, in-house model makers, graphic designers, and architectural visualization teams. Jonathon Broughton is a Design Technology Specialist and self-described Building Data Wrangler. "Design Technologist has the most resonance outside of Allies and Morrison," says Broughton. "That is why I have that as my title. My official title is Data Wrangler and Specialist Modeler. I'm trained as an architect but quite deliberately don't describe myself as one. Technologist can mean working out where the grommets are and how not to let water into the building. Inside the office I don't use that word."

Data wrangler: Funny handle, but is there any truth to it? For example, we once said big data required crunching, but it can be ungainly and unstructured: is *wrangling* a better metaphor? "It is," says Broughton.

Big data hasn't been properly assessed within our part of the industry. It isn't about live, real-time monitoring and social streams. Big data, as I understand it, is grappling with the fact that people are, whether they know

it or not, generating information and generating data. The reason why it is "big," it is not huge quantities as such, but it is massively unstructured. That's because so many times it's depending entirely on who has generated it. While we technically all have the same means of production, we all theoretically have the same sort of deliverables. Ultimately every single person in my organization as well as others I am exposed to, including clients, will make ad-hoc, bespoke data models that briefly fit the purpose. Just because they are unstructured, and just because they are disparate and bespoke, doesn't mean they don't all have meaning. The wrangling side is about knowing where to look and knowing how to filter and offer insight. It's very easy, incredibly easy, with the tools that we have to build really, really, really data-rich haystacks. What we need—and what's missing in our industry—there's a real need for those people who know, maybe instinctively or have a hunch, where the needles may be. And it's those sorts of people that need to apply rigorous algorithmic analyses using analytical tools. Go find me those needles, but what we don't need is people who are just really good at making very good haystacks. [See Figure 6.12.]

Finding Talent to Work with Data

Why would someone with a computer science background go to work in the AEC industry? "For me, the main outcome of my research was to suggest that there is a strong connection between the practices of programmers and architects," says Daniel Davis of CASE. "I expect as more in the AEC industry come to work with data and computation, these connections will become even stronger. So I guess my advice is to look outside the profession; much of what we are trying to do has already been done in some capacity elsewhere." For Davis, "it is

Design as a Filter

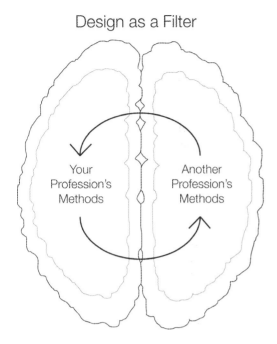

Figure 6.12: Design serves as a filter enabling you to think in terms of others. © R Deutsch

important to differentiate between someone who's good at what they do and someone who's an expert at what they do. We're talking about a tenfold factor of productivity. Because they're not hiring a good person but an exceptional person. There's only a small number of highly skilled people who have an enormous impact on this industry." CASE's managing director, David Fano concurs. "The challenge for our industry is going to be attracting people like Daniel—and frankly, most of the people who work at CASE—to do what we do," says Fano. He continues:

> Folks that are interested in the problems that we're interested in typically don't pursue the careers that we did. There's a specific career path where you pursue some role in the building process because you like buildings or design or creating stuff, and at a certain point you make a very deliberate decision counter to industry pressures to make a career shift.

We work in an industry where, if you pursue architecture, you're looked down upon if you're not the napkin sketcher. You ask students what they want to be—none say they want to be the project architect or project manager. "I don't want to be the technical guy who does the detailing. I want to be the napkin sketcher." That will have to change at an academic level and at the institutional level, such as with the AIA. Contractors don't have this pressure as much. Architects, by accepting specialization and acknowledging that the process is so complex, need to realize it's not just about the napkin sketcher.

"One of the things that we've been trying to do at SOM is to make sure that the folks that we hire have an understanding of the fundamentals of computation," says Robert Yori.

> But we realize not everybody is going to be a computer scientist. We like scripting to be a requirement for entry to our firm. Not because we want everybody to be the rock star. We want our teams to be able to understand that approach. Even if they're not able to do scripting or computation, or data management or hacking to some expert level, there's an understanding of that procedure and how others may be able to execute those things. And then, of course, we will also have those who are highly interested and computationally skilled, leading the teams' and studios' efforts. We look to converge their skill sets rather than keeping them divergent.

"I also don't want to be purely data people," admits Fano. "I absolutely believe there's a place for gut and instinct. I do believe the people who can straddle both and make the judgment calls are going to be the ones who'll be the new breed. These are the type of people we have been fortunate to attract."

How does the AEC industry attract people from computer science? Why would someone with a computer science background go to work in the AEC industry? "Especially when it pays a third of what they were making in their respective industry," says Jonatan Schumacher of Thornton Tomasetti. "We have one computer scientist—after eight years working for a bank he developed some software and came back to work in structural engineering—who is the brains behind a lot of our data. It is obviously hard to find these people. If I were to give smaller firms advice, or firms that don't hire computer scientists, Grasshopper with Google Docs or Google Spreadsheets or Fusion Tables—everybody can do that." Schumacher continued:

> This person wanted to do some real, physical projects. We were lucky. There is obviously a large difference between creating software, or crunching numbers, and designing buildings that will live on for decades, which is attractive to some. It is very hard to find a person who can understand automation but also the subject matter. Sometimes we think we should just hire computer scientists. Obviously, we can't pay them what Google pays them. But get somebody who would otherwise work at Google. We had an intern last year who had two computer science degrees. It was very hard to work with him. He was so far removed from the reality that we are still dealing with paper and drawings—boring stuff. It didn't make any sense to him, coming from a different industry. But it is unfortunately the reality. There needs to be somebody who can at least understand how things are done here. Teaching concepts of computer science to architects and engineers helps us. Most of the people in the CORE studio are Stevens Institute of Technology graduates, and many of us have taught and recruited from here in the past.

"The problem is with the way companies are run, they don't even think about what it would mean if our companies were 20 percent computer scientists and 80 percent engineers," says Schumacher.

> So many big firms could easily support internal research (as small as 0.5 percent), but it's a rarity if they have three people doing research. It's mind-boggling. When you look at our industry, and then at what Google has spent on R&D, for Google it is 13.5 percent. For the AEC industry, it's close to 0 percent. At Thornton Tomasetti, we have 15 people in our CORE studio team, half of which spend their time pursuing R&D tasks, in addition to a healthy annual firm-wide R&D budget for all employees. This is a very big budget for an AE firm. But it is pretty rare—in fact I can only think of Aditazz and one or two other firms with a good dedication to R&D.

"Anywhere where there's a need for technology, where it's not being implemented, there's opportunity," says Jennifer Johnson, Senior Director of Product Development at Reed Construction Data. "It's really the responsibility of the different firms to say this is the direction we are going in, we are going to be about using technology, and we're going to have to attract some smart people with some experience in this arena who are willing to think a little outside the box." She continues:

> I didn't come rushing to the construction industry. I started off in product management. From a software perspective, like what we're in here at Reed, to be a really strong product manager in the technology field you have to have a technical background. You have to understand what the capabilities are of the software and the technology that is out there today. You have to be able to think of ways to exploit that for the industry in which you work.

There are certainly successful technology product managers who don't have that background, but it gives you a definite advantage to think in a much different way. Combining your technical aptitude with certain element of business savvy-ness. Then triangulate that with the customer pain points. You suddenly start thinking about the data that you have and the ways that you would access it much differently. You would start to get really innovative in how you would start to solve problems that really shouldn't be that hard to solve. You've got the data. There's got to be a way to expose it at the right time and to the right people to help them with their workflow. Sometimes it just takes having a customer who's willing to go on that journey with you because oftentimes the solutions for some of our largest customers don't exist. We're saying we have access to this information, or we can buy that information, and I've got to find a way to put those things together and envision what that would look like when loaded on an iPad app. Sometimes that's as much as you have going into it. When you have somebody who thinks the technology is interesting, and who thinks the data is interesting, someone who thinks that the customer problem is interesting—those three things together are really interesting. It's up to the firms to have to pull the technologists into our industry.

Case Study Interview with Greig Paterson

Greig Paterson is a researcher at AHR (formerly Aedas.) His thesis, An Environmental "App" for Architects: Utilizing Artificial Neural Networks and Real-World Data to Predict Operational Energy Consumption of School Buildings Based on Early Design and Briefing Decisions *addresses data use in the AEC industry.*

How did you go about collecting architectural, engineering, and social data from hundreds of schools in England?

Greig Paterson (GP): The aim of my research is to create the prototype of a user-friendly, early-stage design tool that predicts operational energy consumption of school buildings based on the training of artificial neural networks with real-world data. To give some background: It has been argued that traditional building simulation methods can be a slow process, which often fails to integrate into the decision-making process of nontechnical designers, such as architects, at the early design stages. Furthermore, research, such as that carried out by CarbonBuzz, highlights the fact that the actual, measured, energy consumption of buildings regularly exceeds design predictions, often by more than double.

Dr Judit Kimpian from AHR (formerly Aedas) led the development of CarbonBuzz. CarbonBuzz is a crowd-sourcing platform for tracking energy use in buildings from design to operation. The website enables users to upload design, briefing, and energy data in order to compare predicted and actual energy use of their building projects against data from projects entered by other users. The aim of the platform is to show the difference between predicted and measured energy use and help the industry address the sources of this discrepancy.

In view of this, a user-friendly design tool is being developed in the form of a simple "app," which predicts building performance in real time as early design and briefing parameters are altered interactively. As a demonstrative case, the research focuses on school design in England. Artificial neural networks (ANNs), which are a subset of artificial

(Continued)

intelligence, have been trained to predict the heating and electricity energy consumption of school designs by linking measured energy consumption data from the building stock to a range of design and briefing parameters.

The measured energy data used to train the ANNs were sourced from the Display Energy Certificate (DEC) database. Hundreds of schools were chosen from the DEC database based on a set of selection criteria. For each selected school building, geometric, fabric, site, occupant activity, and building services data were collected using various resources, such as digital map software and available databases, such as those offered by the Department for Education. The collected parameters included surface exposure ratios, floor areas, glazed areas, number of pupils, ventilation strategies, and heating degree days.

The artificial neural networks have learned through observations of real-world data—a technique that may help reduce the performance gap between predicted and actual energy consumption. [See Figure 6.13.]

What tools do you use in working with data and what recommendations would you make concerning these tools?

GP: I use MATLAB for the majority of my data analysis. MATLAB is a high-level programming environment for numerical computation. I use the neural network toolbox within MATLAB to train, test, and optimize artificial neural networks. Once I have trained the networks, I export their "weights" to Processing in CSV file format. Processing is a programming language based on Java, designed for the arts and design community. The data visualization and user interface aspects of my research tool are created in Processing.

The strength of Processing is the ability to visualize data with a great amount of freedom. The strength of MATLAB is the ability to organize and analyze large datasets. The online community is considerable for both tools, so I would recommend watching online tutorials, reading user forums, and downloading examples when using these tools. [See Figure 6.14.]

How would you describe AHR's data approach?

GP: The discussion of data-informed versus data-driven is one of semantics and often discussed within the tech industry. Being data-driven is when decisions are made based purely on data. Being data-informed allows for design intuition and engineering wisdom to accompany the analysis of data. A danger of being data-driven is that data is often

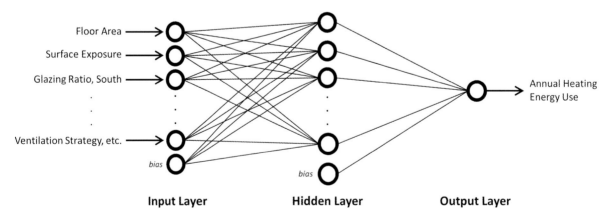

Figure 6.13;   Conceptual structure of the artificial neural network that predicts heating energy consumption. © *AHR*

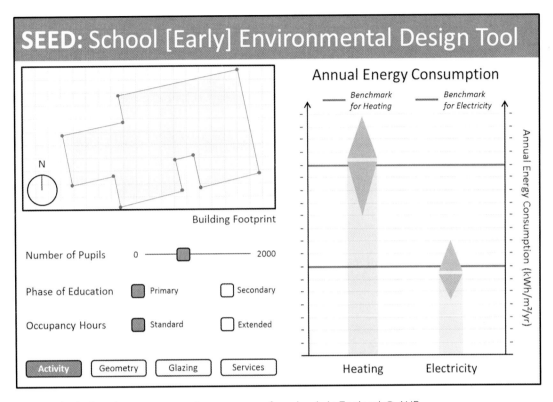

Figure 6.14:   Early design stage energy performance app for schools in England. © *AHR*

biased in some way. Certain micro-decisions of building design may be data-driven, such as when generative design techniques are used, where, for example, the positioning of a modular shading system is optimized based on the path of the sun. However, these computer-generated decisions should be used in conjunction with intuition and experience to keep the project moving toward its global goals. In this way, I prefer the term *data-informed*.

AHR as a practice has been informed by data for a number of years and parts of projects have been driven by simulated data where necessary also. A major source of AHR's information comes from the conclusions of postoccupancy studies, which helps ensure that aspects of a design project that more commonly increase the performance gap are given special attention. AHR is also involved in the creation of bespoke design tools that use real-world data, rather than purely simulated data, to make more accurate energy consumption predictions and thus help designers make more informed design decisions.

Describe a project where use of data led to an improved decision or insight.

GP: Keynsham Town Hall in England is a project where we agreed at the briefing stage to achieve a Display Energy Certificate (DEC) A rating. That is, our goals are based on how the building performs once in operation, rather than how it performs in design predictions alone. The postoccupancy work we have been involved in has helped us target various aspects of the design process to minimize the performance gap, such as ensuring design changes are well documented and commissioning of HVAC systems is adequate.

Leadership in Data

Many design and construction leaders don't know their firm's data capabilities—the talent, the technology, the processes and workflows. What will it take to enable this awareness? Will firm leaders tell their data stories the way they have been telling their collaboration and technology stories? Most importantly, who will lead the data effort within an organization? Who, in other words, will be the glue? (See Figure 6.15.)

"The first reorganization of the traditional design team is to merge the BIM leader and the project architect," says Jill Bergman of dsk architects. "The project leader must be, or must partner on the same leadership level with, the tools expert. I see many young talented design professionals, so well versed in the tools of their craft, and either hiding it, or mak-

Statisticians
Computer Scientists
Planners
Environmental Scientists
Customizers
Design Technologists
Scripters
Analysts
Sociologists
Biologists
Economists
Physicists
Data Scientists
Strategists
Researchers
Mathematicians
Programmers
Coders
Architects
Engineers
Designers
Contractors

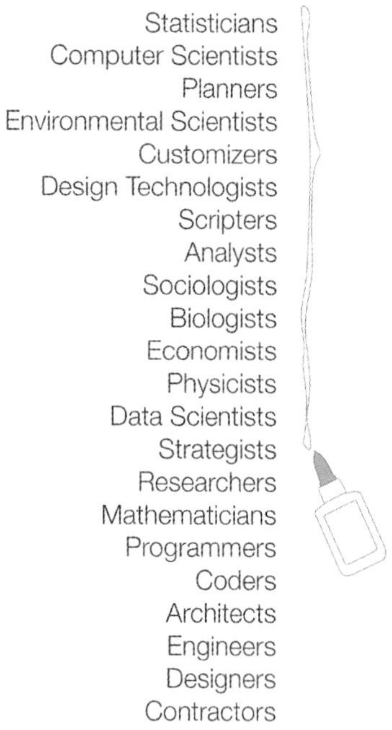

Figure 6.15: Who will define and hold the team together?
© R Deutsch

ing a very clear expectation that they see being a BIM leader as a career-ending path. We need to stop separating the two and merge tool knowledge with building knowledge and give value and reward with leadership." She continues:

> There can be a lot of distraction by adding team members without that leadership in place. An expectation of having a coder or hacker to aggregate building data, without having the full team understand how every step of work they are doing will aid or impede that data path, is a plan for frustration.

Data and Human Behavior

The question of how the AEC industry will adjust to increasing work with data raises a lot of questions. Can data be crunched into a form that can be analyzed by nonexperts? Or will architects and other design professionals need to adapt to working with, and even alongside, analytics experts? If so, how will architects adapt to working with "quants"? Is there a precedent for this situation that architects can learn from and model? If so, what is it?

"To some degree, architects will be the data hackers," anticipates Sam Miller, Partner at LMN and LMNts. "We've always been in this position of diving into the detail of what it takes to create a space or a building that performs in however way we define the performance. In that sense, we're kind of hacking into the code of the building and the code of the program and coming up with a solution. And this will continue. We won't just be sitting among, but to some degree, becoming those coders and finding those solutions. Manipulating the tools to create great spaces."

How can the data be used to achieve the greatest benefits and outcomes for those involved? Reliable, rich data helps architects to do their jobs more effectively and productively, to win jobs and remain competitive, to convince clients to go down a design path, to increase value for owners and reduce waste for the environment.

What are the implications for using manufacturers' data-rich BIM objects that have embedded data and can be dropped right into a building project? When is it appropriate to do this—and when is it best to modify the content?

What are some of the challenges for utilizing data, and the barriers to its use? There are several obstacles: securing commitment within teams and the organization, reinventing internal and external processes, and modifying organizational behavior are just a few. Who will do this?

What are some of the human factors that must be addressed before the use of data design and construction becomes habitual? What skills have to be developed? What training should occur? What are the most effective ways to go about training, learning, and unlearning past behaviors and paradigms? What are the mindsets and behavioral changes that design, construction, and owners' organizations must make to become data driven? What role does intuition—even art and craft—play when data comes to drive the most important of our decisions on building projects?

Communications Director at KieranTimberlake, Carin Whitney, describes the firm culture that enables them to think and act differently. "When Billie [Faircloth] speaks about the way we work here, she's very much speaking about the way it is right now, today, and where we're headed. It's important to note that this was cultivated extremely consciously." Whitney continues:

> The people who lead this firm are very deliberate in evolving behaviors. Some of the behaviors and processes that we use weren't always in place. Something that Billie has done since she has been here has really keyed into how we can think differently. We talk a great deal about how we can think differently and act differently. And it is not without its challenges. These shifts do not come without challenges. With maybe having these things not work across the board. And having to check and recheck. Part of the culture here is to stop and say when things aren't going as planned and what needs to happen in order for those things to change.

Notes

Unless otherwise indicated, quoted text throughout the book is from interviews with the author that took place between February and July of 2014.

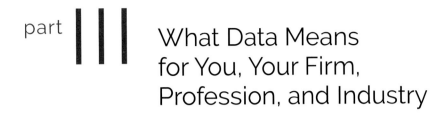

part **III** What Data Means
for You, Your Firm,
Profession, and Industry

Not only are data abstract and aggregative, but also data are mobilized graphically. That is, in order to be used as part of an explanation or as a basis for argument, data typically require graphical representation.
—Lisa Gitelman

Responses to the Question "Why" Will Either Convince or They Will Not

To convince, subjective predilections and preferences have to be backed up with facts, figures, and statistics. Numbers sell. On Twitter, what gets retweeted are tweets containing numbers.

Yet, if all professionals needed to do to make their explanations seem plausible, or their arbitrary predilections seem inevitable, was to sprinkle them with statistics, working with data wouldn't be necessary. It is not enough for decisions to seem plausible: they must actually *be* so. This is where data comes into play.

Many professionals subsist on habits, traditions, conveniences, caprices, prejudices, and specious arguments. Justifications today vacillate between rationalizations and logical proof, conjecture and evidence, intuition and facts, hypotheses and knowledge.

The most effective method for justifying one's decisions consists of appealing to something independent of one's choice, then grounding it in the particular situation, circumstance, or context. When asked to justify a choice, you are not being asked for a historic reconstruction or recounting of how a decision came about. Rather, you are being asked to frame the decision in a larger framework—one that is more objective, public, social, and shared. These require descriptions.

Decisions must be grounded in readily available data, not in personally held beliefs. In fact, design and construction professionals not only design and build buildings, spaces, and places, but also design justifications and build arguments for their actions. And they increasingly do so using data.

chapter 7 Data in Construction and Operations

There are literally hundreds of applications for deep analytics in planning and design projects, not to mention the many benefits for construction teams, building owners, and facility managers.

—David Barista

This book addresses the leveraging of data throughout the entire building life cycle. How can data be applied in the construction phase? When you look at data in design, construction, and operations, the design and operations phases form bookends, each making ample use of available data. Can construction do the same? "You say that data is being incorporated most heavily in the bookends, less so in the middle," says Sam Miller of LMN and LMNts.

But as that model is making its way through, you're going to start to see more and more capturing and leveraging of data in the construction process. It's going to happen. One area is materials. There's a significant body of work that needs to be done in terms of information about materials, performance, life cycle, value and from a sustainability standpoint. Information about what makes up the materials, their safety, that sort of thing. That's one area where the construction piece can start to capture that. Because if you start to track materials in construction, then you can start to get good life cycle information about

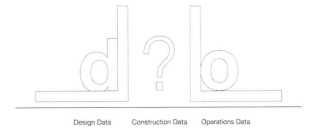

Figure 7.1: When you look at data in design, construction, and operations, the design and operations phases form bookends, each making ample use of available data. © R Deutsch

materials: information that could be really useful for designers and owners. That's one area where there needs to be a lot of movement.

Later in this chapter, we'll have Mani Golparvar-Fard explain how he tracks materials in construction. (See Figure 7.1.)

Design and construction professionals are actively searching for ideas for leveraging data to improve construction quality. Data from earlier phases can be applicable to the construction phase. "For example," says Tyler Goss of CASE, "the near-ubiquity of wi-fi and smartphones helps us understand occupancy and utilization with exacting real-time detail—and this data is as applicable to the construction phase." The real value of data in construction lies in providing contractors and others at the site with real-time, or near real-time, access to cost, schedule, material validation, and installation data. Even the collection, analysis, and reporting of real-time weather-related data can have a positive impact on construction outcomes, especially when preexisting channels for gathering data are used. Data—and the attendant information, knowledge, and insight—enables better decisions to be made in the construction process. As Goss stresses, "Better data leads to better buildings, which is ultimately better business for all of us."

Construction companies have advantages that others in the industry cannot claim. "My experience is that construction entities are much more interested in virtual, digital building technologies and analytic processes than are design firms," says David L. Morgareidge, Predictive Analytics Director at Page. In short, he explains, "If they don't adopt these strategies, they'll lose their shirts." And yet old-school construction culture gets in the way of data having a greater impact, and sooner, at the construction site. Construction culture requires proof—essentially a guarantee based on past outcomes—that a proposed technology or use for data will work. Designers are comfortable working with ambiguity and uncertainty—a necessity when working with data. Construction workers . . . not so much. Those in construction require unwavering predictability and certainty. They're generally not willing to take chances on the unproven. Ongoing management of construction projects continues to this day to be based on habits at worst and best practices at best, and not the near real-time/right-time feedback that data can afford. Furthermore, due to its risk aversion, construction tends not to invest adequately in information technology, training, research and development, or innovation.

We have seen that, to the extent that data—and its associated tools and processes—are already readily available and don't require additional training, equipment, or hardware, the more likely it is that data use in construction will catch on and succeed. Media such

as photographs and video taken at the construction site are two examples where existing technologies can be leveraged to extract valuable information for construction. The thinking goes, once the economic benefits of utilizing data on the construction site (including the automated monitoring of construction progress from one day to the next) are shared and proven, it will catch on. Once a number is applied to the data surrounding the reduction of waste on the jobsite, construction executives will listen.

Data in Construction

Before Deepak Aatresh founded Aditazz, he was a computer chip designer. "What led him on to focus on construction was that he watched a time-lapse video of a construction site," explains Zig Rubel, "and realized that the way they make buildings is the same way they make chips. Just a different scale." Aditazz currently utilizes computer chip design processes for the planning and construction of healthcare facilities. In which of the three stages—planning, construction, operations—is there the most interest? "The most interest is in the project conception phase," explains Rubel. "Our clients want to make sure we're building the right building. Today, a lot of decisions are based on spreadsheets. They are rules-based—based on data—at a very rough level of refinement. We're able to take it down to much more detail granularity and illuminate some of the nuances they wouldn't have otherwise seen." (See Figure 7.2.)

Data in Construction Lags Data in Design

The focus on construction begins at the design stage. "We're focused on how buildings get built and what the complications will be on the construction side," says Jonatan Schumacher of Thornton Tomasetti. "This is why we want to run these kinds of studies during the design phase. Because there's a much greater likelihood that the building will get realized, compared

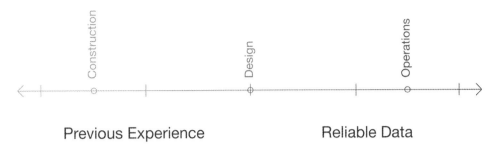

Figure 7.2: Construction historically relies on previous experience and practices over and above reliable data. © R Deutsch

to other high-end engineering firms that mainly work in the conceptual phases of a project." He adds:

> We do this proactively. We have a division called Construction Support Services. They detail the model to the point where the fabricator can order and process all of the steel, and understand every weld, nut, and bolt detail. It's not just structural engineering. It's not just: here's a member with these forces. It's: this has been designed this way because of these forces acting upon the beam. We usually work in Tekla because the fabricator also works in Tekla. We have worked with Digital Project for the fabrication of façade panels. Even if we don't get hired for this initially, we always keep in mind that maybe down the line we will be hired to create a fabrication model. We always design with fabrication in mind, and the quality of our 3D models reflects this from the start.

Strategy No. 21: Construction-Related Data Questions

Data use in design and data use in operations form bookends. How can construction make equal use of data?

Construction is of limited duration compared to the typical lifespan of a building—but we know the goal. In other words, it is not an open-ended process.

We could begin broadly by asking:

> Which data matters in order to construct?
>
> Which data is generated during construction?
>
> What kind of data could be collected such that it becomes a feedback loop or moves the industry toward a certain set of goals?
>
> —Billie Faircloth, KieranTimberlake

"Generally speaking, the goals that we articulate for ourselves during construction are related to productivity and quality," says Billie Faircloth of KieranTimberlake. "I would be curious about what kind of data a contractor could collect." Faircloth continues:

> We know contractors collect data about cost. But as contractors procure they also work in the middle of real-time mass flow. And they have to procure the proper material or product at a point in time. They have no capacity to wait or delay. There's something about their capacity to interface with the market in time, and then collect that information over time, that would permit them to come up with a pretty original dataset about the cost of building and construction as it relates to mass-flow, geopolitics, climate and natural events.

Case Study Interview with Tyler Goss

As the Director for Construction and Manufacturing Solutions at CASE, Tyler Goss works with leading construction clients to help them successfully navigate the dynamic technological landscape of design, construction, and operations. Throughout his career he has managed building information for more than $8 billion in construction volume, where his research and development time have led to significant data analyses and workflow solutions for CASE's innovative construction clients. Tyler has presented to diverse industry audiences at events including the Royal Institute of Chartered Surveyors Summit of the Americas, the national conference for the Construction Managers Association of America, ENR FutureTech, and Autodesk University.

Is data on the contractor's radar?

Tyler Goss (TG): From a financial perspective, construction is far more data driven than the design side. But the actual day-to-day management of the work is still based on rules of thumb: a put-it-all-together, hope-it-all-works-out process in the field. Financials are where construction management really excels. But it doesn't relate back to the product—the building—that is being put in place.

Data-driven construction is not a viable term yet—but it should be. When you talk about data-driven construction, you talk about the classic conundrum of IT spending. Construction has the lowest IT spending of any major industry sector, and the lowest R&D spending of any major industry sector, because it is risk adverse. No one's career or project incentive is to try something novel. Novelty is equated with risk in most people's minds.

How does culture impact the implementation of data use in construction?

TG: Construction is a relationships-driven business. Construction is driven by rules of thumb. How many times has this been executed before?

Working on a project with Turner Construction, we were searching for a document control system that would allow better access to information in the field. My hypothesis was: If you give people mobile access to better data, they can make better decisions on the fly in the field, with less downtime and less waste on the job. But in proposing platforms, what I ran up against culturally was: Show me the 150 projects where this has been deployed successfully. The competing solution was an internal one that had been used on 150 projects. Culturally, not only had it been proven and deployed, it was also a revenue center, and so [they] decided not to choose the innovative path.

> *Data is limited only by the sensitivity of our sensors, our ability to capture it, and the capacity to analyze the results.*
>
> —Tyler Goss, CASE

When you think about how executives within construction management firms are evaluated, they're evaluated very quantitatively. Did you keep your staff-to-volume ratio? Good. This and other key performance indicators.

I don't want to perpetuate the stereotype that architects are running ahead with innovative tools and technologies, then you hand your great dataset over to the construction manager and it's fumbled because construction managers are old school and incapable of handling it. Right now there are very few construction management firms that are looking at their data in an innovative way.

The use of BIM on the construction side has been on a very limited basis. The BIM rubric of 3D, 4D, 5D, 6D, and 7D are, practically, limited uses of data. The practical execution of 3D coordination, I would hesitate to even call that BIM. There's not enough data or information in that process.

Data-driven construction is not a viable term yet—but it should be.

—Tyler Goss, CASE

Most of the attention has been on data use in design, some in operations. You're fond of describing the building life cycle as a series of informational transactions. Can you talk a bit about how data can be used in the construction phase of the building life cycle?

TG: In an elevator pitch: Better real-time access to data and information of the project. To be able to build data up into project knowledge. The overarching goal for using a data-driven approach in construction would be to take that data and synthesize it into valuable, actionable project knowledge in real time.

An example: We're working with a contractor who fabricates and installs high-end custom enclosure systems. They wanted to have better real-time access to their information. Not just how many people they had on a jobsite, but more granular data and a better understanding of how many units they were installing per day. What we did was take their detailed schedule and we decomposed the schedule on an assembly-by-assembly basis. We understood, based on their plan, how many hours they took to install each piece. On the pilot project we managed about 2,500 objects, which was to roll out to 50,000 objects on the next project: an enormous job for them. We were not mounting any new data. What we were doing is synthesizing data that they were already tracking. When they brought a piece to the site, there was a barcode on it. They scan that barcode, and as a part of the automation process, we understood where a piece was and where it was installed. These were things that were not being captured to provide productivity. They were being captured to provide downstream building material validation. Taking data that they already had access to. Something that you have heard David Fano say before: We're all building information managers. All of the data already exists. It's just a matter of capturing it and analyzing it. We captured and analyzed it for schedule performance and productivity. What we found was that they now have a better understanding of what their real productivity is. They can now plan and account for risk better on future jobs. They have a better understanding of what their labor costs and material costs are. There were some things that emerged from capturing that data and reporting it. The most interesting thing I found out during that process was that they had better control of the change management narrative when change ultimately happened, because they had the most robust tracking of the project.

The overarching goal for using a data-driven approach in construction would be to take that data and synthesize it into valuable, actionable project knowledge in real time.

—Tyler Goss, CASE

There was a change management situation that was weather driven. It was weather that drove another subcontractor to not clear an area on time. When they had gone into their change management situation archive, they were able to put all of these daily reports, very robust reports showing where they were, where they weren't, and what constraints they were seeing in the field, in front of the owner. The owner was able to assign liability for that change. In the past, there would have been arguing amongst the high-value, high-cost managers rather than just being able to go with the data and discover and ensure where the liability was in the situation.

(Continued)

There's ambient data that exists already in the business process of building a building, and it's just a matter of capturing that data, putting it in the right buckets, and analyzing it in an intelligent way. It's actually monetizable. It's data that is getting you a better business advantage on future jobs.

If you can make the process predictable and risk-free, you can do it a hundred times. All the economic arguments are more transparent on the construction side.

As an example, having tablets in the field, we wanted to track how many times we walk to the job trailer per day, pre-tablet and post-tablet. About one-and-a-half trips less, post-tablet. It cost on-site job superintendents about 900 man-hours per year. We didn't do GPS-based tracking.

On a fundamental level, two things we have been trying to do with all of our clients now is to make the information available as near to real time as possible, given the sampling rates that are happening; and get it as close to the face of work as possible. Real information has the most value where it is turned from information into decisions in a course of action. Conceptually, we think of the face of work not just as the last guy with a hammer in his hand, but anyplace where you have an informational transaction that's adding value to the process. So, the estimator is the face of work at one point in the project. As the scheduler is the face of work. If we can get the information closer to the face of work, what are the benefits of doing that? For the superintendent study, we looked at 11 employees, and found half a man-year of movement waste over a 6-month period. When you take that number and annualize it, you multiply by the cost of paying a superintendent in the region, it was $130,000 of value we were finding. You put that number in front of the nose of the executive team, it was a no-brainer. They supplied tablets and data infrastructure across all of the superintendents in the region. Either that money was going to be spent in the superintendent walking from place to place, or it was going to be spent on a superintendent actually observing things.

You have written that tedious data-gathering capacities and practices inhibit teams from developing integrated approaches to business processes like estimating, sequencing, or facilities management.

TG: Trying to mount a new data capture is typically going to fail because it's an additional piece of work. This is going to cross all parts of the building life cycle, not just construction: the value proposition of a tap, a swipe, a click, or a data sample, or whatever it is that takes you time. And the value is not immediately apparent to you. While you may do it because you understand the grander vision of the building life cycle, you're going to miss it more often than not. Which means you're going to end up with data that is fuzzy, data that is inconsistent, you won't have well-structured data if it's not drawing off of the immediate value proposition of the people who are creating it.

As an example, I have seen this happen a lot on projects that have lofty visions and complex processes. The task of collecting productivity data falls to a field engineer who doesn't understand what they are doing, with a field superintendent, and they start testing—and that data is captured in a qualitative way. It gets very fuzzy. And gets very hard to standardize and normalize that data across a certain number of people. And because the data collection is tedious, arduous, and stops being done, you have incomplete data, and you cannot mount anything on top of it.

Because money is on the table, and there's risk involved, there's been a historical preference for specificity and actuality in the data. When what you really want to be unearthing is deltas. What is the delta between what you are seeing today and what you have seen historically? And what can you do to assure that you are improving on your historical baseline?

When you start thinking about deltas, as long as you have an internally consistent data structure, an internally consistent model for your data, it doesn't matter what the actual cost is. It just matters if your data is longitudinally getting better. The assumption is that computers are not going to capture the nuance of the data that I can capture given my 30 years of experience as an estimator, or my 30 years of experience as a superintendent. Because it's not nuanced, it's not accurate, it's not reliable, I can't trust it. The beauty of it is, if you capture the same data day after day after day, you have created the deltas. And that's what's valuable. Not the actuals.

I like when people work with data that already exists. With video—with means that are easy to capture with little additional cost. With data that is already being taken on a day-by-day basis. There are a lot of technologies that are on the cusp of being adopted that are going to give us a lot better data about what is actually happening on the construction site. We'll be able to do more elaborate and more complete analyses of what's happening.

The beauty of it is if you capture the same data day after day after day, you have created the deltas. And that's what's valuable. Not the actuals.

—Tyler Goss, CASE

What are you optimistic about concerning where construction is headed in an innovative use of data and building information management?

TG: I'll be optimistic when it's being demanded by owners. For me, none of this changes on the construction side. The root of the cultural issue—for the lack of adoption of new technologies and processes—stems out of the fact that construction is historically and remains a customer-driven, service-driven industry. Until owners are asking for it, it won't be priced into construction. Most customers have not been sophisticated enough to ask for BIM or data analyses of their fleet. Until they ask for that, it becomes a low priority, it gets x'ed out of budgets. When the whole goal is to drive down overall cost, no one is going to ask for add-on technologies or processes. My move to CASE was to get to a better set of clients, both construction managers and also ultimate owners, to help to procure these better. Because at the end of the day it is a procurement issue. It's about understanding how to buy, and what to buy, when it comes to a data-centric project delivery process.

With your experience and perspective in architecture and construction management, knowing what you know now, what advice would you give to an architect entering the field today?

TG: There's a fundamental shift from a document-centric to data-centric delivery methodology in our industry. With a few exceptions, the schools are not preparing people for this. That said, more and more graduates leave school with in-depth practical knowledge of Grasshopper, a parameter-based, rules-based design process. But that shift from a document-centric to data-centric approach, being the one who can lead a practice into making that shift themselves, is going to put themselves in a position of power more quickly than they would otherwise. It's historically been the BIM guy or the CAD manager—the person who works with data—in a practice or a construction management company, who has been a back-room, overhead risk center. What I've found, and what we found at Turner Construction, is that there is no one in the first two years of their career who will touch more parts of the building process than the person responsible for structuring the data. That's the sort of person at CASE that we're looking for. They're coming out of school, or other places in the industry, with a broad understanding of the design and construction process, and the overall business process. Because they've been modeling and thinking in terms of data.

(Continued)

If there's one thing, it's learning to think in a data-centric way. Learn to think about data schemas as opposed to any other way of structuring your design logic.

What's an example of what you mean by document-centric thinking?

TG: I'll use Revit as an example. Revit can be used in one of two ways. It can be used to build a fundamental logic of a project. In terms of a logic of building. Or it can be used to expediently generate 2D documentation for contractual purposes. More often than not, it's the latter way that Revit is used.

The big push to BIM the world—back in 2001–2002—coincided with a downturn in the economy. The promise at the time was that BIM would allow you to mount your documents more quickly, more effectively, and—I saw this in sales pitches—would allow you to eliminate your job captains. You have a promise in the form of a technology that purports to eliminate one of the highest-cost and lowest-utilization employees in a firm in an economic downturn. The job captain—the person whose job it is to set up the logic of the drawing set so that it is usable and understandable. Because the cost of putting a drawing on a sheet in Revit is so low, you don't really worry about it. You just throw them all together. BIM created a way of documentation. Issue 500 sheets for a $1 million project. What was lost was all those job captains all got pushed out of the industry. Their knowledge was lost to the industry to a great extent—and was not replaced. Now people are coming out of school who do not realize that not only are there the requirements to the documents but that there are requirements to develop an internal logic to that document set. It's not necessarily the documents themselves, it's making the documents the end-all and be-all of the process. We should be expressing the data in a logical way in the documents is what we should be shooting for.

Responding to Change

The construction industry is complex, fragmented, and rife with problems such as delays, rework, standing time, material waste, poor communication, conflict, and being over budget, compounded by the global slowdown and the need to address sustainability issues.[1] The construction industry is also risk averse. How receptive has the industry been to change, new apps, gadgets, processes, and data? "The construction industry compared to manufacturing and others is really slow in terms of leveraging new technologies and changing processes," admits Mani Golparvar-Fard. "Though this is changing."

Case Study Interview with Mani Golparvar-Fard, PhD

Mani Golparvar-Fard is Assistant Professor of Civil Engineering and of Computer Science, and the Director of the real-time and automated monitoring and control (Raamac) lab at University of Illinois at Urbana-Champaign. His work in the area of automated building and construction performance monitoring using visual data (images and video streams) and 4D building information models has been recognized by numerous awards. He currently chairs the Data Sensing and Analysis Committee of the American Society of Civil Engineers and is on the editorial board of the ASCE Journal of Construction Engineering and Management *and the* ASCE Journal of Computing in Civil Engineering.

What do you consider data that best helps you achieve your outcomes?

Mani Golparvar-Fard (MGF): My primary interest at this stage of my career is to use photos, videos, and BIM because they are easy to use, because they are already available and don't need training. I am also getting more interested in leveraging commodity smartphones, as they are becoming more ubiquitous on jobsites. My core focus is to contribute to the body of knowledge in computer vision, by creating model-based methods for photo/video analysis, and to contribute to the body of knowledge in construction management, through automated performance monitoring.

In 2008, while working on my PhD, I started working with Turner Construction, where I convinced them to use BIM on the Ikenberry Commons project on campus. I wanted to see how I could extend the value of BIM for contractors using 4D modeling.

We came up with an idea: What if 4D BIM became the baseline for progress monitoring? What are the current practices that contractors have? Every day in the field these guys walked around writing down the paper-based field construction reports, documenting what is happening on the jobsite. The information they get is not necessarily reliable. They also want their contractors to submit their DCRs [Daily Construction Reports]. Every day you end up getting a pile of these DCRs. It is often just too inconvenient for them to accurately capture the exact daily activities of all contractors on the jobsites. In fact, the engineers in charge of the DCRs get so much involved in putting these paper-based documents into the system that they often don't even get the chance to go out of their trailers and do the observation. You collect data for a week from all contractors, assume all information is "complete" and "accurate," and then go into a weekly contractor coordination meeting. This is the time that you're supposed to represent all the data was collected and observed on the jobsite throughout the week, so you can coordinate the tasks for the next three weeks of the schedule. Because the information captured is often incomplete, and sometimes inaccurate, the project manager again asks the representatives of the construction companies to manually color-code the completed tasks on construction drawings—so the process happens three times: contractors document on site; field engineers enter information into a system; and then during coordination meeting, the contractors again provide the same information. This causes the entire team not to have a clear understanding of the actual progress on the jobsite and deviations for a week; that is, there is at least a lag of one week from the time things go wrong until the time the project management is informed on potential or actual delays.

So I wanted to see how I can use BIM—4D BIM—to not only help with constructability review, but also help create the right baseline of monitoring. I started looking into the state of practice and also the state of research for jobsite data collection. If you look into the practice of data collection, people use radio-frequency identification (RFID), barcodes, or laser scan technology. Laser scanning is a very interesting technology, but it comes at a price. It's costly, you need to have two people operate the scanner at the jobsite, you need to provide access to power, and you need to have people post-process the data for you. So you don't use it frequently. The application gets limited to high-profile projects and only a few instances for QA/QC, site verification, and for progress monitoring. This was back in 2005 and 2006. So I started thinking, what are the other means I can use on the jobsite to perform progress monitoring? I don't want to add a new technology because what it does is the following: We try to help people minimize their time performing data collection, because we just want them to focus on identifying alternatives to activities and perform what-if analysis, but instead we need to ask them to spend their time learning and using a new technology. Instead, I want to use things that already exist, because I really did not want them to replace one project management task with another. We came up with the idea of using time-lapse cameras. Back then, time-lapse video cameras were still new, and were just starting to appear on jobsites where contractors could capture work in progress. Today, many projects have cameras: 10, 20—one project in Japan has 40 cameras on site. [See Figure 7.3.]

(Continued)

Figure 7.3: Visualization of construction progress deviations: BIM elements superimposed over a time-lapse image, color-coded based on their progress deviations. Elements behind schedule are color-coded in red, on schedule colored in green. © *MGF*

We have 3D and 4D models superimposed on a photograph of the site, generating an augmented photo. From this photo, we want to go into the schedule and see if we can automatically assess the state of project progress using the simple analogy of traffic light colors: red, yellow, and green. If you're ahead of schedule, in a coordination meeting you would have this image showing elements in green and if behind, in red. [See Figure 7.4.]

Figure 7.4: If you're ahead of schedule, in a coordination meeting this image shows elements in green; if you're behind, it shows in red. © *MGF*

There are a number of problems. Visualizing the state of progress, we can use time-lapse photography. It is easy to relate to: it always shows the site from the same perspective. But, if we want to automate it, we need at least 30 to 50 pixels associated with each element. At the same time, it used to come at a price to buy and operate these at a jobsite. Turner Construction was not interested in having a lot of these cameras on the jobsite, so I showed them another idea. On the jobsite they already collect a lot of photos. Everybody captures photos on the jobsite, for all kinds of purposes: for example, safety documentation, quality documentation, and productivity recording. The challenge was, how could I take these photos and automatically compare them with the same view in the BIM model? [See Figure 7.5.]

I came up with the idea of D4AR technology—4D augmented reality. Here's the process: Given a set of photos captured on a jobsite, on a particular day or over a span of time where not a significant amount of progress has been achieved by the contractor, we automatically put together a 3D point cloud model of the site. This technology by itself so far competes with the laser scanner. It is inexpensive. All you need to have is a camera, have a field engineer walk around and capture a lot of photos, and generate a 3D point cloud. Every day you're taking new photos so we have to create new point cloud models. But we want to do this automatically. So we generate separate point clouds. We have a technique that can generate a 4D point cloud automatically. Now we have sets of photos that are helping you generate

Figure 7.5: A daily construction photolog from a typical building construction site. On average, about 200-250 photos were collected on this jobsite on a daily basis. © *MGF*

(Continued)

as-built models every day. Nontextured surfaces (e.g., finished drywall) are difficult to be picked up by image-based point cloud modeling technology. What is not captured in the point cloud we can see in the photos. The BIM shows us the expected performance. The point cloud plus the photographs show us the actual performance. Now we can create our machine-learning techniques and automatically assess the progress. [See Figure 7.6.]

The point cloud was generated using 160 photos with a resolution of only 2 megapixels. The field engineer in this case walked along the site using just a camera. This is a 3D scene, so we can click on points and take measurements. We can superimpose the photographs that were used to generate the point cloud. Today, of course, we can do this with video and all sorts of fancy data collection techniques (e.g., cameras mounted on aerial robots). At the time of this research, we only wanted to use existing photos. At any position you can jump out of the camera viewpoint and see where the photo was captured with respect to the site. This captures the as-built. We also wanted to use this for construction progress monitoring. It has semantic functionality—that allows a user to search and query cost and schedule information—for construction. For example, we were using this model at the Turner project for concrete billing purposes. We are using IFCs [Industry Foundation Classes], which allows us to integrate a schedule and cost information, both of which we use for progress monitoring. This formulates a 4D augmented reality. Our system, because it is model-based

Figure 7.6:   A daily construction photolog compared with point cloud images. © *MGF*

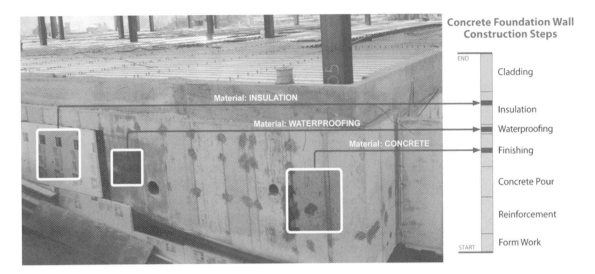

Figure 7.7: Automatically monitoring operation-level details of construction progress requires assessment of building element appearance. Automatically recognizing steps in construction of concrete foundation walls requires image processing that can differentiate between insulation, waterproofing, and concrete. © *MGF*

(model here means the IFC elements), we know if we have photos collected for each element or not. We were the only ones doing this in 2009. Our system today can run as a marker-less mobile augmented reality system, which we have called Hybrid 4D augmented reality. [See Figure 7.7.]

This system had a number of challenges. It is hard, for example, to differentiate between formwork and concrete. We had to look into how we could create an ontology of construction sequences. This led to two projects I am currently working on. One, from small image patches (as small as 30 x 30) I can differentiate different types of material from one another.

The other project is to leverage IFCs to see how we can improve LOD [level of development] in BIM. If we don't have images capturing the building foundations, for example, we can infer those elements. We're looking to see how we can leverage the clouds of points we are generating as well as creating material-based recognition. I've received funding from the National Center for Supercomputing Applications (NCSA) to research autonomous vision-based construction progress monitoring using quadrotors and latest BIM/SfM-based methods to automate data collection on jobsites. Today we have a system where quadrotors can autonomously fly using point clouds that are manually collected. There are safety issues we still have to consider. The point cloud that we have previously collected from photos guides the quadrotor. As it moves we provide feedback as to what areas it needs to fly to in real time. From the collected data, we don't know if the model is going to be complete or not. This is the state of the art in robotics and computer vision. From the BIM we know where it needs to fly because we have an expectation of a new element there. Working with Turner Construction, Okumura in Japan, and another contractor in the U.S. (under NDA), this is a new component: automatically performing quality control. Can we automatically see, for example, if the rebar configuration is laid out according to the specification—either in visual information or via text?

(Continued)

Figure 7.8:   A 3D image-based point cloud model of a rebar cage. Using 15 control points, the up-to-scale point cloud model is transformed into the site coordinate system. © *MGF*

The DC Bridge is an example where a bridge was being replaced. The bridge was supposed to support a track. Here's a brief description of the project. [See Figure 7.8.]

Ensuring compliance with contract documents and the building code applicable to the project under construction requires photographic documentations and close visual inspection by field inspectors. The visual inspection by field inspectors in the current practice, however, is very time-consuming and labor-intensive, although repeated for every project.

Vision-based quality monitoring using unordered digital imagery can help reduce cost and help expedite the current field inspection processes. Our study focuses on detecting and visualizing quality nonconformances for steel and concrete structures. It has the potential to provide a notable improvement in the productivity of both the steel and concrete industry, and ultimately prevents the cost and the loss in time associated with construction defects.

In our proposed methods, a field inspector can carefully walk around a structure and take a complete video footage. Using a pipeline of Structure from Motion and Multi-view Stereo image-based 3D reconstruction algorithms, a dense 3D point cloud model will be generated. Using algorithms developed for checking nonconformances, the as-built 3D point cloud model is inspected. Any nonconformance detected is visualized in 3D on mobile devices to help inspectors identify any problems that need immediate attention.

We can assess this automatically and tell you where the rebar elements are located within 95 percent accuracy. Today, with 300 images, we can do this in 2 hours on the cloud. I have been leveraging images but video is also very rich from a data standpoint in terms of the content it can give us.

I am also interested in capturing video for the purpose of detecting what types of assets and equipment we have on the jobsite. Also, to detect our workers. To focus on each of our resources and know exactly what resource we're looking at—without any tags on the device—for productivity and analysis. It tells you the location without GPS or wireless. Purely based on the content of the video—and the people in action: digging, dumping, hauling, being idle. We formulated this problem to measure both productivity and also the carbon footprint of the operation. [See Figure 7.9.]

We came up with some formulas based on activities we can recognize; we can relate that into greenhouse gas emissions so we can benchmark [the] contractor's performance. We can also relate that to operations efficiency as well as embodied carbon. With workers we can do crew balance charts to understand their productivity. We can understand safety. Why? The second highest rate of fatality is when people work in proximity to the equipment. If we detect them, we can provide an alert mechanism. It is as simple as wiring their safety vests. From a data standpoint, we can set up a constraint—for example, if someone gets within so many feet of the equipment. Or, within the BIM model, we can identify areas that are potential safety hazards. If a person gets into one of those restricted

Figure 7.9:   Details that should be captured in craft worker activities to allow automated activity analysis from site video streams. © *MGF*

areas, we can recognize it. We can map this into the same video feed using a minimum of two video cameras, to triangulate the location. We've attempted to use iPhones for tracking people. Recognizing their activities based on one accelerometer sensor is very difficult today. We tried it; we spent a year on that topic. We can triangulate from a single sensor, but we can't understand what activity they're involved in (at least not at the right granularity). We can differentiate between people walking and not walking, but we cannot tell whether someone is vibrating concrete or handling materials with a single sensor.

Everything I do is purely from a computer vision perspective or what I call Model-based Visual Sensing (again model-based because I like to leverage BIM as the basis of performance monitoring). Analyzing images and video data (resulting in decisions). I want to leverage BIM to see if I can enable computer vision technology. I don't think we should only address problems from image and video. BIM is already rich enough at a preconstruction stage, we just need to extend the application. [See Figure 7.10.]

This is an example of a combination of computer vision and machine learning where we train the program to learn certain behaviors over time. From computer vision we extract features that are these parts. This model was only trained for standing workers. It is not trained to recognize people who are bending or sitting. The body deforms, so we need to learn models that can capture deformity of the object. Activity forecasting takes these machine-learned behaviors and forecasts it, so the resulting data can be predictive. This is a very hot topic in computer vision. [See Figure 7.11.]

(Continued)

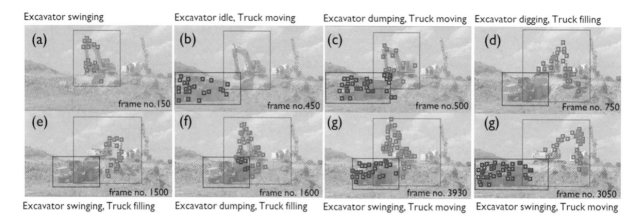

Figure 7.10:   An example of a combination of computer vision and machine learning where the program is trained to learn certain behaviors over time. © *MGF*

Fill Bucket	Dump	Idle	Dump	Idle	Dump	Return to refill bucket

Vibrating Concrete								
Move scaffold	Climb	Idle	Vibrate	Idle	Vibrate	Idle	Vibrate	Climb Down
Worker 1		Unused						
Unused			In use	Unused		Unused		Unused

Placing Concrete							
Move scaffold	Climb	Dump	Idle	Dump	Idle	Dump	Climb Down	Idle
Worker 2		Unused						
Unused		In use					Unused	

Figure 7.11:   To know what activity each person on site is engaged in—what tool they're using, how long they are using it for—requires a massive database. Without detailed data, we won't be able to develop proper machine-learning algorithms. © *MGF*

Very few are exploring video-based activity analysis in construction. I believe it is much more interesting in construction because we have so much prior data to work with. This is where we are going with it: we want to see if we can give you this, at the end of every day, from a productivity perspective.

To know what activity each person on site is engaged in—what tool they're using, how long they are using it for—requires a massive database. Without detailed data, we won't be able to develop proper machine-learning algorithms. As an interim solution, I have created a crowd-sourcing platform that resides on the cloud. We ask contractors to provide us with videos. We upload them into this platform. We plan to pay non-experts to annotate the frames in the video for us, to label people, their role, what type of activity they are engaged in, what posture they have, and how visible they are. This could help us create feedback (crew-balance charts) for contractors, and also produces the rich databases we need for training and testing our machine-learning methods that could help us automate the tasks.

UIUC's David Forsyth was one of the first people to try the idea of crowd-sourcing annotations using images. This work is based on videos—a pretty new concept in computer vision. If we can get people to annotate these, we can cross-validate performance—and guarantee that the result is accurate. At the end of the day, what contractors care about is this: they want to have a time series of the activities, they want to have the crew balance chart. Are we going to provide it to them? What we collect in the interim is the data. Creating the database—for the non-experts to annotate the frames—has been challenging for us. We have an opportunity where we can add labels. If we didn't have the right roles, activities, or tools, we can add them to the system.

You are teaching a course in visual sensing. Can you discuss the implications of such a network for capturing data and how it might be used in construction?

MGF: I'd like to train the next generation of construction informatics experts. Civil engineering and architecture students know the problems and can understand them really well. I'd like to introduce them to the state of the art in computer vision, so they can come up with the "right" solutions. I disagree with those research projects that purely focus on application of a technology. I think we need to fundamentally change the teaching philosophy by allowing students to develop the right technological solutions for the problems in hand. Problem-driven research as opposed to technology-driven work.

Linking Design, Construction, and Operations

What opportunities are there for data to influence the construction side of the building life cycle? "Concerning data, there are missed opportunities for construction," says Sam Miller. "My sense is that there's going to be a closer linkage moving forward between design, construction, and operations. The current vehicle is the digital model. Utilizing the model for design, analysis, performance, and simulation. Then leveraging that model into digital fabrication. Which is just starting to happen. And then that transition into operations." (See Figure 7.12.)

Integrating Cost Data into the Model

Construction and construction management firms can benefit from taking a broader look at project con-

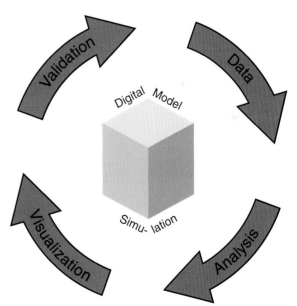

Figure 7.12: Moving forward, we will make greater utilization of the model for design, analysis, performance, and simulation throughout the building life cycle. © R Deutsch

text to see a project from a cost-estimating stand-point. "Astorino has a construction management group with a cost estimating team," explains Brian Skripac.

We were trying to think about how we could integrate our cost information to the model. Thinking about it at a broader scale using an application that allows you to take advantage of historical building cost data. Not just, you have so many linear feet of a wall or square feet of flooring with a general construction cost to it. It contextualizes construction assemblies and their costs based on their "function." For example, you're building a healthcare facility that is so many square feet that will have a Class A definition for the finishes in the space. How do you understand the difference between the situation in a healthcare facility versus a rentable/leasable office space from finishes, to systems, to structure? We started to take a broader look at it based on building type and location, and not just overall quantities of materials that probably aren't yet specified or formalized early in the design. There's an interest in looking at more projects from that perspective in the office.

Interoperability Platform That Allows Exchange of Models between Programs

Thornton Tomasetti has a solution for dealing with data and using data in a meaningful way: have a database that is designed for your own needs. Along these lines, Jonatan Schumacher describes TTX as essentially a repository where programs can talk to each other. "TTX is primarily used by engineers in-house—and it is being developed based on every-day needs of our engineers," explains Schumacher.

TTX is first and foremost an interoperability platform that allows an exchange of mod-els between various programs. Moreover, it tracks every instance of the model over time. So you can go back and say, whatever happened in the month of May was better than what we are doing now. You can then go back and update all the models in the various programs to reflect what was done in May.

We commonly use many programs simultaneously to design a building structure: SAP, Grasshopper, Revit, Tekla, ETABS, RAM, and many more. Certain programs are better for lateral analysis, some are better for slab design, and some are better for documentation. There isn't a single program that can do it all, and I don't think there ever will be. TTX is a repository that all of these programs can talk to, and we can put in their information over time. Since TTX uses a database on the back end, it allows us to keep track of each project revision: every time a project is synched to the TTX database from any of its currently supported programs, a new database entry is added to the TTX project. This entry contains information about the application that synched to the database, such as the sync date, user name, and a user-defined message describing the latest change. It might look something like this:

User: KMurphy

Software: Revit 2014

Sync Date: Dec 07, 2013, 21:15:23

Message: Added roof to the model and moved spacing of grid lines 1 to 10 by 6.

"In addition to this information," says Schumacher, "we keep track of every element that was created, deleted, or modified." He continues:

GitHub is like Google Docs for programmers, mainly used for open-source programmers.

We're basically mimicking GitHub for the development of these models. As with Google Docs, which keeps track of all the versions, we're doing the same but with models. When the model changes, it keeps track of when, who, what the changes were, and also what program was used. So we can look at how the project evolved over time. That allows you to compare two different instances. We don't work in one instance of a design anymore. We keep track of everything.

Recently, the CORE Studio team created a revision history interface [in Grasshopper], which lets the user parse the individual timestamps of the project and review what was changed, when, and by whom. Using the Grasshopper interface we can also compare the stage of the project at different time intervals. We can also run custom queries on the model, such as, "Show me all the changes that we made in May." Or: "Show me all of the changes that were made by SAP or ETABS."

Strategy No. 22: Extract And Transfer What Matters

You've talked about how data can go from software to software. How do you ensure that the tools you—and the teams you work with—use talk to each other? IFCs?

Just follow what matters. Extract and transfer what matters. . . .Interoperability can get very technical. It is pursuing a cure without an original disease. . . .If I'm the architect and you're the engineer, and we need to coordinate on a Revit model, we need to make sure our levels of detail (LODs) are aligned. The technical version of this is that we both need to be using Revit and both need to be using the same version of Revit, we both

need to use Copy Monitor, and both need to use Revit server—that's a very technological approach where you're putting technology first. If you boil down interoperability to its bare transfer, really all we need to know is the elevation of each of those levels. There could be an email on a weekly basis with a list of elevation values. If we can just distill it down to what it really needs to be, that's a web service in front of Revit and a list of auditor's values with their levels and their names and then having some way for whatever platform that the craftsmen wants to use ingest that information to create what you consider the native version of that level. This takes interoperability to a much simpler level.

—David Fano, CASE

Industry Foundation Classes Data Models

Industry Foundation Classes (IFC) is a platform-neutral, open file format specification that is not controlled by a single vendor or group of vendors.[2] "I saw someone posted on Twitter this morning that IFC is anti-innovation," says Brian Ringley. "Shouldn't we always be pushing for change? IFC is just a way to get things to speak. So Revit can speak with Rhino. It is that speaking that contributes to innovation to communication, and innovation through tools. Not about standardization of how we use Revit but about Revit itself."

When important data is missing from the picture, University of Illinois professor Mani Golparvar-Fard uses workarounds based on a construction site's contextual information. "The other project is to leverage IFCs to see how we can improve LOD in BIM," says Golparvar-Fard. "If we don't have images capturing the building foundations, for example, we can infer those elements. We're looking to see how we can leverage the clouds of points we are generating as well as creating material-based recognition."

"Before deciding to develop our own interoperability platform, TTX, we were testing IFC file format on a large fast-paced project," explains Jonatan Schumacher. "Certain companies, like Autodesk, are not motivated to work with IFC. We needed to get all this data from both Grasshopper and SAP into Revit and it was not possible to do so in the workflow that the project required." He continues:

> If the input geometry changes, you lose track of which beams [in Revit] to replace with which beams [coming from Grasshopper]. IFC does not keep track of the unique identifiers that each program assigns to their BIM elements, so we can't use it well to make updates to existing models—especially if that model has changed, too. That is why we came up with TTX. It's an alternative to IFC. It's a file in the end, a database that contains all of the BIM information. It grows over time, and it can talk to all the different programs that we commonly use to model, analyze, document, and fabricate building structures. TTX is the common repository. We can now talk between the individual elements in all programs and keep updating our calculations. Over time we

naturally keep growing this repository, as the project evolves.

I asked Brian Skripac how he would describe an AEC service firm with all of the disciplines that has an in-house approach to interoperability,

> For our office, our architects use Revit Architecture; our structural engineers use Revit Structure and an analogous simulation software that works in concert with Revit; our MEP team is using Revit MEP. Within that core design relationship, it's not really a big deal. Where we've had to extend data and information beyond the local team, everyone has used an Autodesk-based product. Where we're the CM, and we'll lead the collaboration and clash process, we'll work with a .dwg file or an IFC file we've gotten, for example, from a steel fabricator. For us the consolidation of information hasn't been that big of a deal. Looking beyond design and construction, COBie is going to be a very big piece of the puzzle, by distributing information in a way that can be consumed by anything, and working with The Ohio State University, we realized that it will be a key component to interoperability.

Case Study Interview with Bill East, PhD

Bill East, PhD, PE, F.ASCE, is a serial innovator responsible for standards and systems in use across the globe. Bill's Standard Data Exchange Format has delivered earned-value construction schedules to building owners for 30 years. Recently, Bill led standards work resulting in the majority of the technical content in the United States National Building Information Modeling (BIM) Standard. The Construction Operations Building information exchange (COBie) is implemented in more than 20 software products and in contracts worldwide. Bill is an internationally recognized building informatics researcher. He is a Registered Professional Engineer and a Fellow of the American Society of Civil Engineers.

Some people who work with COBie speak almost fanatically about it as the be-all and end-all for the industry.

Bill East (BE): COBie is a means to an end. This—data and Big Data use in the AEC industry—is not really a technology issue. This whole issue is really a process and sociology issue.

How do you see this as not a technology issue?

BE: You have to put it in a context of innovation in our business. When you and I started our careers with punch cards and Fortran, the activity was about, let's automate the slide rule. So people got along great for years. In construction, PCs came around and people were doing cut-and-fill calculations in spreadsheets, and eliminating the need to figure out sines and cosines when surveying. This was really a single use for technology for specific calculations. The computer as calculator. That works pretty well until you get to the place where you have to give your results to someone else.

As soon as you start talking about having to share information, then you have a different kind of problem. It's not a problem that can simply be addressed by replacing a screwdriver with a battery-powered screwdriver.

When I moved from the field to the lab I started looking at the question: How do we eliminate repetitive deficiencies? This is a communication problem that should result in a control cycle that updates criteria much more frequently. This was the first thing: standardizing the process of information exchange. This didn't standardize the content. People still had to look at drawings and still had to make their comments.

Did you see any brush-back for having focused on process in your career?

BE: Yes, there's been quite a bit. We're talking about means and methods. You've got to get this stuff to a place where you can actually get it in a contract, otherwise people won't use it.

This is why my working for the U.S. Army Corps of Engineers Laboratory was pivotal. Because had I been interested in solving process and data problems in academia, I could publish a lot of concepts, but could never actually implement anything at scale.

If you have a process-oriented tool and you're still talking about paper, then you still have to distribute the paper. Whether it's a PDF, e-paper, or paper, it's still document-based. So all of the information is still subject to the interpretation of the viewer.

How do we take the conversation about the design and change it from being a discussion about documents, and turn it into a more substantive discussion of the content of the design?

That's where building information comes into the picture. The mission statement of buildingSMART alliance (bSa) is to create open standard data models.[3] But making data models is not a problem anyone needs. You're not making anything that anybody wants to buy. Nobody changes something unless they're faced with a problem. If there's a crisis, then people need to change. You have two options: either wait for everything to collapse, or point out the failure of the situation and give them a better mousetrap.

As long as people are getting paid, no one has to change. So if you want to have a buildingSMART organization that is meaningful to its constituents, the people who buy construction services, then you have to tell them if you use this stuff, you're going to reduce the cost and improve the quality of your project. Then early adopters might think about it.

What do we manage? Cost, time, quality, and scope. All four of those things could be dramatically improved with shared, structured information. *(Continued)*

We have the process squared away. Now we're going to start investigating the information content. The first bit of the information content was the building's operation and maintenance (O&M) manuals. We have this scenario now, throughout the industrialized world, where at the end of the project, the truck backs up and drops off boxes of paper.

The initial design of COBie, from the 2007 report, said that the information that we're requiring contractors to provide is already specified in our contracts. The problem is that the form of the information is not a form that we can use. What is it that we need? The development of COBie was directly focused on construction process. That made it much more complicated for a software company to look at; they wanted one boiled-down, synthesized data structure.

IFC is the only open standard for buildings but IFC is just a means to an end, not an end in itself. The end is to deliver the useful information about how to manage your facility.

It's an engineering problem. It's not an R&D problem. People just overcomplicate the whole thing. COBie is the set of information that is delivered. Think of it like the optometrist. You go in and your vision is blurry. They put the lens in from of you and it's the way you see now, so that's A. Then they flip a switch, flip the lens, and it's the way you could see, B. So B is COBie.

COBie is the exchange, it's not the use of the information. COBie is the method of the transfer of the information. Ultimately, the implementation format is important, so you have COBie data on tablets and databases. COBie is a contracted information exchange. It's meant to be a performance-based deliverable for information. It doesn't matter what software you use to create it, or what you consume it with at the back end.

> *COBie, a contracted information exchange, is a performance-based deliverable for handing over information. It doesn't matter what software you use to create it, or what you consume it with at the back end.*
> —Bill East, PhD, PE, F.ASCE

Big Data begins with people having correct ground truth about what it is that they have. It's a question of authoritative source.

Even with something as simple as the keying of rooms, we get into the situation needing to have shared structured data in a process, where each group gets access to maintain the keys that belong to them.

What in your own background led you to a career in data and information in the AEC industry?

BE: While I was in the field I worked nights and weekends to design integrated, multi-user construction management software to manage the process I did during the day. There I learned the importance of getting the process right. The next step is unlocking the data inside these processes. I face the abundance of data available to us today by breaking it down into its constituent parts. You're not going to solve everything at once, so you break it down. One of the criteria is where do we waste time and effort? This was the criteria that was presented to me with COBie. When a facility manager gets a new building, they have to retype the information in those paper-filled boxes. But the information all came from someone typing to begin with. So why don't we just get it when they type it to begin with? So then you look at the mass of what is in those boxes. You need to find its constituent parts, you build a data exchange format for those parts.

You're not handing over a building information model, you're handing over the same set of required information that was always required. The only difference is that the format of that information is not consistent across these deliverables.

So, we have COBie and the complied specification. What is now happening with the actual use of COBie is parsing that data set into its parts. Deliverables that used to be made in paper are now going to be made in a subset of COBie. The contractor doesn't necessarily have to concern themselves with what this COBie thing is and is not. All they simply have to do is fill out the template for the installed equipment list correctly, fill out the template for the spare parts correctly, fill out the template for the O&M correctly, then the data through the magic of data modeling collects everything into one data file. This is where COBie is headed. Now that we have the data model, and it is implemented into 30 different pieces of software, now we know how to actually use it. Nobody is going to use COBie. Just like nobody buys a data model. What they're going to do is use a work order system, or a maintenance management system, or they're going to use a CAFM system, or a design system or a construction system.

Where COBie is today. COBie is a requirement in the UK and it is becoming a requirement in the U.S. We're seeing it in contracts in Singapore and New Zealand, it might be occurring in other places as well.

What does it really mean to have that information? What does it mean to have, for the life of that project, to use those resources efficiently? My definition of sustainability is the efficient use of resources in order to accomplish the mission of the building. If the building can't do what people want it to do, then there's no point in having the building there.

How do we solve being able to design and build buildings in this context of ongoing, increasing set of requirements? The way that occurred to me to address this is just by asking what is the data required in order to answer the question? Then it simply becomes a design or an engineering problem instead of having to send somebody to school for a week—they already know how to design and just need the 10 extra pieces of data for this one additional analysis. In the case of total cost of ownership, it's simply an engineering economic problem that anybody with a spreadsheet could solve. Give them a building model and say: add expected life replacement cost to the list.

Do you believe the engineering mindset and approach to data gathering will be sufficient to address today's complex building problems?

BE: I present COBie and some people say we don't need to do all of that. Then they come up with a custom solution, and—after something changes—a few years later they realize they wish they had approached it the standard way. Because now we need to pay extra to fix our custom job. People need to try this on their own so that they'll fail and realize that the only way to do it is by a standard of performance-based specifications for the delivery of building information. And to answer the question, if you want your software to work together, then you'll have to express what it is that you need.

IFC is a flawed idea in the mind of 90 percent of the people who think about this. Because there is no such thing as an IFC file. There is an IFC Model View Definition that is in a particular format. The "information exchanges" such as COBie, from the point of view of IFC, are simply Model View Definitions. The U.S. National BIM Standard has begun to define these Model Views. NBIMS-US v3 has balloted and approved Model Views for building programming, HVAC, electrical, and water systems. The current version of COBie is, of course, another Model View in NBIMS-US V3. Rather than reinvent the wheel, I hope that folks will take advantage of the work done by the buildingSMART alliance.

The only way to get beyond our current situation is through shared structured data. A good way to do that is by having open standards, because then it's the cheapest way to accomplish it. Because everyone can then innovate against the standard, as opposed to arguing that my format is better than your format. This is the efficient way to get there.

(Continued)

When people think of *tool* they're thinking about changing out the screwdriver for the battery-powered drill. They often don't realize that information is a tool and that different people will need different sets of information. COBie and the other information exchange projects in the U.S. National BIM Standard, version 3.0, are the first attempt at a comprehensive set of information standards in our industry. In the next decades these standards will transform our business by extracting the information content off our drawings. Taken to the logical conclusion, such shared structured information will ultimately help us design a more efficient environment.

Standards and Interoperability

To achieve the productivity gains it strives after, the AECO industry will have to make major strides in creating standards, and linking data and interoperability of software. Data linking, compatibility, and homogenization are crucial parts of this endeavor.

Linking Data

Creating standards for the use of Big Data and interoperability of software would establish a foundation for leveraging data in all phases of the project. The linking of data and interoperability of software are the lynchpins in ensuring that data can be leveraged throughout the building life cycle. "I remember when Ecotect first came out and everybody was upset because the boring solar diagrams they formerly had to do by hand now had software for it. Moving into where things are now, with instant analysis," says Brian Ringley. "The point isn't the analysis itself. It's great for communication and doing visualizations. But the fact that I can now associate those pieces of data with the piece of geometry." He continues:

And that theoretically could have ramifications all the way through manufacturing and occupancy. That's of obvious importance. This is what we're moving toward. Toward interoperability in the sense that inherent geometrical data that's important can move through a workflow of different tools, software, and specializations. But also that the data that informs the initial conjectures can also move through datasets.

"Interoperability is a big issue for us," says Sam Miller.

Being able to get across platforms, and to do different things with the same model, is important and will help to facilitate that. The flipside is if there's consolidation—if Autodesk buys up every little analysis tool—then there's the possibility that it's going to squelch the exploration and innovation that comes with that. There's a danger in it all becoming consolidated. But generally the trend has been positive, and beneficial for us, in terms of different platforms playing nice with each other, and there being common platforms everyone can be working off of.

AEC Industry Status on Interoperability

An application programming interface (API) specifies how some software components should interact with each other. Where is the AEC industry in terms of interoperability? Are the various softwares talking to each other? "The approach would be crudely explained as applied with sticky tape and ceiling wax," explains data wrangler Jonathon Broughton. "It takes a hacker mentality." He continues:

I know kind of where I need to get to. I know I have certain tools or facilities or APIs available. None of them are promising to do what it is I want to do. But I know I can get A from X and B from Y. and if I funnel that through Z I'll get D. It's amazing—the availability not only of publicly accessible data but also publicly accessible APIs transformation protocol data. I can plug things in here and get a different answer out here. What would be amazing is if you had an if-this, then-that that you could plug into a CAD package that you could plug into a modeling package that you could plug in with a cost analysis package. I am working as hard as I can on building, not a tool but a workflow, a process. It's being a master of many, many tools at once. Because if we rely entirely on software vendors to—it's never going to happen.

We can distill building elements down to just data. A wall is points, lines, properties, same for floors. As long as software has some programmatic way to interact with it, we can recreate geometry. "With Revit there are certain things we can't do because the APIs don't exist," explains David Fano. "As long as the API is there, then yes."

Case Study Interview with Greg Schleusner

Greg Schleusner, AIA, is responsible for guiding HOK's use of new technologies that pertain to project delivery. In this role Greg works with a broad range of project teams and leaders within the firm to understand workflow and delivery challenges. He then works with researchers, developers, software companies, and others to find solutions to these challenges. Once developed, he then manages the initial implementation of the solutions to prove out their value or need for further development. Greg firmly believes in open source and open standards and has taken part in OGC, buildingSMART, and IES standards development throughout his career.

Looking beyond standards, where is the future focus?

Greg Schleusner (GS): There are two parts to buildingSMART. The first is not necessarily the meat of the work I'm supposed to be doing. Making sure if there are technologies that might be applicable to us. The majority of what I should be doing is solving business needs that happen to be technology driven. The way it works is we identify a problem and work with the internal knowledge groups, define the expertise, then work with them and others to try to find solutions in the market, or see if we can find people with an interest in the same problem. If it's small enough, we'll build the tool in-house.

What are ways you stay on top of the emergent technologies?

GS: I'm not as visible in the Twitterverse and other social media, though I do certainly monitor them. I will unabashedly reach out to people and ask questions, and if there's something we're interested in, I'll make contact. People are aware of the fact that this is my responsibility, so they'll pass along stuff to me to look at. There are multiple ways of doing it. I'm pretty circumspect on the things I'll actually spend time on when it comes time to investigate them. I'll acknowledge something if it's cool but won't go to the effort of contacting folks unless there's a potential value.

Back in the day AIA had CAD standards. They were frequently overlooked or modified for individual use. Who—if anyone—pays attention to the standards and the data?

GS: In our structure at HOK, Lee Miller is in charge of the implementation of the buildingSMART standards. Most local HOK offices have buildingSMART managers. At some level, it's their responsibility. Our view of the world right now is aligned at our technical principals, who serve as the core contact for the local buildingSMART managers. The technical principal is responsible for delivery. I'm not a rah-rah standards guy, working for standards for the sake of standards. They are valuable for the sake of consistency and quality. That's how it makes its way into the process.

Name some benefits of buildingSMART for HOK's clients.

GS: There's quality and consistency. One of the things you see in our industry is the non-farm productivity graph.[4] At the end of the day, the productivity might result in the same building. The fact that we did x-many iterations doesn't reflect in the final product. That's certainly a benefit—and a curse. Clients certainly expect that ability to move quite quickly. It is beneficial, otherwise we're not competing very well.

One of the things we're seeing that is the most rewarding, in the long term, is the development of aligned business propositions that might surround FM handover of different type of data management tasks. These are really nascent things right now, but on a select number of projects we're starting to figure how to do them and offer them potentially as services.

What are some of its challenges?

GS: In our industry, there's a challenge just to determine if we're a design firm that uses technology, or does the current state of the world require that we understand ourselves to be both a technology company that happens to be full of architects? Or something in between?

What do you think the answer is?

GS: The optimum is both. It's a hard balance to meet. Not for unimaginably complex reasons. I went to school to be an architect and didn't think I'd be in technology. The same thing happens for a lot of people. It's just an alignment of what the expectations are.

As an employer you have to manage the expectations of those within the organization.

GS: The big challenge is not, this is the software we use and you should use it. The biggest challenge, and one the design industry has not done very well, is to tease out more interesting reasons why we are moving in this direction. If someone thought the reason we ought to use Revit was now and forever that we wanted to make sure we didn't have to chase down column bubbles, it's sad that they have that opinion. But at the same time, it is not always clear that there are good examples of the longer-term benefits. This is part of that discussion I mentioned before, coming up with the business alignment for future strategies. Once you begin to get those in place, then you're in a situation: if I do x, y, and z, I can get 2, 5, or 10 other things versus if I do one thing, I get one thing; if I do another, I get another.

CAD never improved productivity for our industry, and it appears that BIM technology alone isn't going to do it either. Once we work more collaboratively, perhaps we'll start to see the benefits and productivity will increase.

Do you have any suspicions as to what it will take—whether data, or the interoperability of data—to help turn things around for our industry?

GS: Within software companies, and the state of where we are, there's this discontinuity by the fact that the data—if I build a model I should be able to do ten things with it, not one. Currently, a lot of the processes and workflows require that, even if I have a model, there are 10-15 other things you do as part of the design process that you need to evaluate and analyze. At the end of the day, you have a model but you still have to build a model for two or three other uses. This is the thing that's the biggest problem.

It might be that the uses of the model are by other firms. Then interoperability would be important. We built a Revit model for documentation and it's really hard to get other things out of it in a useful way, whether it's for fabrication or for analytics, anything specific to the building. That's where I see the productivity not coming.

A recent article in *Architect* magazine, "Setting a Standard,"[5] stated: "Although the number of project teams using BIM tools increases each year, the transformative potential of these tools remains checked by barriers that impede the information exchange among participants and across different software platforms. Getting the most out of BIM will require an open exchange of information, which in turn requires defining and implementing common protocols and standards. But who wants this arduous task?" It appears that you and HOK do. Why?

GS: It's not that we're really that interested in making sure everyone follows, for every information exchange, an identical standard. I personally believe that that will never cover everybody's work. Take a web API. There's a standard structure to it. There's a set of documentation that comes along with it. But there is a known set of tools that you need to interact with it. That's more along the lines where I'm interested in seeing these things go.

We're most successful when there's one thing we know how to read well and then manipulate it in such a way that we can produce many results out of it. They aren't standard in that you can only do it one way. But they are standard in the fact that you use the same concepts over and over again, but in slightly unique ways. Like where Jon Mirtschin at Geometry Gym builds custom bespoke stuff, where his transport mechanism is IFC, on top of a standard. Because he uses a standard he knows how to structure the data and how to reinterpret it.

Where is your focus primarily? Geometry? Data? Workflows?

GS: All of the above. Along with the multiple use cases for a model. One of the things I don't see reflected in the hacker mentality is that the people with the expertise are always sitting next to each other and are always using the same set of tools. The workflows are actually quite important. When we can consistently produce something across projects, then the workflows exist that allow a domain expert who has no reason to be in a Revit model. Even if their expertise is not model-driven, they can have access to that data, interact with it; then we have some sort of loop to get it back to wherever we need it to go. Very few of those workflows are close to perfect.

You and James Vandezande, Director of HOK's buildingSMART initiatives, were invited to visit Oslo by your then new strategic software partners—dRofus. HOK and dRofus recently renewed their enterprise license agreement to use

(Continued)

their client-server database solution for integrated program management on a majority of HOK's building projects. How has that worked out? Has it changed the way you work with data?

GS: From a software and implementation standpoint, we're happy with what has happened in that time. The challenge is always on implementation. This is a great example where if we were just to continue to focus on checking program against design, we'd be engaging very few people. If we start to look at a solution like dRofus as a hub for all the key information we need to start a project, it is not because it's the easiest—though we will make it the easiest to work with—but more so for its reliability. That's the part we're delving into now. By reliability I mean: where's the material list for the project? For a project we're doing now, it's probably in an Excel file in a directory somewhere. It doesn't work great if someone doesn't put it in the right spot. Or if 2 or 3, or even 10, different people need to contribute to that. You usually end up with different versions for different things. And the spec writer, when he tries to answer a question about that, is searching all over the place.

Talking about materials: take that concept and start to put it in a project-specific database. Everybody can access it and knows where it is at. It has a well-defined data structure to it. By well-defined, I mean a project that's consistent. That's where we start to engage more than just a few folks that are just checking the program or the building area. That's where we are now. We've done some beta testing on projects but from a usability standpoint it's not where it needs to be.

The buildingSMART data dictionary is one of the key aspects of buildingSMART's vision for interoperability. How useful is it?

GS: There needs to be an understanding of what one concept is in one country versus another. Whether or not that will mean that I, in my model, indicate that this thing is the English word for what I use, and that will then mean that someone else will receive it by that process and it's in French. My view of how this works out is if you build a model and you start off building something with a semantic definition of what things are in a building, you can arrive at the same result without the manual linking process. It s important to have the dictionary so people know what things are across the world. A use case might be where you tell this door that I'm this type of door. Whether a lift is an elevator and what are the properties that are associated with the lift in the two languages. If my structural engineer is French, I shouldn't expect to have him read English to understand the load calculations or the material definitions on that piece of steel.

In that sense, data becomes the universal language.

GS: Yes. In some ways there's a meta-definition. Let's say we're talking about Portland cement. There's a meta-concept that is keyed back to meet this concept of Portland cement. And if you say in English, and you can translate it to understand what I am referring to, if I wanted to know if there's a uniqueness to my language, the properties will then transfer over correctly.

Do you ever work with Big Data?

GS: I would like it to be. It's one of the efforts I am working on to make that possible. Right now, the way the industry works it's a lot of tiny little buckets of little data. And there's no real good way to put it together. It will take a while to see results. We might solve pieces of it, then progress to parts of it, in the firm. Long-term, yes, it has got to move that way toward Big Data. Whether it's an established company in the AEC industry that figures it out or someone that comes from another sector altogether who says, this is stupid, this is not a hard problem to solve if you apply the right technology.

Compatibility Is Key

How does a firm like Thornton Tomasetti address and ensure interoperability—the ability for various pieces of software to talk and play well with each other—among its internal and external teams? "In my opinion, interoperability is the key," says Jonatan Schumacher. "There's a quote from Charlie Thornton, our firm founder, from 25 years ago, when we were first running structural analysis in 3D, who said: 'In spite of the great progress of the last decade, many obstacles must still be overcome.... We now have to zero in on the key issue, the Achilles heel of [structural] computer programs … COMPATIBILITY!'"

Schumacher and Gregor Vilkner taught a programming, BIM, and big data class in 2013 at Stevens Institute of Technology where the assignment—called Solar Monopoly—was about "accessing all the data, all the databases, and constructing tables in such a way that all of these parties talk to each other without really knowing about one another," explains Schumacher. "Just like in today's design-construction scenarios, people barely see the whole picture, and know every party involved."

Today we have buildingSMART, IFCs, COBie, and hacker approaches (using workarounds, design and construction professionals taking matters into their own hands). If one could provide a report card from the interoperability front, how would interoperability be doing? "It's doing really well. And really poorly," says Sean D. Burke. "It depends on the task, on the experience, and on the risk-taking that a team is willing to accept." He explains:

> When it works really well, we're using a lot of those technologies, including open source tools that are able to relay data back and forth. There's this movement where BIM and computational design are starting to smush together. It's going to be harder and harder for these tools to be thought of separately. They're both dealing with large amounts of data. The approach they take to use that data is different. The more they can align with one another, it will be much easier to move the data and geometry between the tools. The teams that are not successful in interoperability are the ones that are less knowledgeable about the different resources that they have at their disposal. It's an education issue. It might be a function of time. They don't have a lot of time to learn these things. A lot are generalists. A lot of folks are very specialized in what they do. For instance, a computational designer. They never do construction documents or visualization. There are other folks who only do those things. Finding what the proper workflows are on both ends, to make sure there's a good handoff, is important. You have to get a bunch of managers to buy-in to make sure that stuff is planned properly from the beginning. If you're planning for these hand-offs, you'll maybe go about your work a bit differently. Versus everybody having a free for all. Recreating a lot of data and being quite inefficient.

"It's our job to implement data but I do think we need some entrepreneurship from the AEC industry, as well as educators to spur curiosity, talk about possibilities, and AEC to integrate the technology," says Ringley. "As far as prepackaging and standardizing what is the IFC for datasets, standardization is important. Some people argue that standardization is a problem for innovation. First of all, stop obsessing over innovation for a second. Let's just try to do something well."

Interoperability as Data Homogenization

Interoperability, at heart, is about trying to get all these tools to talk to each other. According to Andrew Witt of Gehry Technologies, "interoperability is a kind of data homogenization." What does Gehry Technologies' GTeam use to get pieces of technology to play well with each other? "Our system is conformable to IFC specifications," answers Witt, "although our system is both more general and more optimized. In some sense, the more resolution something has, the easier it is to interoperate."

Notes

Unless otherwise indicated, quoted text throughout the book is from interviews with the author that took place between February and July of 2014.

1. www.adjacentgovernment.co.uk/pbc-edition-004/bim-community/
2. http://en.wikipedia.org/wiki/Industry_Foundation_Classes
3. www.nibs.org/?page=bsa_about
4. Teicholz mission statement, 2008.
5. www.architectmagazine.com/bim/setting-a-standard-in-building-information-modeling_o.aspx

chapter 8 Data for Building Owners and End Users

You can have data without information, but you cannot have information without data.

—Daniel Keys Moran

We have seen what role data plays in planning, design, and construction. What role, if any, does data itself play for building owners in their facilities? Do certain building types—technology projects, for example—lend themselves to being data driven while others haven't yet benefited from what data offers? How can consumers of architecture—building tenants and users—benefit from an awareness of building data?

Benefits to the Owner

- Data helps clients understand their facilities in a more data-driven way

- Data facilitates a better understanding of the implicatons of pursuing objectives

- Data enables owners to visualize results almost immediately

The collection, analysis, and transfer of data we have seen so far ultimately benefits the owner. The ability to visualize data goes a long way toward helping nonspecialists, including building owners, understand and evaluate abstractions such as what is communicated by raw data. Sukanya Paciorek of Vornado Realty Trust has high-level ways to evaluate their portfolio. "We use Energy Star Portfolio Manager®, a benchmarking tool that the EPA offers," explains Paciorek. "So, we always had a pretty good idea of where our buildings ranked in their evaluations." As she explains:

> We knew where the problem areas were and where the high-performing buildings were. In the lower-performing buildings, often we suspected that the issues were in the tenant spaces, not the base building. Once we had more data, we could visualize and see this almost immediately. One of the first things that we did when our web-based tool was up and running was to graphically show the portfolio and difference in energy consumption between base building and tenant space. Being able to parse a lot of the data gave us a very good indication as to which buildings we should target for improvements.

Paciorek summarizes this sentiment best when she sa)ys, "The ability to demonstrate the savings was a real success. It not only helped us showcase a great story, but it enabled us to build support for future projects. Having the necessary data underpins an enormous amount of our ability to not only showcase, but build upon our successes."

Case Study Interview with Sukanya Paciorek

Sukanya Paciorek is the Senior Vice President of Corporate Sustainability at Vornado Realty Trust, one of the largest real estate investment trusts in the United States. In this role, she develops and oversees Vornado's corporate strategy and goals, programs and policies, data collection, and disclosure related to energy efficiency/management and sustainability. Paciorek also manages the utilities group for Vornado's New York division, and serves on several boards and advisory groups, including as co-chair of REBNY's sustainability committee, board member of Greenlight New York, Co-chair of the commercial buildings subcommittee of NYC's Building Resiliency Task Force, and board member of the Department of Energy/National Institute of Building Sciences Commercial Workforce Credentialing Council.

As a first mover in this space, your company represents data that is meaningful to different parties: tenants, building operators and engineers, property managers, portfolio-level managers, the accounting team. Who in the end benefits most from the data?

Sukanya Paciorek (SP): The data we collect can be valuable to whoever chooses to use it. In fact, the reason we set up a system where the interface is intended for multiple users is that we feel the end use can be widespread. For example, as a landlord, we benefit from it in that our operators and building engineers have people like me and my team to look at it to enhance our operations and improve what it is that we do everyday. Our tenants are enabled to look at that same data through their own lens and figure out how to make their operations better—to lower their expenses and their needs for electricity. In general, the more meaningful data you collect, the more people for which it is actionable. As our buildings become more efficient, the grid and the community at large receive the benefit of that as we are not calling upon as many resources from the broader society in which we live. Overall, the benefit is pretty widespread.

You have mentioned that at one point you realized you weren't making good use of your data. What are some of the things that you do with the data that you currently have? What did you do to make it meaningful for people who need it?

SP: It's worth providing a little background in terms of how we got to where we are. In most of the commercial market, electricity is either deregulated or it is not deregulated. New York is a deregulated market. Historically, what has happened in real estate—and this is still true for most markets in the U.S.—a landlord would pay the overall electric bill and then charge each tenant either a flat fee (a dollar per square foot amount) or calculate a charge on a per-unit basis. So, if you were 20 percent of the square footage of the building, you would pay 20 percent of the electric bill on an annualized basis.

About 10 to 15 years ago, the public service commission allowed us to introduce submetering, which enabled us to begin to allocate and recover our specific costs per tenant. If a tenant used 10 kilowatt hours in a month, they were charged for those 10 kilowatt hours that month.

What we realized, in 2007–2008, is that we had all of this valuable data coming in through our meters that could be used for a lot more than just billing. Cost recovery is, of course, very important; it is at the core of our business in terms of recovering our operating expenses. But beyond that, the data has provided us with an opportunity to identify areas where we can make improvements to operate more efficiently. We started by looking at the kind of data that we had on a metered basis and then translating that into a web-based tool. As a result, anyone who was interested in this effort, and anyone who was interested in energy efficiency, could log in and start looking at the data—and then make an actionable change that resulted in something that was meaningful.

Would you say that what you were dealing with at this time would today be considered big data?

SP: One of the reasons that we decided to build our own infrastructure and system is that we didn't find what we were looking for in the marketplace. We looked around to see who could help us build a web-based tool that made some sense for real estate, and no one had one. Now, if you go to the market today, it is awash with dozens of different start-up companies that are offering just this type of service. In addition, our submetering partner has also developed a platform, in recognition of the fact that this service is valuable now. So, yes, around 2008, we did raise the question with big data providers in terms of how to make our data collection more meaningful and actionable.

You saw savings beyond just that of the tenants?

SP: Absolutely. After we rolled out our system for tenants, we started to build on the metering infrastructure to have greater visibility into how we were managing our buildings as operators. We did that for electric use in our buildings as well as for steam use. Here in New York we have a pretty large steam-based energy advantage. The system provided us with new visibility into what was going on in the boardrooms and operating pipelines that allowed us to modify either a technology or an operating schedule in order to significantly change energy use in a building.

For example, our headquarters building here afforded us some evidence when our chief engineer logged in for the first time and realized that we were running a lot more steam overnight than we thought we were. We were able to dial it back, and saved quite a bit of steam just by being more aware of what was going on. Visibility allows us to have a more meaningful impact because we are able to clearly see what is happening. And, if reality doesn't track with what we expected, we are able to make changes very quickly.

In addition to the visualization, another important advantage is to help us in making our capital investments in our buildings to upgrade them. The average age of our buildings here in New York is 50 years old. Our objective has been to tie our capital outlay spent on energy efficiency to a robust monitoring and verification process. Our metering has been key in this process, by allowing us to create a baseline for our projects and then verify that we actually achieved a meaningful reduction in energy use. We not only used it then as a good tool to replicate success stories—something we would need to know if we were to do it over and over again—but also to be able to show senior management and our investors that our investments yielded measurable results. We're not only ahead in terms of making investments, but, importantly, we can show that we are doing it very carefully, thoughtfully, and methodically, and that we're capturing the most value.

Did you find that you were telling different data stories to different tenants?

SP: Overall, at a high level, the message is the same. That is, that we have tools that enable you to have access to data and information that you can use to more efficiently manage your operations and make changes as appropriate. It is important to note there is a difference in how we can foster change at the operating level versus the tenant level. Because the operators work for us, we have control over how much money is spent, the kinds of training our engineers receive, how much time they spend on sustainability issues, the incentives we offer, and as a result of all of these things, the kinds of results we achieve. This is totally different when compared with tenants. With tenants, the dynamic is more

(*Continued*)

about partnership, being a good citizen, the bigger picture, and saving money. It's a completely different conversation. In addition, the types of actions tenants can take are very different. They're looking at things such as heat load and whether they are turning their lights off at night. So, while the higher-level message is the same, the tools that we have to utilize are very different.

Your data was used to make a case to your president for saving your company money on a LEED retrofit program. Of this you said: "What this allows us to do is allocate money to stuff that works."

SP: We were assessing what we wanted to do with the portfolio in terms of sustainability. We ultimately decided we would do something involving LEED, to embark on a significant effort to LEED EB (existing buildings) certify our portfolio. What we found, over the first year to year-and-a-half of doing this, was that every time we looked at a building, the operators would say that they had a project that they have been wanting to do, but hadn't been able to get a budget approved when people higher up the ladder didn't understand what the projects were for. So what we did was create a stand-alone energy-efficiency capital budget that helps us finance and implement energy-efficiency projects in our portfolio. One nice thing about our group is that we manage the sustainability budget in New York but we also manage the utilities. We're in charge of paying all of the bills, submetering, and making sure we have all the right technology and infrastructure to make this happen. When we started looking at LEED retrofits through the capital operating program, the first place that we took on was our office. We tested about a dozen different types of lighting options for our office until we found one everyone could be happy with. Once we rolled out the project, the great thing about having all of that data is that the week after the project went into place our manager in charge of sustainability here in New York walked into our office and took a snapshot of the week before and the week after the project was completed. We did a calculation of what we thought the energy savings would be over a year based on our initial findings. And what we saw was a 30 percent reduction of our electrical load in our offices at our headquarters. Within a couple minutes of putting together the necessary data, we sent off an email to our president explaining what it looked like last week versus this week after the retrofit, and showing a 30 percent difference that would save tens of thousands of dollars per year. The ability to demonstrate the savings was a real success. It not only helped us showcase a great story, but it enabled us to build support for future projects. Having the necessary data underpins an enormous amount of our ability to not only showcase, but build upon our successes.

Do you share this data with tenants? For what purpose or outcome? At one point, you gave tenants visibility of what is happening in their own space. How, if at all, did that help them?

SP: Every tenant is different. The ability for a tenant to use data to make changes is directly related to having someone on staff in charge of operations, someone who understands energy and how to look at the data. The data visualization tool we built was pretty easy, both to understand and to manipulate. The only way someone could make a difference with that data was if they were the person paying the bill and very interested—motivated—in reducing energy usage, and if they had an operations background so that they could do something about it. And much like we found errors in operations schedules and building management systems, tenants found the same thing. They had lights running overnight, equipment running overnight. The ability of tenants to make an impact is directly related to whether there is someone at their office or company who is willing and able to take these issues on in order to make a change. I will be the first to tell you that the success we saw early on was due to finding the right partner as a tenant.

Since your initial successes, have you found that there are other types of data that you would potentially share with tenants?

SP: One of the things that we've been thinking about is whether we would want tenants to understand their relative position against other tenants in their building. We know that people are competitive by nature. We know that being able to frame this in that way could have a big impact. The question for us is: we also have limited resources. To be able to spend time thinking about it requires a rethink on our part.

We wouldn't even need to provide tenants with specific data of the other tenants. We could rank-order them—for example, rank them 1 through 35 on an annualized square foot basis. To offer them this information would require us to offer them resources to help them get better or worse. We need to build that capacity to do it effectively.

You mentioned that you were at one time getting 6 million data points on an annualized basis. How much time do you spend analyzing the data? Do you need 6 million data points?

SP: We have this conversation all the time. I just had a conversation about this with one of our chief engineers last week. We're working on a building management system right now. The research associate came back and said, here are all the data points in your building management system that you helped to deploy that we recommend you use. Afterwards, our chief engineer said to me, it's true that we don't use all of the data points. What I need I have. What we're looking at now, and what the industry will have to deal with moving forward, now that the data store is open, there's a real issue of what is signal and what is noise. Being able to figure out which is which requires a very practical orientation. What is the goal? What is the direction we are trying to take? Because more data is not better data. More data just gets in the way, unless there is a goal and direction for the data. In our case, the goal and direction is to be able to enhance what it is everybody does. So that they are getting better information that can then be used to make better decisions on a daily basis. From a submeter standpoint, our goal has always been to recover our energy consumption. Is there a better way to do that while still getting the information we need to recover our costs while also making the data that comes out of that process more meaningful? The goals and direction that we have are very important, as are the means by which we do this. And what is the practical translation of that to get to the endpoint without encumbering ourselves with too much data?

Direction to Work with Data

For data to be implemented and utilized on building projects, often owners need to ask for it. Yet, to ask for it, they need to know what it is they are asking for. Owners need to become informed concerning data and how it can help them in their businesses. Owners also need to understand how data can help them in their building projects after the building is completed and they are operating the facility. Chris Pyke of USGBC is convinced that the entire industry will be shaped by data and, increasingly, the evidence-based practice that it supports. "I believe that this imperative will flow down from the expectations of owners, investors, and other stakeholders—entities that have experience with data and analytics from other industries," says Pyke. "Traditional AEC participants will ultimately respond to these opportunities and, in some cases, requirements."

What will it take to get others to leverage data in their projects? "What will force it is when a client requires it," says CASE's David Fano. "And not in a prescriptive, contract kind of way." He continues:

> But when the client wants to understand facilities in a more data-driven way, they're going to go to an architect and ask, over the last x number of campuses you worked on, what was the ratio of circulation to students? And I want to know the last 10 you worked on. Right now, people can't do that. The same way we do research on the Internet now before we buy a camera, where we visit 15 different websites and read a ton of reviews, the way buildings are procured will change and become a more informed process. It will be a kind of Billy Beane-ism of buildings. It's going to happen. Some owner is going to come out with a story about how much money they saved because of the way they thought about their facilities and some of the things that they've done using data. Other owners are going to get hip to that and it will trickle its way through the industry. That's how I think it would happen. I don't think it's going to be an explicit ask.

Chris Pyke agrees. "Exogenous factors will compel and enable change in the industry," says Pyke. "Stakeholders (owners, investors, the public) will demand that the AECO industry deliver buildings that more effectively and reliably deliver public and private benefits, such as energy efficiency and superior occupant experience." He adds: The expectations of these stakeholders are established outside the AECO industry by experiences with companies like Amazon, Netflix, and so on. Stakeholders will reasonably expect a similar type of evidence-based, data-driven behavior from buildings. The AECO industry will be expected to live up to this standard.

Closing the Building Performance Gap with Data

Keeping owners informed of data, and the decisions they are based on, helps with energy goals/predictions and assists owners in anticipating actual results. "There is a lot of data showing that measured energy consumption of buildings during operation is often higher than the calculated predictions during design," says Greig Paterson, Researcher at AHR. "This 'performance gap' can occur for a number of reasons, such as inaccuracies during the design process, design changes, poor quality of construction; inadequate commissioning of HVAC systems; variation in occupancy patterns; and systems not operating as intended once the building is in operation." He continues:

> Buildings continue to perform more poorly than predicted because there is a lack of transparent design and management data and few incentives to check that a building project achieves its intended performance. A consequence of the performance gap is that buildings often have unexpectedly high annual operating energy costs. This should be made explicit to the project team and in particular the building owners. From this information, operational energy performance goals should be set at the briefing stages, based on how the building performs once in operation.
>
> Taking all of this into consideration, there is a need for more data on design, build quality, building management, occupant behavior, and building systems. As this data grows, research will enable us to understand the complex relationships between performance and determinants.

Engineers and architects are becoming more aware of the benefits of data-informed design. It is therefore necessary for these disciplines to promote the benefits to clients and owners. Buildings often have unexpectedly high annual operating energy costs: this should be made explicit to the project team and in particular the building owners, after which plans can be made to reduce these energy use and costs.

There are many ways data can influence the right approach to take for building longevity. "We are currently looking at the future of flexibility, of sin-gle tenant versus multitenant efficiency on floors, daylight, visibility across floors, and floor to ceiling heights," explains Ryan Mullenix of NBBJ. "There are a number of aspects we intuitively know about these attributes. Now we're putting them into a composite variable system, tying them to a pro forma, and assessing how to create buildings that give short- and long-term returns on investment for owners and occupiers. That to me is how data can influence the right approach for building longevity."

Case Study Interview with Peter Pellerzi

Peter E. Pellerzi, P.E., Senior Staff Engineer, Google Data Centers, is with Google's Data Center Design and Construction group, where he is responsible for the design, standards, and technical execution of data center construction projects worldwide. Google builds substantial global centers requiring a new set of tools with the ability to use data to drive decision-making. These include machine learning to optimize the process plants, BIM to deal with fast-track repeatable projects, reliability and simulation programs to evaluate options, and online collaborative tools to share feedback and changes in real time. Prior to joining Google, Peter held various positions in the construction and consulting professions, including more than 10 years in IBM's data center design group.

How would you describe what you do at Google?

Peter Pellerzi (PP): When I started in Google I was with the Data Center Research group and then became more involved in the operations and construction aspects of the data centers. Today I am fully occupied with design, development, and construction of our data center fleet as a manager in the data center engineering group.

What does a typical day look like for you?

PP: The simplified schedule is, leave the house by 6:20 a.m., at the office by 8:00, breakfast with the team at 8:30, lunch in there somewhere or at the desk, have dinner at the office at 6:30, home by 8:30 p.m. Read emails or documents on the train both ways. At the office: First thing is scan the emails that came in overnight due to all the various teams in different time zones. Address any that are urgent immediately. The rest of the day is spent on various project meetings, staff meetings, and one-on-one meetings with all the individuals on my team biweekly. My personalized statistics from January 21 to February 17, 2014, are 458 new emails created, 5038 received, 82 meetings I accepted totaling 113 hours, and 98 meeting/event invites that I declined.

You work for a company that treasures data. Why is it so hard for others to see the value in data?

PP: I have changed my understanding and problem-solving approach significantly since coming to Google. I am inclined to believe that most people, including my former self, did not understand how much data is available on most subjects and how useful it can be.

(Continued)

I can't imagine not using data for all of the decisions on projects.

—Peter Pellerzi, Google

Strategy No. 23: With Data, the Heart of the Issue Is Culture

There are plenty of tools out there in the marketplace, so I don't think at this stage pointing to this tool or the other is the issue. Pick one that your clients and you are comfortable with and move on.

The heart of the issue is culture. The most successful firms are those that embrace an open feedback loop into their process.

> What did we learn from the last 10 projects like this?
> What worked, what didn't work?
> Did we incorporate those lessons learned into our next design?
> Once that culture starts to take hold it will grow.

—Peter Pellerzi, Google

Can you give an example where you used data to make a decision on one of your projects?

PP: I can't imagine not using data for all of the decisions on projects. Something as simple as paint color has several variations to it that can have impacts on your project in ways such as solar gain or faster production times for equipment. There is, of course, a balance of how much time one should invest in each decision versus the potential return, but often it is as simple as asking why did you pick that product and having a five-minute conversation.

What advice do you have for design firms that are interested in working on data centers?

PP: Don't be data center experts *only*. The business will continue to change rapidly over the next decade, with many more challenges facing the data center operator. Firms that are data center experts only may not be able to provide value long term. For example, things like low power consumption designs, low carbon footprint, and water conservation technologies were not at the top of the list for many data-center-only design firms at one time. I would encourage a core group of mission-critical designers in the firm, but keep a broad base of diverse projects that generate new ideas that can be cross-pollinated, such as medical, pharmaceutical, and other precision manufacturing facilities.

What is the single most important thing to know if you're going to design and construct a data center?

PP: What your client is trying to achieve for their end user, not what you think they need to meet some industry standard or tier level. If the facility is a disaster recovery facility and you design it just like their main data center, that may not have been what the end user wanted at all.

Do the firms you engage work in BIM? How have the projects—and you, as an owner—benefited from using BIM on your projects? Is BIM a good match for data center design, or are you seeing other technologies and tools that can benefit the creation of data centers?

PP: Yes, I try to do all my work using BIM. I have seen some immediate benefits in the work where various spaces connect with each other—mechanical rooms, electrical rooms, networking and server rooms, and so on. BIM is very useful in coordinating the interfaces between all these spaces, which change over time.

Can you talk a little about the energy needs of data centers and what designers can do to assure that energy is used efficiently and that the buildings perform at a higher level?

PP: You should look at the entire building as one integrated assembly. There are simple things that should be done first, such as heating your office areas from server room waste heat—seems obvious but many firms don't do this. You have to champion efforts inside your company that drive energy efficiency and sustainability. The key is having it as part of your culture. When you sit down to start a new data center project, one of the very first items on the whiteboard should be the power usage effectiveness (PUE) calculated target for the region you are planning this center. What can the PUE be at this location and how do you do better than that in a sustainable manner?

What role, if any, does data itself play in the planning, design, construction, and operations of a data center?

PP: Vital. Any large owner/operator should collect, or start collecting, historical records of how reliable, efficient, costly, sustainable, and other lessons-learned data points from past construction and operations.

It would be to their advantage to consider these and any new information, such as present market conditions, in the next project. Why would you use the same roofing system if you have data that shows it performs poorly?

Do you foresee a time in the near future when there will not be as large a demand for data centers?

PP: No, I can't imagine this in the short term, say the next 10 years or so. Beyond that I dare not even guess what excitement may come our way. I think the industry is seeing the benefit of using large-scale data centers to consolidate and perform the work they used to do in smaller distributed data centers.

AECO Firms as Data Intermediaries

Designers and construction professionals can be thought of as data intermediaries—part of a larger system that includes owners—according to USGBC's Chris Pyke. "AECO firms cannot force this transition on their own; however, they can act to accelerate (or slow) its growth," explains Pyke. "They are part of an emerging information ecosystem." He adds:

> AECO firms are fundamentally information intermediaries, sitting between the requirements and resources of project developers and the expectations and experiences of project owners and occupants. AECO can excel in this role by creating strong, systematic linkages between requirements, design solutions, and outcomes. They can retard the growth and impact of data-driven approaches by Balkanizing their work and retreating from the critical analysis of operational performance.

Brian Skripac of Astorino believes that data must be embraced by the entire AECO industry. "If everyone is able to look at analytics, they can then define their own processes for leveraging it," he says. "But when you bring the owner on top of that and the owner has analytics, it's even more powerful." Skripac provides an instance where an owner serves as an example:

> We know what an owner tells us about their space. They tell us how they deal with a specific issue. Their building causes them to function/react in a certain way. And they need to improve upon specific elements. Your job, as an architect, is to fix those items. How are we

going to do that? If we're going to demolish and renovate an entire floor to do it, how is that going to improve upon the owner's particular issues? It's about the tangibles. It works both ways. It's not just about the designers or the contractor reacting to something. It's also about the owner/operator understanding what those impacts are, and being able to share them, so the team members can come back to it. For the design team these become the quantifiable solutions that can drive competitive advantages.

Case Study Interview with Brian Skripac

As the Director of Digital Practice at Astorino (now Astorino—CannonDesign), Brian Skripac has embraced the changing paradigms of architectural practice, integrating BIM technologies beyond the traditional design and documentation processes, including defining how building data can be leveraged to optimize sustainable design outcomes. More recently Brian has focused on the integration of BIM to capture and structure relevant facility data, implementing the value that BIM brings to facility owners from an interoperable life cycle management strategy. He is 2014 National Chair of the AIA Technology in Architectural Practice Knowledge Community.

What are you seeing out there in terms of data use, big data in particular, in the AECO industry?

Brian Skripac (BS): I don't think that the use of data and big data has fully penetrated the AECO industry. It's still at a high level where it's somewhat theoretical for so many people and firms. The point of comparison for big data in the building industry today is understanding more of what you see with large firms like SOM and HOK, who are taking advantage of data which is often used for generative and performative design. At the same time you also see thought leaders like the team at CASE work with data. They're mining all kinds of relevant information from building information models for future use. From a mainstream design firm, it seems a little off to the future, as there are many firms still trying to implement BIM. It makes me try to wrap my head around what to apply it to for my firm's everyday use because it can be so powerful. I look at it from an analysis and simulation standpoint: here data becomes readily available and something tangible, but that real deep dive straight into data, and how to communicate it, still seems further down the road to make it informative and manageable.

On the flip side, I look at what we're doing at The Ohio State University, from an owner's perspective, the information that we're collecting, reviewing and working to structure, all of the facility information falls into big data, too. It's just different. When big data is presented, it's presented as enormous data, huge data—it's like whoa. It's such an all-inclusive thing and you're blown away by it and it can immediately become overwhelming.

I think it's important to capture the idea of big data at a much smaller relative scale. It's about understanding what people are working on in the industry as well as extrapolating how it can impact you and your practice. You can't just plan to consume and apply everything you read about. This understanding and specific application is where AEC firms will be successful with big data.

You look at it first blush and you're like, nah, can't do it. Not for me. It's only for the big firms. You've got to be able to break it down and understand it as an idea, and how to apply it for you. It's like anything else—it was BIM 10 years ago. Oh, this firm did it, so I need to do it … or I can't do that, it won't work for me, it doesn't apply to my project work. It's so cyclical. I'm working hard to get my hands around what I've seen the industry do with big data and understand it.

For many design professionals, the subject of data isn't nearly as compelling as the generation of interesting form. Do you see this as an impediment to data use in the AEC industry?

BS: There is certainly a level of those individuals being enamored by that, and yes, if facets of the AEC industry limit the application of big data only to form generation, it will be an impediment. I've heard the argument in the past where architects are turned off by form generation for the sake of form generation, especially if there may not be a specific problem being solved or criteria being met by the simulation or generation. While this process may be taking advantage of big data and it shouldn't be marginalized, that perception is still out there.

You have to realize that big data is a scalable solution for problem solving and its application is going to be unique based upon its application. Some make take advantage of it for strictly form generation, but others are looking at form generation to understand solar impacts, shading of adjacent buildings, the wind, the optimization of the building's structural members, or the rationalization of façade panels. This is all big data and very applicable.

Just like some architects want to purely be a designer, others want to figure out the nuts and bolts of how things go together. The same is true when you talk about technology. Some people see it only as a means to an end—a production tool; others view it as a design tool. You need to embrace all of the possibilities to integrate it in a manner that enables you to solve problems with quality outcomes. That's where the value of big data is going to come from.

At 110 people, Astorino doesn't have an R&D group. But a firm of your size may need someone like you to either recognize the talent or to recognize that this person is messing around with stuff. Because this person could go to someone else in the organization who doesn't necessarily see how you leverage it or apply it, and it becomes a one-off or dead end.

BS: That's exactly it. Having the opportunity to stretch across the various groups, hear things, communicate it—and distribute it back out to the office—becomes extremely important. That becomes part of that exploitation of the success that we have. He did this, did you hear about that? You can spread that knowledge. It's not like there's this little pocket of BIM stuff going on over there. People become knowledgeable across the board. And the more you share, the more your BIM initiative can progress.

How can firms take the first steps toward applying big data methodologies in their AECO practices? Can firms do this on their own?

BS: Yes, they can do it on their own. You just need to realize that big data is everywhere; it's not something that's inaccessible. The more you learn about it, the easier it is to grasp this idea. To get started you have to have a problem or question that needs solving and realize that big data can help provide the answer. It's about transforming the mindset and culture of how to use technology and merge that with the capabilities in your organization. Once you're able to do this, the expertise will cultivate internally since its value will become immediately apparent.

How much of this is mindset?

BS: Most of it. Somebody has to have an idea. Somebody has to tinker with it. Somebody has to apply it then explain it. You've got to have that thought, that initial question, that challenge. If you're not the person to try to figure it out, but you have the idea, who are you going to team with to do it? That's the cultural aspect of it. You have to understand the personalities. If I have to do this, I know exactly whom I am going to. You have to have those relationships. The tools are there to do things, you have to identify who wants to take advantage of them to investigate it and solve problems.

(Continued)

What qualities would you recommend others develop in order to work with data?

BS: It's a thirst for understanding. They experiment without a fear of messing it up. Because they're going to figure it out, or find an even better solution through the trial-and-error process. There's a drive to find a solution to a problem. They've got a "there's got to be a better way" mentality.

Can you think of a project where you've used data in your office that led to an improved outcome?

BS: We've recently had two projects that looked at the impacts of passive solar strategies early in the design process. After following up on a series of iterative performance studies with massing models in Autodesk's Vasari that optimized the building's orientation/form and glazing distribution, the design team was interested in exploring the value of exterior light shelves from both an esthetic and performance perspective. We were able to quickly model the design concept and test the outcomes and found that the ROI [return on investment] just wasn't there based on our building design for a site-specific location. Any saving from shielding the unwanted solar gains in the summer months were outweighed by the missed opportunities to capture that same solar gain throughout the winter months.

On another project we started using a tool from a cost-estimating standpoint. We were trying to think about how we could integrate our cost information to the model, thinking about it at a broader scale using an application that allows you to take advantage of historical building cost data. Not just, you have so many linear feet of a wall or square feet of flooring with a general construction cost to it. It contextualizes construction assemblies and their costs based on their "function." For example, you're building a healthcare facility that is so many square feet that will have a Class A definition for the finishes in the space. How do you understand the difference between the situation in a healthcare facility versus a rentable/leasable office space from finishes, to systems, to structure? We started to take a broader look at it based on building type and location, and not just overall quantities of materials that probably aren't yet specified or formalized early in the design. There's an interest in looking at more projects from that perspective in the office.

That ventures into big data, in that you are contextualizing it.

BS: In that case, we're using historical data from other buildings that are similar to what we are doing. To do this we're using a tool called Building CATALYST. We at first ran it in parallel with a project we were doing to see how it could validate what we're doing. We're currently working through how this technology integrates into our overall project delivery process. We're trying to figure out how to merge our model data further downstream. Not for just an initial programmatic understanding, but how does it validate against what we're creating? How do we start to bridge that downstream gap? We shared historical project data with the program developer and made that part of the process. We're also looking at how to link data further in the process. There have to be checks and balances along the way.

How much are security and privacy an issue when sharing data?

BS: The data shared was from projects where we were the CM and had all of the close-out information as the construction manager. It wasn't a case where we were sending other people's data; we were sharing our own data, so it wasn't an issue.

There haven't been any issues that we've run into. There's always the contract language that you fill out, this type of process/sharing/liability documentation has gotten better. Rather than a security issue—nobody is running off with our plans and building another building—the real issue becomes people being released to use the data and the model for a specific task. If I build something, I'll define that it can be used for the following applications—you can be trusted with the model to this level. We call it *prescribed reliability*.

We look at it as sharing information that leads to the betterment of the industry. If it makes a project better and helps the community as a whole, we want to share it. We see a value here, let's help drive that change. Maybe that's a little idealistic. You gain knowledge and you share knowledge. I've worked in environments where that's not part of the culture.

Data is convincing because it's numeric and tangible. It's easy data, you can't really argue it. You're trying to validate a design strategy one way or another. In the end, you have to have numbers to do it.

—Brian Skripac, Astorino

How have you been utilizing BIM data?

BS: BIM information and data have to be about connectivity, not just serving as a storage receptacle for product information and the owner's manual. Our project at Ohio State has been eye-opening concerning this. Putting all the information in the model and then giving it to an owner, that's not what they want. They want the model to be structured in a way they can use it. We as the AEC community need to understand what an owner's needs are so we can help them. They want to partner with us on that. They don't want to be told. That's where the breakpoint is: You need BIM— here's everything. You might as well just wish them good luck with that. They're going to get buried in all of that data. They can't use it that way and don't want to use it that way. You have to formulate what data is needed, about what assets, who/where it is going to come from, how it is going to be used/shared, and what structure and format it will best be delivered in. That's what we've been working a great deal of detail on, generating spreadsheets of data to understand what data the university is using to maintain their facilities. You can tell them 40 things about a VAV box, but if they only need 9 things the rest is just waste. They might just want to know who the manufacturer is; do I have digital access to the operations manuals; do I have access to a parts list; when was it installed and how long is it supposed to last; and who do I call if it breaks?

It's about pairing up geometry and data in a structured way so it can be connected with other applications; the rest of the data (outside of the model) can come from a COBie spreadsheet. Once I can match this information up in a way that's useful, I can share it with the other CAFM, CMMS, GIS, BAS technologies to use on my iPad, I don't need a BIM authoring platform to look at something. I can take advantage of my task-centric technologies, get mobile with the information on my tablet device, and be assured that I'm working from connected data that originated from a single source of truth—BIM.

Data Visualization Helps Owners Make Decisions

In Chapter 4, Brendon Levitt spoke about using data visualization to help make large datasets understandable. Here, we focus on how data visualization specifically helps owners with their decision-making. The introduction of various analysis and data visualization tools ensures that the transparent communication of information takes place, and the ability to communicate design issues and recommendations to the owner in nearly real time goes a long way to help build trust. "Now, with these visualization methods," says Jonatan Schumacher, "we can comfortably go to the owner, convey our findings, and thus create trust from the beginning."

If data helps owners make decisions, data visualization helps owners understand the data. It is in this way that data visualization enables decisions to be made, and projects to move forward. Schumacher provides examples where visualization reacts directly to analysis, in 3D, without the need to produce additional reports. In other words, instead of farming out the work into a separate visualization to make it understandable for nonspecialists—ostensibly dumbing it down into bar charts and diagrams—here the work *is* the visualization. "This is more and more the case," explains Schumacher. "In an ideal scenario, engineers would be able to concentrate on running analyses, and not so much on documenting the results in reports and drawings. We are working toward this goal more and more—and a big part is to exchange 3D model information with embedded performance feedback visualization."

LMN is another firm that is doing some very interesting things with data visualization to try to graph output in a way that allows viewers to quickly assess performance and identify a promising subset for further exploration. "It even goes down into the file naming protocol," says Sam Miller.

> One of the ways we are going at that is the files are being generated, and the performance is being determined, we're embedding coding literally in the name of the file. So you don't

even need to open the file to get a sense of how the performance is working. If you get a list of a hundred files in the morning when you come in, after running it overnight, you can quickly sort through those and identify which ones are the most promising ones for further exploration.

Erik Olsen says Transsolar's people spend a lot of time thinking about how they are going to present the results to an architectural audience, so that the recommendations are as clear as possible, "especially of high-quality graphics of our data to make sure the visualizations are very clear." "Because then we're more likely to be understood by a design audience." Olsen continues:

> We don't have any graphic designers on board. We're a bunch of engineers who pretend we're graphic designers. We certainly make sketches and charts that are clear and simple. We're trying to make sure that the idea, and the data, speaks for itself, so that what we're recommending is as clear as possible. We're trying to learn as much as we can from fields such as data visualization without having someone external necessarily for that purpose. We're optimizing our diagrams. We've got everybody in the company agreeing not to show a chart without thinking about what every piece of ink of the chart is there for. Charts need to be designed, they're not by-products given to us automatically.

Case Study: Data Viz Using Revit

Michael Kilkelly, principal at Space Command, is currently working on an interesting data visualization (data viz) project using Revit and shares the following:

The client is a wholesale company with 50 or so warehouses across the country. I'm using BIM software to model and visualize their warehouse inventory data. Given the volume of data they collect and the speed at which it changes, they need a system to quickly visualize and identify problem areas in their warehouses. Spreadsheets and typical 2D reports just aren't cutting it. Fortunately, BIM is great for this type of work. Though this isn't a typical architectural service, I feel this is an area where data-driven architects can really help clients understand their data and transform it into actionable business knowledge. [See Figure 8.1.]

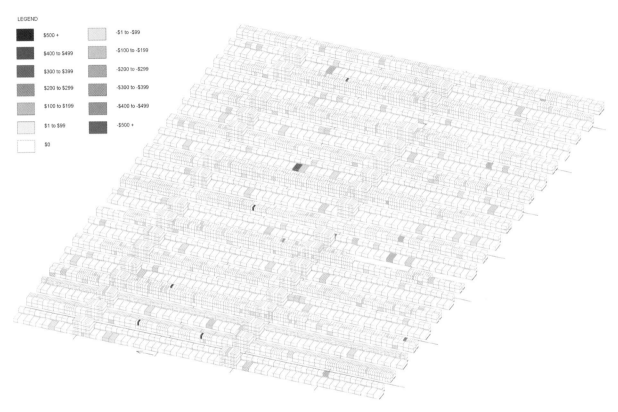

LEGEND

■	$500 +	▨	-$1 to -$99
■	$400 to $499	▨	-$100 to -$199
■	$300 to $399	▨	-$200 to -$299
■	$200 to $299	▨	-$300 to -$399
■	$100 to $199	▨	-$400 to -$499
■	$1 to $99	▨	-$500 +
□	$0		

Figure 8.1:   We can help clients visualize problems. A building is just one outcome. Data visualization is another. © *Space Command*

I used to work with one of the data analysts in a previous architecture firm. He ended up leaving. He had a varied IT and business background. He also had a background in relational databases. He ended up working as a data analyst, doing a lot of the reporting, dealing a lot with their data. They were trying to figure out how they could better visualize some of the data they were getting out of the warehouse. They have to parse through it because it is strictly tabular. They can't tell if something is a global issue with regard to row or aisle in the warehouse because it is just coming up as numbers. You can sort the data, but it doesn't give you a good picture as to what is really happening.

Internally, they were looking for a way to start to visualize some of the data. This former coworker of mine saw that I started to work on my own. I have a pretty strong technology background, even though I am an architect. In this firm, I bounced back and forth between working directly in IT and then would also do project work. He did know that I had

(Continued)

some chops as far as technology goes. More or less on a whim, he called to ask if this would be something I would be interested in. Is this something that Revit could work in? I built a very schematic model of their warehouse. [See Figure 8.2.]

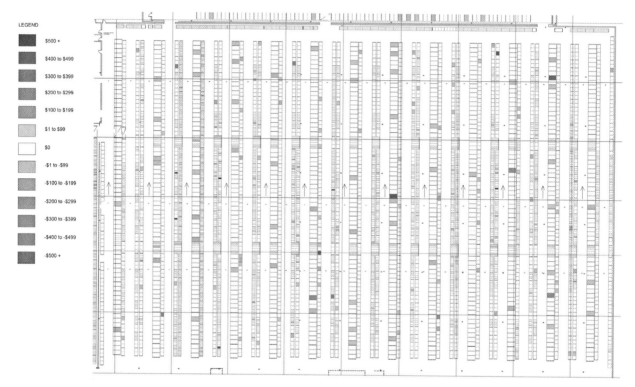

Figure 8.2:   One of the major advantages BIM software has over data visualization tools is the ability to view data in three as well as two dimensions, helping clients better understand their data as it applies to the physical environment. © *Space Command*

To get into some of the technology itself: it is real simple. There's an AutoCAD background. On top of that I built a series of boxes in Revit that represent all the products. There's one (Revit) family in there, but it has a whole lot of variations depending on the size. There are probably 100,000 to 200,000 of these boxes. The file size got pretty large. It's a warehouse. Within each product box we can track as much data as we want. They have a couple metrics that they look at. The families themselves within the Revit model are just containers for the data. They give me an Excel file, though we'll move to something that's a direct draw from a database. Then I can get the value straight into the objects. From there we can filter and color-code them based on the values themselves.

As I've started to work on it and work with them, I've been interested to see what other opportunities there are out there for this type of work. There are definitely data visualization companies. There are a whole bunch of data visualization products out there as well. It's interesting plunging into it not knowing too much about it or coming fully up to speed. [See Figure 8.3.]

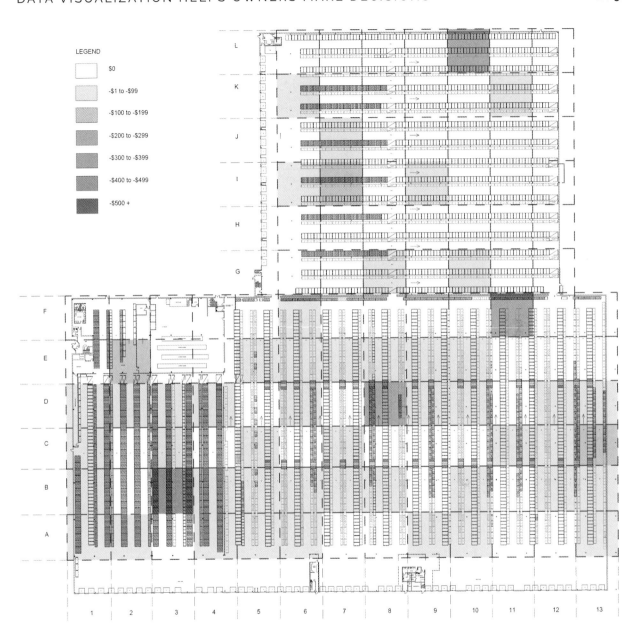

Figure 8.3:   There are a number of really good data visualization applications on the market, such as Tableau and Spotfire. However, these products work best with 2D data. © *Space Command*

I've always been sort of a data guy. Right out of grad school I worked for a start-up. I started playing around with databases. Got comfortable working with raw data in that format. I haven't shied away from that. When I worked for Gehry's office I would build databases for them. For construction observation, various things where you'd do room data.

(Continued)

We would have to do room data sheets for very big projects, it was just easier to do in a database than in something like Excel. Having had some exposure to that, I wasn't afraid of big data in that capacity.

As far as pure data points, 100,000-200,000 objects is a lot. They're giving me the raw data in Excel, and whoa, that's a big Excel file.

The data is passing through some filters before it gets to me. It sounds like their back end is a little complicated. I get the sense that they have a lot of legacy systems. To get the information, it's going out of one database into another, and then they're doing an extraction from that. They give it to me and I clean it—I clean out what I don't need. I still have 100,000 pieces of data, but I can work with that. At some point we'll be able to tap this into the actual live data and then have a near-real-time representation. It's still in an R&D phase. What's interesting for me is to see how this might potentially roll out for the whole organization. [See Figure 8.4.]

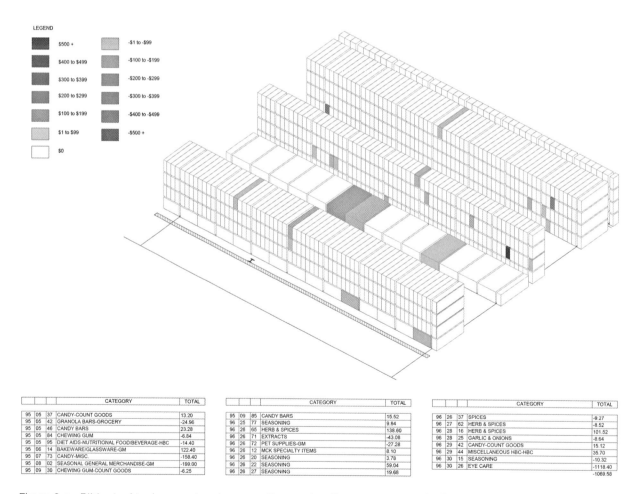

LEGEND

$500 +	-$1 to -$99
$400 to $499	-$100 to -$199
$300 to $399	-$200 to -$299
$200 to $299	-$300 to -$399
$100 to $199	-$400 to -$499
$1 to $99	-$500 +
$0	

			CATEGORY	TOTAL
95	05	37	CANDY-COUNT GOODS	13.20
95	05	42	GRANOLA BARS-GROCERY	-24.96
95	05	46	CANDY BARS	23.28
95	05	84	CHEWING GUM	-6.84
95	05	95	DIET AIDS-NUTRITIONAL FOOD/BEVERAGE-HBC	-14.40
95	06	14	BAKEWARE/GLASSWARE-GM	122.40
95	07	73	CANDY-MISC.	-158.40
95	08	02	SEASONAL GENERAL MERCHANDISE-GM	-199.00
95	09	30	CHEWING GUM-COUNT GOODS	-6.25

			CATEGORY	TOTAL
95	09	85	CANDY BARS	15.52
96	25	77	SEASONING	9.84
96	26	65	HERB & SPICES	138.60
96	26	71	EXTRACTS	-43.08
96	26	72	PET SUPPLIES-GM	-27.28
96	26	12	MCK SPECIALTY ITEMS	8.10
96	26	20	SEASONING	3.78
96	26	22	SEASONING	59.04
96	26	27	SEASONING	19.68

			CATEGORY	TOTAL
96	26	37	SPICES	-9.27
96	27	62	HERB & SPICES	-8.52
96	28	16	HERB & SPICES	101.52
96	28	25	GARLIC & ONIONS	-8.64
96	29	42	CANDY-COUNT GOODS	15.12
96	29	44	MISCELLANEOUS HBC-HBC	35.70
96	30	15	SEASONING	-10.32
96	30	26	EYE CARE	-1118.40
				-1069.58

Figure 8.4:   BIM, a tool to document and manage the construction process, can also be used as a data visualization tool.
© *Space Command*

I've always liked the "information architect" moniker. In a lot of ways that's what architects do. We manage information and the flow of information and the distribution of it. It's too bad the web guys got to it first. It wouldn't necessarily be a full-on coup to take it back. Working at Gehry's office, the position I was hired for was Information Architect. They were looking for somebody who had a technology background but who was also an architect. Someone who could in essence manage the flow of information for this one particular project. That was what drew my eye when I saw the opening. This is a little between both.

Looking at the data, a lot of that came out of this warehouse project. They definitely had a need. Because it aligned with their business goals. That would be one way of offering my skills to their business needs that's not necessarily architectural in the sense that I'm designing a building.

The challenge has been working for myself, just managing my own time. This one client is a big organization, so they don't move that fast and they're seeing this as an R&D project. It has the opportunity to scale up quickly. I need to make sure I'm in a situation where I can scale as I need to. I have been able to move this along by myself. There have been parts that have been very data-input intensive. That has been a challenge. That is one area where I can use help. The client sent out someone to the warehouse who went out aisle by aisle doing a survey because they don't have a good system for documenting where everything is in the warehouse. I received an Excel file that listed all of the product numbers and the aisle numbers, and so on. Translating that into Revit was very time-consuming. And because this one older warehouse was so idiosyncratic, I couldn't automate it. It is really low tech.

There are a lot of time-consuming parts and building the Revit model took a whole lot longer than I would have hoped simply because I'm juggling that project with some other projects.

Wherever possible, I try to automate it. If I could have written a script that would have built the warehouse by itself, that would have been great. Everything was slightly different enough from aisle to aisle that it wasn't possible.

When I first spoke with the client, and they talked about what they wanted to do, they wanted to do some sort of heatmap so they can identify problems. The data that they would want to look at may change. To me, it seemed like a perfect fit for using BIM software because I could create fairly generic objects, then I could customize what type of data goes into them. We could also look at it three-dimensionally. That I could create 3D objects and add information to them, that I could filter and color-code that information, and that I could look at it from multiple views, if these were my criteria puts you in the BIM camp. I spoke with someone today that does data dashboard software, Tableau. One potential problem I see is that because it is not 3D, I can create a heatmap but it's only going to be based on x/y coordinates. Warehouses are three-dimensional, so they have products that stack, so I'm not sure how that's going to work. The thing I like about the dashboard is that you can get the data connection in real time. You can deploy the dashboard so that somebody who doesn't have specialized knowledge can interact with the data. You can move sliders and change parameters and it will update information.

One thing that's really nice about the BIM model is that I can look at it in a plan cut; I can do elevations. With the potential of being able to discover where potential problems may lie in the warehouse, having these multiple views is really helpful. You may see something in plan, you may see something altogether different in elevation or in 3D.

It's outside the typical range of architectural services. But it's solving some interesting problems that businesses are having. I'm trying to figure out how I can extrapolate this. For example, in healthcare, they're tracking all sorts of stuff within hospitals; is there a potential application for something similar there? Who knows where else? There are any number of industries that can benefit from a visualization like that.

Visualizations Enable Data to Tell Its Story

Gregory Janks describes his role at Sasaki in terms of data visualization. "In my own head, I strive to understand what kinds of things can be measured, and which cannot, and how both groups can contribute to decision making," says Janks. "I work hard to allow data to speak qualitatively when it can't speak quantitatively, and above all, to make data accessible through visualization techniques and to express itself through storytelling. This last is fundamental. We've all been through those endless presentations of number after number that amounts to not very much. If the data is meaningless, keep it to yourself. Find the meaning. Tell its story." (See Figure 8.5.)

"It's all about the data," says David Sawdey of Jones Lang Lasalle, Strategic Consulting. "If you have great data, there are great, easy-to-use visualization tools. There are data visualization tools out there that you

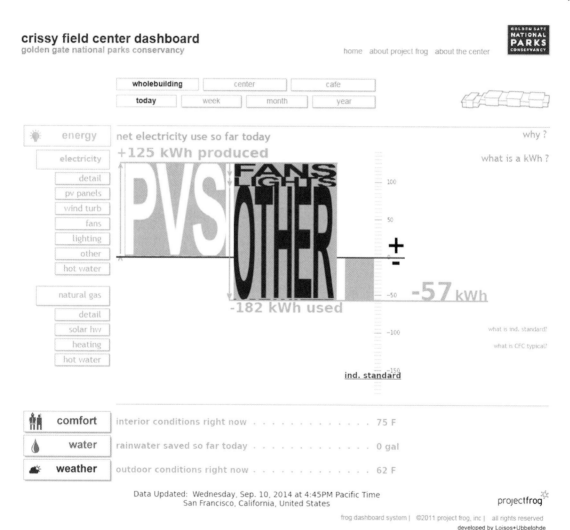

Figure 8.5:   Dashboard for the Golden Gate National Parks Conservancy for the Project Frog modular building developed for Crissy Field Center. The dashboard tells a story about the building. © *Loisos + Ubbelohde*

can use to find opportunities, uncover insights." He continues:

> And tell a story through data. Not anecdotal storytelling as when you say what is happening in the business in a touchy-feely manner. But in a measurable way. The fact-based business where it is all about the numbers, it's all measurable numbers. With that, you have an unbiased understanding of what's going on in the business. Working with our clients, we're past the mindset. Our clients already understand where they are in the journey and where they want to go.

Case Study Interview with Evelyn Lee

Evelyn Lee is a Senior Strategist at MKThink. A licensed architect and dual MPA/MBA degree holder, Evelyn is a recipient of the AIA National Institute Associate of the Year award and presently holds the position of Regional Director of AIA California Council to the AIA National Board.

You're in the strategy group at MKThink. How would you describe your relation to data?

Evelyn Lee (EL): All of the work that we do with strategy we say is data-enabled and human-centered. In many cases we've used data to help eliminate emotion from the decision-making process. It helps our clients find thought processes that are objective when it comes to the ultimate solutions we help them to create using data that supports how we move forward in the project. A lot of the time we just see ourselves as conveners for these projects and what we're doing is helping the client understand the best outcome for the current portfolio of assets. We use a lot of data in a lot of different formats—anything from a card swipe upon entering a building, to understanding how far students are traveling to determine if there are enough schools in a school district, to how many offices are occupied by a major contingency on a regular equipment basis—or do each of them need private offices? All different types of data.

You've had a conversation with Zigmund (Zig) Rubel about some of the work MKThink has been doing around data-driven design. Zig says: "Here's a firm that's actually doing it—using data in day-to-day practice—they do real projects." Does this sound like an accurate description of your firm?

EL: MKThink is in an interesting place. We may not be as bleeding-edge as some because our architecture studio, for example, is run very much like a traditional architecture studio. What we are consistently having to do in Strategy was responding, for instance, to RFPs for campus planning, or programming a new building. Every time we respond to an RFP we are excited about the services we can offer: have you thought about doing this? The time we spend on RFPs when compared to the return is not very great. It takes a smart client to really understand the value that we bring. Many times we're asking them to back up and take a little time to investigate their process, which means that we have to shake hands with them 20 times before the "aha" moment happens. Or you're searching for that needle in the haystack until the client gets it.

At the same time, we're a medium-size firm with a model that other firms could potentially copy. It's doable. A lot of firms are looking at their services and strategy is one way you can go about it.

What qualities would someone need to have to thrive in an environment like MKThink?

EL: Architects are horrible communicators—especially with the general public. In terms of what we look for in a new hire, it's the ability to illustrate a compelling story graphically. We're looking for a good fit with our team. We're happy to train you. We're looking for individuals with a keen graphic eye. We've hired architects with an architectural background and

(Continued)

some with more of an urban planning background, some with more of a design background. We're looking for someone with the ability to take all of this data and distill it into a simple infographic that tells a story that a client can understand just by looking at it in one minute. Because what we're doing most of the time clients don't understand. This ability to communicate is being taught more in schools these days.

I'd call this ability *data visualization*. We don't have dedicated data visualization people on board because our more recent hires have data visualization as part of their toolkit. Because we're so small, people within Strategy wear a lot of different hats. We look for well-rounded individuals who can also think graphically.

Can you give an example of how computers are utilized in the capturing, mining, analysis, or application of data at MKThink?

EL: Depending on the project, we ask for a variety of different data points. At The Nature Conservancy (TNC), everyone was screaming that they needed their own desks. But they're also scientists. We collected card swipes going around their building. On any given day, even a busy day when you have an all-hands meeting, they're only at 80 percent occupancy. That type of data is very different from the type of data we get for school and classroom use. We get all kinds of data. We can use 4Adaptive as a software platform to begin to make cross-comparisons across datasets for us. And also begin to create a visualization in a very technical way. Then Strategy pulls out the visualizations and annotates them in a way that our clients understand. Or we turn them into infographics.

For instance, we're working for one school district that everyone is moving into. One high school is anticipating growth from 1,200 to 2,000 students in 5 years. The school district was interested in building out the adjacent site that they owned next to the high school as another middle school. The high school said no, we are over capacity and need to build an extension. They brought us in. We could have done this without visiting the school. We did a visualization and occupancy study that showed that over 80 percent of the classrooms that were scheduled were over capacity but, during almost every period during the day, because each teacher was assigned one classroom, 40 percent of the classrooms were empty. There we used the data to say yes, we understand why you feel like you are over capacity, but, if you change some administrative rules on how you run the school, you'll be able to get a higher utilization rate out of it. The PTA had been surveyed. The principals had been surveyed. The faculty and administrative staff had been surveyed. They all agreed they're over capacity. Then they saw the data and saw that they were not over capacity.

With The Nature Conservancy, they were all screaming "we need our own offices." Classroom size was just one data point. We pulled many other data points. We did a lot of observation data points: for example, 30 percent of you aren't in your offices 3 days per week. Rent is going up by this much. If we can shrink the floor plate by sharing office space— and you can break down your silos by talking to one another—not having your own office can make for better research outcomes. So nobody has their own office now.

The other thing we do—in terms of our data sources, and where we are comfortable getting our data—we mine public data, we get data from our clients, and in many cases we go out and collect our own data in the field.

If the data resulted in a recommendation to not build or expand, would MKThink make that recommendation, even if it meant killing a potential project for the office?

EL: Absolutely. From a strategy standpoint. One of our taglines is: We believe the most sustainable building is the one that's not built. We find, on average, that many of our clients and organizations that we're working with are utilizing only 60 percent of their building, and that we can help increase their use of the space to 80-85 percent.

Do you feel that owners are receptive to the data you share with them?

EL: They're convinced by the data. The fact that we can turn what is seen as subjective solutions into objective ones supported by data is very meaningful to them. Ultimately, they feel that they are reducing their risk associated with any future architectural project because we've done the research and the data has challenged them. We find if we get ourselves in front of the CFO, especially for universities, that's where our best entry point is, because they get it right away.

Talk a bit about the data analytics people at MKThink. Will architects in the near future be sitting side by side with data science folks?

EL: The principal who runs our Strategy group came from the culture of a big consulting firm. If you aren't on-site learning something about your client, that's an opportunity for someone else to steal your project. He'd rather us be out of the office than in the office. Being able to then bring that knowledge ahead to the process as we move from strategy to programming into what we call implementation. Moving from strategy into architecture. We help serve as a kind of owner's representative in that capacity, and bring to them all of the information that we found in our previous research. Which helps any architecture project to be much more successful.

I am of the personal notion that the idea of the traditional architecture firm is not going to last. That it is going to be hard for traditional practice to continue. We—as architects—do a lot of complaining about not being at the table. But in order to be at the table we're going to have to offer something special. If architects want to be at the table, when it comes to sustainability or what is happening to the future of our cities, they'll need to find themselves partnering with people from other backgrounds. There will be more models where all of the partners of the firm will not be architects. They may be sociologists or biologists or economists as partners in the firm. That will enable them to think a little more broadly about things that are of value to the client. That's where I feel things are headed.

One of the things that we need to do a better job of on our website, especially as we go after RFQs, are the various degrees we hold. We have a rocket scientist, we have a lot of analysts, we have a psychologist, we have a cultural anthropologist and mathematicians. It is truly a diverse firm and I believe more firms would benefit greatly if they brought in other individuals from different backgrounds.

Does it take a certain amount of courage to work in design alongside hard data?

EL: Data is different—it's new and it's scary. It's different from what designers view. With the current architecture curriculums, I don't think any of the students graduating right now have an issue with working with data. A lot of these programs have a cross-over with GIS and energy modeling, which requires data. If you asked any of these graduates, they would tell you they would love to find a firm where I could put all of this into action. You ask a majority of firm leaders, though, in the architecture profession—and we all know that the architecture profession suffers from a generation gap— and they don't know what to make of it [data] and specifically how to apply it in a meaningful way. Individuals who have been around 10-20 years tend to be averse to it. In many instances, they are scared of finding out that the post-occupancy evaluation results tell them that their design was horribly designed. At the same time, I would argue maybe that's the result of the program you were given to design from. Because many architects are not given the correct program.

How does MKThink deal with big data?

EL: It's about finding the right balance in everything. We try to pull the smart data from big data. Development people say: If you want to have the most sustainable building on the block, never turn the lights on. Never run any of the

(Continued)

mechanical systems. At the same time, we're trying to produce a productive workplace for your employees. What is the right amount of everything that will get you the highest level of productivity? We do use big data, and we have a system that can mine it really quickly, but it's really about being smart about the data you're collecting. So we talk about it as smart data.

Data-Driven Design Driven by Owners

What should we be optimistic about concerning where design, construction, and operations are headed in an innovative use of data and building information management? When should we be optimistic that data will be leveraged throughout the building life cycle? "I'll be optimistic when it's being demanded by owners," says Tyler Goss of CASE. "For me, none of this changes on the construction side. The root of the cultural issue—for the lack of adoption of new technologies and processes—stems out of the fact that construction is historically and remains a customer-driven, service-driven industry. Until owners are asking for it, it won't be priced into construction."

Building owners need to know their audience—and what motivates them to act on the data. As Sukanya Paciorek of Vornado points out, there is a difference in how owners can foster change at the operating level versus the tenant level, based on each entity's relation to the owner and the types of actions each can take. Landlords and building owners can benefit from having access to building data to improve maintenance, management, and operations of the facility. End users, such as building tenants, find that having access to building data can lower their expenses and energy consumption. The benefits of accessing and using building data are widespread. As Paciorek says, "As our buildings become more efficient, the grid and the community-at-large receive the benefit of that as we are not calling

upon as many resources from the broader society in which we live."

Building data provides building owners and end users with a chance to identify ways to operate buildings more effectively and efficiently. Owners have concluded that for end users, the data matters, but who the tenant is, and who they have on board to monitor the data and situation, matters too. Data provides a feedback loop of sorts, enabling both building owners and users to circle back and make adjustments to their habits and use patterns. The reduction in energy use and cost also results in success stories—data stories—for leadership to tell and marketing to retell. The bottom line for owners is leveraging data to assure stakeholders and shareholders that measurable results are being achieved. A new awareness brought about by the collection, analysis, and (importantly) visualization of data can help owners address problems and solutions for underperforming buildings. The data helps owners not only to identify but also to demonstrate savings—and pinpoint where the problems are; confirm their hierarchy, extent, or impact; and determine how to react.

Notes

Unless otherwise indicated, quoted text throughout the book is from interviews with the author that took place between February and July of 2014.

chapter **9** Building a Case for
Leveraging Data

*Data is a precious thing and will last longer than the
systems themselves.*

—Tim Berners-Lee

In addition to helping design and construction professionals, what is the best case for implementing
a data transformation within one's organization? We
have seen that design and construction professionals leverage data to create and construct high-performing buildings, and to help create safer buildings
and construction sites via building information models infused with rich data. Despite all that has been
presented so far in this book, many design professionals want to better understand the role data
plays in advancing their practices, how it leads to
increased ROI, added value, reduced waste, and
greater productivity.

Business Intelligence (BI) and
Current-State Assessment

When it comes to technology and data, the AEC
is anything but a first adopter. "If you want to see
what's coming up for the AEC industry, just look at
articles in *TechCrunch* five years ago," says David
Fano in Strategy No. 3. "You can see where the world
is going. If anything, we're behind."

"How long has business intelligence been around?"
asks Fano. "It's old news. For the AEC industry, it's a
new, innovative, groundbreaking thing—it's really
not. Others have figured this out for us already.
The technology's figured out. The software's figured out. Processes are mostly figured out. We
just have to readapt them to our industry." Fano
adds:

> Our data problems just aren't that big. People
> talk about Hadoop and R, we don't need any
> of those. We can get away with Microsoft
> Access for really sophisticated problems. You
> can use Alibre, Office, or Google Docs and do
> some pretty sophisticated things. Once you
> start to talk about a full portfolio of projects in
> an AE firm, and you're bringing in sensor data,
> occupancy data, energy data—if you're tak-
> ing about a retailer, all of their POS data—then
> yes, that's big data and we're not talking about
> Excel anymore. Then we're talking about a
> large, MapReduce effort and full-on business
> intelligence.
>
> To be able to even start to think this way,
> we don't want the tail wagging the dog. The
> architect, the owner, needs to say the impli-
> cations of space could result in these busi-
> ness outcomes. What do we need to do
> then? Is it as simple as getting some already

297

synthesized reports from your ERP system? I doubt many architects ask their clients for their sales records. There needs to be a transformation of the architect to business consultant. Data is going to help make a lot of those decisions.

One way to keep an eye on project outcomes is by monitoring data visualizations such as dashboards. "We're keeping a real close eye on CASE's Project Dashboard," says NBBJ's Sean D. Burke. "The idea of aggregating data across multiple projects, then putting it in a dashboard-type interface so you can learn several different things, both at the project team level and the business intelligence level for the firm, is quite interesting."

"People who have already figured out to send me an email or call me on the phone, I don't have to tell them that BI and data analytics are important," explains David Sawdey of Jones Lang Lasalle, Strategic Consulting. "They already figured that out. Because what they are then coming to me with is, they don't know where to start from a technology standpoint. Aggregating and integrating that data." He continues:

> They have space and occupancy data, they have lease data, and critical actionable data, they have some financial system over here that's doing all their total cost of occupancy

data. And somewhere there's the property list. If those systems aren't all interconnected, then all of a sudden they can't do cost per person, cost per square foot, and get down to those metrics, that help me to do an apples-to-apples comparison of the portfolio. They just can't look at total cost, one building might be twice as big as the other. We use a visualization tool on top of that to communicate what's in the data.

"I have found that if you want to have a meaningful conversation about the future, you must first agree on where you are today," says David L. Morgareidge, Predictive Analytics Director at Page. "Many organizations, surprisingly, do not have monitoring and reporting systems that quantitatively and in exhaustive detail document how they are performing." He adds:

> I've been hired on occasion just to do a current-state assessment because the client didn't have a fully developed, comprehensive current-state dashboard. The current-state assessment is a way to get everybody grounded, using the same language, and understanding from what springboard they are collectively leaping into the future. Once that foundation is laid, predictive analytics and simulation technology allow us to scenario-plan.

Fee and Profitability Data Case Study

Here's a specific example of how Jonathon Broughton of Allies and Morrison captured, mined, analyzed, and applied organizational data.

Most of the work that I've done in data mining has been about tracking sector-based profitability. There's been a view for a long time within the partnership that if we do a certain amount of work that brings in high fees, it will allow us to do a certain amount of work that really interests us: the artsy project, the little boutique house." He continues:

One of the most interesting recent pieces of work has been to mine all of the fee and profitability records and map that against hours worked by those people who weren't doing it for their own satisfaction. There's a separation of the view of those people in charge of a project of what profitability is, and at its most basic, I get a certain amount of money paid to me, I've expended a certain amount of money, therefore I have a profit. We haven't been including people working the three or four extra hours a day, the twelve extra hours a week. Whether they're the projects that we like doing, or the ones where we were delivering high profitability.

The most interesting insight and visualization I was able to give was that the application of the workforce didn't change. It reaffirmed that the smaller projects were much loved by them and made less profit. It was all true. What was interesting was that it didn't matter if you weren't in a position to take satisfaction in a project. Or how much you were applying yourself. If you're on the front line, one of the foot soldiers, no matter what project you were on, your focus is your next deadline. Getting those drawings out. Regardless of how nice the project is, you have the same pragmatic set of variables. And people were applying themselves absolutely equally. While profitability should have been higher on the bigger jobs, what the insight should have been, is that actually if we're not loving these projects as much—we apply ourselves conscientiously and professionally to all of our jobs—why are we asking our staff to apply themselves equally? Two things could come out of that: one is, people just work less. Or, if this is already making us a lot of profit, and therefore allowing us to do those projects we like more, let's just do more of those projects, make more money and do more of those projects we really like. The point is we presented the data against a supposition that was never tested.

Monitoring Office Performance by Tracking Data for The 2030 Challenge

To slow the growth rate of emissions and then reverse it, Architecture 2030 issued The 2030 Challenge, asking the global architecture and building community to adopt various targets.[1] "One of the challenges we have right now at NBBJ as one of the signers of the 2030 Challenge—where we've got to keep track of the reporting to the AIA of the projected energy use of our projects—is every project does their analysis in their own way, or may not be using the same tools," says NBBJ's Sean D. Burke. He continues:

> Some may be using Green Building Studio, IES, or a consulting engineer to do energy modeling for us. We're getting data back, but it's all in these disconnected reports. We're trying to figure out, how do we aggregate all of that? And put in a place where it can be reported on, where the data can be sliced and diced in different ways, so you can make better decisions when starting a project? It's very manual right now, and we want to eliminate that by getting as much data as we can directly into the model. And if we can't do this, we have to ask ourselves why?

Later in this chapter, Mark Frisch of Solomon Cordwell Buenz discusses how capturing 2030 data can be viewed as a snapshot of how his office is performing.

Case Study Interview with David Fano and Dr. Daniel Davis

A founding partner and Managing Director of CASE, David Fano leads the firm's strategic initiatives with an emphasis on business development, knowledge capture and sharing, and data management efforts. Trained as an architect, David's interests and expertise lie in connecting technology and data within the building industry. Working with leading AECO firms, he enables new insights into the knowledge management of technology, and develops approaches that leverage data to deliver value and drive business performance. David received his Master of Architecture degree with honors from Columbia University and has been an adjunct professor at Columbia University's GSAPP since 2007.

Dr. Daniel Davis is a senior building information specialist at CASE. Originally trained as an architect in New Zealand, Daniel holds a PhD in computational design from RMIT University. He currently leads CASE's research program, focusing on the impacts of data, computation, and technology on the AECO industry. His research has been published in AD, ACADIA, ArchDaily, Architect magazine, AUGI, CAADRIA, ENR, and IJAC, as well as books.

Is CASE basing its whole business plan on data-enabling designers?

David Fano (DF): We're enabling the building industry, not just designers. We see them as a very important part of what is a much broader life cycle of building information. With that small adjustment, the answer would be yes. We are changing the way we describe ourselves to a building information consultancy. That is our core business value. We are experts in building information.

Is the emphasis moving forward more on the data than the technology?

DF: I read an article the other day that says the real definition of *technology* is "making processes better." If you need a hardcore definition, yes, we do technology. But it's really about bringing an analytical approach to the building process. And the medium we do that with is data. The data itself is just the raw resource. We see experts in the building industry who leverage that data to bring about insights and ultimately make better buildings and better places for people to inhabit. [See Figure 9.1.]

The advent of technology and data has led to the creation of roles and titles never before seen in our industry. Daniel, you are a senior building information specialist, where you lead research efforts focused on the impacts of technology on the building industry. Are we going to see a need for more people in a similar research-oriented role?

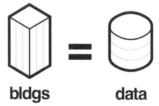

bldgs   data

Figure 9.1 CASE is a company founded on the notion that data is the medium of the building industry. Image by CASE. All Rights Reserved. © *CASE*

Daniel Davis (DD): Most of our industry is based on knowledge and information from which we derive insights—whether insights from data or computational tools.

Strategy No. 24: Big Data in Practice

Once you start to talk about a full portfolio of projects in an AE firm, and you're bringing in sensor data, occupancy data, energy data, then yes, that's big data and we're not talking about Excel anymore.

The architect, the owner, needs to say that the implications of space could result in these business outcomes.

What do we need to do then?

Is it as simple as getting some already-synthesized reports from your ERP system?

I doubt many architects ask their clients for their sales records. There needs to be a transformation of the architect to business consultant.

Data is going to help make a lot of those decisions.

What's the business problem I'm trying to solve? Then go find that data.

I don't think we're at the big data thinking of just give me everything. We don't even know what to ask yet. Go ahead and collect it—especially since the price of storage has gone down—but before you start any kind of exploratory exercise, you should at least have a hypothesis of what you are looking to solve.

—David Fano, CASE

Are firms sitting on data that they aren't even aware of?

DF: Yes. Any firm that is working in BIM. Their own internal enterprise resource planning (ERP) to better understand how they work. The traffic on their websites. Timesheets, calendar schedules for clients. There's lots of data that's going unused or not considered as useful information.

Can firms do this on their own?

DF: Yes. It is more a mindset than a toolbox of technologies and skills. And they all need to spend some quality time with their financial software. It starts there. If you look at any of the industry surveys undertaken by management consultants, firms' profitability numbers in the building industry are just not there. Firms need to align their operational goals with their business goals. Firms need to take a whole new approach to how they think about business. They have to bring this kind of thinking to their own business. Really understand efficiencies. Really spend time with their ERP data. Really capture information about their own business. Then they'll be in a better place to relate to their client and better able to accomplish building this building. They need to be able to talk about their design project in terms of the business impact that the construction project is supposed to have.

(Continued)

Others have figured this out for us already. The technology's figured out. The software's figured out. Processes are mostly figured out. We just have to readapt them to our industry.

—David Fano, CASE

The AECO industry is said to be going through a historic transformation, moving from a document-centric to a data-centric approach. But can't documents also be considered data?

DF: Everything is data. Our gripe is not with documents or with paper. Paper's fine. Paper serves a very valuable service. Our issue is with the status quo, saying that a 24 x 36 or 36 x 48 sheet size is the only way building information is conveyed. Why? That's an old thing that came from modes of production at that time. We have iPads now. We have laser printers that can go on the jobsite. Why shouldn't a drawing set be the size of a book? We can zoom in and zoom out now. Scale had to do with the size of a pencil and how much information you can put on paper. We need to recognize the opportunities that current mediums allow for.

Documents are fine. If you look at the latest trends in databases, they're document-based databases rather than table or relational databases.

What we want to challenge is the presentation of the information. A lot of the thinking in the industry has been about CYA, document it so you can go back and say you did. If it's about giving the right amount of information to the right people at the right time, then we can challenge what all the principles are for what a drawing set is: the documents that are required to build a building. A document for me is a video file. Let's use video. Let's not confine ourselves to 2D abstraction. [See Figure 9.2.]

If you look at the rest of the world, data visualization has become this very powerful thing. The *New York Times* will spend a lot of money on the top data visualizer in the world because now you can understand very complex things in a very simple way. So for me, a drawing set is a data visualization. And it is time for that data visualization to evolve.

[See Figures 9.3 and 9.4.]

How important is consideration of the audience for the consumption of the data visualization?

DF: It is absolutely critical. There's exploratory analysis you do for yourself. That's how designs can get better. What we're producing is always for someone else. If you're working on a building that's going to get built, everything is for someone else.

Past			
	Data	vs.	Geometry
	Data	vs.	Documents
Present			
	Data	=	Geometry
	Data	=	Documents

Figure 9:2   If you look at the latest trends in databases, they're document-based databases rather than table or relational databases. © R Deutsch

Firms that are going to be able to talk about design and construction in those terms will be the ones that do this and succeed. The ones that don't will become design departments inside construction companies.

—David Fano, CASE

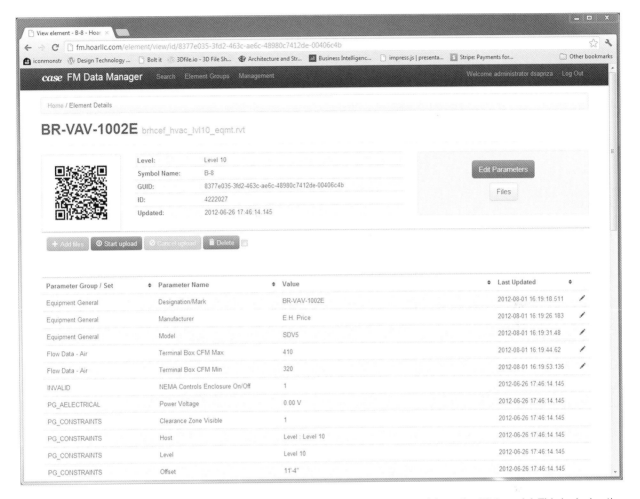

Figure 9:3   Each asset has its own page, presenting data that has been extracted from the BIM model. This includes the location of the asset, its unique ID, and manufacturer. This allows someone on site to access the data without needing to open up a BIM model. © *Hoar Construction and CASE*

How receptive are you seeing others to the message that building data is the basis for good design and construction?

DF: The expectation for owners is going to change. Owners are requiring BIM right now as an intermediary step. They're asking: How will this building—this configuration of this building—help to make me a better business? I think there's another way—by leveraging data—to make that argument. When Google proposed that they were going to build a new building, I want to give them a spreadsheet that talks about bottom-line costs, construction costs, operational costs, maintenance costs, mobilization costs. Companies—owners—are going to ask for this. It is inevitable. Firms that are going to be able to talk about design and construction in those terms will be the ones that do this and succeed. The ones that don't will become design departments inside construction companies. [See Figures 9.5 and 9.6.]

(*Continued*)

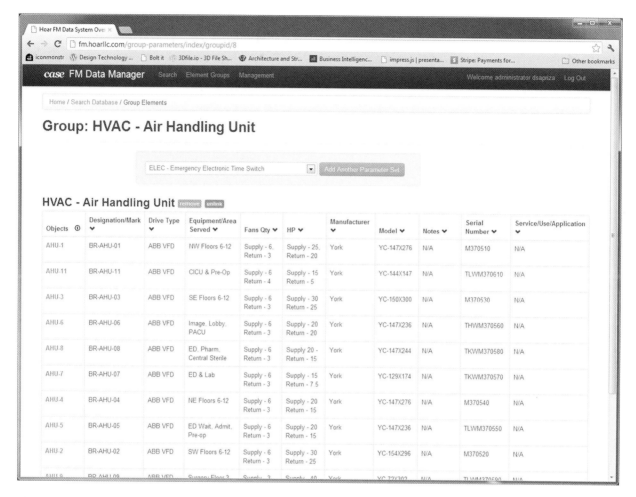

Figure 9:4   Categories of assets are grouped together to improve discoverability. In this case, all the HVAC air-handling units are shown. © *Hoar Construction and CASE*

Beyond accomplishing specific tasks, does data help people make informed decisions?

DF: They might be misinformed decisions. Garbage in, garbage out. But I think at a high level data enables decisions. Rather, it is the leveraging of data that enables decisions. Data itself is a raw resource. Conceptually, I believe in the data, information, knowledge, wisdom (DIKW) progression. What the industry needs to realize is this is what they've been doing. Part of the reason architects are so valuable and come into trouble later in their career is because they have accumulated a lot of wisdom. I don't think that can be trivialized. What I think is happening is—if we can capture this stuff which is really only in passive knowledge—now we have all of this more retrievable stuff. We can expose the wisdom to a different demographic and one that thinks about things in a different way. I do see this as a watershed moment for the AEC industry. When we could end some of these long-lasting traditions—modes of working—as people begin to leverage information.

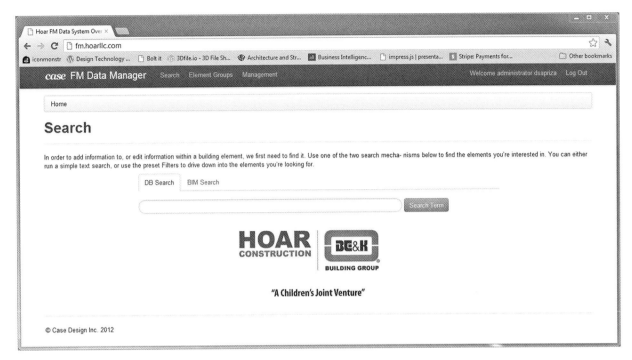

Figure 9:5   The HOAR FM Data Manager provides data on the assets within a building. From the home page, a user can search for a particular asset and bring up all the data in the BIM model pertaining to that particular asset. © *Hoar Construction and CASE*

What more does data provide?

DF: Data makes decisions defensible. But it also allows for more confidence. Data allows designers to design with more certainty. The reason design isn't defendable or defensible right now is because it's "I think this is a good idea." That's my opinion and you're entitled to have your opinion because you're the client and you're paying for it. If I run the numbers and know that this spatial configuration, based on past projects and the sensors I had on 20 projects for other clients I've done them for, will result in this kind of thing. Data sources are not missing. It's the thinking. The other part of it is the validation. We're scared to validate. All of the energy calculations on the building model said it is going to be this. Then they go back and measure it and it is not anywhere near that. We can't be scared of that. We have to embrace those failures, learn from them.

Is there a downside to data-enabling designers?

DF: Yes. Like all things, if used poorly, it will result in poor outcomes.

Does this sound like an accurate description of CASE's approach: Keep things simple, address what is there, and don't try to overcomplicate things by making them "smarter"?

(Continued)

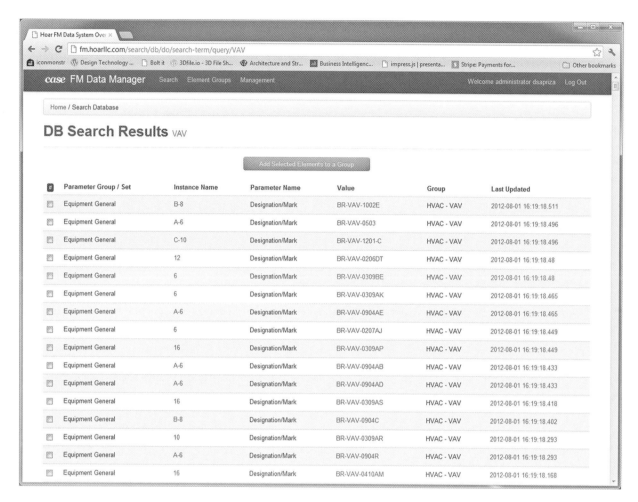

Figure 9:6   After searching for "VAV," the user is presented with all the HVAC variable air volume controllers within the building. The user can also search using a product name, description, serial number, or other associated data. © *Hoar Construction and CASE*

DF: Yes. It's all out there already. For the most part, everything we need to do incredible things already exists. We just have to find the right people. I don't know how you convince someone who wants to do data science and work for Google to think that urban problems are more interesting. People are the big part of this. The reason CASE is successful, or is what it is, is because of the group of people we've been able to carry. We haven't invented any software. We've used off-the-shelf stuff. We're not inventing a programming language. We're just using stuff that's out there. All the stuff we do is open-source technologies. It's all PHP, off-the-shelf frameworks. I'm not filing patents for any of that stuff. We're using other industries as precedent. We're using off-the-shelf stuff, even a lot of free stuff.

As building information consultants and specialists, CASE has looked at how people are using data and information. How much of the data in the models is making its way into operations?

DF: That's not happening.

CASE has worked with a number of clients to help them take the first steps toward applying big data methodologies in their various AECO practices by making use of dashboards. Is that a preferred way for less technical players to interact with the data?

DF: In a broader sense, it's about visualizing data. The drawing set is actually a data visualization. Eero Saarinen was a phenomenal data visualizer. His drawing sets were terse, precise, and elegant. He was able to succinctly visualize data in order to accomplish buildings without a computer. So really, at its core it's about communication. This is why data visualization and infographics have taken hold, because people then could really understand information and knowledge in a much clearer way. Dashboards are one manifestation of a data visualization. As are the drawing sets. We as an industry are going to have to recognize it's really about communicating stuff. The notion of the drawing set needs to be challenged. I don't think paper should go away. Paper is just a medium. It doesn't matter if the drawing is printed on an iPad or in the cloud or projected in the middle of space through an Oculus Rift. It's irrelevant. The information that is communicated has the potential to be much richer. It's the sole reason dashboards have bar graphs and pie charts, to better communicate what's in the building so you can more accurately create what's in the field. [See Figure 9.7.]

BIM—it's just a spreadsheet. A firm could dig down 10 key data points for every project they've done. All they have is a significant amount of information. Most firms don't even do that. They just see every project as start-from-scratch. Architecture school teaches us that we need to start from scratch every time.

What importance does the format that data is delivered in have on translating it from raw data to knowledge and decisions?

DF: How many firms have a full-time specifier on staff? The people who work on words and data. How many firms have off-loaded that role, because they don't want that person in-house? Then look at the size of the spec writing consulting groups. The spec is one of the most valuable things. Putting lines on paper is a whole lot easier than writing words and quantifying things. There's less and less interpretation, and you have to take a firmer and firmer position. And that's what people are scared of doing. As soon as you put a number on there, I can measure you against that number. You said there were 32 lights? Actually, there were 36. I'm going to back-charge you for that. It's your fault. I'm going to sue you for that.

> *One of the biggest hurdles for using data in our industry is going to be embracing certainty.*
> —David Fano, CASE

One of the biggest hurdles for using data in our industry is going to be embracing certainty. Being able to say, yes, I know it's that. Most people want to be able to say: It could be this. It could be that.

This is one of the challenges we have right now. We have the technology evangelists who say it's in the model. And that's not necessarily true. You could have hired an intern who didn't know to place that right kind of light, or drafted it instead of modeled it, and it's wrong. Here's an instance where the architect is disconnected from what the team is doing. Here's an instance where the quality of labor is way better than the quantity of labor. I honestly believe that we produced with two very, very good people what an AE firm would produce with eight. A small group of all-stars versus one all-star with a group of pretty good people, which is generally the

(Continued)

Figure 9:7   An early version of the CASE Building Analytics dashboard. The dashboard helps architects and building owners see trends in their projects' geographic locations, sizes, and program types. © *CASE*

approach firms have taken. They have two or three BIM specialists and say let's put one on each team. What they really should do is take those three, and make them their own swat team, and they will just carve right through the projects without a problem. Very few firms are willing to do that.

Is the ultimate goal to automate the capturing and applying of data so we don't have to attend to buildings?

DF: I don't think so. I'm a firm believer in our capacity to think. Those of us who can leverage data to make better decisions will be successful. Buildings can benefit from people who think of running facilities that way. The building itself is still very much an instrument that needs to be played and not an automated thing like a player piano. I met with some people recently who come at buildings from a technology standpoint, who had a very strong push to automate and leverage computation. It would be so dehumanizing. It is so far from what we want to be pushing.

There is this utopian world where we have so much data that, when you move a room, it's the equivalent to running a Google query that indexes a gazillion websites and tells you what's the right one. I don't think you're ever going to be able to structure a way to capture that experience. You won't want to sit there—it will feel terrible to be there. To come up with an algorithm that can capture that is trying to solve the wrong problem.

To what extent are computational design tools such as Grasshopper central to leveraging data in design, construction, and operations?

DD: If you are working with data, you are going to need to use a computer at some stage to manipulate it. This is especially true if you are working with large datasets or real-time data. Tools like Grasshopper are interesting because they make computation more accessible, which has the effect of making data more accessible.

Is it just the technology that needs to be flexible or also the technologist?

DD: In the long term, technologists have to be extremely flexible simply because mostly they're working with technology that is constantly evolving. But on the timescale of a project, I think technologists have to be careful about being too flexible. Technologists need to be a little inflexible, a little demanding, and push back against the status quo in order to move it forward.

Talk about data for design analysis in Rhino and Grasshopper; for example, visual programming.

DD: The Grasshopper definition in the Snohetta project worked by trying every louver orientation, running the analysis, and presenting the results on a spreadsheet. A designer could then go back to the spreadsheet and say, "At this orientation I get this performance." So the Grasshopper definition wasn't giving a designer an optimized solution, it was rather giving the designer the data about the performance potentials. The designer can then look at that data and use their judgment evaluate the options. They might go with the theoretical optimum, or they might decide to use a configuration that is slightly less than the theoretical optimum but more aesthetically satisfying. This is a type of reasoning computers are terrible at. It's the best of both worlds: The computer is doing the analysis the designer would find far too tedious, and the designer is using that analysis data to make a decision that is far more sophisticated than anything the computer could make.

(Continued)

How would you describe the main outcome of your research for your thesis?

DD: For me the main outcome of my research was to suggest that there is a strong connection between the practices of programmers and architects. I expect that as more in the AEC industry come to work with data and computation, these connections will become even stronger. So I guess my advice is to look outside the profession; much of what we are trying to do has already been done in some capacity elsewhere.

Security and Privacy

While the security of private information is a much-discussed issue in our time, most of the professionals I spoke with for this book had varying degrees of concern for the security and privacy of data. Transparency of data and information, in contrast, was considered to be of critical importance.

While the subject of data security is still being played out, many questions arise. Who owns the data? What role do security and privacy play in data sharing, and in maintaining and building trust on project teams? What are the ethical implications for sharing private data? Whose responsibility is it to keep this top of mind? How does one go about seeking consent to capture, analyze, store, or apply private building data? When do the benefits brought about by using data outweigh any caution of data sharing?

What changes when the data is not private, but open, public, and readily available to anyone? "Privacy is controllable by keeping the data anonymous—by anonymizing the data," says Toru Hasegawa of Columbia University, Proxy, and Morpholio. "The caveat is, what is truly reliable data? That's what it comes down to. Crowdsourcing is an example where it is exciting and you can gather a lot of data, but how reliable is it? You might just be ending up with more unreliable data. That's the danger of public open-source data."

How much security/privacy becomes an issue when leveraging data depends on the type of data under study. "Most types of data we make use of don't really have an impact on security or privacy," says Andrew Heumann, "but in both healthcare and corporate examples, it was critical to guarantee that data involving people was 100 percent anonymized."

The context of where the data is leveraged—and one's role and demographics—can impact privacy concerns. This is especially true in education. "As an educator I work with students and am very sensitive to their right to privacy and their right to not be exploited through their personal data," says Brian Ringley. "Personally, I'm very torn on the issue—as someone caught between Generation X and the Millennials, and not really identifying with either, I'm sensitive to others' desire for privacy without really expecting it or considering it practical for myself, at least viewed through the lens of contemporary technology, politics, and marketing." Ringley continues:

> The other side of this is that the contribution of our personal data could also be used to improve life for others, whether it's the contribution of medical data to fight disease, or our attitudes and emotions toward different spaces for the benefit of the AEC industry. Unfortunately, we're at a point where even the positive usage of our data will likely be simultaneously utilized for marketing purposes.

The sharing of data often concerns the front office from a liability standpoint. "Contracts are often holding us back—everybody is scared of being sued for providing the wrong information," says Jonatan Schumacher. "We can calculate the sizes of every beam and column, automatically in real time. But in reality, unless the contract is very secure, we don't feel comfortable sharing this information with the client early on. It might be misused for early bidding for construction, and then we'll be held to it and the flexibility in the design process is reduced. So we have to pick how much information we share. We certainly like the contracts where 3D models are being shared, and want to see more of these."

Confidentiality is a big concern for SOM. "There are a lot of examples where the toolsets out there aren't as sensitive about the confidentiality as we have to be for some of our projects," says Robert Yori. "Sometimes it's more challenging to leverage technologies that exist because of that, and it's always a significant consideration." He continues:

> There's a proprietary nature to a lot of what we do. There are confidentiality agreements that we have with our clients. It's a struggle sometimes. Perhaps that's one of the reasons why we may be a little more inwardly focused on the information that we gather, collect, and maintain than other firms. It's of paramount concern to us. Just because the data is stored on our computer, it doesn't make it any less confidential or less important than the drawing sets that we might have, or the confidential project that we have with a particular client. It's information, it's all data. It just happens to be on our computer. We still apply the same level of discretion to it and value it the same way we would any other source of information.

Security and privacy issues are an intrinsic part of dealing with large amounts of data. "We address these issues in everything we do, but I don't feel that they are real barriers," says USGBC's Chris Pyke. "They are technical and operational challenges that

can be addressed with technology and appropriate business rules." He adds: "The fundamental challenge for big data is to create value that outweighs the cost of realizing this value." With numerous issues associated with security and privacy, Pyke mentions the balancing of public and private good:

> Many recent conversations end with great pains taken to protect the privacy of building-related data, notably energy consumption data. This is useful conversation, but it has often been divorced from a practical discussion about the balance between public and private good. In practical terms, energy consumption creates social, economic, and environmental impacts at local, regional, and national scales. The public has an interest in understanding and reducing these impacts. We should have an open discussion about how, as a society, we should balance privacy concerns with the legitimate need to address these impacts.

Transparency versus Risk

The real estate industry, according to Pyke, needs to have a conversation about the relationship between risk and transparency. "In most financial situations, transparency is inversely related to risk-adjusted returns. Transparency about assets or transactions can be used to understand and price risk appropriately," says Pyke. "The same should apply to buildings and other built environments. Regardless of the purported rationale, a relative lack of transparency about an asset is a source of risk for investors. Action to promote transparency—ideally in the form of electronically accessible information—reduces risk for investors and should be applied to permit markets to more reasonably allocate capital and price risk. Today, we experience the legacy of long-standing practices that reduce transparency in the operational performance of buildings. Going forward, this lack of transparency should be weighed as a significant liability for owners, investments, and other stakeholders."

Case Study Interview with Mark Frisch, FAIA, LEED AP BD+C

Mark Frisch is a creative, award-winning thought leader at the forefront of integrated project delivery. Focused on increasing collaboration among design teams, builders, manufacturers, and fabricators, Mark is able to realize thoughtfully integrated building systems, precedent-setting sustainable design solutions, and artfully detailed architecture. As Principal-in-Charge of Technical Design at Solomon Cordwell Buenz, Mark is responsible for initiatives in innovative building systems and materials, technical oversight, and delivery strategies for all client projects. In recognition of the immense importance of data driving today's architectural practice, Mark has developed applications to facilitate access to the silos of information used to monitor projects, market work, drive evidence-based design, and validate building performance.

Mark Frisch (MF): I am really interested in the various types and scales of data generated and available in an office and how best to capture it and apply it. In my case, it seems that the most efficient way to get it is to use those who may benefit from it and to filter the collection through the various groups I work with, such as the studio technical directors. [See Figure 9.8.]

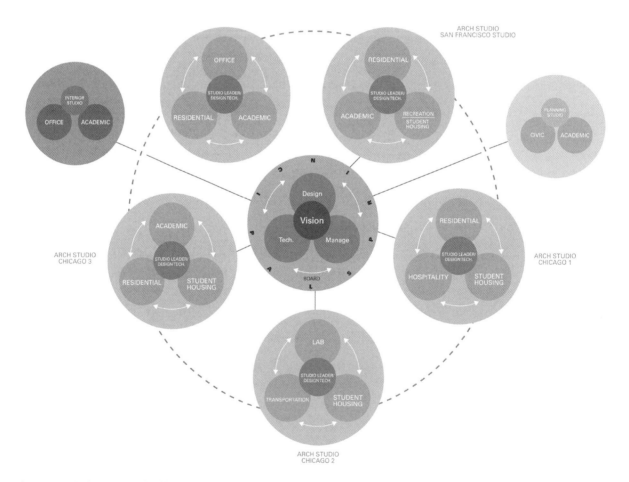

Figure 9.8   Solomon Cordwell Buenz Studio and Design Services infrastructure. © *Solomon Cordwell Buenz*

I have been involved with attempts to collect "all the data that is perceived to be required." As you would expect it, overwhelmed our capabilities; the end result is a totally constipated program, lots in, nothing out. In reflection, our problem was we simply tried to capture too much data, too granular. In part it stems from the fact that everyone in the office has their own needs, which results in an unlimited attitude about what is required—after 10 years of attempting to solve a global problem, we are still without a central database.

If we ask those benefiting from using the data to help collect it, we have a better chance of getting it.
—Mark Frisch, SCB

Lately, as I mentioned above, I have focused more on the individual project scale. I asked myself what happens if we collect and allow it to filter up or sideways. While we as a profession understand the usefulness of office metrics, I wanted to know: If I apply the same sensibilities to project metrics, could we positively influence a project? Further, if we ask smaller groups—say, each team—to collect some of the data, we have a better chance of getting it. If we ask those benefiting from using the data to help collect it, we have a better chance of getting it. [See Figure 9.9.]

For example, as it relates to sustainability, there's aggregated data we collect from our projects that we feed up to the 2030 national database. Capturing 2030 data is a snapshot of how our office is performing, as opposed to understanding, from a project level, what drives better design. Although I understand the role of aggregated data, that's not enough to improve the performance of our buildings. I believe that we need to focus what we're doing on a project level—how the decisions we make are influencing our building's performance. This is meaningful.

I ask the people charged with this area of the practice to give the project teams smaller bites of information, more specific to a component of a project, and to develop an understanding of how it is influencing the performance of the building. Further, I suggested that when you collect information about a building, you need to understand how they are using the data; whether the information you are providing is being applied; and if so, how the performance is trending. Specifically, we are interested in the make-up of the exterior wall. Or, how the barrier levels are being detailed and how the performance criteria are being applied. Further, we know that the exterior wall and the mechanical systems are intimately related, therefore based on the decisions we make on the exterior wall, the mechanical systems we're using should be tuned: Are they? We need this project data to do our work and we need a simple way to abstract it (learn). Finally, I contend that until you hear the studio members chatting about these metrics, we have not solved our data enrichment goal. [See Figure 9.10.]

Following, if you have data for three or four projects, you can chart how the data is trending and whether the process is working or driving you to the same conclusions. If we're using a component three times: Are they all performing at the same level of efficiency? Is there a correlation between the wall system and the mechanical systems? If not, why not? It can be applied very early in the process; for example, if we are sitting in a room with an owner on a project, and they want to know what glass we are proposing to use. It would be better if, based on our database, we can describe what it should be rather than deferring a decision based on further research. We should have precedent information available and be able to talk about it with some level of intelligence based on the building. Bottom line: We are collecting a great deal of information for the 2030 database; my challenge is to collect project data that impacts our decision-making process.

Returning to the topic of responsible parties, while I firmly believe that we need to design a data collection system that rewards those collecting data with information to support their decision-making process, we also need local

(Continued)

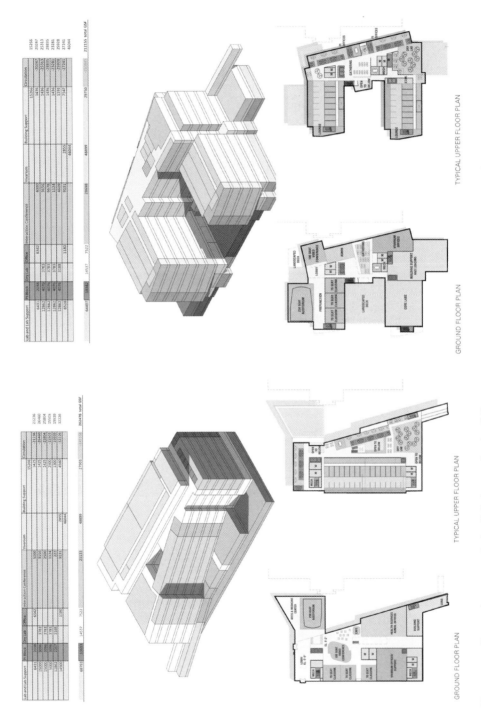

Figure 9.9 Dynamic area analysis. © Solomon Cordwell Buenz

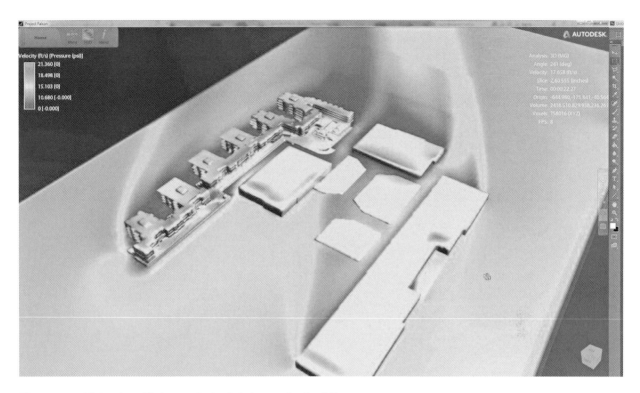

Figure 9.10   Natural ventilation analysis. © *Solomon Cordwell Buenz*

data coordinators. In our case, as we have a technical director in every studio—each studio being a baby office—they by default become the logical arbitrators. Further, each studio technical director has an office "area of expertise"—one is focused on building core, one is focused on construction administration, and one is focused on the building enclosure. As a resource, it is logical that they each gather and maintain data that will support their focus area, so not only are they helping the team to collect project data, they are abstracting from that data specific information to support their work.

[Besides] the data we generate internally, we are recipients of data generated externally, some simply a recitation of who bids on and builds what we design (i.e., subcontractors/contractors), and some is the costs and buildability of what we design. This is valuable data that improves our process and improves our design. This data has a lot to do with how our work is perceived in the community, how accurately we are able to mediate design and budget, and ultimately how well our buildings are performing. [See Figure 9.11.]

There are at least two types of data we work with: building/project data and office data. Most of what I have discussed is building/project data. What I call office data; how our process works from a business perspective, in my opinion is more mature. Interestingly, our profession knows more about the business side than we do about the building/project side. While the office data is relatively sophisticated, it would seem to follow that the building data would be at a similar

(Continued)

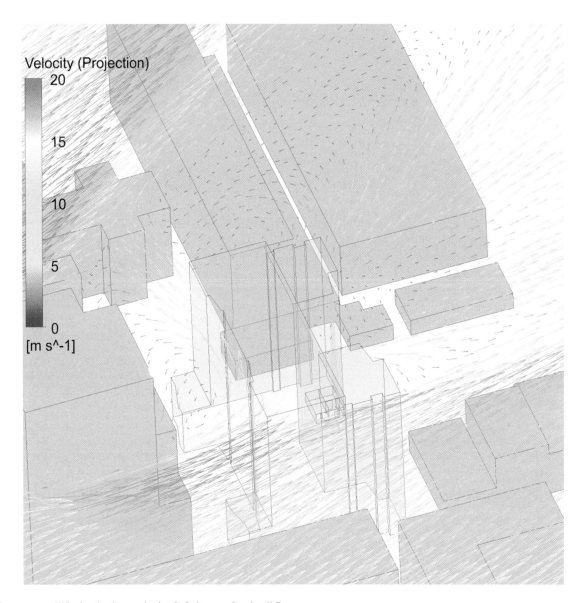

Figure 9.11   Wind velocity analysis. © *Solomon Cordwell Buenz*

level, but my experience is that it is not. Better understanding of the relationship between the two is in its infancy and in my opinion ripe for attention. [See Figures 9.12 and 9.13.]

Regarding the office side, I am interested in how to apply what we are learning from a business perspective into the design side. For example, during the design phases, I know that if jobs are getting fatter in terms of [file size, number of views, number of details] or in terms of hours spent on the project, it may indicate a weakness in the design process and

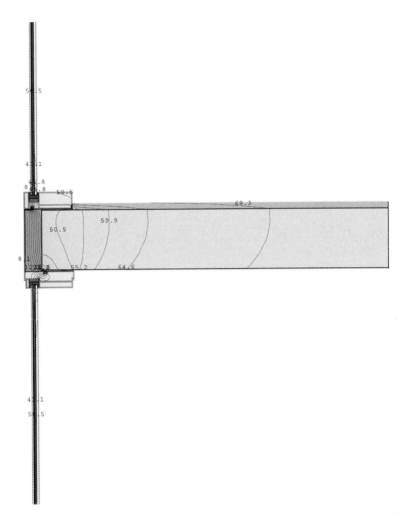

Figure 9:12   Therm heat transfer; color gradation and isobar analysis. © *Solomon Cordwell Buenz*

therefore require an intervention. In the construction administration phase, I might be interested to know how many RFIs we're getting—for example, how many per 1000 square feet—and what the builders are asking about as a possible clue as to how thoroughly we understood the design and whether we did an adequate job communicating our ideas.

Do technical coordinators need to be trained to collect data?

MF: The studio technical directors each generally have 15–20 years of experience and are skilled project managers. They have sound technical skills in terms of our markets (high-rise and institutional), so they deeply understand our projects. So no special training in terms of understanding what is important, but being supported by someone who

(Continued)

Figure 9:13   Therm heat transfer; color gradation and iso-bar analysis. © *Solomon Cordwell Buenz*

knows how to collect data efficiently, how best to store it, and how best to abstract it and apply it would be a very useful partnership. There are a lot of people collecting data in our office; there are not many whose sole interest is data.

Any concerns with the sharing of data?

MF: In general, I'm more inclined to share than not to share. I recognize the benefit of transparency as opposed to opacity and would lean toward being as transparent as possible. Transparency drives innovation and improves a product immeasurably. With that said, growth comes from identifying problems and solving them. This is a "critical" process and has complex business ramifications, some associated with proprietary information and some associated with critical reviews. Information that drives better products also drives litigation. Especially in this regard our industry would benefit from protective legislation that protects a firm's peer review data. As we believe in aggressively reviewing our work, it makes me very sensitive to how this data is shared.

There's a need in the profession for people trained in this process. I think that higher education should be developing this specialized skill set.

—Mark Frisch, SCB

Don't the studios get defensive?

MF: Of course, we all want to do a "good job" and be told how well we performed. The corollary to this is that if the data improves our product, we are inclined to suffer through the process. What we find is that there are two components to successful peer reviews: useful information and nonsubjective prose. We constantly work to improve both and use feedback loops to identify improvements to the peer review process. Currently the project teams feel that there is a benefit from the peer reviews and seek them.

How did your interest in data evolve in your career?

MF: I realized that many problems we face have information-driven solutions and being able to access information increased the speed and quality of solutions. That led to an interest in the process of knowledge sharing. Quite frankly, there's a need in the profession for people trained in this process. I think that higher education should be developing this specialized skill set. [See Figure 9.14.]

I do not subscribe to the notion that mechanization and craft are mutually exclusive.

—Mark Frisch, SCB

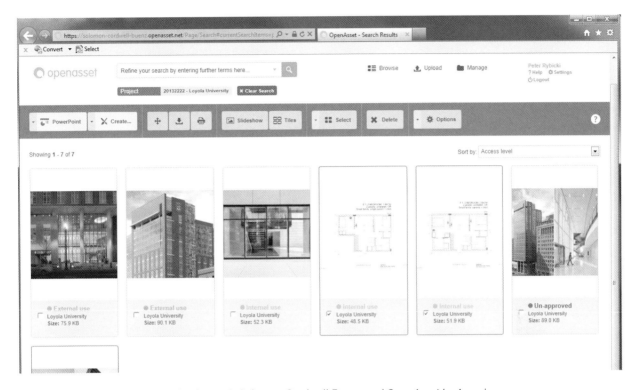

Figure 9:14   OpenAsset visual database. © *Solomon Cordwell Buenz and OpenAsset by Axomic*

Why do you suppose the AEC industry is the last to discover—and utilize—data for its own benefit?

MF: Although critically important, I think the profession conceives itself as a craft and thus is slow to embrace mechanization and all the ancillary components. I do not subscribe to the notion that mechanization and craft are mutually exclusive.

How would you utilize that person in your office?

MF: Some of what I am talking about are skills that everyone should be familiar with. Project information needs are constant; in order to gather it, store it, and access it, every architect should have a fundamental understanding of information processes. Further, in many offices there is the need for an information specialist. Ideally they would have a thorough background in information management and the associated tools. In order to be strategic they need to understand how to apply the information, which requires that they understand the architectural needs; that is, they should be very familiar with the architectural working process. I think that this position lives outside of the traditional information management group and is more closely allied with the library. I might have a harder sell [with my partners] on creating a totally new position—not because it's overhead, but because nobody understands its value. The people in the more traditional data intensive silos, such as our CFO, are understood. On the other hand, project data management has not been around long enough for offices to understand where or whether it fits in. [See Figure 9.15.]

(Continued)

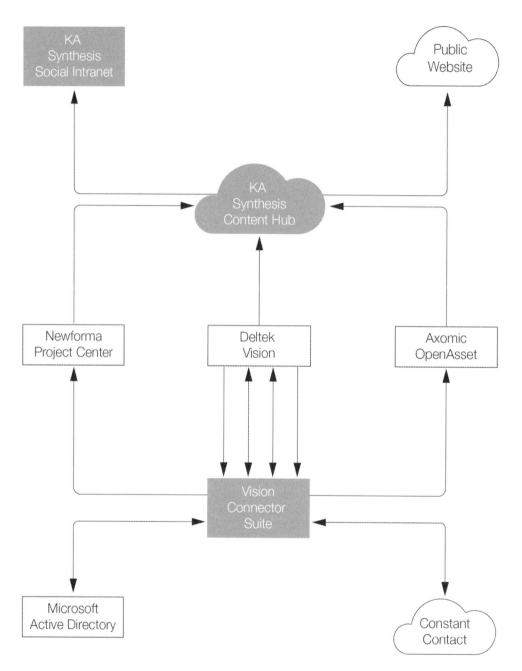

Figure 9:15   Connected systems diagram. © *Knowledge Architecture*

Advantage or disadvantage for hiring a data person from the data science/analytics realm over an architect with analytics skills?

MF: The same question could be asked about what is the best background for a visualization specialist: Are they architects trained in graphics, or are they graphic specialists working on architecture? We have one of each. The truth is that the one with no architectural background approaches the work with a graphic sensibility and the one with an architectural background tends to be interested in the newest technology. They're both good. They work very well together and with their complementary skill sets produce a very rich and ever-evolving product.

In the case of data, I don't know if it's an architect who understands all the things that we do and has a real affinity for data, or someone who understands analytics and applies it to architecture. If I could only have one, I would probably start with the former.

I sit on the AIA Large Firm Roundtable (AIA LFRT). There were recently 40 or so of us in a room answering what is on our minds. When it got to me, I said: Data. I know we're sitting on a mountain of it, I know it can help us—but at present it's stagnant, an untapped resource. We're simply not thinking about it enough. The act of saying it out loud has heightened my interest; I've been ruminating on it ever since.

So many things that we do are about optimization: the form, the materials, the process—and I found the way we progress most rapidly on these fronts is to understand as much about the context as we can. In my mind, data which captures this knowledge and experience is how best to optimize decisions. Today we have tools to manage even bigger mounds of stuff. The science of harnessing it and applying it has yet to be applied to our practices.

When I was at Murphy/Jahn, a colleague and I would be working on a difficult problem. I would always say, "Just give me everything you got, I am not afraid of the information." I knew intuitively that somewhere in that pile of stuff we would see a path, and be able to use it to solve the problem. Back then all we had were folders and file cabinets, and truthfully the information we had to manage could be difficult. I would say that a lot of people were and still are afraid of having too much information. While the amount of information has grown exponentially, I am convinced that rather than an impediment it is a resource for solving bigger, more complex problems. We have the tools, we now need the science.

Does data drive or inform the decisions you make?

MF: I would say it informs decisions. Your mind thinks; information informs. Say you are interested in detailing a door opening. Ultimately, someone is going to ask you: "What's the gauge of the hollow metal frame?" As long as you know exactly where to go and find out easily, you do not need to store that information in your head. You can focus on the most appropriate design solution and look up the appropriate gauge when required. Both are important, but the driver is the detail, not the gauge. In my view of the world of architecture and the process of solving technical problems, your head should to be able to think-drive decisions that the information warehouse is there to inform.

How can you make the BIM process faster, beyond using templates for kitchens and bathrooms? Any other ways that you're working to make the BIM process more efficient?

MF: Building Information Modeling (BIM) is information management. Anytime you want to manage information more efficiently, you need to organize it. In our case, looking carefully at all of our processes and applying more rigorous

(Continued)

standards improves efficiencies. Two recent examples of how we are optimizing the BIM process is integrating hyperlinked keynoting and building standard Revit partition details. By virtue of standardizing both of these processes, we have harnessed the power of continuity across an entire office platform. It makes the process of applying the information more efficient and it reduces the occurrence of errors.

An area where we continue to struggle is our rapid design/visualization workflow. The minute we introduced Revit into the process, the legacy workflow broke down. While Revit is our default production platform, it is not yet ready, nor are we convinced it needs to be our default modeling or visualization platform.

Have you looked at the metrics on a project and realized that there are certain things that you do that save time?

MF: We know that the building enclosure is a large file. You can really slow down the model and the drawing process, depending on the level of detail you apply to the building enclosure. In this case, metrics on the size of the model is driving "less" rather than "more."

Another metric driving efficiency is content creation and storage. Building libraries, standardizing the families, and organizing the information so that it can be easily accessed is high on the time-saving list.

Assigning an individual to "own" the model allows teams to share information easily through collaboration meetings and ensure that office standards are applied to each project. Central model management is a tool we use to bridge the information divide between teams, studios, and offices.

You mentioned that design and management mesh well in your office. That isn't always the case. Elsewhere, you stated that an office is just a chunk of silos of data. Can you elaborate?

MF: It is not always the case that these work well together; however, the stated goal is to collaborate. Creating an environment which rewards senior leadership for successes and challenges the same leaders when a project is not performing from a design, technical, or financial standpoint helps to break down these silos. The argument for the project team to collaborate is best made when you can show your team collaborating. Further studio resources such as the Technical Directors are invested in the success of the entire studio and help to arbitrate issues that may be the result of responsibility silos.

What would you recommend to someone who's studying to enter the profession or industry in terms of skill sets and mindsets to help them acquire the non-siloed approach that you take?

MF: Understand the kinds of information it takes to solve a problem. Hone your skills in gathering this information quickly and putting it in a place that is easily retrievable. Watch how information is used in your project and how it impacts decisions. Look at how different information leads you to different solutions. Ask yourself if the different solutions represent multiple ways to solve a problem or whether there was a flaw in applying the information. Evaluate whether there was an appropriate allocation of time for information gathering and make commitments about the amount of time one should spend in information gathering. Test your assumptions to become comfortable with the process and in the end evaluate the effectiveness of your process.

Keep in mind that you will be doing many things in your career. When you become confident in one area, ask yourself what's next? Do not get complacent. We all know people whose skill sets are general and consequentially their contributions are less significant. Try to avoid this situation in developing your career. Be disciplined and drive toward multiple and deep levels of competence in a variety of areas. Be patient, you can't learn everything at once. Using the analogy of a room, see what the parts of projects you touch are, break them down into an understandable number of parts. Remember them all but tackle one at a time. Know what interests you the most and tackle that one section first and become competent at it. While you're conquering that part, look for the next item which interests you. Take a look at it, dip your proverbial toe in that water. After working on those items, you're probably going to see something else that interests you; be sure to move on.

Throughout your career you will cycle through silos of problems and your depth of knowledge will grow. Manage this process; force yourself to experience new things.

One of the greatest learning experiences I had in my career was working with an extremely young façade company. Our design was a glass box: I detailed it and believed I had a very thoughtful solution. The group said we can do it like that but it will be costly. Alternatively, if you're willing to try something new, like this, we can build it easier and it will cost less. I stopped drawing, joined them in the factory, and we developed a new product. I will never forget that experience; I gained an understanding of how critical the builder is in design. They propelled that and other commissions into a world-renowned enclosure company.

My interests are varied. Primarily I like the way buildings go together. I'm interested in the design process. I'm very interested in information technology: hardware, software, networks, and communication. I'm interested in design technologies such as visualization and physical modeling and how they interface and inform the design process. I'm also very interested in knowledge: How do you continue to be current, how do you get information to others who need it, and how do you use information? And lastly, research and investigation: How do you identify problems and spend time on them? In my mind, this package is all interrelated.

Has keeping track of your data allowed you to make more informed practice decisions regarding project staffing, project billing, and staff hiring?

MF: There are two aspects to this type of information: one relates to the relevance of the information and the other relates to its timeliness. In short, yes, office-level data informs decision making.

You mentioned that "we are ripe to mine the data." How so, and why now?

MF: Since mining data requires time and resources, I think that there is a generally greater appreciation of how data can positively inform a variety of processes in our profession. Furthermore, there are people capable of developing the protocols and technology capable of managing the datasets all triangulating now.

What is the business case for your implementing a data transformation within your organization—like the one you describe?

MF: It allows the profession to better understand problems, focus on solutions that solve these problems, and allocate resources more efficiently. The end result, if done correctly, will allow more time to create, more creative solutions, and more beautiful products.

Sharing Data

Despite advances in technology and the opportunities to share, many firms are still cautious about sharing data and information. "I think it is going to change," says Jonatan Schumacher. "We alone don't have that much of an impact. But, by having open conversations on the web, and at symposiums, and by learning more from the open-source mentality of computer scientists, we'll be able to work it out eventually." Schumacher continues:

> If people aren't sharing, we wouldn't be learning. Imagine what would happen if all of us in our industry just started sharing their knowledge, as it's done in the computer science communities? I think we would advance much faster from a technological perspective. This is also the reason why we are organizing events such as the AEC Technology Symposium and Hackathon. We really want people to openly share ideas, and even better, to team up outside of their corporate environments and start developing software and solutions together!

To come up with its structural designs, Thornton Tomasetti (TT) makes use of databases. Do these belong to the owner? Are there public or private sources that TT turns to for data on a regular basis, or does it depend on the project? Does TT collect and warehouse its own data for use in projects or to improve performance? "As part of our intranet solution, we have a private webpage for every project that features high-level project information: who is the key contact, services offered, construction date, etc.," explains Schumacher. He adds:

> We can use this intranet to ask: What do we do in healthcare? What do we do on high-rise projects? What do we do in Dubai? Every project page also has inputs for structural system, average building weight/sq. ft., and for embodied carbon. I have been considering adding the TTX model for every project in there, too. So that in the future, we can always look back and extract BIM and analytical data. It's just a database, so we'll be able to open and read it. It won't get outdated, like a Revit model or a Grasshopper definition would. And it doesn't use up much storage capacity. We can open it in 10 years and run very detailed queries down to a single BIM element or structural analysis node.

"As far as giving away tools and ideas, there aren't too many concerns from our leadership," says Schumacher. "Everybody is interested in creating better buildings, and having more fun in the process, which is why we are encouraged to share."

Data has to be made intelligible before it can be shared, and data which is intelligible for one use may be noise for another.

—Andrew Witt, Gehry Technologies

Mark Frisch is also someone who is more inclined to share than not to share. "I recognize the benefit of transparency as opposed to opacity and would lean toward being as transparent as possible. Transparency drives innovation and improves a product immeasurably," says Frisch, who then cautions:

> With that said, growth comes from identifying problems and solving them. This is a "critical" process and has complex business ramifications—some associated with proprietary information and some associated with critical reviews. Information that drives better products also drives litigation. Especially in this regard, our industry would benefit from

protective legislation that protects firms' peer review data. As we believe in aggressively reviewing our work, it makes me very sensitive to how this data is shared.

Andrew Witt has said that in 10 years, people will be sharing vastly more information than they are now. What will this primarily be attributed to? "It's the opportunistic availability of both data and the means to share it," says Witt, then adds:

> It's not necessarily based on some new requirement to share. There's a greater and greater expectation of higher and higher fidelity communication. People will have the means to execute high-resolution communication. People won't necessarily be communicating more frequently, but the resolution of that communication will be much higher.

Professor Aimee Buccellato of the School of Architecture at the University of Notre Dame sees ubiquitous data as the crux of the problem. "We're doing a lot of work. We want people to see it. But how much do industry professionals want people to see our data, the collection of which is the fruit of many hours of labor?" asks Buccellato.

We all need to be pulling from the same streams of data and pushing our data into the same structured streams. What's preventing us from doing this? What are the barriers?

—Aimee Buccellato, Notre Dame

In terms of this idea of data sharing: anything from the data I've gathered, all the materials and methods I'm going to use in the construction of a building, I've done it all manually because frankly right now that is how it is done. Even with the tools we have to use at this point, it is like we are still using big, dull crayons. However, what we could be saying is that there's potentially great reward in large-scale data sharing across our industry. Especially with respect to the potential to manifestly improve the way we make buildings—and the way we make our buildings perform. But with the increased reward, there's got to be a cost or risk. How do you anonymize the data? How do you balance out "what do I get for what I give?" At the beginning there's going to be a lot of tension between what we have and what we want to do, and the tools we currently access to incorporate this information.

Case Study Interview with David Sawdey

Dave Sawdey is a senior vice president and the Director of Business Intelligence in Jones Lang LaSalle's Corporate Solutions group. He is responsible for developing and leading the Jones Lang LaSalle Business Intelligence Center of Excellence. He is an advocate, advisor, trainer, and promoter of business intelligence and data analytics to derive actionable insights that shape smarter business decisions and improve overall outcomes for clients, and he brings a best-practice approach to delivering portfolio data advisory services related to measurement, reporting, analytics, and business intelligence. Earlier in his career, he helped many companies connect databases to CAD drawings.

Most people in our industry are not yet using BIM for its capacity as a database.

David Sawdey (DS): We were on that right away. Part of my role is predictive analytics and statistical modeling, but an even bigger part is visualizing your data. When I make my first pitch to an organization, they have all this information about what

(Continued)

goes on within the four walls of your building, it's very hard to understand that in just a tabular list. We saw the opportunity to marry the data that's in your database with the design of your 2D CAD floor plans. That was a huge win. You can maybe better understand financial data in a pie chart or bar graph. You can better understand your facility assets on a floor plan.

I came from an IT database background. Most of my competition when I was in that business were architecture firms. Any time we would compete against architecture firms I always knew we had an advantage because we understood this was about data and they came at it from an architecture perspective. They couldn't wrap their heads around the fact that all this data didn't belong on the drawing, it belonged in the database. All the CAD drawing was really was a visualization tool of relational data that was somewhere else. That's where you had all your connections, where you could so elegantly bring in employee needs or assets, anything you'd want to attach to that Desk 101 kind of concept.

Are there any tools you're currently working with that take advantage of that information?

DS: We're in the process right now of building a more robust and sophisticated client data mart, or enterprise data warehouse on top of those data marts, where we can better leverage the sheer knowledge that's in all of the client data marts. We're not married to any single tool. We let the client make the call as to what tool we use to visualize the space and occupancy data on our floor plans.

You have said: "I've seen a single data visualization change an entire strategy, by highlighting unintended consequences or unforeseen opportunities. It's a powerful force."[2] Can you elaborate?

DS: We have absolutely seen that. Where we have seen that the most is in uncovering insights from a portfolio strategy. On a global level, you're dealing with a scale of property information of, say, a thousand. The senior executives we're working with, they don't know where all of these properties are, they don't know what they're all about. They have at best a third of them. Some of the properties are acquisitions they didn't have anything to do with where they came from. The empowerment you get from the data visualization tools—and the interactivity with them—help you to uncover the variability. Where are my correlations and variability aligned or misaligned? And why am I getting that? That's the sort of data discovery that you get.

Where do I have high vacancy and high cost? Where is cost per square foot 30 percent higher than my average? And where is vacancy above 30 percent? We have algorithms in there that also show distance to the nearest related site. With the growth a lot of our clients are getting, it's surprising but not surprising that they don't even realize that they have two buildings in the same city, both of which have 50 percent vacancy in them. That's the obvious strategic decision there. You just don't see those things on a piece of paper. The paper in and of itself won't connect all of those dots. It's the fact that you're seeing something that piques your interest that doesn't look right, and the ability to drill up and drill down to find them.

Strategy No. 25: Use Data to Provide Better Service

How do JLL's clients—global Fortune 500 company real estate departments—work with data?

JLL is in the middle of a culture change where we're not only trying to data-enable our own clients, but use our client's data to provide better service.

More efficiently, effectively, at a better price.

We're no different than Target stores—trying to use customer data to increase profit while delivering better service.

A big portion of the corporate solutions business is IFM (Integrated Facilities Management)—outsourced FM.

What can we learn about work order performance, cost, cycle time, and vendor performance management by geography, by work order type—beyond just a single client, but across those clients, to help us provide better service and delivery?

What does best-in-class facilities management look like?

It's not just janitorial cleaning at a certain cost per square foot. It's the alignment of service delivery at the cost point where it aligns perfectly with our target customer satisfaction level. In reality we're not shooting for 99.9 percent satisfaction. That would be too expensive.

Our clients—starting with corporate real estate (CRE): If I think of them holistically, they're still data-enabled or aware. They want to take more advantage of data. See the opportunities that the data-informed level provides. But they're still figuring what that means and how to get there.

Suggestions for how they can get there:

They know they want to get there. What they really struggle with is the investment that it takes to get there. Because it's not just making a culture change. It is an investment in additional people as well as technology.

But the largest component is the change management, the additional process, and valuing the data. Today, it's one-off spreadsheets. Thirty percent of the data is entered, of which you need 90 percent of the data to do anything strategic. That's where they get caught up. They're ready to do it when they look at the paper, but once you throw the budget against it, they get challenged.

—David Sawdey, Jones Lang Lasalle, Strategic Consulting

Where does your interest in data come from?

DS: It goes way back, because I have always been passionate about good design in general. The ability to make better decisions to predict where my business is going is really best communicated in pictures, which really means visualizations and graphics. And the subject-matter expertise to know how to transform that data from a table to a chart.

Now, today's analytics and visualization tools are at an economical price point, as well as a level of skill that can empower the end user to create these visualizations. What would have taken months and thousands of dollars, now takes an hour and the cost is almost negligible.

> I try never to say big data. I sit with clients and because they have 10,000 rows of data they think it's big data. It's really not how much you have, it's what you do with it. In terms of the value it's going to get you.
> —David Sawdey, Jones Lang Lasalle

When are you brought into the process?

DS: There are firms that come in on the back end. You can basically make statistics tell any story you want. People do that as a post-decision rationalization. We're actually very lucky with our clients here. I lead our Strategic Consulting Business Intelligence and Analytics Practice. What I'm going to describe is along the broader things we do within the Strategic Consulting group. We have clients who have decided that they are clearly ready to run a fact- and data-driven corporate real

(Continued)

estate organization. They are very often coming to us ready for the change management that's required to run that kind of organization. We're lucky that we were in on the front end of that. We have probably done some of that where we are coming in on the back end. We've been advocating this to our clients for a couple years. The fact [is] that they are not just hearing it from us, but they're hearing it from their CEO, they're hearing it from the market, they're hearing it at trade shows. They're really coming around. We've had some great success stories with accounts. They have their monthly and quarterly meetings. There's no anecdotal storytelling. Dashboards get pulled up—dashboards that are based on operational core systems. There's no pulling data off into Excel and manually making your charts and graphs, and then coming to meetings with your own point of view. Data's pulled from the warehouse. The warehouse data is set by operational systems. Governance is put in place as well as the appropriate resources to make sure data is managed through the process in those source systems correctly so we can rely on the data in the data warehouse. [We deal with] senior management, for whom if it is not written down it didn't happen. No one wants to hear some story about the project, why it's behind or not behind. We should be able to see that in the data. It's up in the dashboards, available on the weekly or monthly report. That accountability is what drives a lot of that culture change. Meetings happen faster. It's been great for our clients.

We're typically dealing with the corporate real estate group. The more they run their business that way, the more they change the conversation with the different revenue-generating divisions whom they are there to support, to help them understand the challenges of real estate, dealing with the cost of occupancy, with vacancy, change management around new ways of working. You're now coming to these meetings not just with the strategy that's written in the paragraph, but you can show true utilization, true vacancy, as it relates directly to that line of business. And show a real measured value—or lost value—in the strategy.

Is it possible to present data objectively, without putting an angle on it, or changing it in some way, which usually is in favor of some preferred outcome?

DS: That is hard. I'm a believer that as much as you can take bias out of anything, there's always bias in it. Having data governance as a process well defined has a value. But how do you define that process? How do you determine the terms and taxonomy of your value? How you define a service-level agreement and a key performance indicator [KPI] goes a long way. But you can't get around the system. There are always the politics, the nuances, the interpretation of a date or a time or a deliverable. To your point, JLL does that better than average. A lot of that is due to how important ethics is to the firm. Even in a perfect process, the perfect operational connection and the whole vision I just gave you, there's always room to filter out the business unit that's underperforming, or the region that had a lot of churn, and get the numbers to tell the story you want to tell.

Can you describe how JLL's clients work with data?

DS: We work primarily with corporations. My day-to-day experience is with global Fortune 500 companies—specifically, their real estate departments. JLL is also in the middle of a culture change where we're not only trying to data-enable our own clients, but use our client's data to provide better service. More efficiently, effectively, at a better price. We're no different than Target stores—trying to use customer data to increase profit while delivering better service. A big portion of the corporate solutions business is IFM (Integrated Facilities Management)—outsourced FM. What can we learn about work order performance, cost, cycle time, and vendor performance management by geography, by work order type—beyond just a single client, but across those clients, to help us provide better service and delivery? What does best-in-class facilities management look like? It's not just janitorial cleaning at a certain cost per square foot. It's the alignment of service delivery at the cost point where it aligns perfectly with our target customer satisfaction level. In reality we're not shooting for 99.9 percent satisfaction. That would be too expensive.

Our clients—starting with corporate real estate (CRE)—if I think of them holistically, they're still data-enabled or aware. They want to take more advantage of data, see the opportunities that the data-informed level provides. But they're still figuring what that means and how to get there.

Any suggestions for how they can get there?

DS: They know they want to get there. What they really struggle with is the investment that it takes to get there. Because it's not just making a culture change. It is an investment in additional people as well as technology. But the largest component is the change management, the additional process, and valuing the data. Today, it's one-off spreadsheets. Thirty percent of the data is entered, of which you need 90 percent of the data to do anything strategic. That's where they get caught up. They're ready to do it when they look at the paper, but once you throw the budget against it, they get challenged.

We really are going through a culture change. We're training account resources how to use these tools, and how to think smarter about their data. We're rethinking what best-practice data governance looks like. We're creating a centralized, global pool of data scientists that clients can leverage. We see it as a competitive differentiator for us.

In this and in the preceding chapters, you have met industry innovators and thought leaders who, together, provided information, knowledge, and wisdom to help you build a compelling case for leveraging data in your own firm or organization, demonstrating in myriad ways how data can be used for the greatest impact for each project stakeholder. Now that you have completed the book, may data empower you to accomplish whatever it is you set out to achieve in your practice, career, and life.

Notes

Unless otherwise indicated, quoted text throughout the book is from interviews with the author that took place between February and July of 2014.

1. www.architecture2030.org/2030_challenge/the_2030_challenge
2. www.joneslanglasalle.com/SaltLakeCity/en-us/Pages/NewsItem.aspx?ItemID=27301

EPILOGUE: THE FUTURE OF DATA IN AEC

Let me be hyperbolic and assert that we are entering into the dataverse.

—Geoffrey C. Bowker

The future is already here—it's just not very evenly distributed.

—William Gibson

Building as Building	Building as Documents	Building as Database

Figure 10.1: In the future, buildings will increasingly be valued in terms of data. © *R Deutsch*

Imagine a world where architects, engineers, and contractors backed up their predictions, predilections, and preferences with data. Architects would be less marginalized and trusted more. Decisions would be made more quickly and assuredly. Productivity would improve. Outcomes would be visualized and understood sooner, resulting in fewer unwanted surprises. The leveraging of data would be introduced in the academy, followed by on-the-job learning and professional growth.

Our Data-Driven Future

In the future, due in part to an increased, widespread, and more assured use of data, there will still be an AEC to leverage data. Using data will assure that the design professions and industry will not be replaced by someone—or something—else. Data will enable those in design, construction, and operations to work with more confidence, relying less on spurious arguments and "that's how we've always done it." (See Figure 10.1.)

Data Landscapes and Geo-Everything

We're learning, living, and working at a time when no one knows conclusively what the future of BIM, architecture, or construction will look like. Every day we read or see stories on the Internet of Things (IoT)—the internet of buildings, internet of *everything*—and are not sure what to make of it. How will smart objects, devices, and manufacturer's products interface with the buildings we devise and construct? While no one can say with certainty what the future holds, this book has tried to describe a world where the data from smart phones, devices, and products already informs design, construction, and operations, and will increasingly do so in the years ahead.

Data's future will be two-pronged: data use will continue to increase due to its presence earlier in one's tutelage, playing a more central and integrated role in school; and due to advances in technology. The role of data in practice will increase equally, in part due to students' and practitioners' familiarity with the impact of data throughout the building life cycle from commission and concept to construction and decommission—and the increased awareness and implementation of data in practice and the field.

Smart buildings, smart cities, smart infrastructure, and smart landscape will increase in intelligence not due to technology alone, but because in each of these instances smart equals connected. As long as we recognize that a building doesn't end at its walls, and think in terms of flows, we will make greater use of everything connected through data.

Ever-Expanding Horizons and Unlimited Opportunity

MKThink's Evelyn Lee believes that the idea of the traditional architecture firm is not going to last—that it is going to be hard for traditional practice to continue. "We—as architects—do a lot of complaining about not being at the table," says Lee. "But in order to be at the table we're going to have to offer something special from our firm." She adds:

> If architects want to be at the table, when it comes to sustainability or what is happening to the future of our cities, they'll need to find themselves partnering with people from other backgrounds. There will be more models where all of the partners of the firm will not be architects. They may be sociologists or biologists or economists as partners in the firm. That will enable them to think a little more broadly about things that are of value to the client. That's where I feel things are headed.

Leveraging data amongst multidisciplinary partners is one way to distinguish and differentiate oneself, and one's firm, and provides a compelling way for a firm to continue to offer *something special*.

Predictive Analytics

I wouldn't just say that the future looks good for predictive analytics. I'd say the future is predictive analytics. Period. It is the core enabler of the two major trends in the AEC industry today.
—David L Morgareidge, Predictive Analytics Director, Page

The two major trends in the AEC industry today are performance analyzed, optimized, and forecast; and performance guaranteed across disciplines and time. "Clients want a design team to deliver more than just an attractive facility which will function as required, and keep them dry and thermally comfortable," says Morgareidge. "They want their complete 'business platform' operationally and financially simulated, including space, technology, staffing models, product or service supply and demand curves, and work processes, so that they can know with certainty that the key financial and operational performance benchmarks that are critical to make their business successful will all be achieved." This is performance analyzed, optimized, and forecast, and is what predictive analytics delivers.

"Clients increasingly want more than just a good design narrative," adds Morgareidge. According to Morgareidge,

> They want long-term, quantifiable performance guarantees that are backed by financial commitments from the full AECO-M team—architects, engineers, contractors, and facility operations and maintenance teams. This is evidenced in particular by the growth of P3 (public-private partnership) projects and of 'guaranteed facility performance' projects in the private sector. In these situations the design/build/operate-and-maintain consortium is financially responsible for the facility's performance for 20 to 30 years. If performance falls below one or more of the agreed-to metrics for a month, the consortium's fee for that month is proportionally reduced.

Thus the second major trend in the AEC industry today: performance guaranteed across disciplines and time, which is also what predictive analytics delivers. It represents a change that has "forced the shift of the formerly 'academically oriented' post-occupancy evaluation (POE) or facility performance evaluation (FPE) toward a 'put your money where your mouth is' contractual commitment that ties the full AECO-M team's compensation to their ability to deliver as promised."

GEO and GIS

The future will invite more expansive, impactful, and transformative uses of data in our tools. Data wrangler Jonathon Broughton sees himself as helping to report the measurement of things, windows, doors, people … time. "The geo-spatial data mantra: 'everything happens somewhere' is a call to arms for GIS specialists but more fundamental than that would be that 'everything is a thing,'" Broughton explains. "What about those things are we actually interested in? Where they are? Sure. How many? Of course. More interesting to me is when BIM and GIS will answer the question of a fund holder investing in construction: 'Steel is rocketing in price due to the trade embargo with Elbonia.[1] What is my exposure to that right now?' Only then is BIM anywhere near approaching big data class."

Brian Ringley points to the problem of sourcing data, rather than technology, as the largest hurdle for the AEC industry. "It's no problem for me to use DIVA or Ladybug within a Rhino/Grasshopper workflow to directly reference certain elements of environmental data, or Elk or Meerkat for GIS data," says Ringley, "but what if I want city data on acoustics at a given intersection, or foot traffic data to determine siting or egress, or anything really?"

The Future Is Already Here

Buildings and Cities as a Tangible Interface to Data

SmartGeometry's Projections of Reality—augmenting design processes involving physical models with real-time spatial analysis—developed a system where objects placed on a table were identified by a Kinect sensor and then fed into a simulation that was projected back over the table, resulting in a "cityscape that could be intuitively manipulated and simulated; a tangible interface to data." [2] Projections of Reality suggests a future where virtual data is overlaid with objects architects manipulate in the real world. I asked Daniel Davis of CASE if this how we would describe reality in the near future: buildings and cities as a tangible interface to data? "Building sites are already augmented to some degree," responded Davis. "If I go to a jobsite I can open up my email and see informational data that I wouldn't have had access to in any other way. What is happening is that increasingly the separation between what is happening in the visual and what is happening in the physical world are becoming more and more blurry and hard to keep apart. The way we interact with buildings and the way we make buildings will change because of that."

"I think that's a great point," says David Fano. "A lot of people think about this literally. That there needs to be an image projected in front of your face. That we'll be wearing goggles. The Blade Runner version of the future. The reality is that I can get access to all of that stuff on a phone right now. All I need is the mindset." Fano explains:

> If I walk through a building will I want to know the day it was built? All I have to do is pull that information from Wikipedia. Everyone thinks the building is going to flash all these things in front of my face. It's all about the interface and the desire to know. The painted picture of the future is like in the film *Idiocracy*, there's a time when a character physically goes to the Internet, and he's walking around the halls, people jumping out all over the place. That is a dramatic version of the cartoon of augmented reality. We live in that world *now*. The way we interface with it is different. We're just as capable of living in that information world right now.

Whether mixed reality, hybrid reality, or mixed virtuality, in the years to come we'll be seeing an increase in the data-driven merging of virtual and real worlds.[3]

Automation

Another instance of "the future is already here" can be found at Thornton Tomasetti. It is common practice on high-rise projects to undertake column removal studies asking how a building would react if certain columns were to be removed. Jonatan Schumacher explained that conventionally, engineers would just pick (by hand) 5 or 10 columns to be tested in an analysis. "One of our engineers set up a tool that does this analysis for every single column in the tower; it automatically takes one column out, runs the analysis, takes the next column out, runs the analysis, and so on, running overnight," says Schumacher. "Every single iteration is recorded into the TTX database, including all of the forces acting in all of the building elements, for thousands of runs. So in the morning we have millions of lines of information about all the forces acting on all the members in all possible cases of column collapses. Then we can use our BIM query and visualization tools to understand how the building would behave, and make informed design decisions thereafter."

Many in AECO are concerned that automation will replace design and construction professionals. There are people who believe that architecture and construction will become a computer-and-robotic culture in the end, and that there won't be a place for them. "In all fairness, to some degree they're right," says Zigmund Rubel. "I don't want to minimize their fears but I think the reality, though, is that data-driven computer use in the industry will allow for a much more creative process for those who participate."

Man-Machine Collaboration

Designers, engineers, and contractors who rely on computers and various digital devices to complete their work are already participating, to some extent, in man-machine collaboration. In the months prior to completion of this book, Flux, a startup spin-off of the semi-secret Google[x] research moonshot lab and incubator at Google, dedicated to projects such as the driverless car and Google glass, set out to automate the AEC industry. "We noticed that real estate developers, land-use specialists, and architects were spending considerable time gathering and consolidating data from a multitude of sources to understand development potential and constraints."[4] To help integrate and manage data, Flux uses a series of tools to look at how those in the AEC industry could leverage data and design and build buildings more efficiently and sustainably, and asks: What if there was a standard library where people could build upon the work of others, as opposed to solving the same problems over and over again? What if, in other words, more rote and repetitive parts of the design and construction process could be automated, thereby (at least ostensibly) freeing up design and construction professionals to do what they do best?

Data will continue to play a vital role in design, construction, and operations due to its increased presence in education and because of recent advances in technology, but it will not flourish in the design professions or construction industry without the right mindset. Moving forward and looking ahead, our creative acts—if they are to be realized—will look to be informed by data. But what's the right proportion in terms of algorithms and human intervention? For David L. Morgareidge, that's the wrong question. "Everything in technology today is human-generated. Every bit of processing logic, every algorithm that was written, involved 'human intervention,'" says Morgareidge.

The value of technology is that it accelerates the exploration of things that are so complex that even the most advanced human minds can't accomplish the task alone. Technology is just the repository of collective human experience. To the extent that there is a human override needed, that would only indicate that the heuristics, the internal design logic, was flawed. People overlooked something—not computers. "That algorithm clearly didn't take into account *x*. We'll need to fix that." It's an iterative process by which each one of those circumstances suggests an improvement. You cycle that back into your knowledge management portal in terms of the simulation and the optimization behind it, and you get better and better each time you cycle through.

It's *all* "human intervention." Every piece of code was developed by someone. Whether you're using commercial applications or your own, you're just building on someone else's smarts. If you're not comfortable working with numbers, you're probably not going to be working, period.

Notes

Unless otherwise indicated, quoted text throughout the book is from interviews with the author that took place between February and July of 2014.

1. http://en.wikipedia.org/wiki/Dilbert#Elbonia
2. Daniel Davis & David Fano, "Practice 2.0: 10 Years of Smart Geometry"; www.archdaily.com/398406/practice-2-0-10-years-of-smart-geometry/
3. http://referaat.cs.utwente.nl/conference/2/paper/7089/the-use-of-mixed-reality-in-architecture-for-conceptual-design.pdf
4. "A+U Interviews Co-Founders of Google[x] Startup, Flux"; www.japlusu.com/news/flux-encoding-logic-design

APPENDIX

Experts, Innovators, and Thought Leaders Interviewed

- Jill Bergman, Healthcare Principal and Vice President at HDR

- Jonathon Broughton, Data Wrangler, Allies and Morrison

- Aimee Buccellato, Assistant Professor, School of Architecture at the University of Notre Dame

- Sean D. Burke, LEED AP, Digital Practice Leader, NBBJ

- Daniel Davis, Senior Building Information Specialist, CASE Inc.

- Bill East, PhD, PE, F.ASCE, bSa Projects Coordinator, Founder, Prairie Sky Consulting LLC

- Billie Faircloth, AIA, LEED AP BD+C, Research Director and Associate, KieranTimberlake

- David Fano, Partner and Managing Director, CASE Inc.

- Mark Frisch, FAIA, Managing Principal, Solomon Cordwell Buenz

- Mani Golparvar-Fard, PhD, Assistant Professor of Civil and Environmental Engineering and Computer Science, University of Illinois at Urbana-Champaign

- Tyler Goss, Director of Construction Solutions, CASE Inc.

- Toru Hasegawa, Columbia University GSAPP Cloud Lab Co-director, Proxy Co-creator, Morpholio Co-creator

- Marco Hemmerling, MA, Prof. Dipl.-Ing. Professor at Detmold School of Architecture

- Andrew Heumann, Leader of NBBJ's Design Computation team

- Gregory Janks, Principal, Sasaki Associates

- Mads Jensen, CEO, Sefaira

- Jennifer Johnson, Senior Director of Product Development/Management, Reed Construction Data

- Michael Kilkelly, Principal, Space Command

- Evelyn Lee, Strategist, MKThink

- Brendon Levitt, Loisos + Ubbelohde

- Peter Liebsch, Global Head of Design Technology, Grimshaw Architects

- Sam Miller, Partner, LMN Architects

- David Morgareidge, Predictive Analytics Director, Page

- Tom Mulhern, SVP, Chief Innovation Officer, Dātu Health, (formerly with Gensler)

- Ryan Mullenix, Design Partner, NBBJ

- Erik Olsen, PE, Managing Partner & CEO, Transsolar Climate Engineering

- Sukanya Paciorek, Vice President of Corporate Sustainability, Vornado Realty Trust

- Greig Paterson, Researcher, AHR (formerly Aedas)

- Peter Pellerzi, Manager, Data Center Global Engineering Team, Google

- Chris Pyke, USGBC

- Brian Ringley, Fuse Lab Technology Coordinator, City University of New York; Design Technology Platform Specialist, Woods Bagot

- Zigmund Rubel, AIA, Co-Founder Aditazz Inc.

- David Sawdey, Director of Business Intelligence, Jones Lang Lasalle Strategic Consulting

- Greg Schleusner, Director buildingSMART Innovation, HOK

- Jonatan Schumacher, Director of CORE studio, Thornton Tomasetti

- Brian Skripac, Director of Digital Practice at Astorino (now Astorino-CannonDesign)

- Clayton Starr, Associate Vice President, RTKL

- Carin Whitney, Communications Director, KieranTimberlake

- Andrew Witt, Director of Research, Gehry Technologies

- Robert Yori, Senior Digital Design Manager at SOM

Organizations and Universities Represented

- Aditazz

- AHR (formerly Aedas)

- Allies and Morrison

- Astorino (now Astorino-CannonDesign)

- buildingSMART

- CASE Inc.

- City University of New York

- Civil and Environmental Engineering and Computer Science, University of Illinois at Urbana-Champaign

- Columbia University

- Dātu Health

- Detmold School of Architecture

- HDR

- Gehry Technologies

- Google

- Grimshaw Architects

- HOK

- Jones Lang Lasalle

- KieranTimberlake

- LMN Architects

- LOISOS + UBBELOHDE

- MKThink

- Morpholio

- NBBJ

- Page

- Prairie Sky Consulting LLC

- Proxy

- Reed Construction Data

- RTKL

- Sasaki Associates

- School of Architecture at the University of Notre Dame

- Sefaira

- Solomon Cordwell Buenz

- SOM

- Space Command

- Thornton Tomasetti

- Transsolar Climate Engineering

- USGBC
- Vornado Realty Trust
- Woods Bagot

The 25 Data-Driven Strategies

- **STRATEGY No. 1:** Hone in on key information

- **STRATEGY No. 2:** Demonstrating works, explaining doesn't

- **STRATEGY No. 3:** Look outside the industry

- **STRATEGY No. 4:** Not Big Data, smart data

- **STRATEGY No. 5:** Eight questions to ask for data preparedness

- **STRATEGY No. 6:** Four steps toward making the change to be more data-centric

- **STRATEGY No. 7:** Ask good questions

- **STRATEGY No. 8:** Play with data

- **STRATEGY No. 9:** Create a data collection strategy

- **STRATEGY No. 10:** First steps to becoming data-centric

- **STRATEGY No. 11:** First steps in applying data analysis

- **STRATEGY No. 12:** Two ways to think about energy analysis

- **STRATEGY No. 13:** Analysis for sustainable design

- **STRATEGY No. 14:** How analysis informs decision making

- **STRATEGY No. 15:** Start simple, technology optional

- **STRATEGY No. 16:** Leverage data as means to an end

- **STRATEGY No. 17:** First steps before applying data

- **STRATEGY No. 18:** Plan for the data

- **STRATEGY No. 19:** Should the data team be integrated or stationed in the corner?

- **STRATEGY No. 20:** Computer scientist vs. emerging professional

- **STRATEGY No. 21:** Construction-related data questions

- **STRATEGY No. 22:** Extract and transfer what matters

- **STRATEGY No. 23:** With data, the heart of the issue is culture

- **STRATEGY No. 24:** Big Data in practice

- **STRATEGY No. 25:** Use data to provide better service

Software Mentioned

The book strives to be vendor-agnostic. Software listed is not an endorsement. Please note: Software changes frequently and may have evolved since the compilation of this list.

- Alibre
- Apache OpenOffice
- Athena
- Autodesk 3ds Max
- Autodesk AutoCAD
- Autodesk AutoCAD Architecture
- Autodesk Dynamo Visual Programming for BIM
- Autodesk Dynamo BIM

- Autodesk Ecotect
- Autodesk Green Building Studio
- Autodesk Maya
- Autodesk Revit Architecture
- Autodesk Revit MEP
- Autodesk Revit Structure
- Building CATALYST
- CASE Pro Apps
- CASE/SOM BIM Dashboard
- Chameleon
- CodeBook
- Copy Monitor
- D3
- Dassault Systèmes CATIA
- Dhour
- DIVA
- dRofus
- DynaRobo
- EES: Engineering Equation Solver (Transsolar)
- Elk
- EnergyPlus (U.S. DOE)
- Energy Star Portfolio Manager
- Etabs
- eQUEST
- Firefly
- FlexSim Healthcare
- Galopogos
- Gehry Technologies Digital Project
- Geometry Gym suite
- Graphisoft ArchiCAD
- Grasshopper plug-in Ladybug
- Grasshopper plug-in Honeybee
- GreenScale Tool
- Hadoop
- IES
- KieranTimberlake Research Group, Tally plug-in
- Lyrebird (LMNts and Robert McNeel & Associates)
- MapReduce
- McNeel & Associates Grasshopper
- Meerkat
- Microsoft Excel
- Microsoft Word
- MKThink 4Adaptive
- Mobile Augmented Reality System (MARS)
- Oasys MassMotion
- R
- Radiance
- RAM
- Robert McNeel & Associates Rhino (Rhinoceros)
- SAP
- Sefaira
- Sefaira for SketchUp plug-in
- Shade 3D
- SolidWorks
- Tableau
- Tekla

- Therm

- TRACE™ simulation

- Trelligence Affinity

- Trimble SketchUp

- TRNSYS

- TTX (Thornton Tomasetti CORE studio/ACM Team)

- ViziCalc

Recommended Reading

Aiden, Erez, and Jean-Baptiste Michel. *Uncharted: Big Data as a Lens on Human Culture*. Riverhead, 2013.

Ayres, Ian. *Super Crunchers: Why Thinking-by-Numbers is the New Way to Be Smart*. Bantam, 2008.

Borner, Katy, and David E. Polley. *Visual Insights: A Practical Guide to Making Sense of Data*. MIT Press, 2014.

Brandt, Robert, Gordon H. Chong, and W. Mike Martin. *Design Informed: Driving Innovation with Evidence-Based Design*. John Wiley & Sons, 2010.

Carr, Nicholas. *The Big Switch*. W. W. Norton, 2013.

Cook, Gareth, ed. *The Best American Infographics 2014*. Houghton Mifflin Harcourt, 2014.

Davenport, Thomas H. *Big Data at Work: Dispelling the Myths, Uncovering the Opportunities*. Harvard Business Review Press, 2014.

Davenport, Thomas H., Jeanne G. Harris, and Robert Morison. *Analytics at Work : Smarter Decisions, Better Results*. Harvard Business Review Press, 2010.

Davenport, Thomas H., and Jinho Kim. *Keeping Up with the Quants: Your Guide to Understanding and Using Analytics*. Harvard Business Review Press, 2013.

Few, Stephen. *Now You See It: Simple Visualization Techniques for Quantitative Analysis*. Analytics Press, 2009.

Foreman, John W. *Data Smart: Using Data Science to Transform Information into Insight*. John Wiley & Sons, 2013.

Fung, Kaiser. *Number Sense: How to Use Big Data to Your Advantage*. McGraw-Hill, 2013.

Gitelman, Lisa. ed. *"Raw Data" Is an Oxymoron*. MIT Press, 2013.

Goldstein, Brett, and Lauren Dyson. *Beyond Transparency: Open Data and the Future of Civic Innovation*. Code for America Press, 2013.

Gurin, Joel. *Open Data Now: The Secret to Hot Startups, Smart Investing, Savvy Marketing, and Fast Innovation*. McGraw-Hill Education, 2013.

Harris, Phillip A. *Data-Driven Design: How Today's Product Designer Approaches User Experience to Create Radically Innovative Digital Products*. K & R Publications, 2013.

Hey, Tony, Tansley, Stewart, & Tolle, Kristin. *The Fourth Paradigm: Data-Intensive Scientific Discovery*. Microsoft Research, 2009.

Hubbard, Douglas W. *How to Measure Anything: Finding the Value of Intangibles in Business*. John Wiley & Sons, 2014.

Kelly III, John E., & Hamm, Steve. *Smart Machines: IBM's Watson and the Era of Cognitive Computing*. Columbia Business School Publishing, 2013.

Kolb, Jeremy. *Business Intelligence in Plain Language: A Practical Guide to Data Mining and Business Analytics*. Applied Data Labs Inc., 2012.

Lanier, Jaron. *Who Owns the Future?* Simon & Schuster, 2014.

Mayer-Schönberger, Viktor, and Kenneth Cukier. *Big Data: A Revolution That Will Transform How We Live, Work, and Think*. Houghton Mifflin Harcourt, 2013.

Isard, Michael, and John MacCormick. *Nine Algorithms That Changed the Future: The Ingenious Ideas That Drive Today's Computer*. Princeton University Press, 2011.

Milton, Michael. *Head First Data Analysis: A Learner's Guide to Big Numbers, Statistics, and Good Decisions*. O'Reilly Media, 2009.

Minelli, Michael, Michele Chambers, and Ambiga Dhiraj. *Big Data, Big Analytics: Emerging Business Intelligence and Analytic Trends for Today's Businesses*. John Wiley & Sons, 2012.

O'Reilly Radar Team. *Big Data Now: Current Perspectives from O'Reilly Radar*. O'Reilly Media. 2011.

Provost, Foster, and Tom Fawcett. *Data Science for Business: What You Need to Know about Data Mining and Data-Analytic Thinking*. O'Reilly Media, 2013.

Redman, Thomas C. *Data Driven*. Harvard Business Review Press, 2008.

Rudder, Christian. *Dataclysm: Who We Are (When We Think No One's Looking)*. Crown Publishing Group, 2014.

Sathi, Arvind. *Big Data Analytics: Disruptive Technologies for Changing the Game*. Mc Press, 2012.

Schmidt, Eric, and Jared Cohen. *The New Digital Age: Reshaping the Future of People, Nations and Business*. Knopf, 2013.

Scoble, Robert, and Shel Israel. *Age of Context: Mobile, Sensors, Data and the Future of Privacy*. Patrick Brewster Press, 2014.

Segal, Leerom, Aaron Goldstein, Jay Goldman, and Rahaf Harfoush. *The Decoded Company: Know Your Talent Better Than You Know Your Customers*. Portfolio, 2014.

Segaran, Toby, and Jeff Hammerbacher, eds. *Beautiful Data: The Stories Behind Elegant Data Solutions*. O'Reilly Media, 2009.

Shron, Max. *Thinking with Data: How to Turn Information into Insights*. O'Reilly Media, 2014.

Siegel, Eric. *Predicative Analytics: The Power to Predict Who Will Click, Buy, Lie, or Die*. John Wiley & Sons, 2013.

Simon, Phil. *The Visual Organization: Data Visualization, Big Data, and the Quest for Better Decisions*. Wiley and SAS Business Series, 2014.

Simon, Phil. *Too Big to Ignore: The Business Case for Big Data*. John Wiley & Sons, 2013.

Smolan, Rick, and Jennifer Erwitt. *The Human Face of Big Data*. Against All Odds Productions, 2012.

Steiner, Christopher. *Automate This: How Algorithms Took Over Our Markets, Our Jobs, and the World*. Penguin Group, 2012.

Surdak, Christopher. *Data Crush: How the Information Tidal Wave Is Driving New Business Opportunities*. AMACOM, 2014.

Takahashi, Mana, and Shoko Azuma. *The Manga Guide to Databases*. No Starch Press, 2009.

Townsend, Anthony M. *Smart Cities: Big Data, Civic Hackers, and the Quest for a New Utopia*. W. W. Norton, 2013.

Tucker, Patrick. *The Naked Future: What Happens in a World That Anticipates Your Every Move?* Penguin Group, 2014.

Yau, Nathan. *Data Points: Visualization That Means Something*. John Wiley & Sons, 2013.

INDEX

AAC (Adaptive Architecture and Computation) master's program, 222
Aatresh, Deepak, 75, 78, 244
Abstract nature of data:
  as challenge for architects, 19–20
  Zigmund Rubel on, 77, 113
Access to data, 36
Adaptive Architecture and Computation (AAC) master's program, 222
Adaptive challenges, 13
Aditazz, 6
  catalog of building products at, 77
  client data at, 153
  data-driven approach at, 75, 76, 79, 85, 86, 107
  data utilization at, 84
  decision making at, 79, 83
  productivity at, 79
  project teams at, 222
  Realization Platform, 19
  research at, 234
AEC industry:
  Big Data in, 228
  business intelligence in, 297–299
  computer scientists in, 232–234
  data-driven design in, 198
  data in, xvi–xix
  data strategies from other industries in, 32, 33
  data utilization in, 319
  decision making based on data in, 79–80
  design teams in, 183
  firms as data intermediaries in, 281–282
  future of data in, 331–335
  interest in data vs. form in, 44
  interoperability in, 266–267, 271–272
  productivity in, 78–79

AECO industry:
  acceptance of data by, 162–163
  Big Data in, 1–2, 14–15, 54, 115, 282
  culture of, 199
  data preparedness of, 107–110
  leveraging data in, 29–36, 87
  stakeholder expectations of, 278
  technical vs. adaptive challenges with data in, 13
  transparency in, 18, 19
  trends in, 71–74
  views of data in, 164–165
AEC Technology Symposium & Hackathon, 324
AHR, 222, 235–237
AIA (American Institute of Architects), 233, 268
AIA Large Firm Roundtable (AIA LFRT), 321
Algorithms:
  form-making, 204
  improving building performance with, 65–66, 204
  improving human performance with, 229
  monitoring performance with, 197
Alibre, 297
Alinea, 109
Allegory of the Cave (Plato), 78
Allies and Morrison Architects, 97
  data-driven design at, 102–103
  data wranglers at, 232
  intranet of project data at, 99
  web application by, 98
Allison, Markku, 1
Amazon, 278
Amazon Web Services, 83
American Institute of Architects (AIA), 233, 268
American Society of Civil Engineers, 250

Analytical approach to building process, 4
Analyzing data, 179–211
  by building owners, 277
  and data analytics, 179–180
  for decision making, 171, 172, 200–203
  with Dhour, 209–210
  for improving performance, 191, 197–198
  Mads Jensen on, 182–190
  Brendon Levitt on, 203–209
  Erik Olsen on, 193–197
  with predictive analytics, 180–182
  Chris Pyke on, 198–200
  synthesizing data vs., 211
  tools for, 190–191
ANNs (artificial neural networks), 235–236
Apache OpenOffice, 83
APIs, see Application programming interfaces
Apple, 106
Application of project data, 213–239
  by data wranglers, 232
  Billie Faircloth on, 216–221
  firm and project size as factors in, 213–216
  hiring candidates for skill in, 232–235
  by leadership, 238–239
  Grieg Paterson on, 235–237
  problem as focus of, 216–216
  by programmers, coders, computer scientists, and data scientists, 230–232
  by project teams, 222–226
  steps in, 213
  Andrew Witt on, 226–229
Application programming interfaces (APIs), 99, 266, 267, 269

343

Aptitude, data, 124–125, 227
Architects:
    benefits of data to, 5–12
    challenges with data for, 19–21
    changing role of, 238
    communication with, 67
    coordinating of data and
        information by, 228–229
    data as tool for, 104, 105
    data-driven design for, 207, 208
    data-intensive roles of, 230–232
    and data scientists, 295, 321
    education of, 99
    information, 230, 291
    as producers of knowledge, 211
    and programmers, 310
    understanding of databases by,
        38, 39, 42–43
Architectural justification, xv
    and data-informed decision
        making, 27
    rationalization vs., 120
    using data for, 21, 109, 141, 241
Architecture. See also AEC industry;
    AECO industry
    computers in, 75
    data in, xiii, xiv, xviii–xix
    form in, xiii, 35–36
    information in, xiii, xiv
Architecture 2030 Challenge, 60,
    200, 299, 313
Architecture programs, learning to
    use data outside of, 131, 132,
    137
AR.Drones, 118, 166
Arduino microprocessors, 117, 118,
    154–156
Artec EVA, 170
Artificial neural networks (ANNs),
    235–236
Arup, 109
ASCE Journal of Computing in Civil
    Engineering, 250
ASCE Journal of Construction, 250
ASHRAE Journal, 14, 199
Assumptions, testing, 186
Astorino, 94, 110, 282–284
Audience for data visualization,
    302

Augmented reality, 253–255,
    333–334
AutoCAD, 64, 137, 231
AutoCAD Architecture, 60
Autodesk, 56, 65, 130, 262
Autodesk University, 45
AutoLISP, 137
Automation:
    of construction data collection,
        255
    of decision making, 17–19
    in future of AECO industry, 334
Awareness of data, 36, 301
Azure, 83

Backaitis, Virginia, 179
Background:
    and comfort with data, 113
    and data aptitude, 124–125, 227,
        265
    and preparation for data-driven
        practice, 220
    of project team members, 230–
        235, 321
    and signal processing ability, 131,
        132
Barista, David, 243
The Bartlett, UCL, 222
Behavior, human:
    analysis of, 198
    and building performance, 114
    changes in, 4
    and data utilization, 239
    predicting, 181, 197
Belcher, Dan, 114
Bergman, Jill:
    on challenges with data
        collection, 176
    on data-ready approaches, 97
    on leadership, 238
    on planning for data use, 215
    on value of investing in data, 13
Berners-Lee, Tim, 297
BI (business intelligence), 32,
    297–299
Bias, in presentation of data, 328
Big Data:
    in AEC/AECO industries, 1–2,
        14–15, 54, 115, 228, 282

applying, 216
in architecture, xiii
and business intelligence, 297
at CASE, 307, 308
defined, 52–55
firm/project size and integration
    of, 213
for governments, 195
and instrumentation, 71
interest in, 283
Evelyn Lee on working with,
    295–296
at LMN/LMNts, 163
meaningful data vs., 54–55
at NBBJ, 91
Sukanya Paciorek on working
    with, 275
in planning process, 174–175
David Sawdey on, 327
Greg Schleusner on working with,
    270
security/privacy of, 313
sharing of, 55–56
solving business problems with,
    301
structuring, 227–228
and unstructured data, 71, 175,
    232
wrangling, 97, 232
BIM (building information
    modeling):
in architecture education, 129
benefits of, 280–281
Big Data in context of, 55, 56
collaboration and, 29–32
and computational design, xix,
    271
construction data in, 247, 249,
    251, 254
as database, 2–3, 8, 11, 215–216
data visualization with, 15, 286–
    288, 290
and data vs. information, 52
and data wrangling, 97
document-centric use of, 250
early uses of, 66
ERP data in, 301
and IMB approach, 83–84
improving efficiency of, 321–322

improving level of development in, 255–256
interacting with data via, 307
and interest in performance vs. form, 204
mining project data in, 165–167
and past experience, 209
and productivity, xvii, 269
and radar factor in data preparedness, 109, 110
real-time analysis in, 60
at SOM, 45–49
standards for, 269
supplemental data from, 50, 51
for sustainable design, 192
uses of, 285, 325–326
value of, xvi, 2
BIM and Integrated Design (Randy Deutsch), xvi
BIM Benchmark Tool, 30–31
BIM leaders, 231, 238
BIM objects, using, 239
BIM Standard, *see* United States National Building Information Modeling (BIM) Standard
BIPV (building integrated photovoltaic) systems, 207
Blender, 83
Böke, Jens, 131–133
Bowker, Geoffrey C., 331
Brain Hacking Studio, 128
Broughton, Jonathon, 225
    on background and data aptitude, 124–125
    on data-driven design approaches, 97–106
    on data preparedness, 109–110
    on data scientists, 231–232
    on data visualization, 122
    on data wrangling, 232
    on decision making, 201–202
    on demonstrating vs. explaining value of data, 20, 102
    on fees and profitability, 298–299
    on future of AECO industry, 333
    on interoperability, 266–267
    on intuition and data, xv, 9, 12, 103, 105
    on "playing" with data, 123

Brown, Brené, 179
Brown University, 171, 172, 175, 201
bSa (buildingSMART alliance), 263
Buccellato, Aimee, 134–136, 325
Building Analytics dashboard, 10, 308
Building CATALYST, 284
Building construction courses, xvi
Building façade performance, 166, 168
Building information modeling, *see* BIM
Building integrated photovoltaic (BIPV) systems, 207
Building lifecycle, 179, 243, 266, 331
Building longevity, 279
Building management systems, 182, 277
Building owners, *see* Owners
Building performance:
    algorithms for improving, 65–66, 204
    analyzing data to improve, 197–198
    computational design for improving, 150
    creating project teams to improve, 225
    data for improving, 136
    as factor in leveraging of data, 35–36
    and geometry, 229
    human behavior and, 114–115
    human performance and, 191, 229
    interest in form vs., 204, 205
    optimizing, 63–64
    organizational performance and, 191
    in practice of design, 216–217
    structure, skin and, 66–67
    warehousing data to improve, 69
buildingSMART alliance (bSa), 265
buildingSMART data dictionary, 270
buildingSMART standards, 267, 268
Burke, Sean D.:
    on building, human, and organizational performance, 191

on business intelligence, 298
on computer scientists, 230
on data, 55–61
on data generalists vs. specialists, 224, 225
on decision making, 200
on energy analysis, 191, 192, 299
on human resources, 34
on interoperability, 271
on learning to work with data in practice, 137
on monitoring organizational performance, 299
on multi-factor analysis, 7
on simulations, 191
on teaching data-driven design, 129, 130
Business case for leveraging data, 297–329
    and business intelligence in AEC industry, 297–299
    David Fano and Daniel Davis on, 300–310
    fee and profitability data in, 298–299
    Mark Frisch on, 312–323
    David Sawdey on, 325–329
    and security/privacy concerns, 310–313
    and sharing of data between firms, 324–325
Business intelligence (BI), 32, 297–299

CAD (computer-aided design), 39, 44, 269, 326
CAD managers, 231
CAD standards, 268
California College of the Arts, 203
Capacity, utilization and, 170, 294
Capturing data. *See also* Collecting data; Mining project data
    Mark Frisch on, 312–317
    Brian Ringley on, 117–118
    at USGBC, 200
    with visual sensing, 259
CarbonBuzz, 235
Card-swipe readers, 156–157
Carnegie Mellon University, 149

CASE Inc., 246
  Big Data at, 282, 307, 308
  Building Analytics dashboard of,
      10, 308
  data analysis at, 179
  database work of SOM and,
      37–41, 48
  data-enabled design and
      technology at, 300, 305–307
  data mining in BIM by, 165, 166
  data preparedness at, 109, 110
  FM Data Manager of, 303–306
  noncompensated learning at, 137
  predictive analysis with
      dashboards at, 180, 182
  Project Dashboard of, 56–57, 298
  skills of job candidates at, 249
CASE Pro Apps, 114
Certainty, 21, 180–181
CFD (computational fluid dynamics)
      modeling, 146, 147, 149
Chameleon, 114
Change, advocating for, 59–60
Change management, 247–248
Charles Street Car Park (Sheffield,
      United Kingdom), 103–105
Chicago, Illinois, 195
Christenson, Clayton, 76
Citi Bike, 157
City Tech, CUNY, 63, 113, 114, 137
Clients:
  communication with, 8, 10, 67
  direction on data use from, 278
  as drivers of data-driven design,
      106
  planning for data use by, 215
  project data from, 153
  promoting data-informed design
      to, 278–279
  use of data by, 328–329
  using data to persuade, xv–xvi
  views of data by, xxi
Client data marts, 326
Climate analysis, 192, 194–196
Climate change, 195–196
Cloud computing:
  at Aditazz, 83
  as factor in leveraging of data,
      32, 33

project data in, 187
  at Sefaira, 184–185
Cloud Lab, 126–128
COBie (Construction Operations
      Building information
      exchange), 262–266
CodeBook, 56
Coders, 230
Cognitive data, collecting, 128
Collaborations:
  of computers and design
      professionals, 334–335
  of design and management, 322
Collecting data:
  benefits of, 170
  from clients, 153
  in construction industry, 245,
      248–249
  from field, 154–157
  at Sasaki Associates, 176
  strategy for, 169–170
  by technical coordinators,
      317–318
Collins, Mark, 126
Columbia University, 63, 126, 127
Comfort, 193
Communication:
  at Astorino, 283
  with clients, 8, 10, 67
  high fidelity, 229
Comparison Engine, 42
Compatibility, software, 271
Compilation of data, 203
Complexity, 5, 177
Compromises, designers', 76, 77
Computational design:
  and BIM, xix, 271
  intuition in, 147, 148
  leveraging data with, 309
  at NBBJ, 150, 153, 190–191, 213
  predicting human behavior with,
      197
Computational fluid dynamics
      modeling, see CFD modeling
Computers:
  in architecture and construction,
      75
  and automation of decision
      making, 17–19

collaborations of design
      professionals with, 334–335
  data mining with, 294
  hardware limitations of, 17
Computer-aided design, see CAD
Computer scientists:
  in AEC industry, 232–234
  emerging professionals vs., 231
  hiring, 65, 230–232
Computer vision, 257–259
Concrete problems, 216
Confidence, 6, 305
Confidentiality, 313
Connected systems, 320
Consensus building, 180
Conservation, energy, 194, 281
Construction industry, 243–272. See
      also AEC industry; AECO industry
  awareness of data in, 36
  computers in, 75
  data use in, 91, 92, 244–245
  Bill East on, 262–266
  Billie Faircloth on, 220
  Mani Golparvar-Fard on, 250–259
  Tyler Goss on, 246–250
  interest in technology in, 244
  interoperability of AEC software
      with, 266–267, 271–272
  linking data in design, operations,
      and, 259–262
  owners as drivers of data use in,
      296
  risk aversion in, 250
  Greg Schleusner on, 267–270
  standards for, 266
Construction Operations Building
      information exchange (COBie),
      262–266
Construction phase, 243–245,
      247–248
Consumption, energy, 196, 208, 278
Contextualizing data, 16–17, 284
Contractors:
  benefits of data to, 12
  challenges with data for, 21, 23, 24
  data collection by, 245
  interest in data by, 246
ConXtech, 72
Cooling tower (Doha, Qatar), 22

CORE Studio, 63
   computer science background of
      members in, 234
   data visualization at, 64
   project with Property Loss
      Consulting Group, 66, 67
   research at, 234
   revision history interface project
      of, 261
   TTX at, 114
Corporate real estate (CRE),
   327–329
Cost estimation, 259–260, 284
Cost savings, data visualization for,
   275, 276
CRE (corporate real estate), 327–329
Creativity, 75–77
Crissy Field Center (San Francisco,
   California), 292
Critical thinking, 20, 58–59, 120
Cross-checking datasets, 120
Crossing the Chasm (Geoffrey A.
   Moore), 45
Cross-referencing datasets, 17
Cross-ventilation experiment in
   Dhour, 209–210
Culture:
   AECO industry, 199
   construction industry, 244,
      246–247
   firm, 20, 33, 34, 239, 280
   school, 120–122
CUNY, see City Tech, CUNY

D3 approach, see Data-driven
   design approach
D3 program, 99
D4AR technology, 253–255
Daily construction photolog, 23
Daily Construction Reports (DCRs),
   251
Dashboards. See also Project
   Dashboard
   Building Analytics, 10, 308
   data visualization with, 307
   Zero Net Energy Design, 7
Data, 29–69
   in AEC industry, xvi–xix
   in architecture, xiii, xiv, xviii–xix

benefits of using, 4–13
in building construction courses,
   xvi
Sean D. Burke on, 55–61
challenges with using, 13–17
definition of, 50–54
demonstrating value of, 20, 102
design professionals' view of, 1–4
documents vs., 61–63
future of, in AEC industry, 331–335
and information, 228–229
interest in form vs., 44, 115–117,
   130, 188, 189, 196–197, 282–283
justifying use of, 141
as means to an end, 201–203
mindset for using, 2–3, 239,
   322–323
persuading clients to follow
   design direction with, xv–xvi
Jonatan Schumacher on, 63–69
time and effort for working with,
   21–24 as tool for architects, 104,
   105
unstructured, 17–21
value of, 13, 279
Robert Yori on, 37–49
Data analysis, see Analyzing data
Data analytics:
   accomplishments of, 202
   data analysis vs., 179–180
   predictive, 180–182, 332
Data approach to buildings, 39, 40
Data aptitude, 124–125, 227
Data architects, 230
Data-backed decision making, 174
Database(s):
   architects' understanding of work
      on, 38, 39, 42–43
   BIM as, 2–3, 8, 11, 215–216
   Display Energy Certificate, 236
   document-based, 302
   drawings as, 62
   at Gehry Technologies, 289–291
   OpenAsset, 319
   of SOM and CASE Inc., 37–41, 48
   SQL, 160
Data centers, 165, 280, 281
Data-centric thinking:
   document-centric vs., 62, 302

improving firms', 87–88, 174, 218
   shifting to, 249–250
Data coordinators, 315
Data-driven construction, 246
Data-driven decision making, 33,
   183–184
Data-driven design:
   in AEC industry, 198
   for architects, 207, 208
   building owners as drivers of, 296
   future of, 331–333
   teaching, 129–133
Data-driven design (D3) approach,
   71–106
   Jonathon Broughton on, 97–106
   clients as drivers of, 106
   continuum for, 84–86, 94–95
   data-informed vs., 236, 237
   Andrew Heumann on, 86–92
   hybrid, 96
   and ideal firm approach, 44
   at LMN Architects tech studio,
      157–158
   Zigmund Rubel on, 75–84
   at Sefaria, 185
   and trends in AECO industry,
      71–74
Data-enabled approach, 44, 85, 305
Data-enabled project teams,
   222–226
Data-informed approach:
   at AHR, 236, 237
   data-driven vs., 87, 96
   defined, 85
   as ideal firm approach, 44
   professionals/firms using, 94–95
   at Sasaki Associates, 171
Data-informed decision making, 27,
   304, 321
Data-inspired approach, 44
Data literacy, 87
Data marts, client, 326
Data-nimble approach, 96, 216
Data preparedness, 73, 107–110
Data-ready approach, 96
Data scientists:
   and architects, 295, 321
   Jonathon Broughton on, 99
   on project teams, 231–232

Datasets, 17, 120
Datatization, 71–73
Data visualization (data viz):
    as AECO industry trend, 74
    in architecture workplace, 138
    audience considerations in, 302
    with BIM, 15, 286–288, 290
    at CASE, 307, 308
    cost savings related to, 275, 276
    with Dhour, 209–210
    and documents, 62
    flexibility in, 204, 205
    importance of, 206, 207
    learning to work with data via,
        119–120, 122–123
    Evelyn Lee on, 294
    at LMNts, 161
    monitoring, 298
    by owners, 285–293
    portfolio strategy and, 326
    Revit for, 286–291
    at Thornton Tomasetti, 68–69
    tools for, 206–208
Data wrangling, 97, 232
Davis, Daniel:
    on behavior change, 4
    on business case for leveraging
        data, 300–310
    on computer scientists in AEC
        industry, 232–233
    on data analysis for decision
        making, 200
    on future of AECO industry, 333
    on insight, 51
DC Bridge project, 256
DCRs (Daily Construction Reports),
    251
DeBono, Edward, 124
DEC (Display Energy Certificate)
    database, 236
Decision making:
    in AEC industry, 79–80
    analyzing data for, 200–203
    by architects, 6–9
    automation of, 17–19
    collecting data for, 313
    data analysis for, 171, 172
    data-backed, 174
    data-driven, 33, 183–184

data-informed, 27, 304, 321
data visualization for, 326
format of data and, 307, 309
improving, with data, 45–49,
    88–91, 116, 199, 207–209, 237,
    280, 293
justifying, 241
office data for, 323
using data in, 2, 6–8
DEC (Display Energy Certificate)
    ratings, 237
Deltas, 248–249
Deming, W. Edwards, 143
Department of Transportation
    (DOT), 169
Deproductization, 72
Design:
    collaboration of management
        and, 322
    data as compliment to, 3, 12
    data in, 91, 92
    data in construction vs., 244–245
    as filter, 233
    linking data in construction,
        operations, and, 259–262
    as search, 127–128
Design computation, see
    Computational design
Design direction, xv–xvi, 170
Designers:
    compromises by, 76, 77
    data-intensive roles of, 230
Design phase, 186
Design professionals:
    architectural justification by, 141
    collaborations of computers with,
        334–335
    data as must-have for, 3
    interest in form vs. building
        performance for, 204, 205
    interest in form vs. data for, 44,
        188, 189, 196–197, 282–283
    leveraging of data by, 176
    use of data by, 91–94
    views of data by, 1–4, 200
Design teams, 183
Deutsch, Randy, xvi, xx
Dhour, 204, 206, 209–210
Differentiation factor, data as, 101–102

Digital-data referees, 229
Digital Project, 65, 245
Digitization, 71, 72
DIKW progression, 5, 6, 50–52, 304
Diller Scofidio + Renfro, 66
Display Energy Certificate (DEC)
    database, 236
Display Energy Certificate (DEC)
    ratings, 237
Distrust, of data, 19–20
DIVA:
    applying data from, 117, 118
    data on façade performance in,
        166
    noncompensated learning about,
        137
    and physical models, 120
    referencing environmental data
        in, 116, 333
Diversity, project team, 226
Document-centric thinking, 62,
    249–250, 302
Documents:
    data in, 144, 145
    as output of architects, 61–63
DOT (Department of
    Transportation), 169
dRofus, 56, 269–270
Dynamic area analysis, 314
Dynamic data, 169–170
Dynamic thermal simulation, 193
Dynamo, 58, 137
DynaRobo, 112

East, Bill, 262–266
Easy data, 13
EBD (evidence-based design), 202,
    277
Ecotect simulation, 60
Education:
    of architects, 99
    and data in school culture,
        120–122
    learning to work with data during,
        110–111, 128–133, 137
    security/privacy of data in, 310
EEG (electroencephalography), 128
EES (Engineering Equation Solver),
    196

Efficiency:
    of BIM, 321–322
    energy, 274–276
Effort:
    for collecting data, 176–178, 248
    for working with data, 16, 21–24
Eisenman, Peter, 120
Electroencephalography (EEG), 128
Elk, 116, 333
Emerging professionals, 231
End users, 296. *See also* Tenants
Energy analysis:
    Sean D. Burke on, 191, 192, 299
    data in, 59
    at Transsolar, 194
Energy benchmarking, 194
Energy conservation, 194, 281
Energy consumption, 196, 208, 278
Energy efficiency, 274–276
Energy generation, 208
Energy monitoring systems, 74
Energy Star Portfolio Manager®,
    273
Engineering, *see* AEC industry;
    AECO industry
Engineering Equation Solver (EES),
    196
Enterprise Resource Planning
    (ERP), 156, 298, 301
Environmental impact, comfort and,
    193
Erwin, Kim, 156
Estimation, cost, 259–260, 284
Evidence-based design (EBD), 202,
    277
Expectations, owners', 303
Experimentation with data, 123–124
Exploration, in design process, 161,
    186
External generative data, 50, 51

Facility performance evaluation
    (FPE), 332
Faircloth, Billie, 239
    on application of project data,
      216–221
    on data-enabled project teams,
      222, 224
    on data in construction phase, 245

on data-nimble approaches, 96
    on data synthesis, 211
False positives, 12
Fano, David:
    on business case for leveraging
      data, 300–310
    on business decisions, 7–8
    on business intelligence, 297–298
    on certainty in AECO industry, 21
    on computer scientists in AEC
      industry, 233
    on data mining in BIM, 165
    on data missed by firms, 156
    on data preparedness, 109
    on data strategies from other
      industries, 32, 33
    on datatization, 72
    on data visualization, 62
    on data vs. information, 50–52
    on defining Big Data, 53
    on direction for data use, 278
    on documents, 61
    on extracting and transferring
      meaningful data, 261
    on fabrication of tools by
      students, 111–112
    on future of AECO industry, 333
    on information management, 247
    on integrated vs. nonintegrated
      project teams, 226
    on interoperability, 267
    on quality of data, 16
    on Quantified Self movement,
      156
    on school culture, 121
    on social media, 157
    on validation, 74
Fear of working with data, 77, 103,
    295
Fees, productivity and, 298–299
Field data, collecting, 154–157
Field inspections, 256
Firefly, 117, 154
Firm culture:
    as challenge in working with
      data, 20
    as factor in leveraging of data,
      33, 34
    and leadership in data use, 239

Peter Pellerzi on importance of,
    280
Firms:
    data applications and size of,
      15–16, 213–214
    data-centric, 87, 174
    as data intermediaries, 281–282
    research at large, 234
    sharing data between, 324–325
    small, 136, 162, 231, 234
Fletcher, Paul, 27
Flexibility:
    of buildings, 149, 150
    in data visualization, 204, 205
    of technology, 309
FlexSim Healthcare, 191
Flux, 334
FM Data Manager, 303–306
Form:
    in architecture, xiii, 35–36
    as driver of design, 65–66
    interest in building performance
      vs., 204, 205
    interest in data vs., 44, 115–117,
      130, 188, 189, 196–197,
      282–283
    and performance optimization,
      63–64
Format, data, 307, 309
Forsyth, David, 259
Founders Effect, 137, 227
4Adaptive, 154, 294
4D modeling, BIM for, 251
FPE (facility performance
    evaluation), 332
Frisch, Mark, 299
    on business case for leveraging
      data, 312–323
    on construction industry, 36
    on data-informed approaches, 95
    on data mining in BIM, 165
    on hiring computer scientists,
      230–231
    on learning to work with data, 111,
      129
    on sharing data, 324–325
Fuel3D, 170
Fuse Lab, 113, 114, 118
Fusion Tables, 234

GBIC.org, 144
Gehry Technologies (GT), 226
    as digital-data referee, 229
    interoperability at, 271–272
    Michael Kilkelly on use of
        databases at, 289–291
Generalists, data, 224–225
Gensler, 144
Geographic information system
    (GIS), 163, 333
Geometry:
    and building/human
        performance, 229
    computational design for
        improving, 150
    interest in data vs., 56, 58, 66
    in practice of design, 216–217
Geometry Gym, 114
Georgetown University, 175
George Washington University, 198
Geo-spatial data, 333
Gibson, William, 331
GIS (geographic information
    system), 163, 333
Gitelman, Lisa:
    on data mining, 141
    on disciplines, 107
    on graphical representation, 241
GitHub, 260–261
Golden Gate National Parks
    Conservancy, 292
Goldstein, Brett, 195
Golparvar-Fard, Mani:
    on challenges with data
        collection, 177, 178
    on construction industry,
        250–259
    on documents, 62
    on IFCs, 261
    on risk aversion, 23
    on technology, 250
    on tracking materials, 243
Good, public and private, 313
Google:
    as building owners, 303
    collaboration with computers at,
        334
    data centers for, 279
    data sharing facilitated by, 187

    importance of data-driven design
        to, 106
    research at, 234
Google Bay View campus
    (Mountain View, California),
    145–149, 153
Google Docs, 234, 260, 261, 297
Google Spreadsheets, 234
Goss, Tyler:
    on challenges with data
        collection, 176–177
    on construction industry,
        246–250
    on documents, 62
    on learning to work with data in
        school, 128–129
    on leveraging data in
        construction phase, 243–244
    on owners as drivers of data use,
        296
    on predictive analytics, 182
    on risk aversion, 23
Governments, Big Data for, 195
Grasshopper:
    analysis for decision making with,
        200
    carbon calculator in, 192
    data handling by, 64–65, 114
    design analysis in, 309
    frit pattern analysis with, 67
    IFCs for transferring data from,
        262
    learning to work with data in, 99
    leveraging data with, 309
    optimizing performance with, 63
    prototyping visualization for, 204
    referencing environmental data
        in, 116, 333
    revision history interface for, 261
    at small firms, 234
    students' knowledge of, 62, 129,
        249
    TTX vs., 324
Green building design, 183–184, 199
Green Building Information
    Gateway, 198, 199
Green Building Studio, 60, 299
Green Group, LMN, 157
Green Permit Program, 193

Green roof vegetation study,
    220–221
GreenScale Tool, 134–135
Griffin, Duncan, 145
Grimshaw Architects, 95
GT, see Gehry Technologies
GTeam, 227–229, 271–272

Hacker mentality, 222, 225, 238,
    269
Hadoop, 297
Hamer Andy, 20
Hangzhou Stadium (Hangzhou,
    China), 12, 88–93, 130
Haot, Rachel, 195
Happold Consulting, 109
Hardware, limitations of, 17
Harvard University, 227
Harvests (SOM), 41
Hasegawa, Toru:
    on background factors in data
        aptitude, 125
    on learning to work with data,
        126–128
    on security of data, 310
HDR (high dynamic range)
    photography, 208
Healthcare projects:
    data-driven design for, 106
    mining project data for, 166, 168
    predictive analytics for, 181
Hemmerling, Marco, 109, 230
Heumann, Andrew, 145
    on Big Data, 54
    on card-swipe data, 156
    on data-driven design
        approaches, 86–92
    on data-enabled project teams,
        224
    on data sources for healthcare
        projects, 166, 168
    on roles of designers, 230
    on security/privacy of data, 310
    on teaching data-driven design,
        129
High dynamic range (HDR)
    photography, 208
High fidelity communication, 229
Hiring:

candidates with data application skills, 232–235
computer scientists, 65, 230–231
data scientists vs. architects, 321
HOAR FM Data Manager, 303–306
HOK, 267
    Big Data at, 282
    buildingSMART standards at, 268
    data preparedness at, 110
    and dRofus, 269–270
Holland, Nate, 89
Homogenization, data, 271–272
Honeybee, 67
Horizon Cloud, 36
Hudson Yards Culture Shed (New York, New York), 66
Human intervention, in future of design, 334–335
Human performance:
    algorithms for improving, 229
    analysis of, 198
    and building performance, 191, 229
    cross-validating, 258–259
    and geometry, 229
    and organizational performance, 191
    in practice of design, 216–217
Human resources, 33, 34, 108
Hurricane Sandy, 66, 67, 196
Hybrid data-driven design approaches, 96

IES, 299
IFCs, see Industry Foundation Classes
IFM (Integrated Facilities Management), 327, 328
IIT Institute of Design, 156
Ikenberry Commons project, 251
IMB approach, 83–84
IMMERSIVx, 176
Implementation of data strategies, business case for, see Business case for leveraging data
Industry Foundation Classes (IFCs):
    data models using, 261–262
    Bill East on, 265, 265

Mani Golparvar-Fard on, 261, 263–266
and Revit, 58
with standards, 269
and TTX, 65
Information:
    in architecture, xiii, xiv
    coordination of data and, 228–229
    from data, 202, 203
    data vs., 50–52
    honing in on key, 17
    sharing, 229, 263
    sharing of, 229
Information architects, 230, 291
Information intermediaries, 223
Information specialists, 230–231, 319
Inherent geometrical data, 50, 51
Insecurity in working with data, 109
Insight, 51
Instrumentation, 71, 72
Integrated Facilities Management (IFM), 327, 328
Integrated project teams, 225–226
Intelligence, business, 32, 297–299
Intergovernmental Panel on Climate Change, 198
Intermediaries:
    data, 281–282
    information, 223
Internet of Things (IoT), 71, 331
Interoperability, 17, 114
    and access, 36
    in AEC and construction industries, 266–267, 271–272
    and buildingSMART data dictionary, 270
    and extracting/transferring meaningful data, 261
    repositories for improving, 260–261
    in simulations, 163
    Brian Skripac on, 262
    and TTX platform, 65
    and workflow, 160
Intuition:
    Jonathon Broughton on data and, xv, 9, 12, 103, 105

in computational design, 147, 148
in data-driven approaches, 158
at Sefaria, 186
IoT (Internet of Things), 71, 331
Iterative design process, 158–161, 163, 185

Janks, Gregory:
    on applying data analysis, 180
    on bad data, 211
    on data generalists vs. specialists, 224
    on data-informed approaches, 94
    on data visualization, 292
    on decision making, 201
    on mining project data, 170–176
    on preparing to apply data, 214
Jensen, Mads:
    on analyzing data, 182–190
    on Big Data, 53
    on cloud computing, 32
    on data analysis vs. analytics, 179–180
    on data as means to an end, 203
    on data preparedness, 109
    on diversity of project teams, 226
    on risk aversion, 14
    on technology, 33, 107
Job captains, 250
Johns Hopkins University, 175
Johnson, Jennifer:
    on analyzing data, 202, 203
    on contextualizing data, 16
    on data collection strategies, 169
    on data in documents, 144, 145
    on honing in on key information, 17
    on technology, 234–235
Jones Lang LaSalle:
    clients' use of data at, 328–329
    improving service with data at, 326–327
    use of BIM at, 325–326

Keynsham Town Hall (Keynsham, England), 237
Kieran, Stephen, 220

KieranTimberlake, 216
  culture at, 239
  data application at, 220–221
  data-driven approach at, 85
  data-nimble approach at, 96, 216
  project teams at, 222, 224
  research at, 217, 218
Kilkelly, Michael:
  on information architects, 230
  on "playing" with data, 124
  on Revit for data visualization,
    286–291
Kimpian, Judit, 235
King's Cross Central Master Plan
    (London, England), 106,
    122–123
Knight Frank, 109
Knowledge, producers of, 211
Koo Foundation (Taipei, Taiwan),
    149, 168

Ladybug, 67, 116, 333
Large firms, research at, 234
Leadership:
  application of project data by,
    238–239
  at Sasaki Associates, 173
Learning:
  how to learn, 112–113
  noncompensated, 137
  speed of, 6
Learning to work with data, 107–139
  and background factors in data
    aptitude, 124–125
  Jonathon Broughton on, 99
  Aimee Buccellato on, 134–136
  for contractors, 21
  and data preparedness factors,
    107–110
  data visualization in, 122–123
  with existing tools, 111–113
  Toru Hasegawa on, 126–128
  in practice, 137
  Brian Ringley on, 113–120
  and school culture, 120–122
  in schools, 128–133, 137
  in workplace, 137–139
Le Corbusier's Modulor, xiii
Lee, Evelyn:

on analytical approach to
    building, 4
on architect's views of data, 20
on benefits of collecting data, 170
on Big Data vs. meaningful data,
    54
on building owners, 293–296
on collecting field data, 154–155
on data-enabled approach, 85
on data mining, 143
on diversity of project teams, 226
on field data, 154
on future architecture firms, 332
LEED certification, 199, 276
LEEDOnline, 143–144
Leonhardt, Anne, 137
Level of development (LOD),
    255–256
Leveraging data. See also Business
    case for leveraging data
  in AECO industry, 29–36, 87
  Big Data, 53, 115
  in construction phase, 243–244
  by design professionals, 176
  mindset for, 45, 88, 301
  over building lifecycle, 243
Levitt, Brendon, 209, 285
  on analyzing data, 197, 203–209
  on data sources for building
    façade performance, 165–167
  on decision making, 6
  on simulations, 182
Liability with sharing data, 310–311
Liebsch, Peter, 95, 121
Lifecycle, building, 179, 243, 266,
    331
Light, David, 29
Literacy, data, 87
LMN Architects, 157
  acceptance of data at, 162
  Big Data at, 163
  data-driven approach at, 85, 158
  data-informed approach at, 95
  data visualization at, 286
  energy monitoring system of, 74
  simulations at, 163–164
LMN Architects tech studio
    (LMNts):
  Big Data at, 163

data-driven approach at,
    157–158
Lyrebird project at, 114
research project with Thornton
    Tomasetti, 67–68
technology at, 160
tools used by, 160–161
Local data, using, 194
Local Law 11, 145
Location-based analytics, 169
LOD (level of development),
    255–256
LOISOS + UBBELOHDE, 6, 203, 206
Longevity, building, 279
Lyrebird, 114

Machine learning, 257, 258
Mcinturf, Michael, 120
MacLeamy graph, 16
Magnetic resonance imaging (MRI),
    128
Management, collaboration of
    design and, 322
MapReduce, 297
Marble Fairbanks Architects, 126
MARS (Mobile Augmented Reality
    System) platform, 62–63
Materials, tracking, 243
Mathematicians, 183
MATLAB, 236
Maya, 114
Meaningful data, 54–55, 261
Mechanization, 318, 319
Meerkat, 117, 333
Metrics factor (data preparedness),
    108–109
Microsoft Access, 297
Microsoft Excel:
  handling of project data in, 64,
    114
  Michael Kilkelly on Revit and,
    288, 290
  potential of, 215
  project data in, 43
  as report card vs. database, 224
Microsoft Office, 83, 297
Miller, Lee, 268
Miller, Nathan, 137
Miller, Sam:

on changing role of architects, 238
on construction industry, 259
on data and sped of learning, 6
on data-informed approaches, 95
on data visualization, 286
on firm size, 16
on interoperability, 266
on leveraging data over building lifecycle, 243
on mining project data, 157–165
Mindset:
    for addressing complex building problems, 265
    of AECO industry, 14
    for leveraging data, 45, 88, 301
    and school culture, 121
    and technology, 45, 190, 190, 199
    for using data, 2–3, 239, 322–323
    for working with data, 77, 88, 160, 190, 190, 199, 218, 220, 283–284
Mining project data, 143–178
    benefits of, 170
    in BIM, 165–167
    on building façade performance, 166, 168
    challenges with, 176–178
    from clients, 153
    collecting field data, 154–157
    with computers, 294
    Mark Frisch on, 323
    for healthcare projects, 166, 168
    Gregory Janks on, 170–176
    Sam Miller on, 157–165
    Ryan Mullenix on, 145–153
    at NBBJ, 88–89, 91
    from private sources, 153–157, 165–168
    from public sources, 143–145
    Brian Ringley on, 115–118
    strategy for, 169–170
Mirtschin, Jon, 269
MKThink, 4
    data for owners at, 293–296
    field data at, 154–155
    requirements for job candidates at, 111

Mobile Augmented Reality System (MARS) platform, 62–63
Mobile devices:
    data collection with, 177–178
    private data from, 154–155, 176
Model-based Visual Sensing, 257–259
Moore, Geoffrey A., 45
Moran, Daniel Keys, 273
Morgareidge, David L.:
    on future of AECO industry, 332, 334
    on organization performance, 298, 299
    on predictive analytics, 180–181
    on technology for construction firms, 244
Morpholio Project, 126
Motivation, for using data-driven design, 78–79
MRI (magnetic resonance imaging), 128
Mulhern, Tom:
    on Big Data, 55
    on client data, 153
    on defining projects with data, 5
    on human performance, 198
    on instrumentation, 71
    on public sources of data, 144
    on Quantified Self movement, 156
Mullenix, Ryan:
    on building longevity, 279
    on computational design, 190–191
    on mining project data, 145–153
    on value of data, 50
Multi-factor analysis, 7, 17, 18, 181
Murphy/Jahn, 321
MyBuilding tool, 175
MyCampus tool, 175
MyCommunity tool, 175

National Center for Supercomputing Applications (NCSA), 255
Natural experiments, buildings as, 199, 201
Natural ventilation analysis, 315

Nature Conservancy, 170
The Nature Conservancy (TNC), 294
NBBJ, 55, 86
    Big Data at, 56, 91
    capabilities of, 145–147
    capturing data at, 89
    computational design at, 150, 153, 190–191, 213
    data-driven approach at, 85, 87, 148
    data for improved decision-making at, 88–91
    mining project data at, 89, 89
    monitoring organizational performance at, 299
    simulations at, 191
    use of data at, 92–92, 149
    validation of data at, 59
NCSA (National Center for Supercomputing Applications), 255
Netflix, 278
New York, New York, 195, 196, 274–276
New York City College of Technology, see City Tech, CUNY
New York Times, 62, 302
New York University (NYU), 37, 119, 138
Nike Fuel, 156
N Maeda Atelier, 126
Noise problem with data, 16, 17, 131, 132, 227, 277
Noncompensated learning, 137
Nonintegrated project teams, 225–226
Non-siloed approach to data use, 322–323
Notre Dame University Sustainable Data Community, xvi–xvii, 134
NREL, 60
NYC Open Data initiative, 145
NYU, see New York University

Oakland, California, 205
Oasys MassMotion, 198
Occupancy, utilization and, 182, 243

Office data:
    applying, 316–317
    decision making based on, 323
    relationship of project data and,
        315, 316
    sources of, 165, 167
Ohio State University, 262, 282, 285
Okumura, 255
Olsen, Erik:
    on analyzing data, 193–197
    on card-swipe readers, 156
    on data visualization, 286
    on form and performance in
        architecture, 35
    on open data, 145
    on sustainable design, 192
    on technology, 202
OpenAsset database, 319
Open data, 145, 195
Open-source software, 83
Operations, linking data in design,
        construction, and, 259–262
Operators, 275–276
Organizational data, 173
Organizational performance:
    integration of building and
        human performance with, 191
    monitoring, 298, 299
    in practice of design, 216–217
Outsourcing, of data mining, 176,
        333
Overall View Analysis Diagram, 8
Owners, 273–296. See also AECO
        industry
    and AECO firms as data
        intermediaries, 281–282
    benefits of data for, 21, 273
    closing performance gap for,
        278–279
    data analytics for, 202
    data visualization by, 285–293
    demand for construction data
        by, 249
    direction on data use from,
        277–278
    as drivers of data-driven design,
        296
    expectations of, 303
    Evelyn Lee on, 293–296

Sukanya Paciorek on, 274–277
Peter Pellerzi on, 279–281
planning for data use by, 215
promoting data-informed design
    to, 278–279
Revit for data visualization by,
    286–291
Brian Skripac on, 282–285
views of data by, xxi, 295

P3 projects, 332
Paciorek, Sukanya:
    on building owners, 273–277, 296
    on contextualizing data, 17
    on defining projects with data, 5
Pascal, 125
Past experiences:
    benefits of data vs., 105
    in BIM, 8, 11, 209
    decisions based on data vs., 20
    mining data from, 165–167
    warehousing data on, 69
Paterson, Grieg:
    on application of project data,
        235–237
    on building performance gap,
        278
    on data-enabled project teams,
        222, 223
Pellerzi, Peter:
    on building owners, 279–281
    on data centers, 165
    on data-driven design for
        Google, 106
Performance, see specific types, e.g.:
    Building performance
Performance-based design, 185,
    190, 190
Performance gap, closing, 278–279
Performance wheel, 9
Petronas Towers (Kuala Lumpur,
    Malaysia), 66
Photos, construction data in, 251,
    253–255
Physicists, on design teams, 183
Planning:
    Big Data in, 174–175
    for use of data, 215
    of work at Sasaki Associates, 171

Plato, 78
"Playing" with data, 123–124
POE (post-occupancy evaluation),
    332
Point cloud models, 253–256
Portfolio strategy, 326
Post-occupancy evaluation (POE),
    332
Power usage effectiveness (PUE),
    281
Pratt Institute, 113
Predictive analytics, 180–182, 332
Preferences, data and, xvi, 27
Prescribed reliability, 284
Presenting data, 328
Privacy, 284–285, 310–311
Private data sources, 153–157,
    165–168, 176
Private good, 311
Problem solving:
    as critical process, 318, 324
    and focus of data application,
        214–216
    working with data for, 301
Processing (program), 236
Productivity:
    in AEC industry, 78–79
    and BIM, xvii
    in construction industry, 247, 269
    and data, 2
Productization, 72
Profitability, 298–299
Programmers, 230, 310
Progress monitoring, 251–255
Projects:
    application of data and size,
        213–214
    defining, 5
Project conception phase, 244
Project cQ, 145
Project Dashboard:
    of CASE Inc., 56–57, 298
    of Skidmore, Owings and Merrill,
        11, 38, 40, 41, 43, 45–47
Project data:
    at Allies and Morrison Architects,
        99
    application of, see Application of
        project data

collecting, 313
mining, *see* Mining project data
relationship of office data and, 315, 316
technologies for handling, 43–44, 114, 187
Projections of Reality, 333
Project Model Page (SOM Dashboard), 47
Project Page (SOM Dashboard), 46
Project teams, 222–226
application of project data by, 222–226
data-backed decision making by, 174
data-enabled, 222–226
data-intensive roles on, 230–235
data specialists vs. generalists on, 224–225
diversity of, 226
integrated vs. nonintegrated, 225–226
use of data by, 313
Prototyping visualization, 204
Proxy Design Studios, 126, 127
Proxy models, 18, 116, 117
Public data sources, 143–145, 176, 294
Public good, private and, 311
PUE (power usage effectiveness), 281
Pyke, Chris:
on AECO firms as data intermediaries, 281
on analyzing data, 198–201
on Big Data, 14–15, 53, 54
on data collection strategies, 169–170
on data generalists vs. specialists, 225
on data-informed approaches, 95–96
on data preparedness, 107
on direction for data use, 277, 278
on public sources of data, 143–144
on risk and transparency, 311
on security/privacy of data, 311
Python, 137, 209

Quality:
data, 16
project, 164
Quantified Self movement, 156

R (programming language), 297
Radar factor (data preparedness), 109–110
Rapid Serial Visual Presentation (RSVP), 127–128
Rationalization, 120, 327–328
Readiness factor (data preparedness), 107–108
Real-time analysis, 60, 248
Redfin, 227
Reed Construction Data, 144, 145, 169, 234
Referees, digital-data, 229
Reliability, 16, 284, 310
Remapping data, 118–119
Remote solving, 67–68
Repositories, 260–261
Research:
at KieranTimberlake, 217, 218
at large firms, 234
by Grieg Paterson, 235–236
on practice of programmers vs. architects, 310
on technology in building industry, 300
Resilient cities, 196
Return on investment (ROI), 284
Revision history interface, Grasshopper, 261
Revit:
in architecture education, 129
carbon query tools in, 192
for data visualization, 286–291
document-centric use of, 62, 250
and efficiency of BIM, 322
as introduction to databases, 38, 39, 42
limitations of, 58
project data in, 43, 44
reasons for using, 268
at small firms, 162
at SOM, 45–49
transferring meaningful data in, 261

and TTX, 65, 324
using IFCs to transfer data into, 262
Rhino, 113, 114, 309, 333
Ringley, Brian:
on challenges with data collection, 176
on collecting data, 154, 170
on concrete problems, 214
on critical thinking, 20
on data preparedness, 107, 108
on firm/project size and data application, 213–214
on future of AECO industry, 333
on IFC, 261
on integrated vs. nonintegrated project teams, 225–226
on interoperability, 271
on learning how to learn, 112–113
on learning to work with data, 113–120, 138
on linking data, 266
on noncompensated learning, 137
on school culture, 120–122
on security/privacy of data, 310
on teaching data-driven design, 130
on types of data, 50
Risk, transparency and, 311
Risk aversion:
as challenge with using data, 14–15
in construction industry, 244, 250
of contractors, 23
and validation, 74
Risk management, 4, 5
Rogers Place Arena (Edmonton, Canada), 64
ROI (return on investment), 284
Roudsari, Mostapha, 63, 67
Roundhouse One, 154, 155
RSVP (Rapid Serial Visual Presentation), 127–128
RTKL, 86, 154
Rubel, Zigmund, 293
on abstract nature of data, 113
on automation of decision making, 18

Rubel, Zigmund (*continued*)
  on client data, 153
  on confidence, 6
  on construction industry, 244
  on data-driven design
     approaches, 75–84, 86, 106
  on documents, 63
  on future of AECO industry, 334
  on human behavior, 181
  on instrumentation, 71
  on productization, 72
  on project teams, 222, 226
  on validation, 73–74
Rules-based design processes,
  128–129

Saarinen, Eero, 307
Safety, on construction sites, 256,
  257
Sajda, Paul, 127
Samsung, 150–152
Sangenjaya residence (Tokyo,
  Japan), 126
SAP, 65, 262
Sasaki Associates, 170
  Big Data at, 175
  data analysis for decision making
     at, 171, 172
  data collection at, 176
  data-informed approach at, 94,
     171
  leadership at, 173
  Sasaki Strategies in, 173
  tools for working with data at, 175
Sawdey, David:
  on business case for leveraging
     data, 325–329
  on business intelligence, 298
  on data visualization, 292, 293
Scan data, collecting, 170
Scarangello, Tom, 66
Scenario planning, 181, 298
Scene design approach, 204
Schleusner, Greg, 267–270
Schmoker, Mike, 71
School culture, 120–122. *See also*
  Education
Schumacher, Jonatan:

on computer scientists in AEC
     industry, 234
  on construction industry, 244, 245
  on data, 63–69
  on data visualization for owners,
     285–286
  on future of AECO industry, 334
  on IFCs, 262
  on open data, 145
  on sharing data, 310–311, 324
  on software compatibility, 271
  on sustainable design, 192
  on TTX, 260–261
Search, design as, 127–128
Security, 284–285, 310–311
Sefaira, 182
  cloud computing at, 184–185
  comparing design options in, 14,
     34, 35
  data analysis vs. analytics at,
     179–180
  data-driven analysis at, 185, 186
  design teams at, 183
  green building goals of, 182, 183
  intuition at, 186
  outputs from, 33
Sefaira for SketchUp plug-in, 189
Sensors:
  private data from, 154–155, 176
  wireless sensor network, 218, 219
Service, improving, 326–327
Shade 3D, 126
Shading analysis, 61
Shading tests, 32
Sharing data:
  barriers to, 187
  Aimee Buccellato on, 134–136
  Sean D. Burke on, 55–56
  concerns about, 18, 19, 284–285,
     310–311
  between firms, 324–325
  Mark Frisch on, 318
  and privacy/security, 284–285,
     310–311
  Andrew Witt on, 227
Sharing information, 229, 263
Shoebox daylight study, 160
SHoP Architects, 129

Shron, Max, xvi
Sim City, 33, 185
Simulations:
  and cloud computing, 185
  data analysis for, 191
  dynamic thermal, 193
  Ecotect, 60
  at LMN Associates, 163–164
  and predictive analytics, 181, 182
  at Transsolar, 193, 194, 196
Site selection, 55, 144
SketchUp, 83, 114
Skidmore, Owings and Merrill
  (SOM), 37
  Big Data at, 282
  confidentiality of project data at,
     311
  database work of CASE Inc. and,
     37–41
  data-informed approach at, 94
  data preparedness at, 110
  hiring at, 233
  Project Dashboard at, 11, 38, 40,
     41, 43, 45–47
  Revit and BIM standards initiative
     at, 45–49
Skin, building, 66–67
Skripac, Brian:
  on AECO firms as data
     intermediaries, 281–282
  on analytics, 202
  on applying Big Data, 214
  on computer scientists vs.
     emerging professionals, 231
  on cost estimation in
     construction, 260
  on data-informed approaches, 95
  on data preparedness, 110
  on easy data, 13
  on interoperability, 262
  on owners, 282–285
Small firms, 136, 162, 231, 234
SmartGeometry, 333
Smart objects, 331
Smartphones, 177–178, 182
Snohetta office (Oslo, Norway), 200,
  309
Social media, 157, 267

Sociometrics, 153
Software. *See also* Interoperability
  and diversity of project teams,
    226
  as factor in leveraging of data, 29
  fluency in multiple types of,
    138–139
  learning to use, 121–122
  open-source, 83
  for sharing data, 187
Software developers, 183
Solar isolation, 116
SolidWorks, 114
Solomon Cordwell Buenz:
  data collection system at, 313,
    315
  design and management at, 322
  infrastructure of, 312
SOM, *see* Skidmore, Owings and
    Merrill
Specialists:
  data, 224–225
  information, 230–231, 319
  visualization, 231
SQL databases, 160
Stabile Center, 126–127
Stakeholders:
  expectations of, 278
  transparency and risk for, 311
Standard Data Exchange Format,
  262
Standardization, 271
Starchitects, 35
Starr, Clayton:
  on Big Data, 54
  on collecting field data, 154
  on data-driven approaches, 86
  on data generalists vs.
    specialists, 224, 225
  on data preparedness, 108
  on data sources for healthcare
    projects, 166
  on focus for data application, 214
Static data, 169
Steinfeld, Kyle, 209
Stevens Institute of Technology, 63,
  234, 271
Storytelling:

  with data, 132, 327–328
  data visualization for, 292–293
Strategies for working with data, 2
  applications of data analysis, 180
  big vs. meaningful data in, 54–55
  in construction stage, 247
  creating a data collection
    strategy, 169
  and data as means to an end, 203
  in decision making, 201
  demonstrating value of data, 20
  and determining data
    preparedness, 73
  for emerging professionals, 231
  in energy analysis, 191
  experimentation/play in, 123–124
  extracting and transferring
    meaningful data, 261
  and firm culture, 280
  honing in on key information, 17
  to improve service, 326–327
  with integrated vs. nonintegrated
    teams, 225–226
  making firms data-centric, 87–88,
    174
  and mindset for working with
    data, 88
  from other industries, 32, 33
  planning for data use, 217
  and preparing to apply data, 214
  to solve business problems, 301
  in sustainable design, 192
  technology in, 202
Strategy (program), 293–295
Structure, building, 66–67
Students. *See also* Education
  fabrication/manipulation of tools
    by, 111–113
  interest in form vs. data for, 115–
    117, 130
  necessary skills of graduating,
    118–120
  preparing, for non-siloed
    approach to data use, 322–323
  teaching data-driven design to,
    129–133
Studio Klashka, 109
SunSys Pavilion project, 131–133

Supplemental BIM data, 50, 51
Sustainable building data, 134–135,
  143
Sustainable design, 192
Synthesizing data, 211

Tableau, 99, 291
Tally, 217
Teaching data-driven design,
  129–133
Technical challenges, with data, 13
Technical coordinators, 317–318
Technology(-ies):
  adoption of, 106, 187
  and business intelligence,
    297–298
  at CASE Inc., 300
  in construction industry, 244,
    250
  emergent, 267
  flexibility of, 309
  for handling project data, 43–44,
    114, 187
  Jennifer Johnson on, 234–235
  for leveraging data, 29–33, 45, 88
  and mindset, 45, 190, 190, 199
  for working with data, 160, 190,
    190, 199, 202
Teicholz, Paul, xvi, 78
Tekla, 192, 245
Tenants, 274–277
Thermal heat transfer, analysis of,
  317, 318
Thornton Tomasetti, 63. *See also*
  CORE Studio
  automation at, 334
  compatibility of software at, 271
  Construction Support Services at,
    244, 245
  data visualization at, 68–69
  Property Loss Consulting Group,
    66, 67
  research at, 234
  research project with LMNts,
    67–68
  sharing data at, 324
  TTX at, 114, 260
  warehousing of data at, 69

3DS Max, 64, 83
Timberlake, James, 220
Time:
   for collecting data, 176–178
   as data preparedness factor, 107
   for working with data, 21–24
Tisch School of the Arts, NYU, 119, 138
TMY3 (Typical Meteorological Year, version 3) data, 218
TNC (The Nature Conservancy), 294
TRACETM simulation, 60
Training, see Learning to work with data
Transparency:
   of AECO practices, 18, 19
   Mark Frisch on, 318, 324–325
   and risk with sharing data, 311
Transsolar, 193, 194, 196, 286
Trelligence Affinity, 56
TRNSYS software, 193, 194
TTX:
   as interoperability platform, 260–262
   Brian Ringley on, 114
   Jonatan Schumacher on, 65, 69, 324, 334
Tucker, Patrick, 145
Turner Construction, 246, 249, 251, 253–255
Twitter, 63, 241, 267
Typical Meteorological Year, version 3 (TMY3) data, 218

UCL (University College London), 222
U.S. Army Corps of Engineers Laboratory, 263
United States Green Building Council (USGBC), 198
   data analysis at, 199, 200
   data collection strategy of, 169–170

data-informed approach at, 95–96
   public data from, 143
United States National Building Information Modeling (BIM) Standard, 262, 265, 266
University College London (UCL), 222
University of California, Berkeley, 203
University of Chicago, 156
University of Illinois at Urbana-Champaign, 250
Unstructured data:
   and Big Data, 71, 175, 232
   challenge of working with, 17–21
   structuring, 227–228
Utilization:
   and capacity, 170, 294
   improving, 294–295
   and occupancy, 182, 243

Validation:
   with data, 20, 305
   of data use, 59
   as trend in AECO industry, 73–74
Vandezande, James, 269
Vasari, 284
Video data:
   collecting, 177
   in construction industry, 249, 251, 256–259
Video games, 33, 185
Vilkner, Gregor, 271
Vision, computer, 257–259
Vision-based quality monitoring, 256
Visualization specialists, 231
Visual programming, 309
Visual sensing, 259
ViziCalc, 124
Vornado Realty Trust, 5, 274

Warehousing data, 69
Warnings functionality (SOM Dashboard), 48–49
Weather data, 195
Whitney, Carin, 239
Wind velocity analysis, 316
Wireless sensor network, 218, 219
Witt, Andrew:
   on application of project data, 226–229
   on background factors in data aptitude, 125
   on Big Data, 55
   on collaboration and BIM, 29, 32
   on data-enabled approach, 85
   on data mining, 144
   on interoperability, 271–272
   on learning data outside of architecture programs, 131, 132, 137
   on performance algorithms, 197
   on sharing data, 324, 325
Woods Bagot, 113
Workplace, learning to work with data in, 137–139
Wyatt, Scott, 145

Yori, Robert:
   on applying data, 214
   on background factors in data aptitude, 125
   on confidentiality, 311
   on data, 37–49
   on data-informed approaches, 94
   on documents, 62
   on hiring at SOM, 233
   on learning to work with data in the workplace, 138–139
   on selecting tools, 217

Zero Net Energy Design Dashboard, 7
Zillow, 227